CAT PARADISE ❹

Yuji Iwahara

Translation: Amy Forsyth

Lettering: Alexis Eckerman

GAKUEN SOUSEI NEKOTEN! Vol. 4 © 2008 Yuji Iwahara. All rights reserved. First published in Japan in 2008 by Akita Publishing Co., Ltd., Tokyo. English translation rights arranged with Akita Publishing Co., Ltd. through Tuttle-Mori Agency, Inc., Tokyo.

English translation © 2010 by Hachette Book Group, Inc.

Yen Press
Hachette Book Group
237 Park Avenue, New York, NY 10017

www.HachetteBookGroup.com
www.YenPress.com

Yen Press is an imprint of Hachette Book Group, Inc. The Yen Press name and logo are trademarks of Hachette Book Group, Inc.

First Yen Press Edition: May 2010

ISBN: 978-0-316-07736-1

10 9 8 7 6 5 4 3 2 1

BVG

Printed in the United States of America

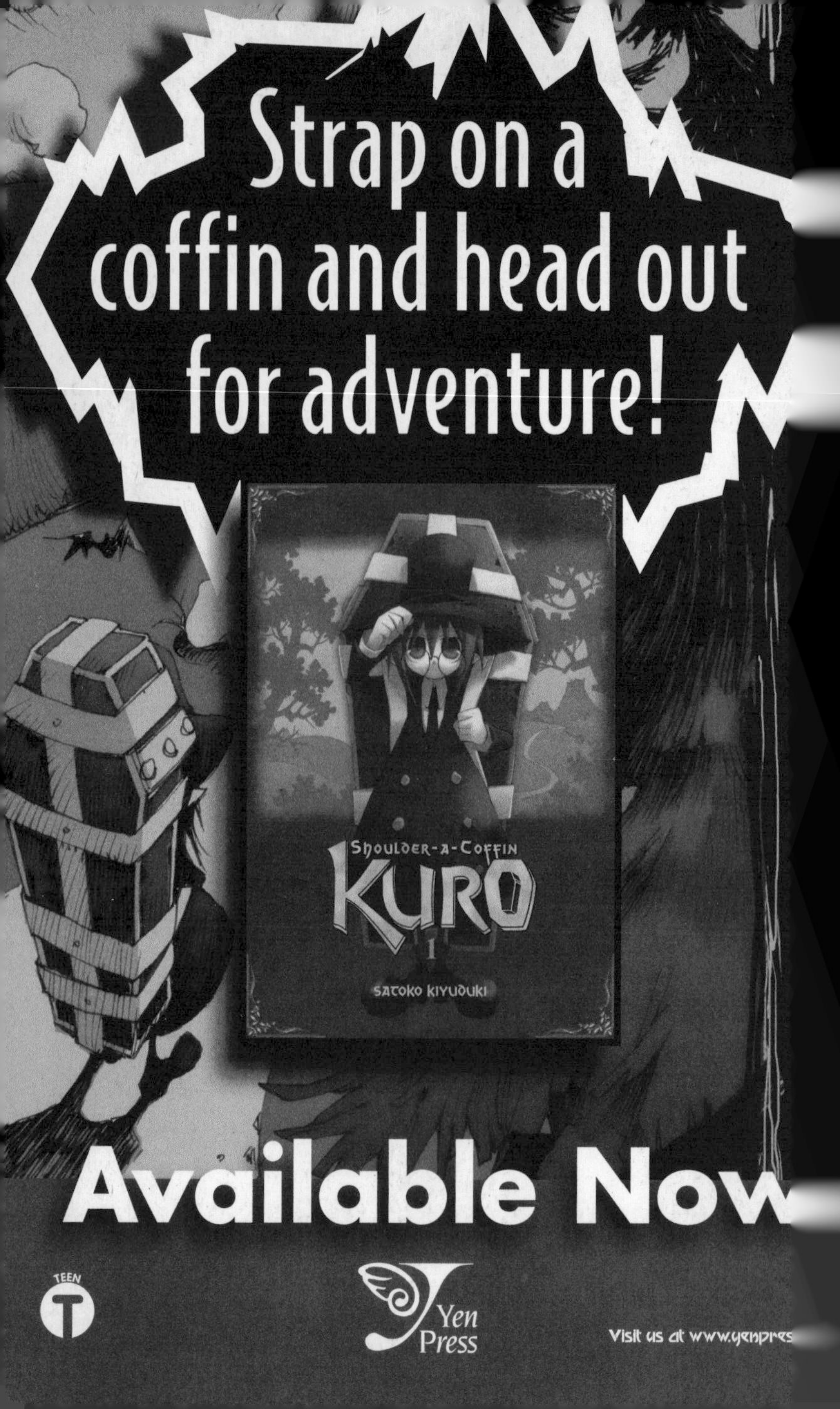

Strap on a coffin and head out for adventure!
Shoulder-a-Coffin
KURO
1
SATOKO KIYUDUKI
Available Now
TEEN
T
Yen Press
Visit us at www.yenpres

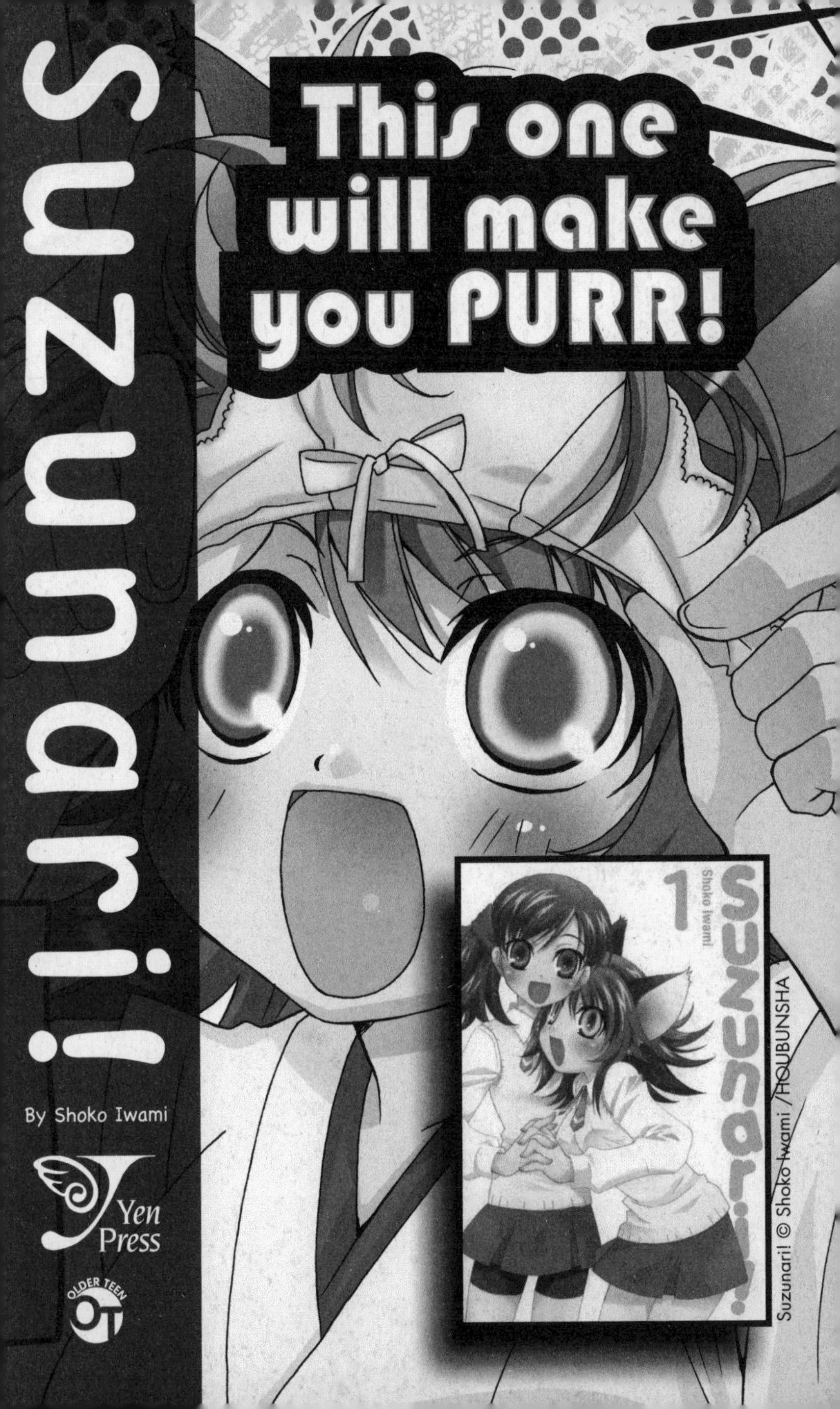
Suzunari!
This one will make you PURR!
By Shoko Iwami
Yen Press
OLDER TEEN
OT
1
Shoko Iwami
SUZUNARI!
Suzunari! © Shoko Iwami /HOUBUNSHA

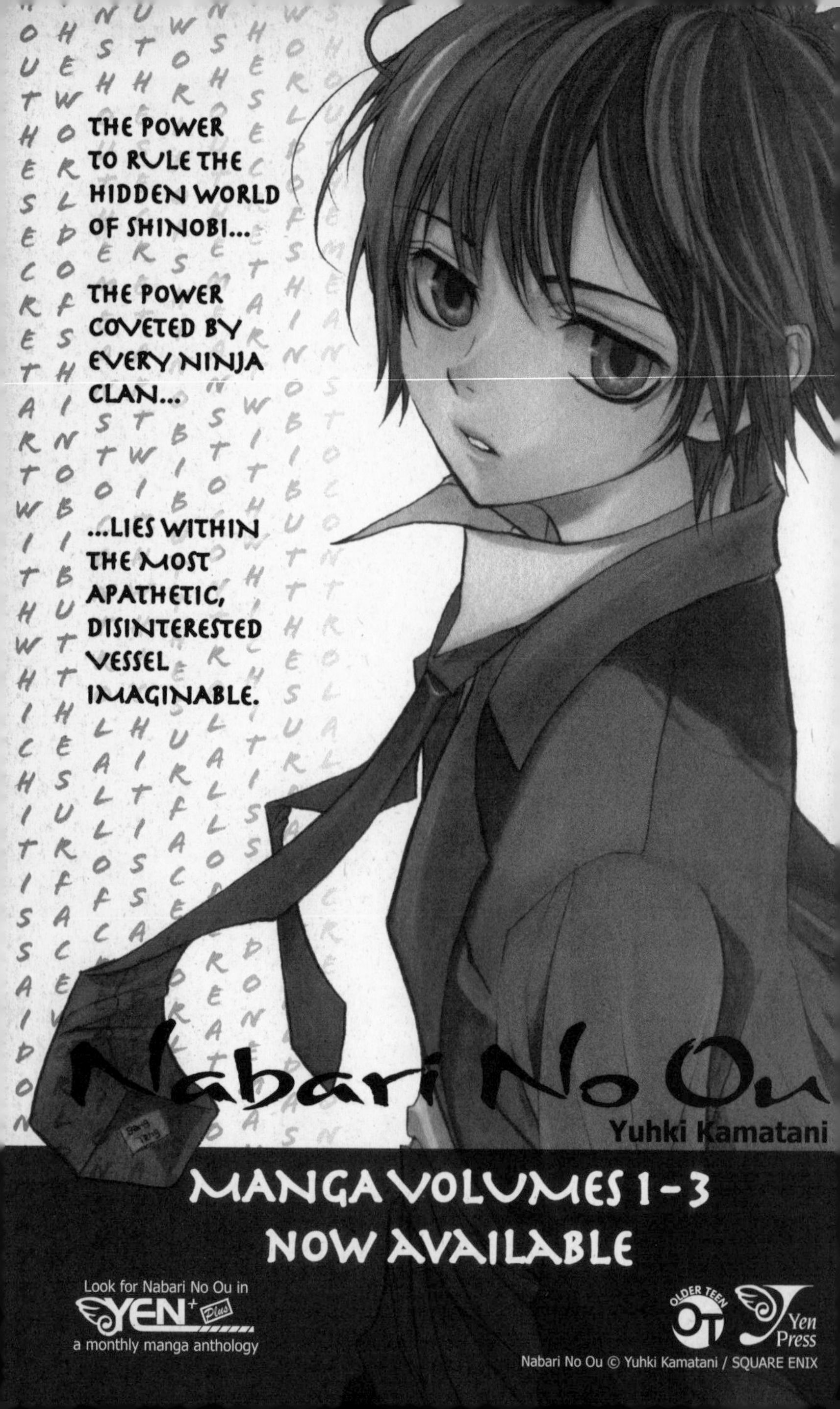
THE POWER TO RULE THE HIDDEN WORLD OF SHINOBI...
THE POWER COVETED BY EVERY NINJA CLAN...
...LIES WITHIN THE MOST APATHETIC, DISINTERESTED VESSEL IMAGINABLE.
Nabari No Ou
Yuhki Kamatani
MANGA VOLUMES 1-3 NOW AVAILABLE
Look for Nabari No Ou in YEN+ Plus a monthly manga anthology
OLDER TEEN OT
Yen Press
Nabari No Ou © Yuhki Kamatani / SQUARE ENIX

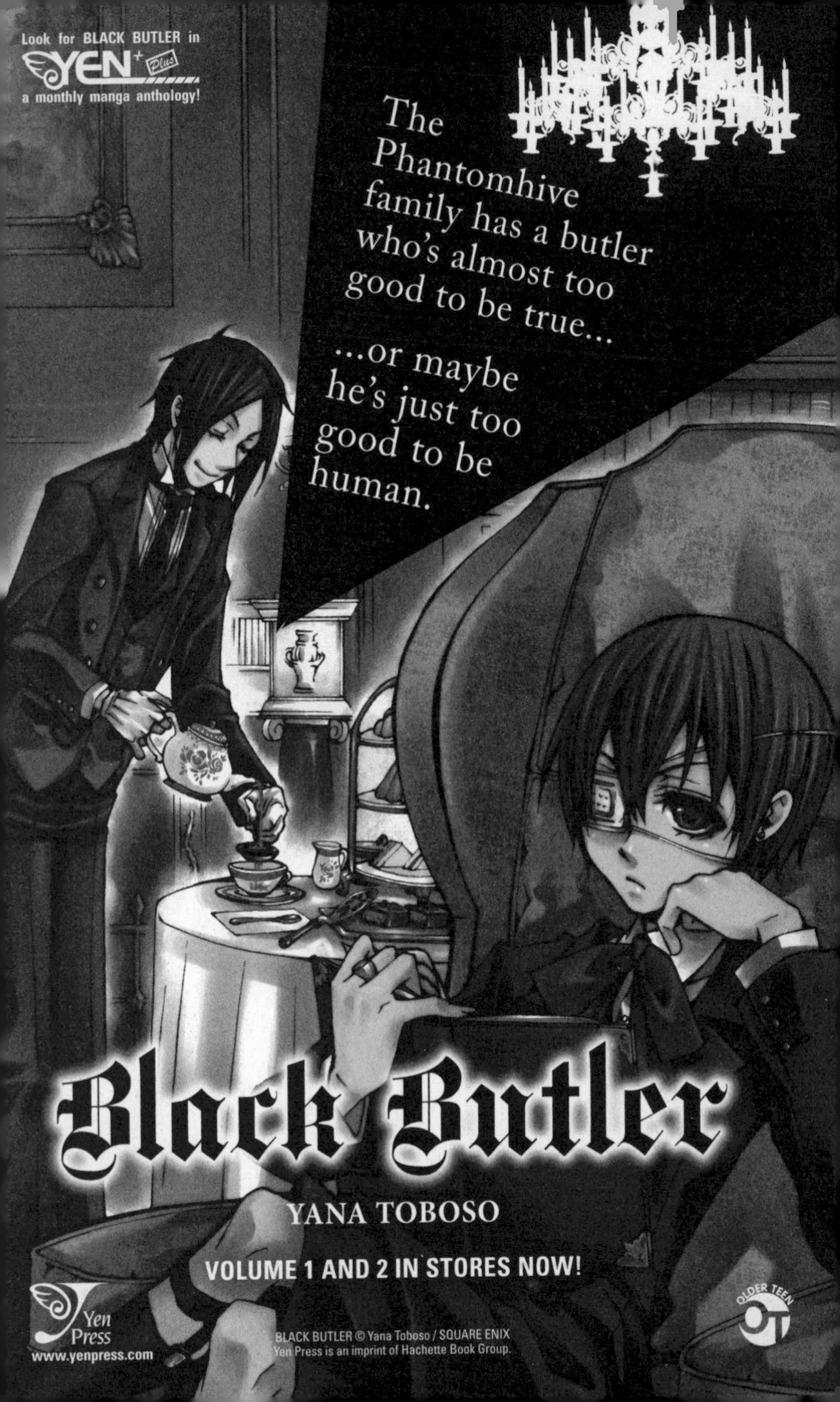

Look for BLACK BUTLER in
YEN+ Plus
a monthly manga anthology!
The Phantomhive family has a butler who's almost too good to be true...
...or maybe he's just too good to be human.
Black Butler
YANA TOBOSO
VOLUME 1 AND 2 IN STORES NOW!
Yen Press
www.yenpress.com
BLACK BUTLER © Yana Toboso / SQUARE ENIX
Yen Press is an imprint of Hachette Book Group.
OLDER TEEN
OT

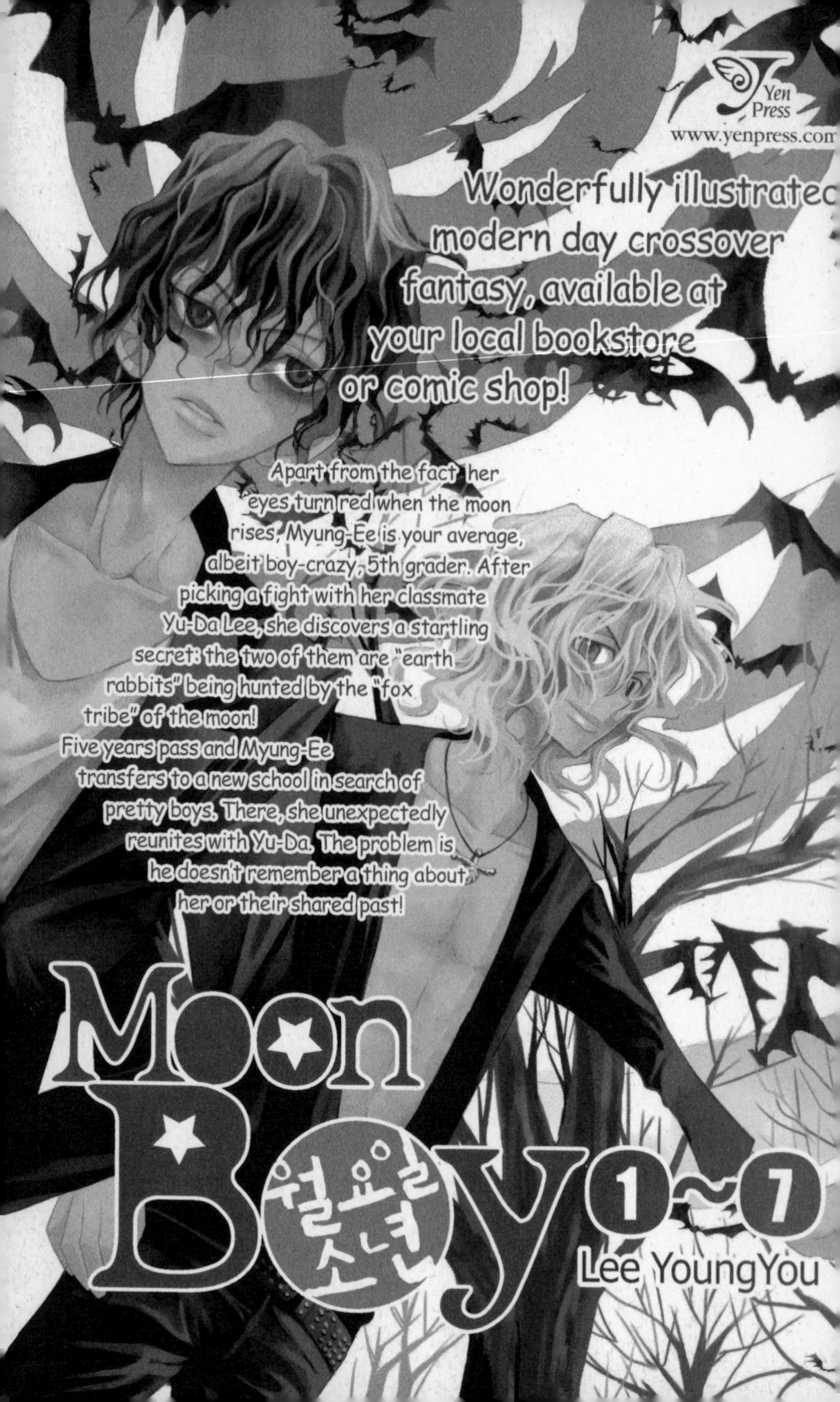
Yen Press
www.yenpress.com
Wonderfully illustrated modern day crossover fantasy, available at your local bookstore or comic shop!
Apart from the fact her eyes turn red when the moon rises, Myung-Ee is your average, albeit boy-crazy, 5th grader. After picking a fight with her classmate Yu-Da Lee, she discovers a startling secret: the two of them are "earth rabbits" being hunted by the "fox tribe" of the moon! Five years pass and Myung-Ee transfers to a new school in search of pretty boys. There, she unexpectedly reunites with Yu-Da. The problem is he doesn't remember a thing about her or their shared past!
Moon Boy
월요일 소년
1~7
Lee YoungYou

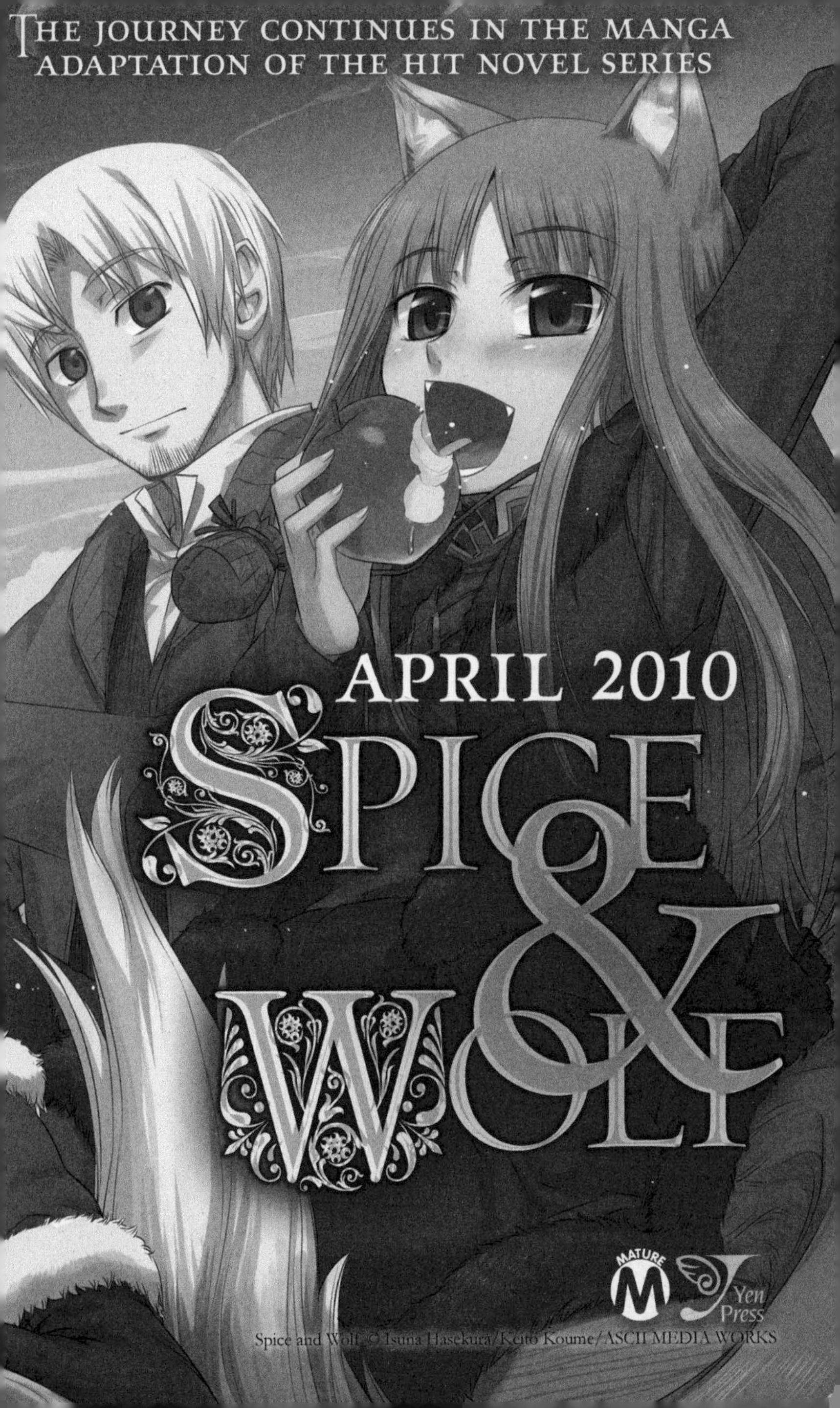
THE JOURNEY CONTINUES IN THE MANGA
ADAPTATION OF THE HIT NOVEL SERIES
APRIL 2010
SPICE & WOLF
MATURE
Yen Press
Spice and Wolf © Isuna Hasekura/Keito Koume/ASCII MEDIA WORKS

I always paint my color pages with an acrylic gouache from Turner* (the backgrounds I do in watercolor and color ink), but since the painting method is simple, I think it would be faster to do it with a computer. I even have some experience with CG. But for some reason I just don't feel like really getting into CG. And well, if I do it by hand, at least I have an excuse if it turns out bad. Keeping it as a raw image is better after all.

----

*Gouache is a type of paint in which the pigment is suspended in water. Turner is the name of an art supply company that produces this kind of paint.

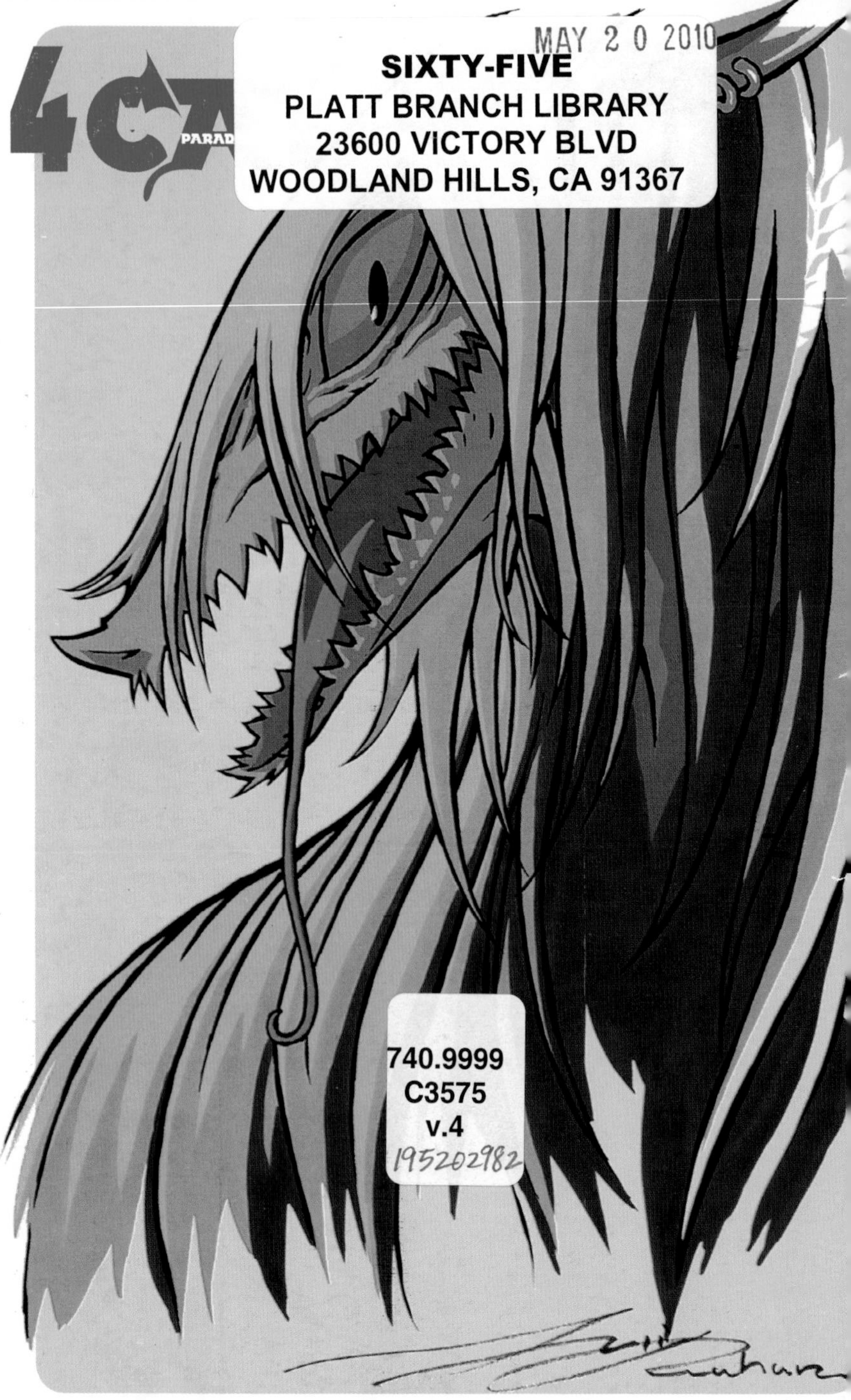

YUJI IWAHARA

CAT PARADISE

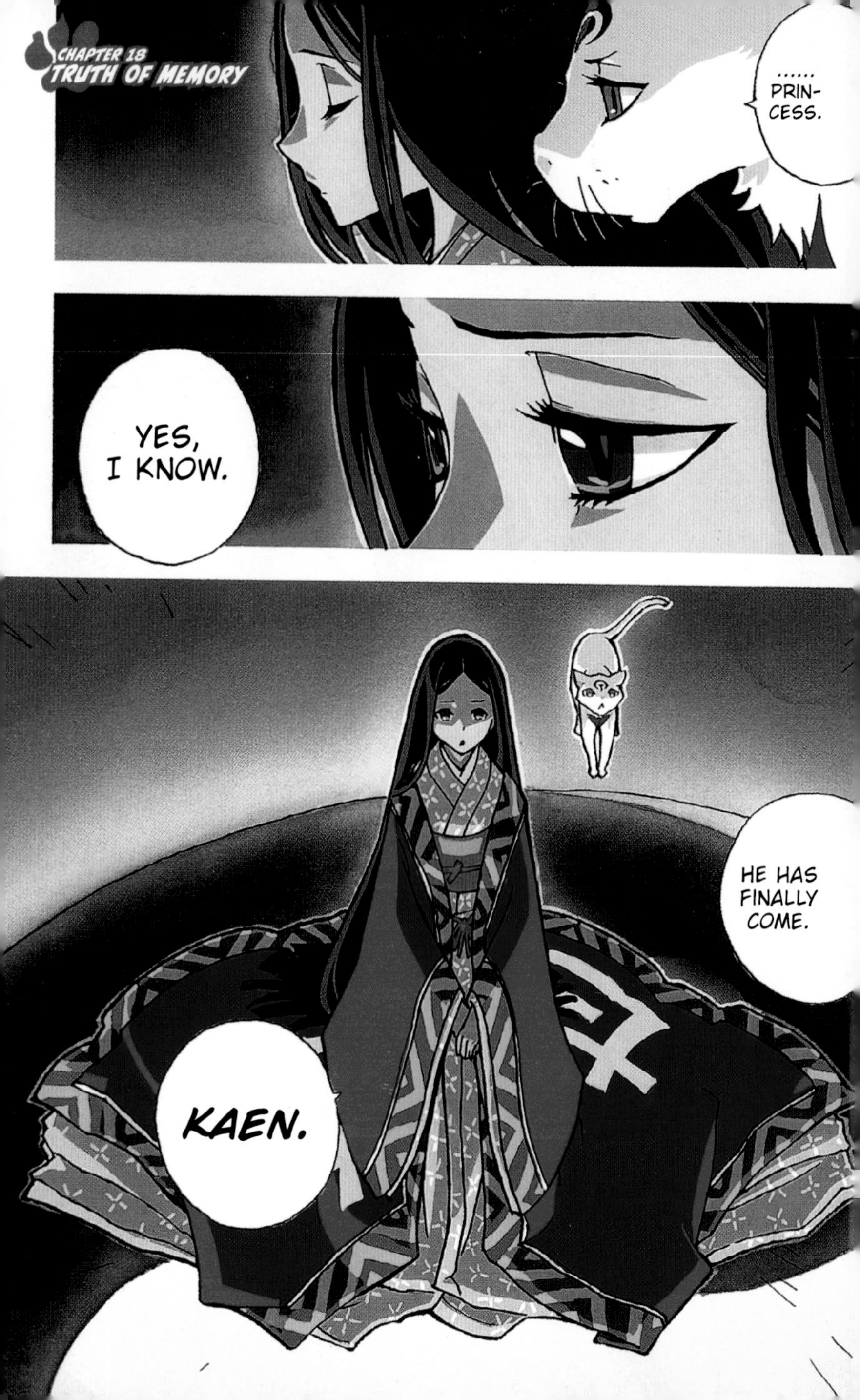
CHAPTER 18
TRUTH OF MEMORY
......
PRINCESS.
YES, I KNOW.
HE HAS FINALLY COME.
KAEN.

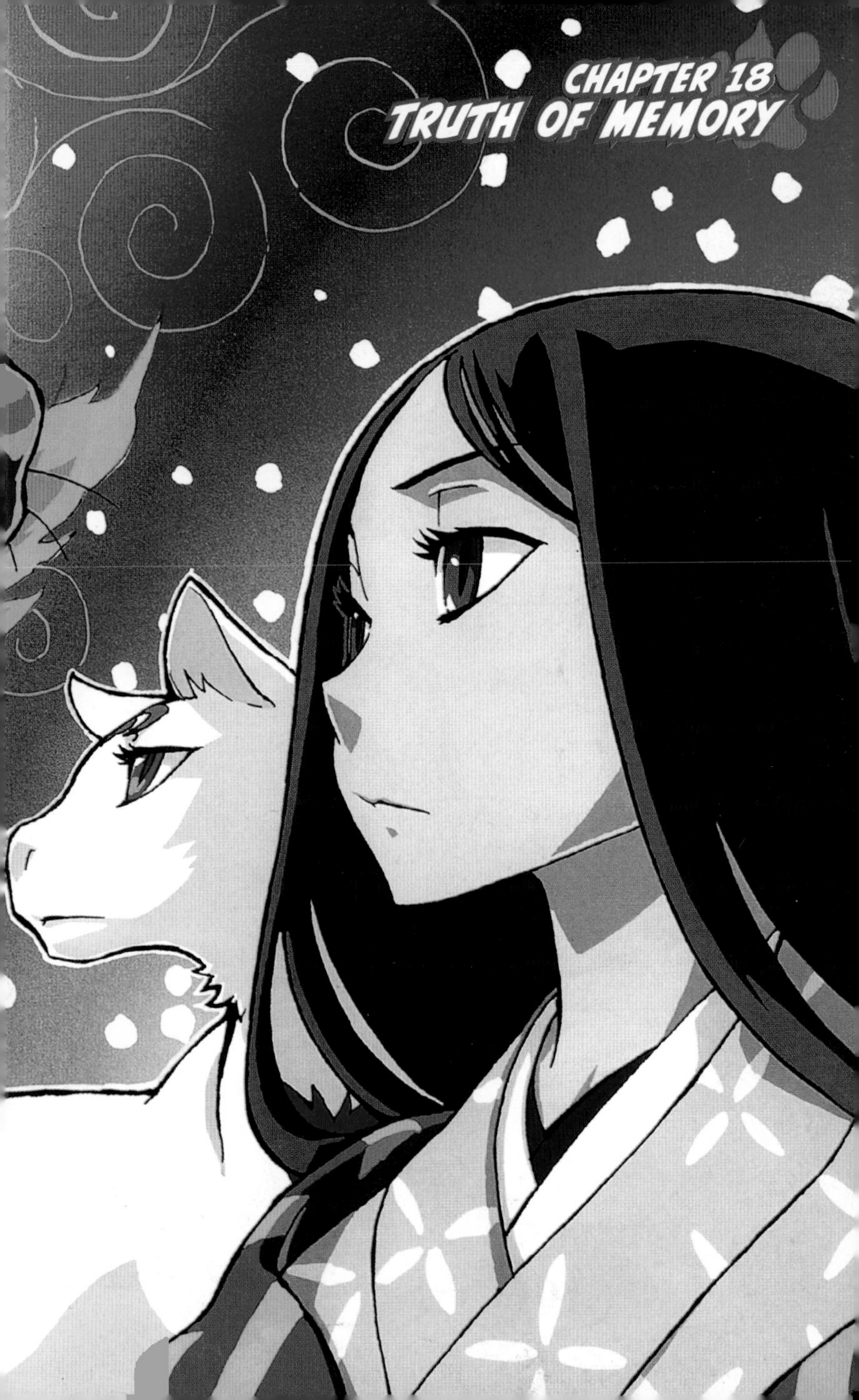
CHAPTER 18
TRUTH OF MEMORY

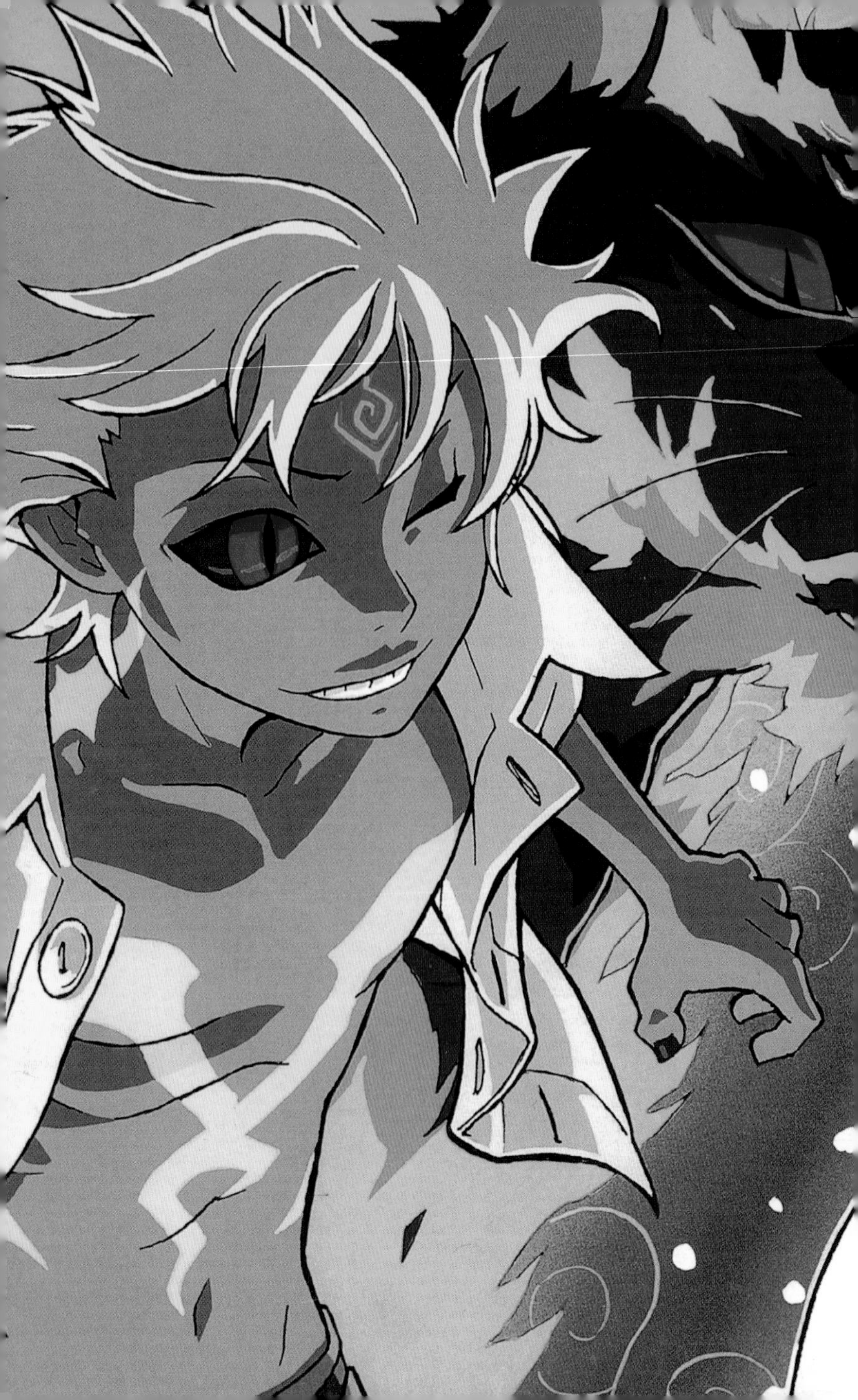

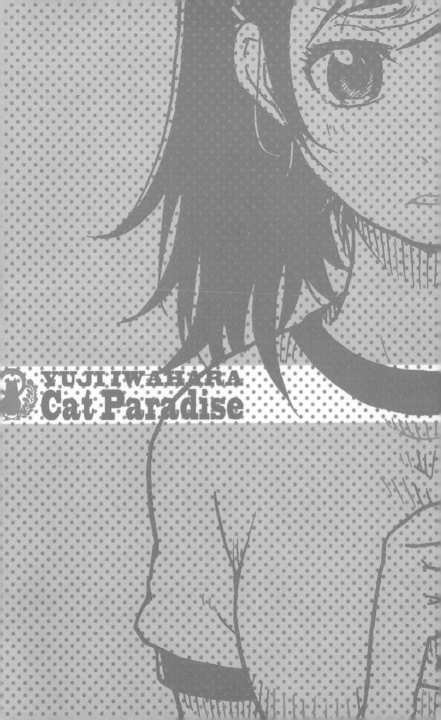

YUJI IWAHARA
Cat Paradise

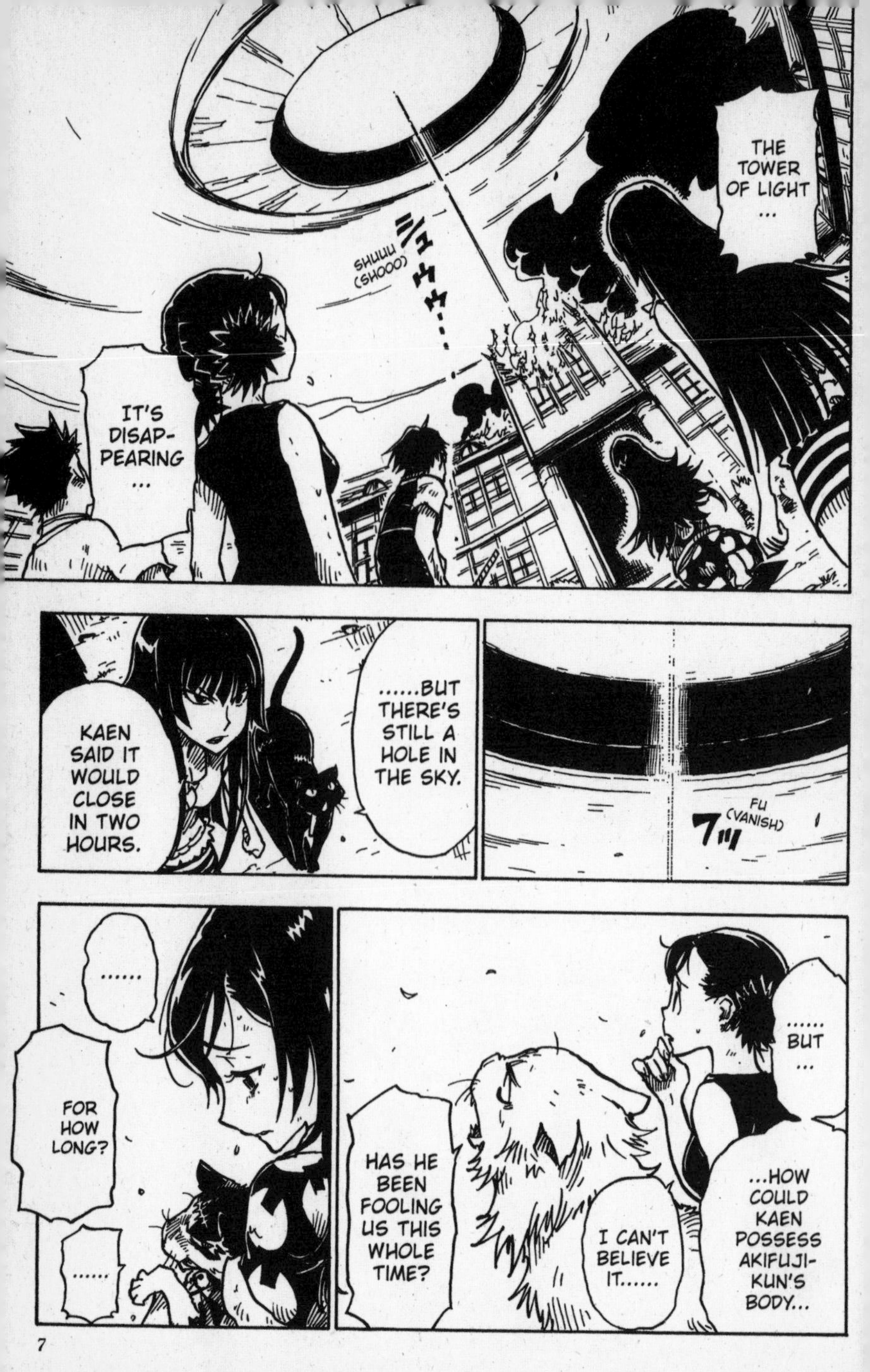
THE TOWER OF LIGHT ...
シュウウ・・・
SHUUU (SHOOO)
IT'S DISAPPEARING ...
フッ
FU (VANISH)
......BUT THERE'S STILL A HOLE IN THE SKY.
KAEN SAID IT WOULD CLOSE IN TWO HOURS.
...... BUT ...
...HOW COULD KAEN POSSESS AKIFUJI-KUN'S BODY...
I CAN'T BELIEVE IT......
HAS HE BEEN FOOLING US THIS WHOLE TIME?
......
FOR HOW LONG?
......

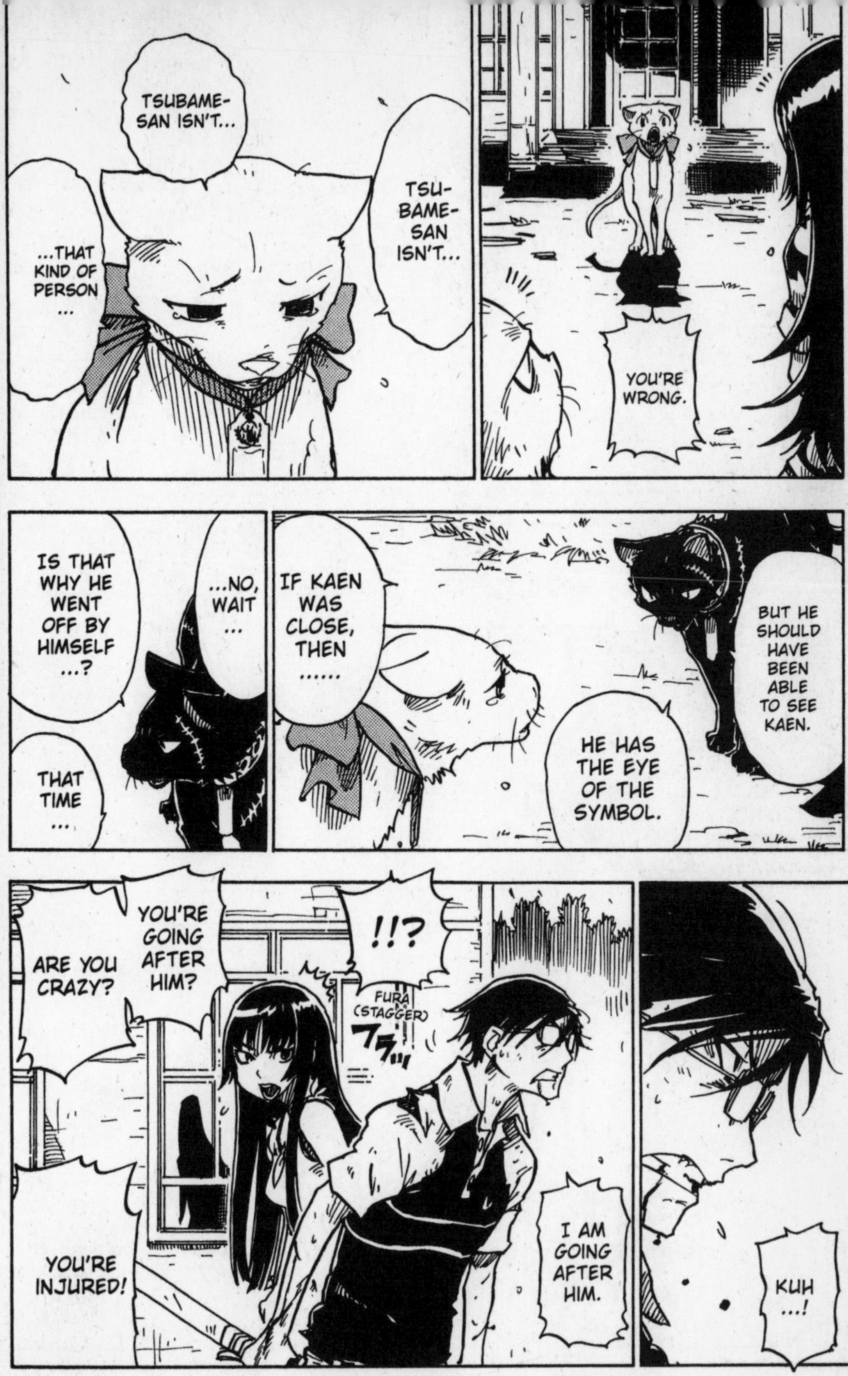
YOU'RE WRONG.
TSUBAME-SAN ISN'T...
TSU-BAME-SAN ISN'T...
...THAT KIND OF PERSON ...
BUT HE SHOULD HAVE BEEN ABLE TO SEE KAEN.
HE HAS THE EYE OF THE SYMBOL.
IF KAEN WAS CLOSE, THEN ......
...NO, WAIT ...
IS THAT WHY HE WENT OFF BY HIMSELF ...?
THAT TIME ...
KUH ...!
I AM GOING AFTER HIM.
!!?
FURA (STAGGER)
YOU'RE GOING AFTER HIM?
ARE YOU CRAZY?
YOU'RE INJURED!

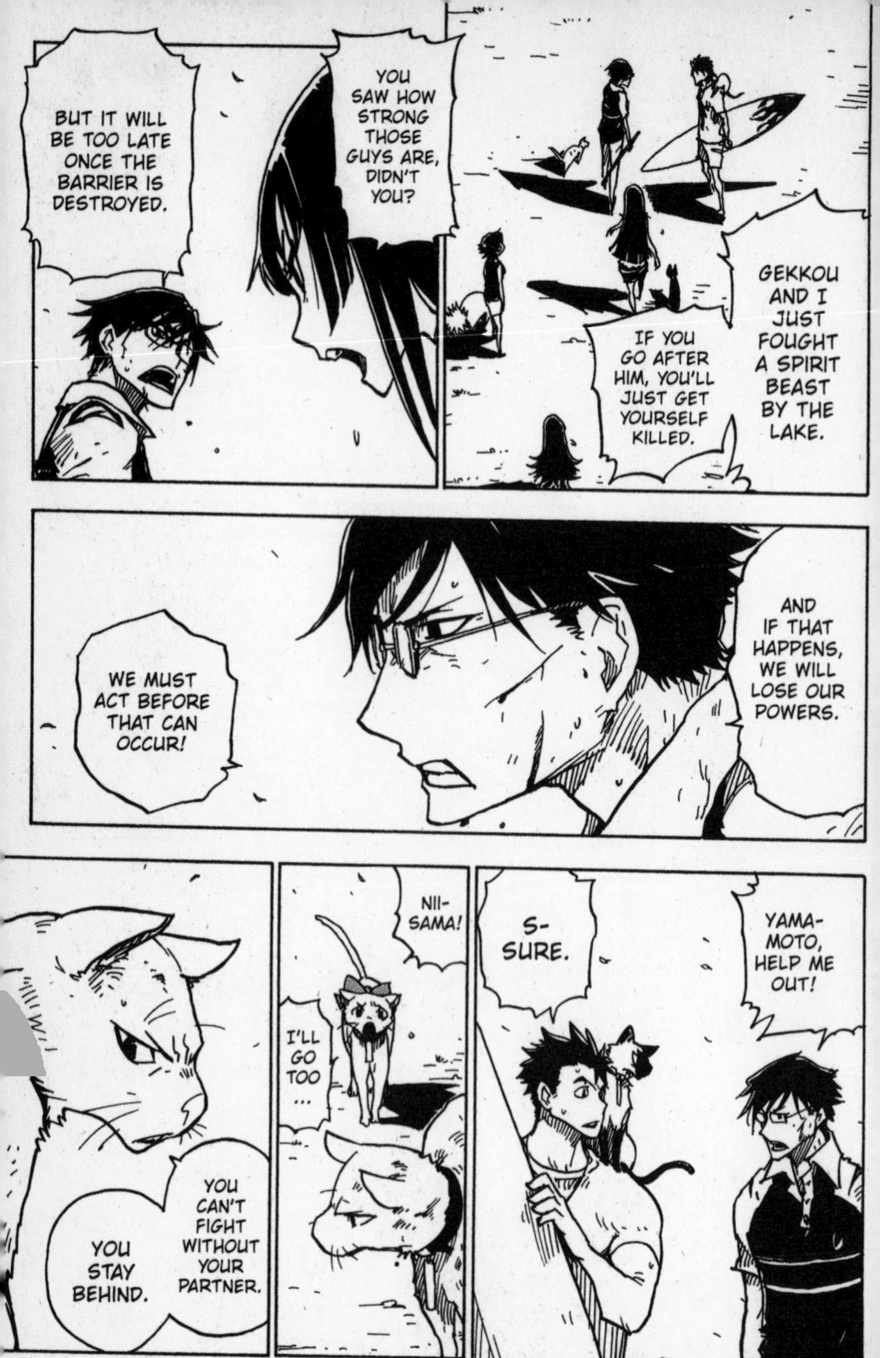
GEKKOU AND I JUST FOUGHT A SPIRIT BEAST BY THE LAKE.
IF YOU GO AFTER HIM, YOU'LL JUST GET YOURSELF KILLED.
YOU SAW HOW STRONG THOSE GUYS ARE, DIDN'T YOU?
BUT IT WILL BE TOO LATE ONCE THE BARRIER IS DESTROYED.
AND IF THAT HAPPENS, WE WILL LOSE OUR POWERS.
WE MUST ACT BEFORE THAT CAN OCCUR!
YAMAMOTO, HELP ME OUT!
S-SURE.
NII-SAMA!
I'LL GO TOO...
YOU CAN'T FIGHT WITHOUT YOUR PARTNER.
YOU STAY BEHIND.

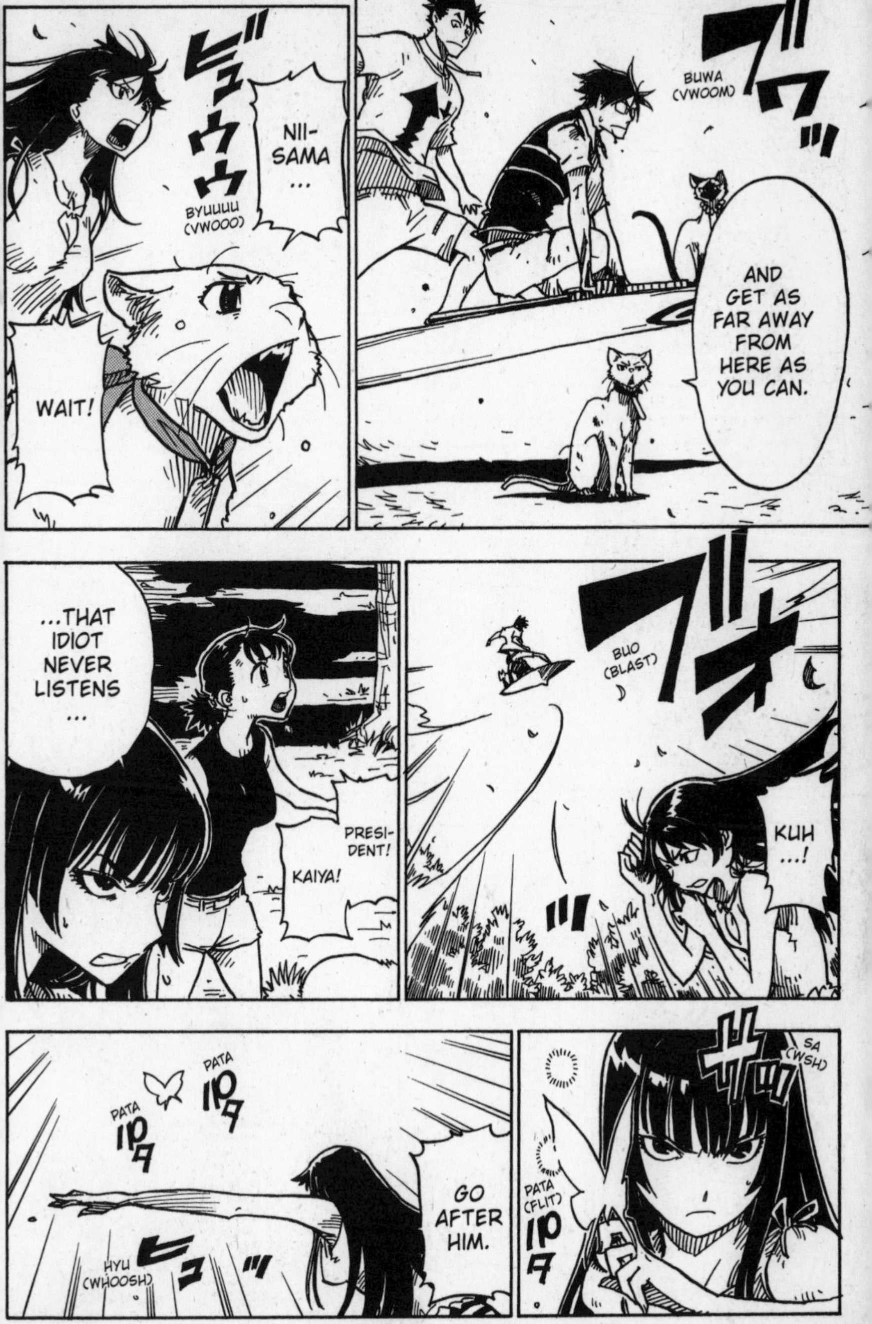
ブワッ
BUWA (VWOOM)
AND GET AS FAR AWAY FROM HERE AS YOU CAN.
ビュウウ
BYUUUU (VWOOO)
NII-SAMA...
WAIT!
ブオ
BUO (BLAST)
KUH...!
...THAT IDIOT NEVER LISTENS...
PRESI-DENT!
KAIYA!
ザッ
SA (WSH)
パタ
PATA (FLIT)
GO AFTER HIM.
パタ
PATA
パタ
PATA
ヒュッ
HYU (WHOOSH)

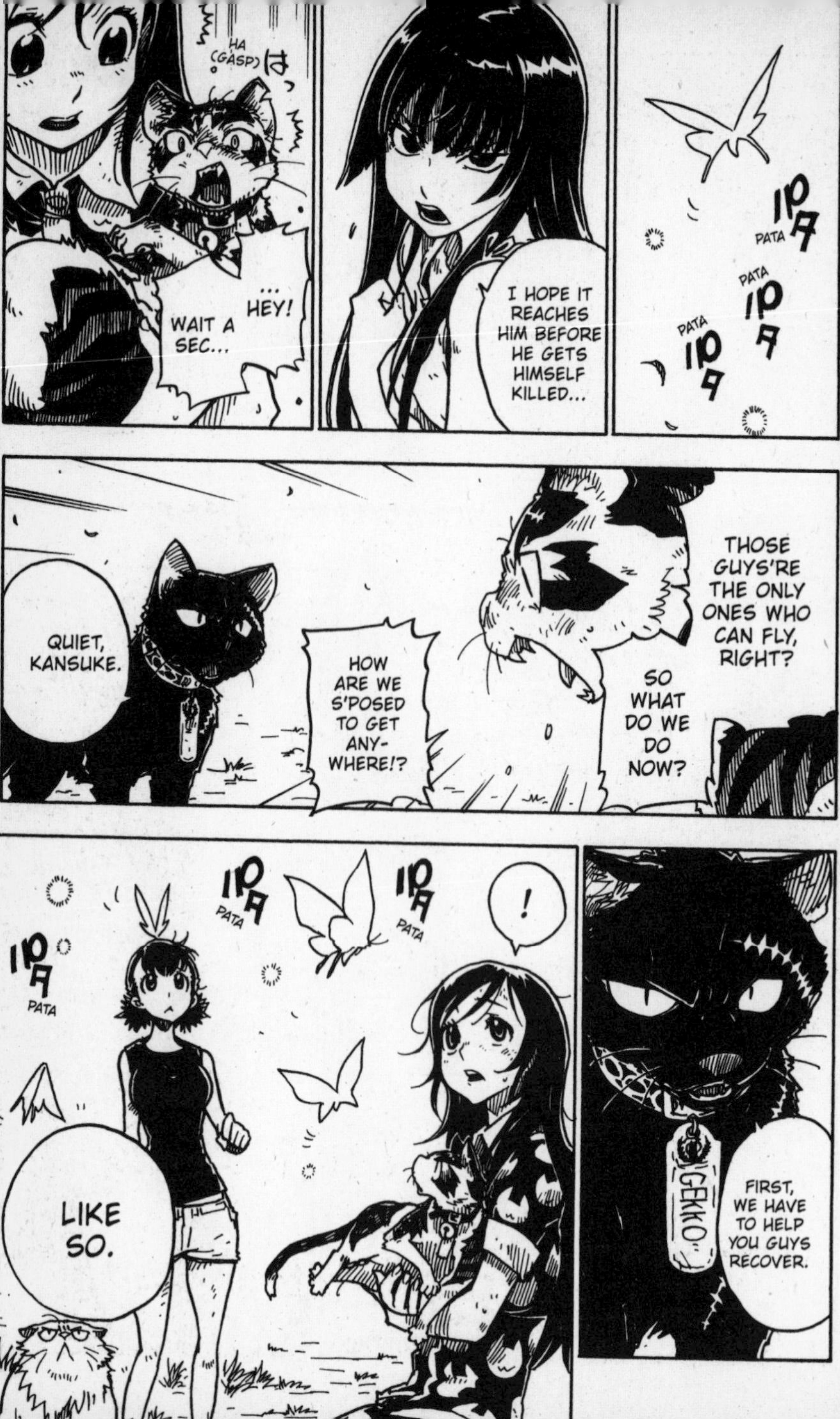
PATA
PATA
PATA
I HOPE IT REACHES HIM BEFORE HE GETS HIMSELF KILLED...
HA (GASP) は
...HEY!
WAIT A SEC...
THOSE GUYS'RE THE ONLY ONES WHO CAN FLY, RIGHT?
SO WHAT DO WE DO NOW?
HOW ARE WE S'POSED TO GET ANY-WHERE!?
QUIET, KANSUKE.
FIRST, WE HAVE TO HELP YOU GUYS RECOVER.
GEKKO
!
PATA
PATA
PATA
LIKE SO.

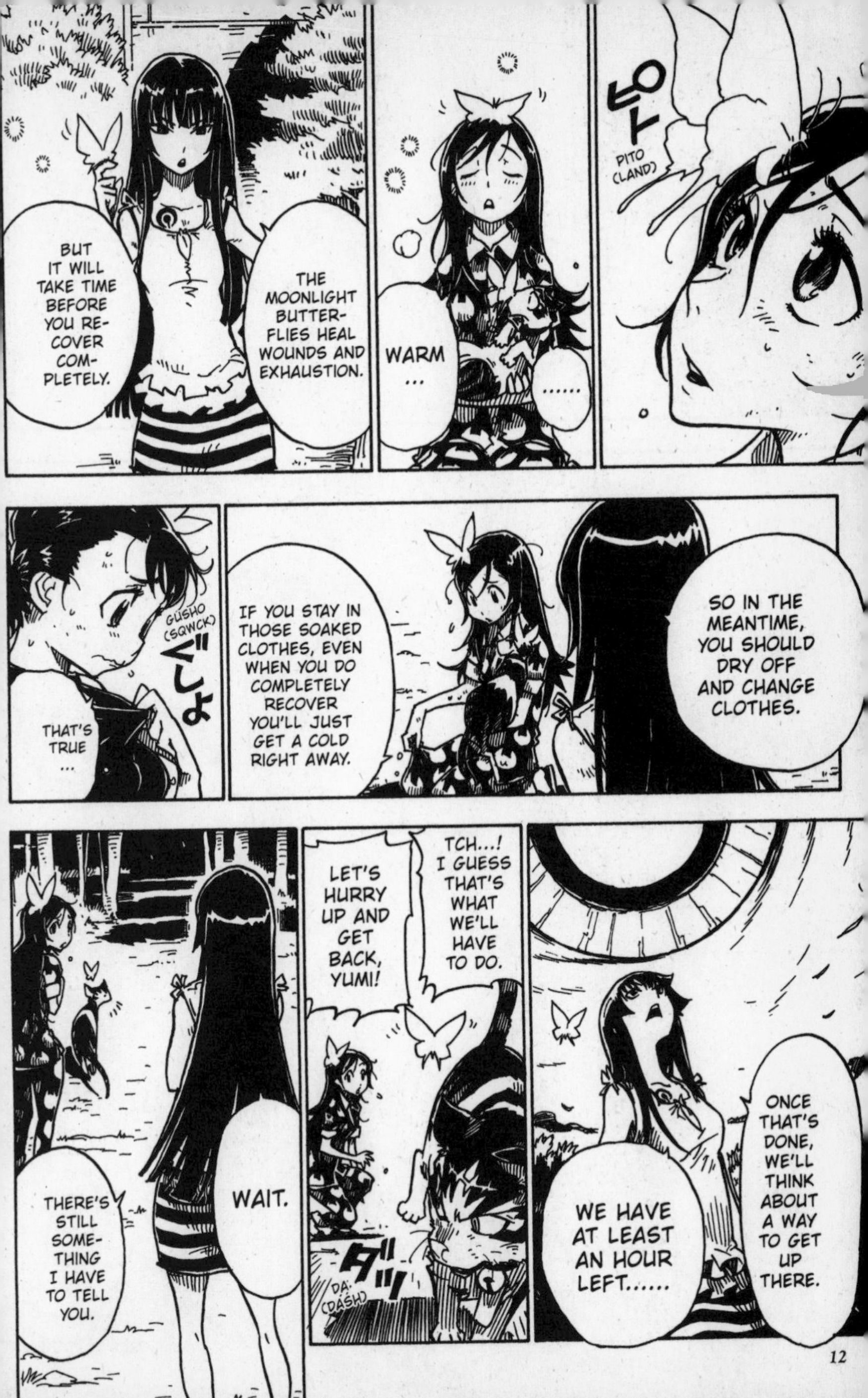
ピト
PITO (LAND)
WARM ...
......
THE MOONLIGHT BUTTERFLIES HEAL WOUNDS AND EXHAUSTION.
BUT IT WILL TAKE TIME BEFORE YOU RECOVER COMPLETELY.
SO IN THE MEANTIME, YOU SHOULD DRY OFF AND CHANGE CLOTHES.
IF YOU STAY IN THOSE SOAKED CLOTHES, EVEN WHEN YOU DO COMPLETELY RECOVER YOU'LL JUST GET A COLD RIGHT AWAY.
ぐしょ
GUSHO (SQWCK)
THAT'S TRUE ...
ONCE THAT'S DONE, WE'LL THINK ABOUT A WAY TO GET UP THERE.
WE HAVE AT LEAST AN HOUR LEFT......
TCH...! I GUESS THAT'S WHAT WE'LL HAVE TO DO.
LET'S HURRY UP AND GET BACK, YUMI!
ダッ
DA (DASH)
WAIT.
THERE'S STILL SOMETHING I HAVE TO TELL YOU.

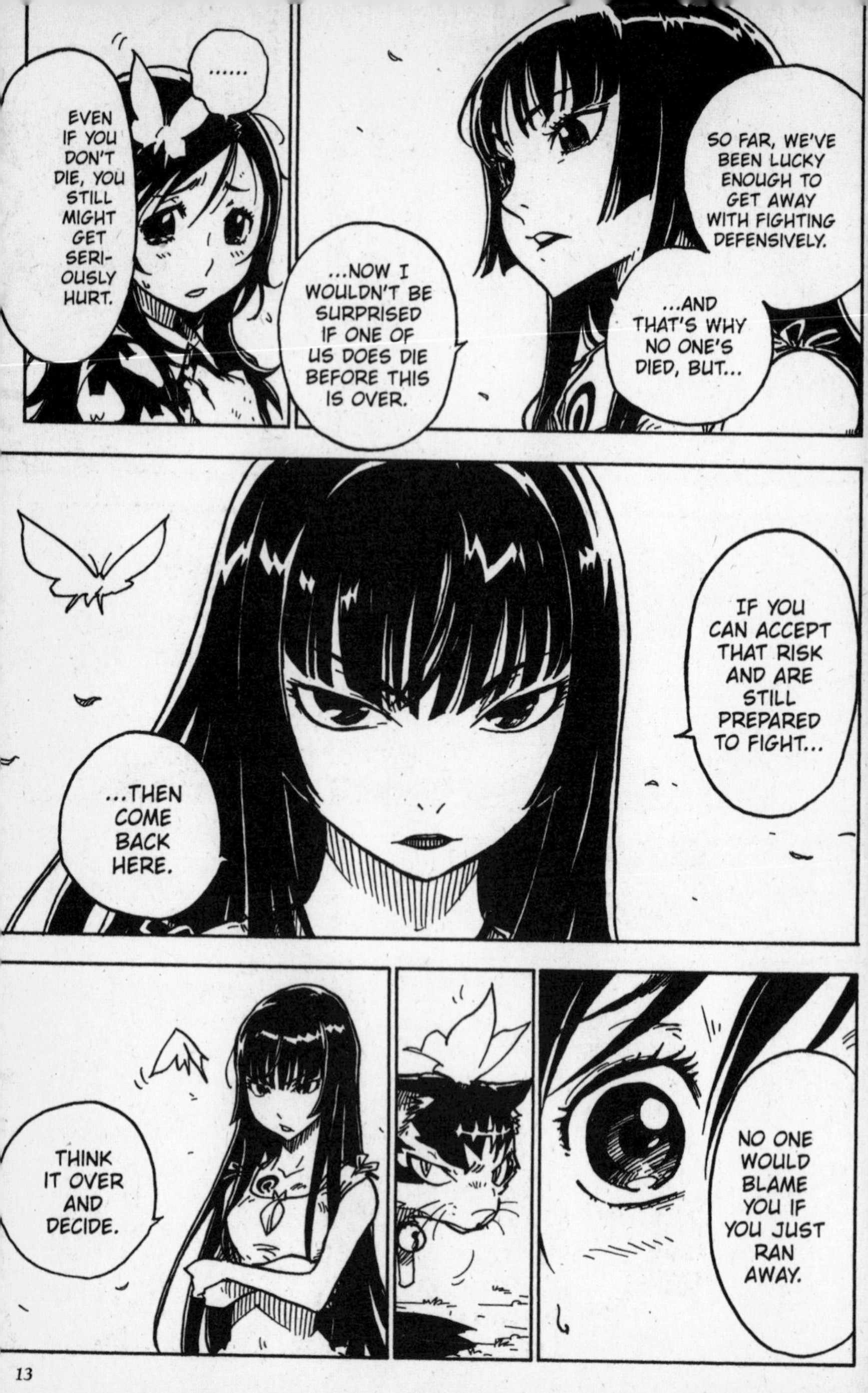
SO FAR, WE'VE BEEN LUCKY ENOUGH TO GET AWAY WITH FIGHTING DEFENSIVELY.
...AND THAT'S WHY NO ONE'S DIED, BUT...
...NOW I WOULDN'T BE SURPRISED IF ONE OF US DOES DIE BEFORE THIS IS OVER.
......
EVEN IF YOU DON'T DIE, YOU STILL MIGHT GET SERI-OUSLY HURT.
IF YOU CAN ACCEPT THAT RISK AND ARE STILL PREPARED TO FIGHT...
...THEN COME BACK HERE.
NO ONE WOULD BLAME YOU IF YOU JUST RAN AWAY.
THINK IT OVER AND DECIDE.

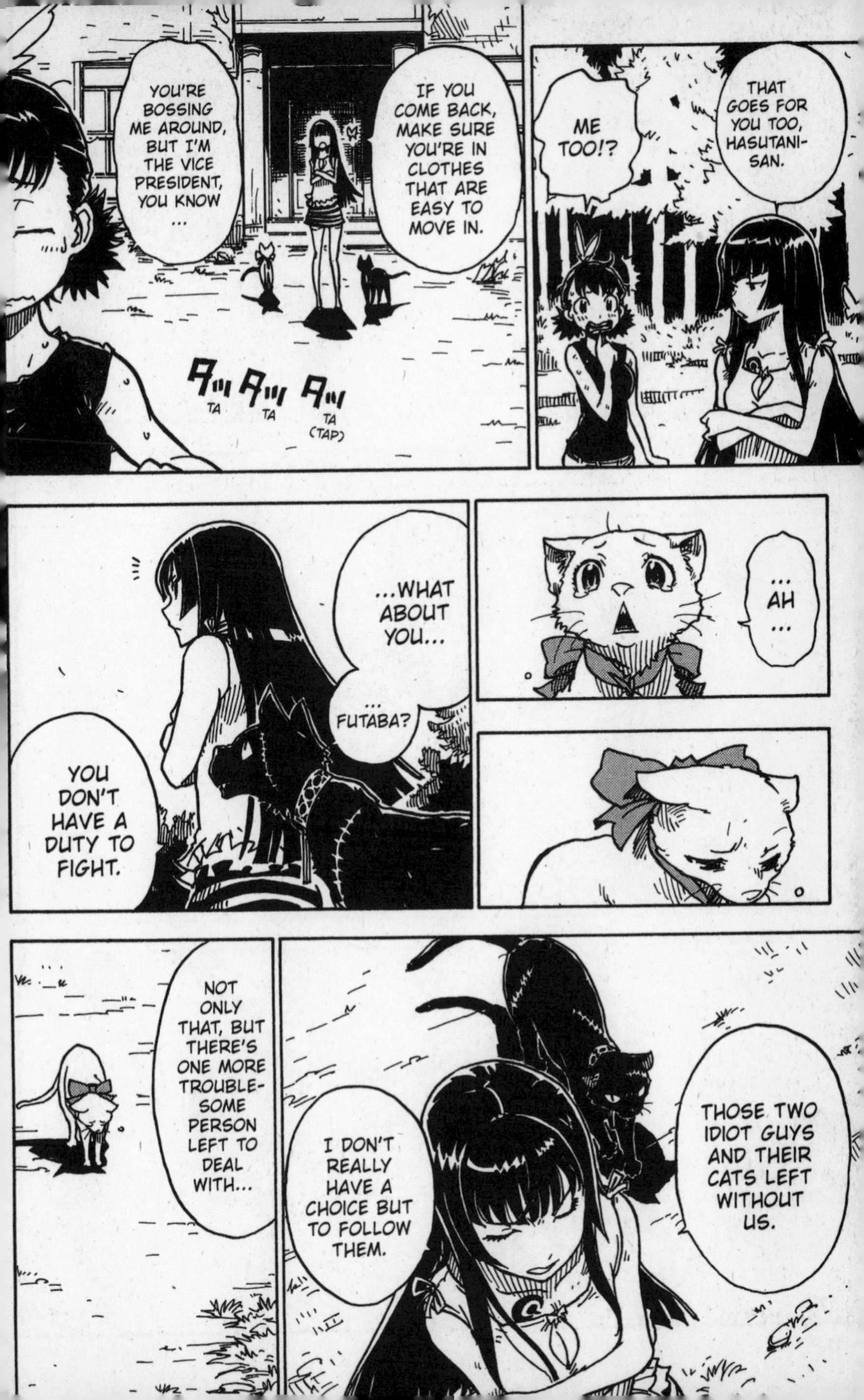
THAT GOES FOR YOU TOO, HASUTANI-SAN.
ME TOO!?
IF YOU COME BACK, MAKE SURE YOU'RE IN CLOTHES THAT ARE EASY TO MOVE IN.
YOU'RE BOSSING ME AROUND, BUT I'M THE VICE PRESIDENT, YOU KNOW ...
タッ TA
タッ TA
タッ TA (TAP)
... AH ...
...WHAT ABOUT YOU...
... FUTABA?
YOU DON'T HAVE A DUTY TO FIGHT.
THOSE TWO IDIOT GUYS AND THEIR CATS LEFT WITHOUT US.
I DON'T REALLY HAVE A CHOICE BUT TO FOLLOW THEM.
...
NOT ONLY THAT, BUT THERE'S ONE MORE TROUBLE-SOME PERSON LEFT TO DEAL WITH...

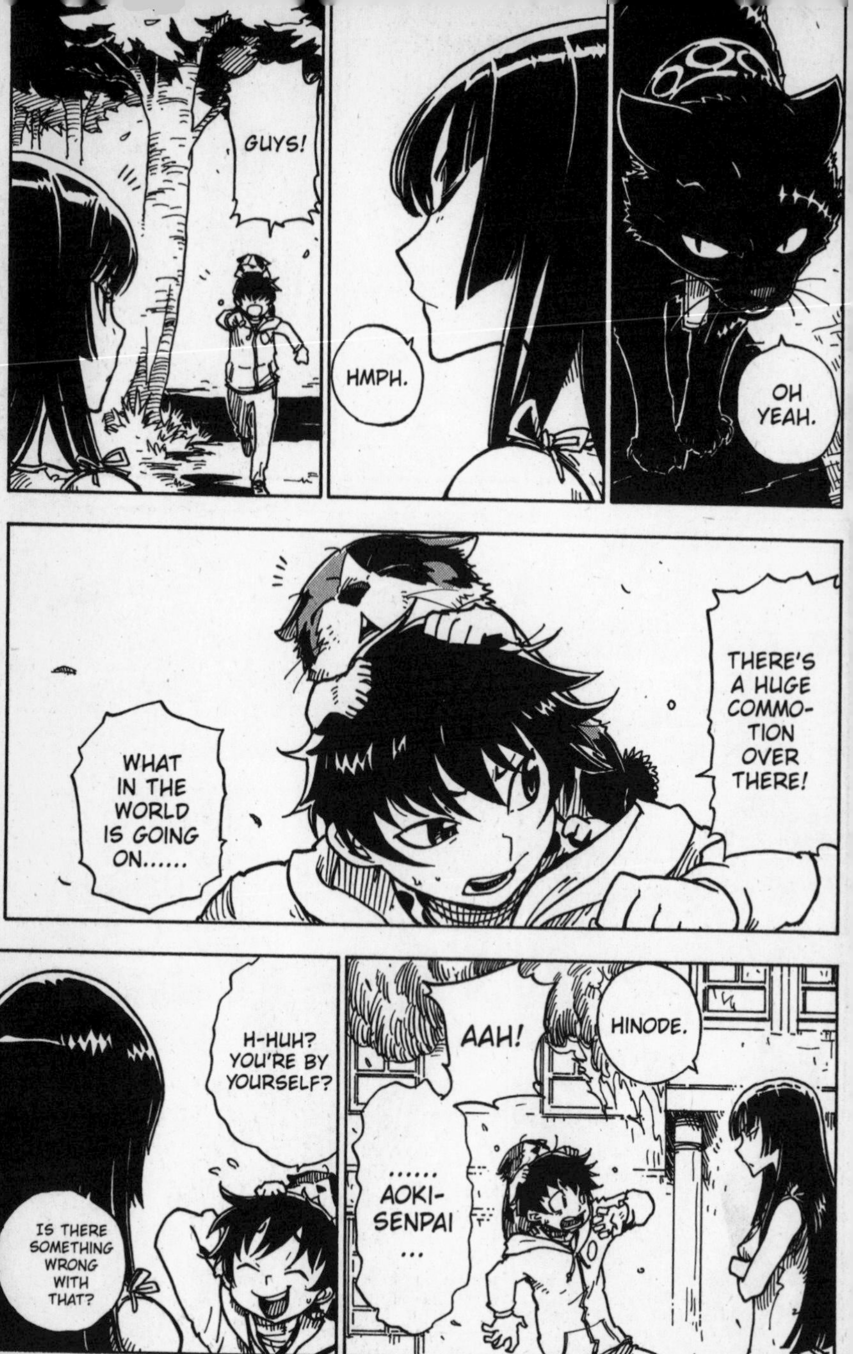
OH YEAH.
HMPH.
GUYS!
THERE'S A HUGE COMMO-TION OVER THERE!
WHAT IN THE WORLD IS GOING ON......
HINODE.
AAH!
......AOKI-SENPAI...
H-HUH? YOU'RE BY YOURSELF?
IS THERE SOMETHING WRONG WITH THAT?

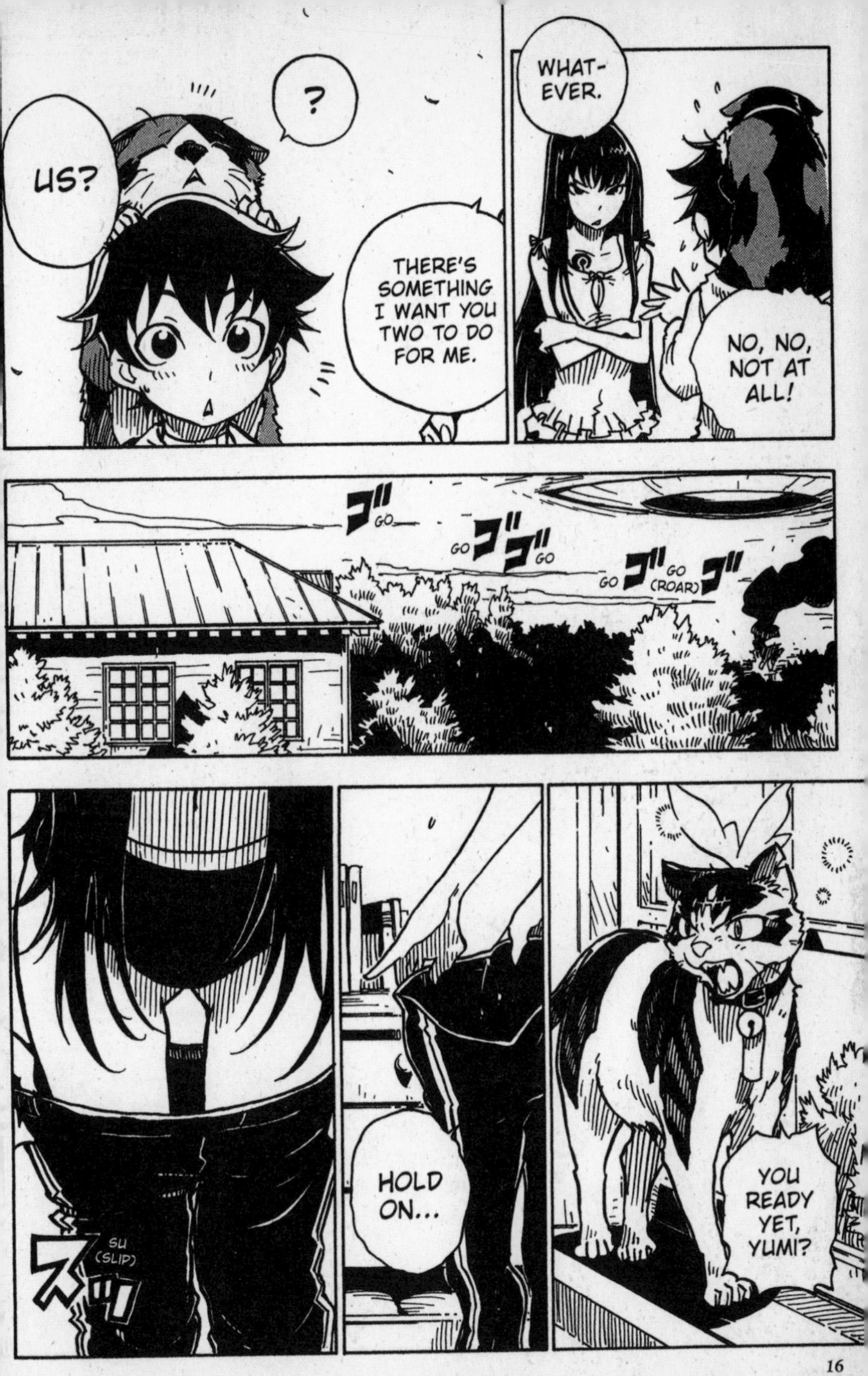
WHAT-EVER.
NO, NO, NOT AT ALL!
THERE'S SOMETHING I WANT YOU TWO TO DO FOR ME.
?
US?
GO GO GO GO GO (ROAR)
YOU READY YET, YUMI?
HOLD ON...
SU (SLIP)

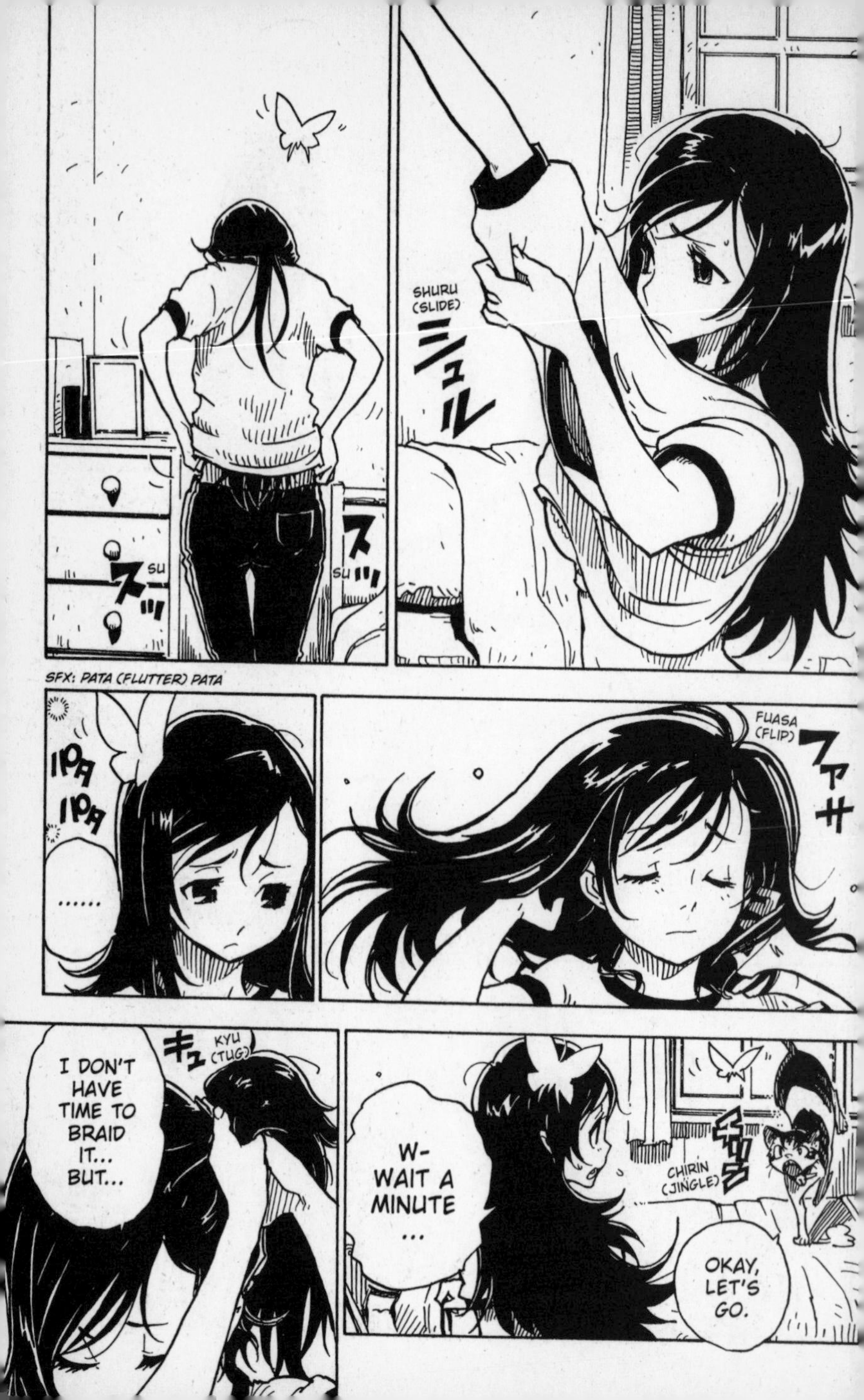
SHURU (SLIDE)
シュル
SU
スッ
SU
スーッ
SFX: PATA (FLUTTER) PATA
FUASA (FLIP)
ファサ
パタ パタ
......
KYU (TUG)
キュ
CHIRIN (JINGLE)
チリン
W- WAIT A MINUTE ...
OKAY, LET'S GO.
I DON'T HAVE TIME TO BRAID IT... BUT...

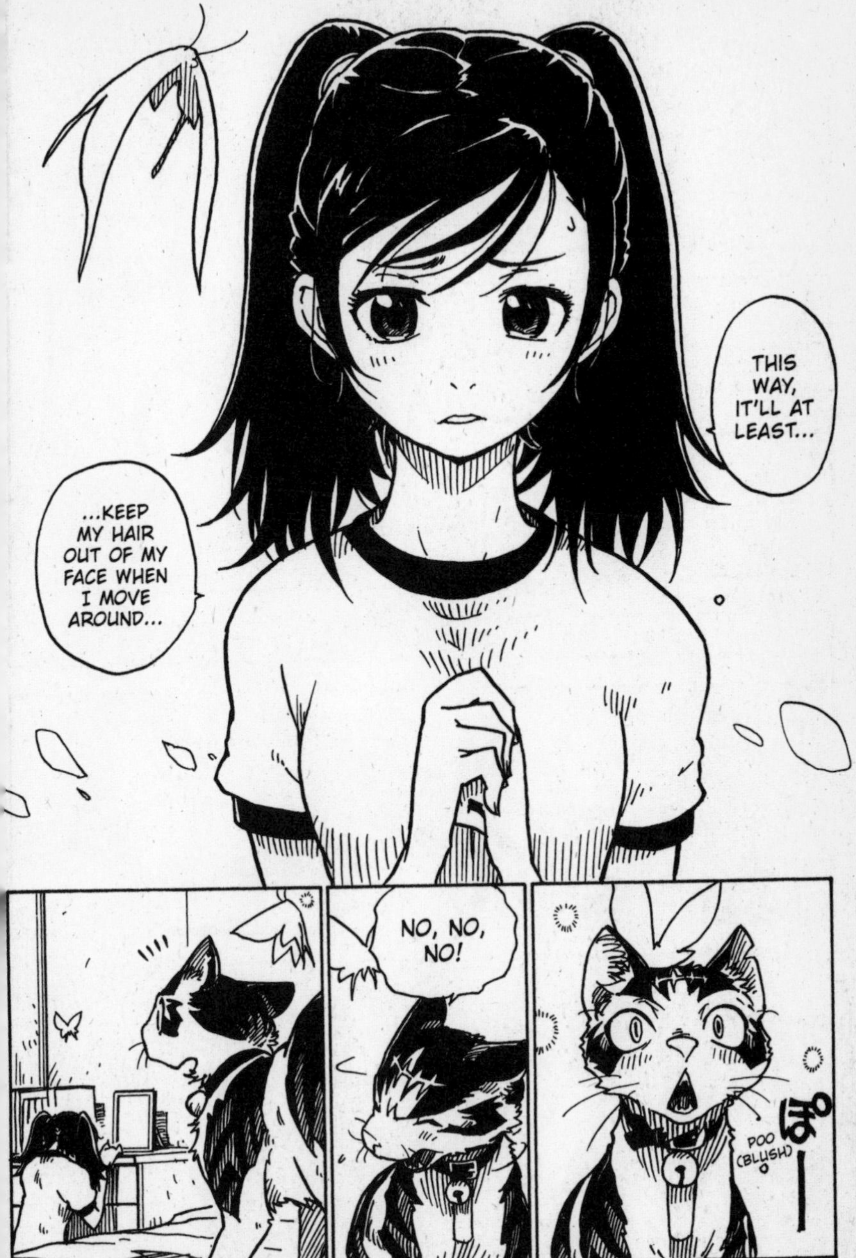
THIS WAY, IT'LL AT LEAST...
...KEEP MY HAIR OUT OF MY FACE WHEN I MOVE AROUND...
ぽー
POO (BLUSH)
NO, NO, NO!

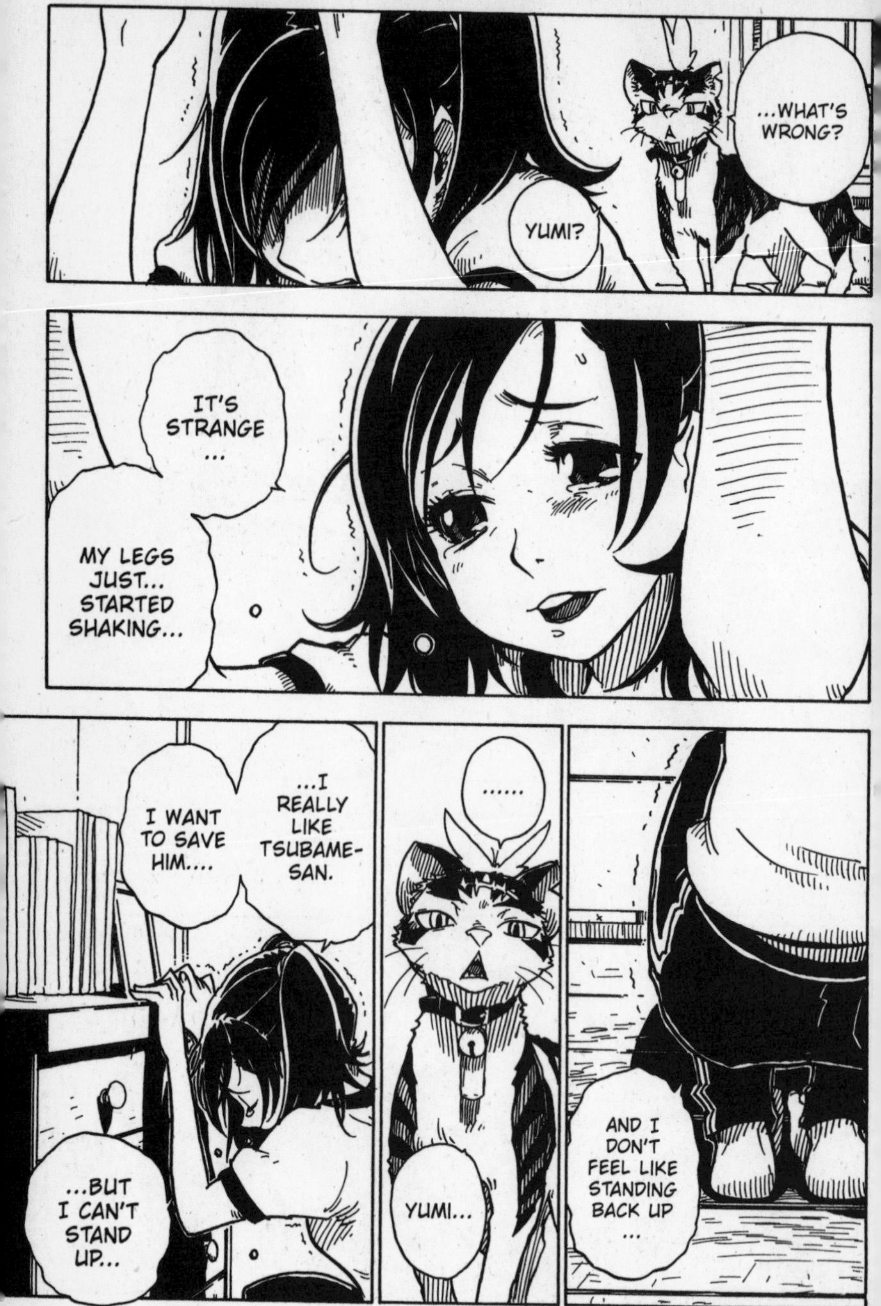
...WHAT'S WRONG?
YUMI?
IT'S STRANGE ...
MY LEGS JUST... STARTED SHAKING...
AND I DON'T FEEL LIKE STANDING BACK UP ...
......
YUMI...
...I REALLY LIKE TSUBAME-SAN.
I WANT TO SAVE HIM....
...BUT I CAN'T STAND UP...

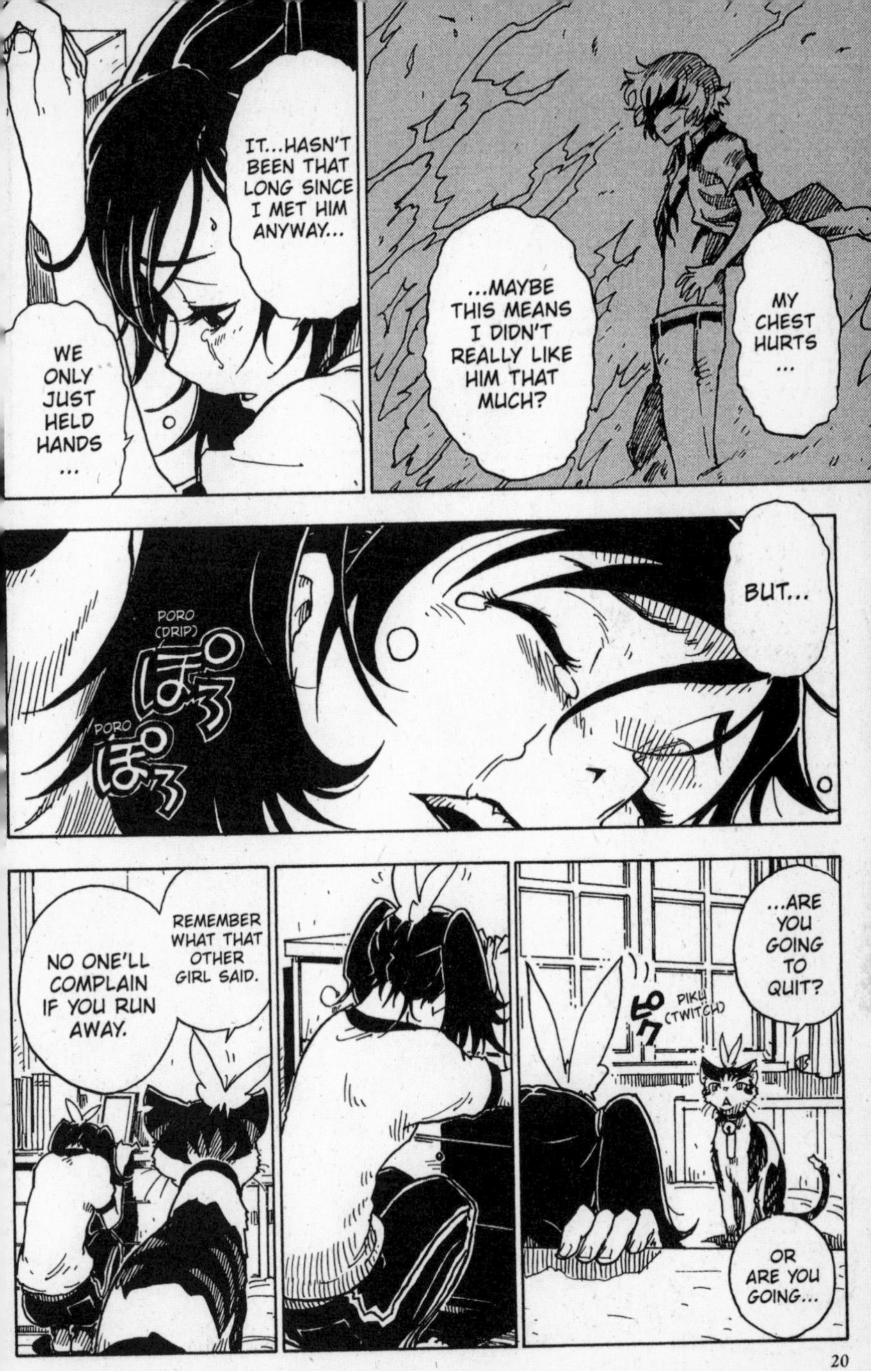
MY CHEST HURTS ...
...MAYBE THIS MEANS I DIDN'T REALLY LIKE HIM THAT MUCH?
IT...HASN'T BEEN THAT LONG SINCE I MET HIM ANYWAY...
WE ONLY JUST HELD HANDS ...
BUT...
ぽろ PORO (DRIP)
ぽろ PORO
...ARE YOU GOING TO QUIT?
ピク PIKU (TWITCH)
OR ARE YOU GOING...
REMEMBER WHAT THAT OTHER GIRL SAID.
NO ONE'LL COMPLAIN IF YOU RUN AWAY.

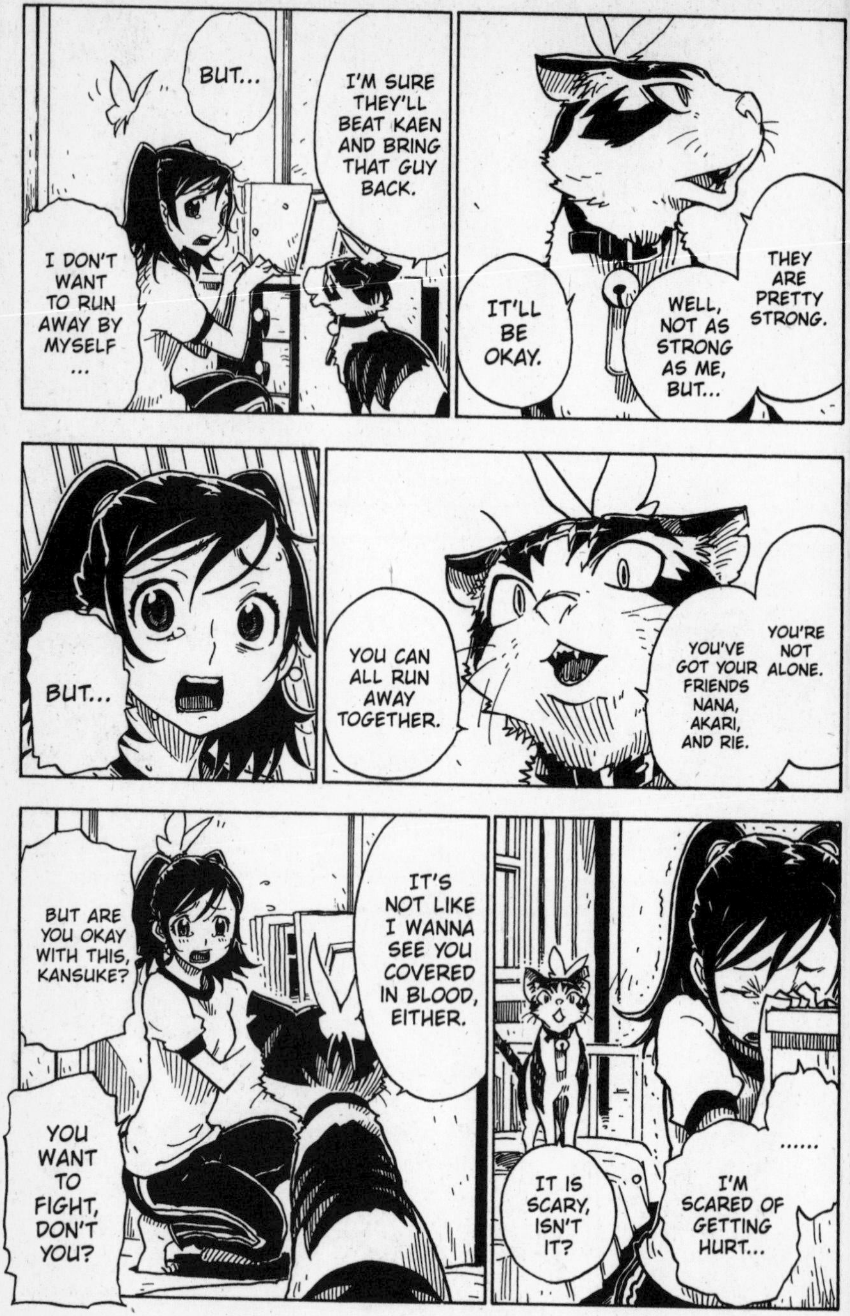
THEY ARE PRETTY STRONG.
WELL, NOT AS STRONG AS ME, BUT...
IT'LL BE OKAY.
I'M SURE THEY'LL BEAT KAEN AND BRING THAT GUY BACK.
BUT...
I DON'T WANT TO RUN AWAY BY MYSELF ...
YOU'RE NOT ALONE.
YOU'VE GOT YOUR FRIENDS NANA, AKARI, AND RIE.
YOU CAN ALL RUN AWAY TOGETHER.
BUT...
......
I'M SCARED OF GETTING HURT...
IT IS SCARY, ISN'T IT?
IT'S NOT LIKE I WANNA SEE YOU COVERED IN BLOOD, EITHER.
BUT ARE YOU OKAY WITH THIS, KANSUKE?
YOU WANT TO FIGHT, DON'T YOU?

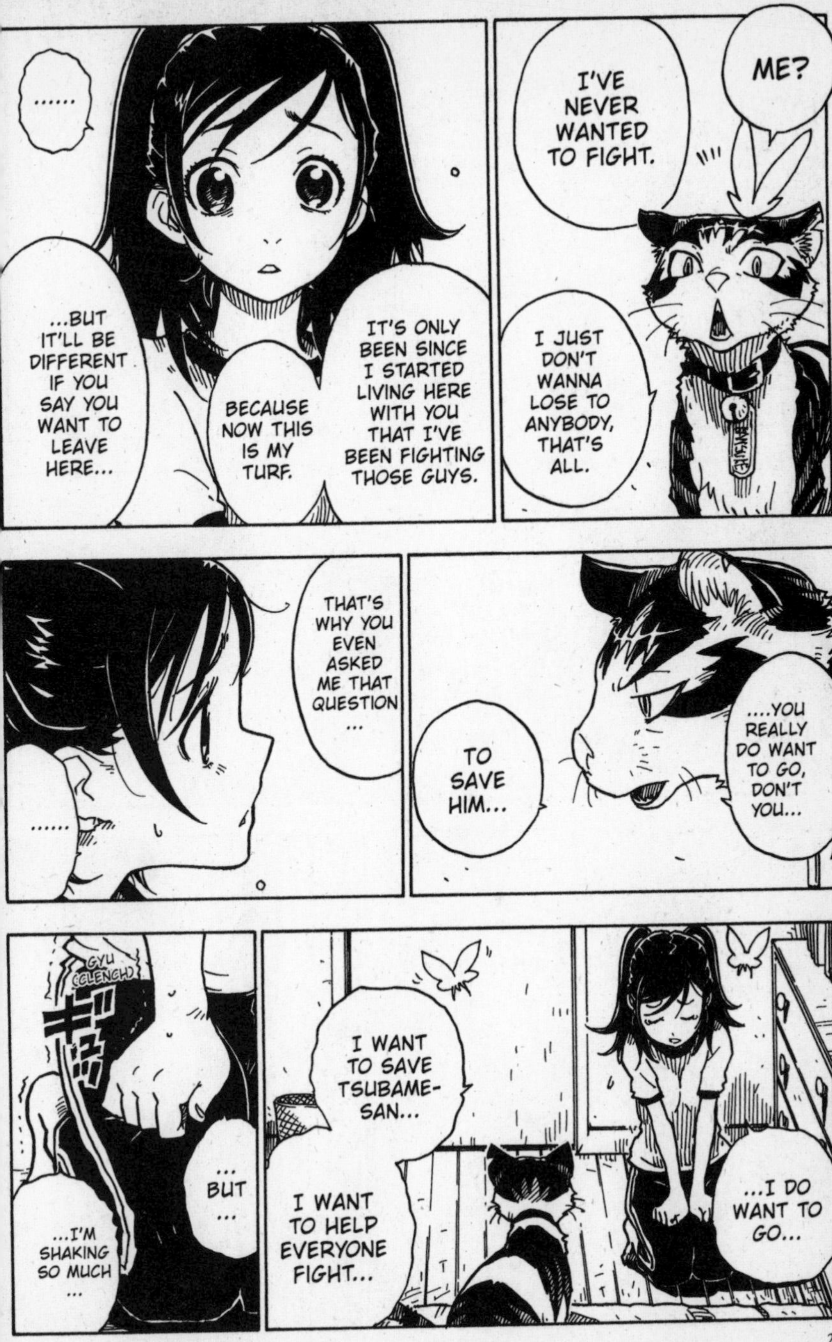
ME?
I'VE NEVER WANTED TO FIGHT.
I JUST DON'T WANNA LOSE TO ANYBODY, THAT'S ALL.
......
IT'S ONLY BEEN SINCE I STARTED LIVING HERE WITH YOU THAT I'VE BEEN FIGHTING THOSE GUYS.
BECAUSE NOW THIS IS MY TURF.
...BUT IT'LL BE DIFFERENT IF YOU SAY YOU WANT TO LEAVE HERE...
....YOU REALLY DO WANT TO GO, DON'T YOU...
TO SAVE HIM...
THAT'S WHY YOU EVEN ASKED ME THAT QUESTION ...
......
...I DO WANT TO GO...
I WANT TO SAVE TSUBAME-SAN...
I WANT TO HELP EVERYONE FIGHT...
GYU (CLENCH)
... BUT ...
...I'M SHAKING SO MUCH ...

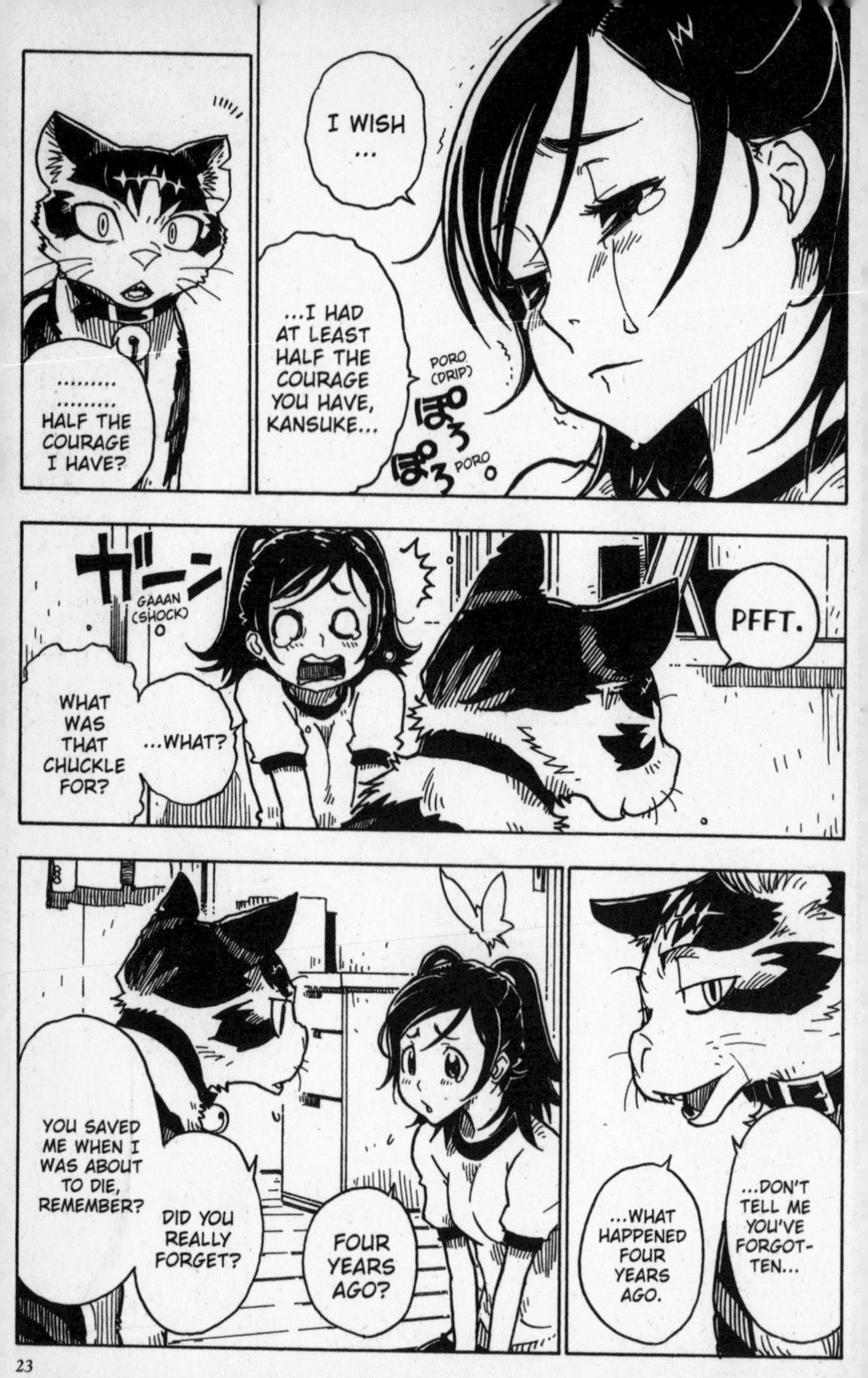

I WISH ...
...I HAD AT LEAST HALF THE COURAGE YOU HAVE, KANSUKE...
ぽろ PORO (DRIP)
ぽろ PORO
.... HALF THE COURAGE I HAVE?
PFFT.
ガーン GAAAN (SHOCK)
...WHAT?
WHAT WAS THAT CHUCKLE FOR?
...DON'T TELL ME YOU'VE FORGOT-TEN...
...WHAT HAPPENED FOUR YEARS AGO.
FOUR YEARS AGO?
DID YOU REALLY FORGET?
YOU SAVED ME WHEN I WAS ABOUT TO DIE, REMEMBER?

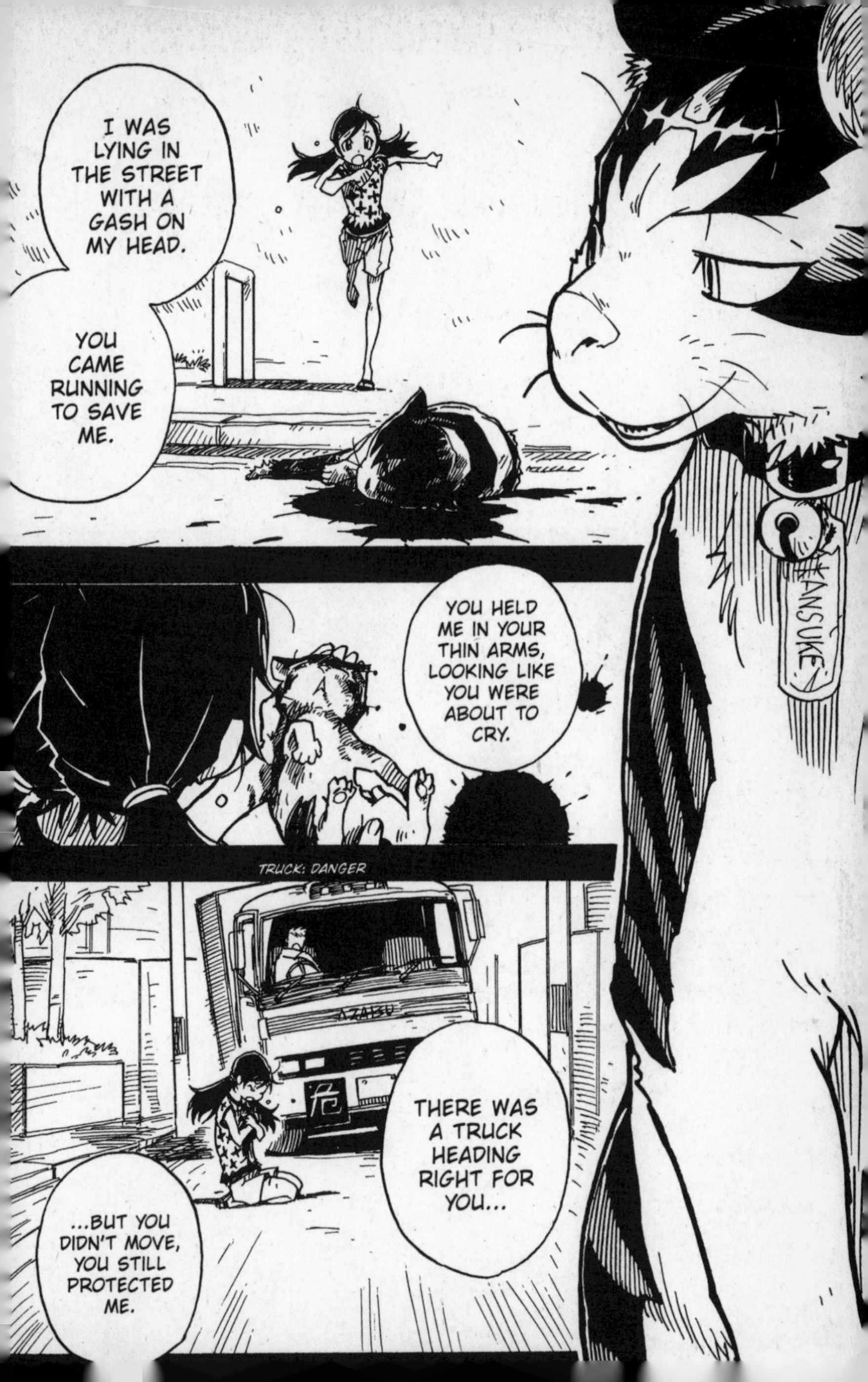
KANSUKE
I WAS LYING IN THE STREET WITH A GASH ON MY HEAD.
YOU CAME RUNNING TO SAVE ME.
YOU HELD ME IN YOUR THIN ARMS, LOOKING LIKE YOU WERE ABOUT TO CRY.
TRUCK: DANGER
THERE WAS A TRUCK HEADING RIGHT FOR YOU...
...BUT YOU DIDN'T MOVE, YOU STILL PROTECTED ME.

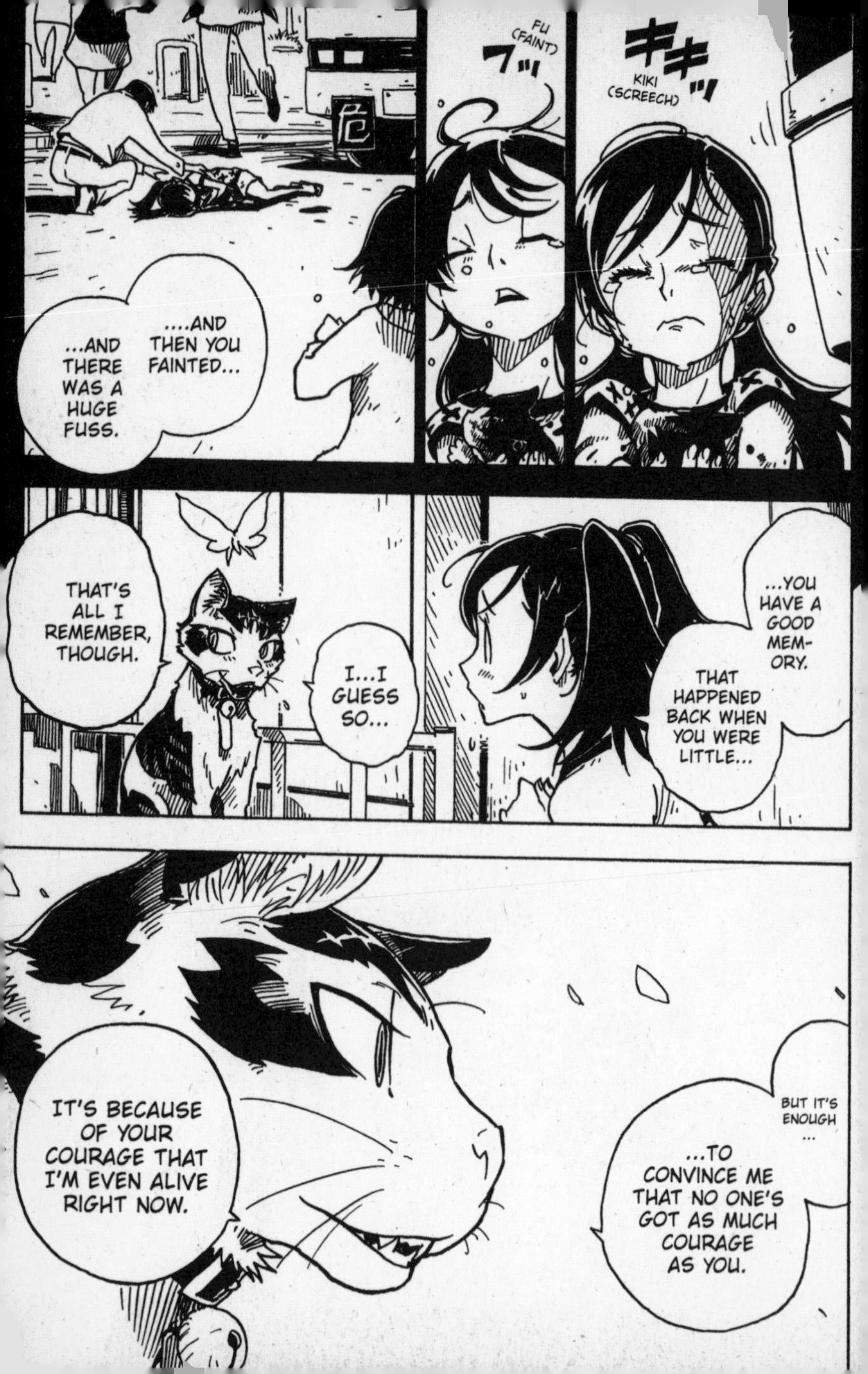

キキッ
KIKI (SCREECH)
フッ
FU (FAINT)
....AND THEN YOU FAINTED...
...AND THERE WAS A HUGE FUSS.
...YOU HAVE A GOOD MEM-ORY.
THAT HAPPENED BACK WHEN YOU WERE LITTLE...
I...I GUESS SO...
THAT'S ALL I REMEMBER, THOUGH.
BUT IT'S ENOUGH ...
...TO CONVINCE ME THAT NO ONE'S GOT AS MUCH COURAGE AS YOU.
IT'S BECAUSE OF YOUR COURAGE THAT I'M EVEN ALIVE RIGHT NOW.

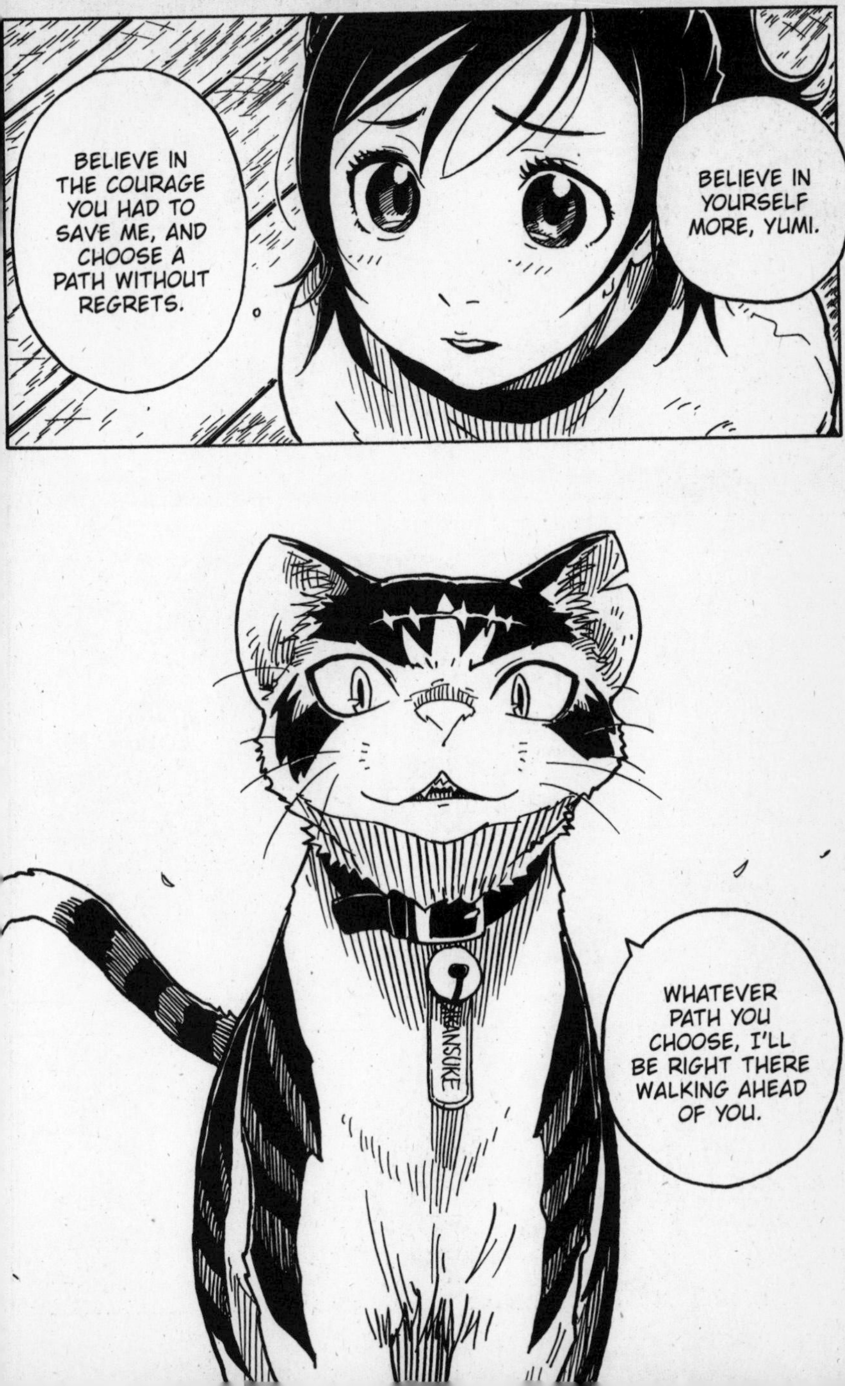
BELIEVE IN YOURSELF MORE, YUMI.
BELIEVE IN THE COURAGE YOU HAD TO SAVE ME, AND CHOOSE A PATH WITHOUT REGRETS.
WHATEVER PATH YOU CHOOSE, I'LL BE RIGHT THERE WALKING AHEAD OF YOU.

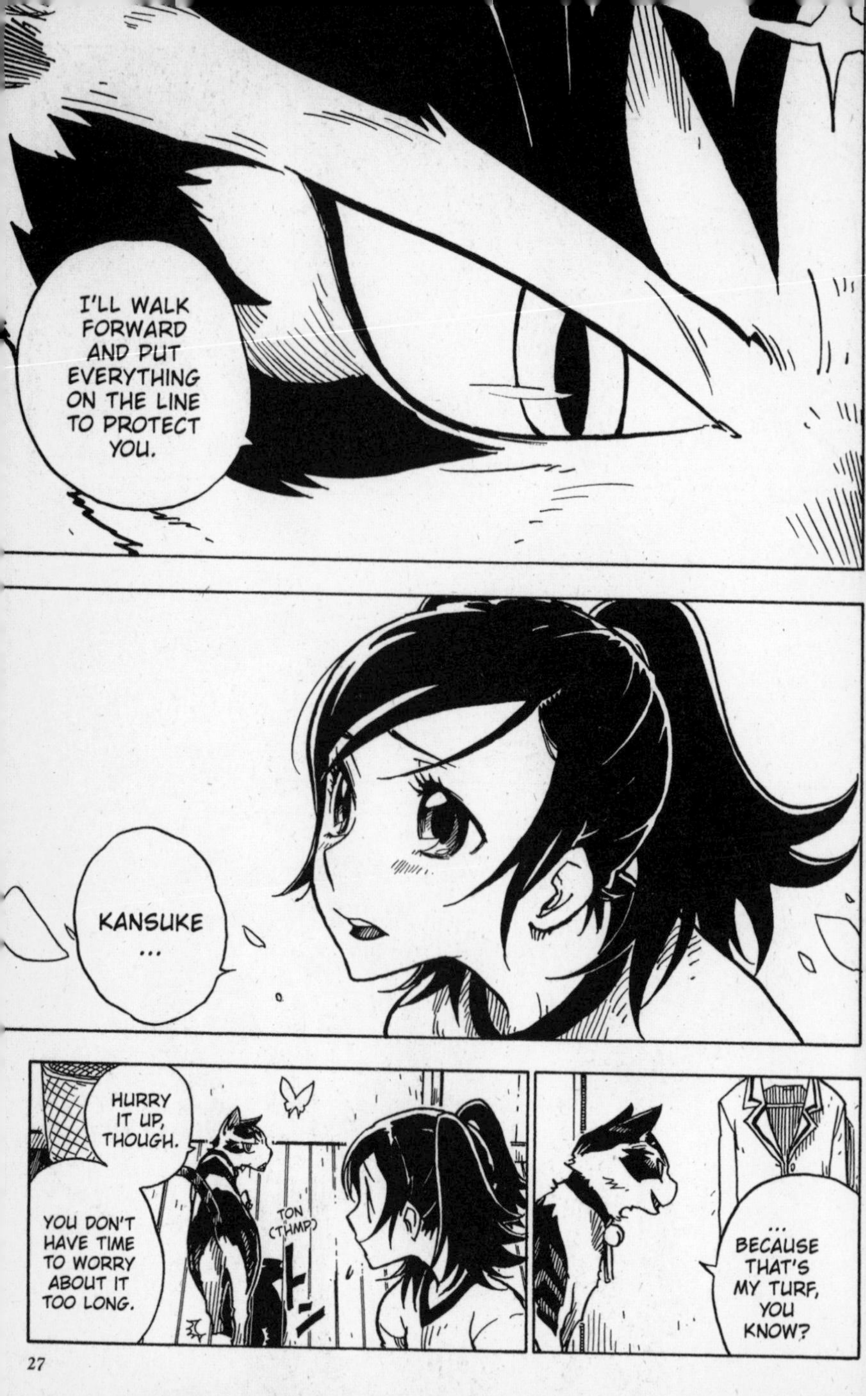
I'LL WALK FORWARD AND PUT EVERYTHING ON THE LINE TO PROTECT YOU.
KANSUKE ...
... BECAUSE THAT'S MY TURF, YOU KNOW?
HURRY IT UP, THOUGH.
TON (THMP)
YOU DON'T HAVE TIME TO WORRY ABOUT IT TOO LONG.

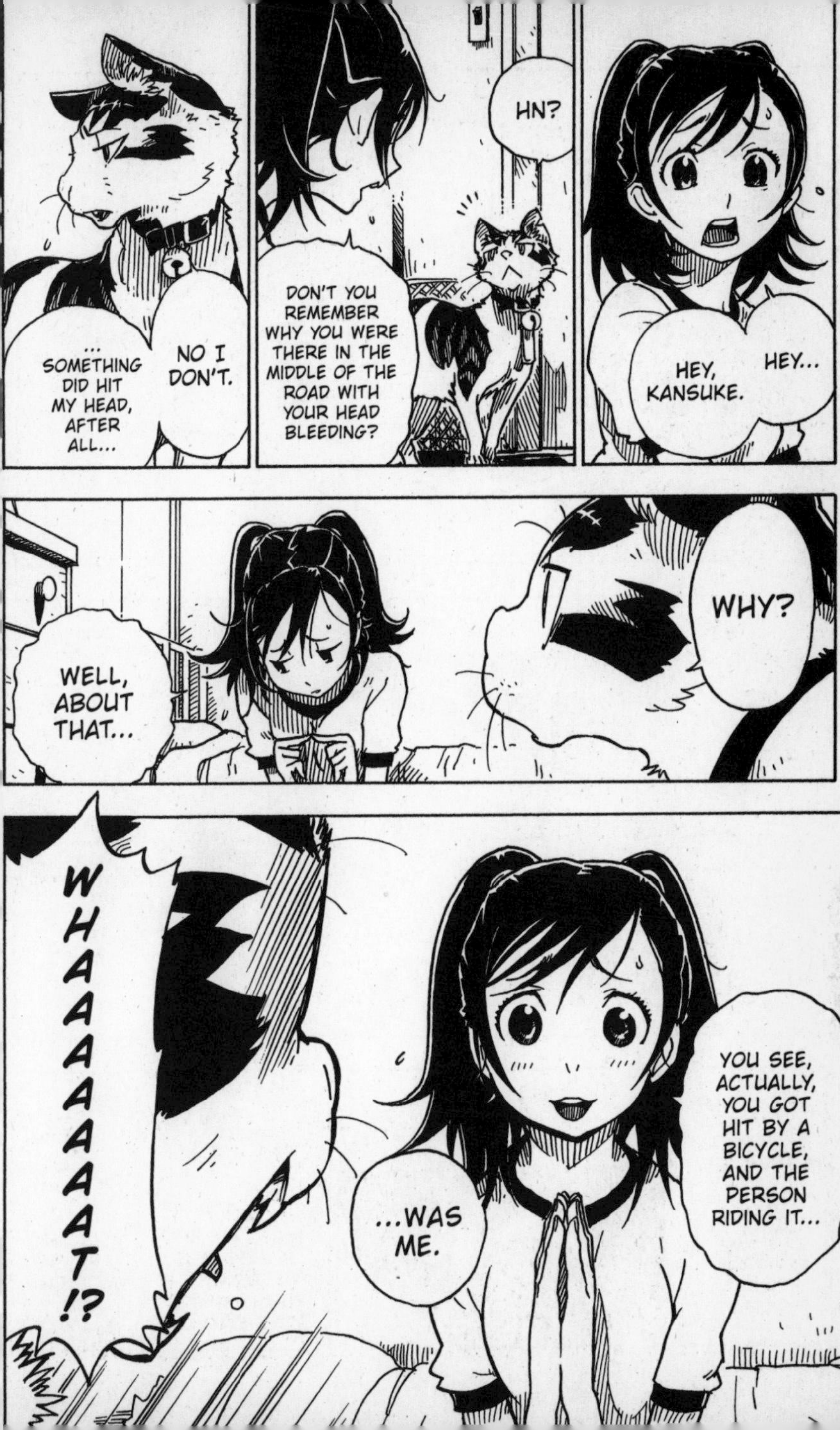
HEY...
HEY, KANSUKE.
HN?
DON'T YOU REMEMBER WHY YOU WERE THERE IN THE MIDDLE OF THE ROAD WITH YOUR HEAD BLEEDING?
NO I DON'T.
... SOMETHING DID HIT MY HEAD, AFTER ALL...
WHY?
WELL, ABOUT THAT...
YOU SEE, ACTUALLY, YOU GOT HIT BY A BICYCLE, AND THE PERSON RIDING IT...
...WAS ME.
WHAAAAAAAAT!?

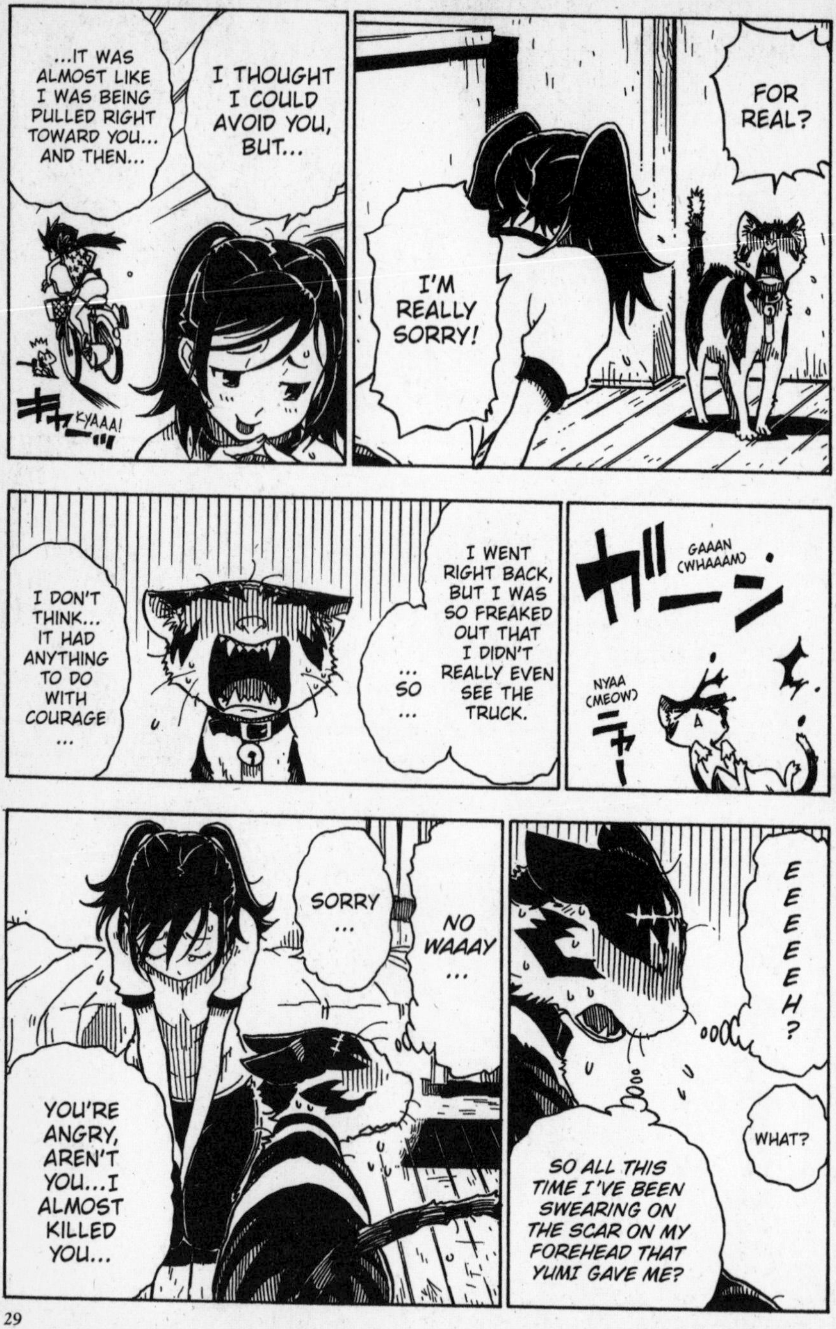
FOR REAL?
I'M REALLY SORRY!
I THOUGHT I COULD AVOID YOU, BUT...
...IT WAS ALMOST LIKE I WAS BEING PULLED RIGHT TOWARD YOU... AND THEN...
KYAAA!
GAAAN (WHAAAM)
NYAA (MEOW)
I WENT RIGHT BACK, BUT I WAS SO FREAKED OUT THAT I DIDN'T REALLY EVEN SEE THE TRUCK.
...SO...
I DON'T THINK... IT HAD ANYTHING TO DO WITH COURAGE...
EEEEEEH?
WHAT?
SO ALL THIS TIME I'VE BEEN SWEARING ON THE SCAR ON MY FOREHEAD THAT YUMI GAVE ME?
NO WAAAY...
SORRY...
YOU'RE ANGRY, AREN'T YOU...I ALMOST KILLED YOU...

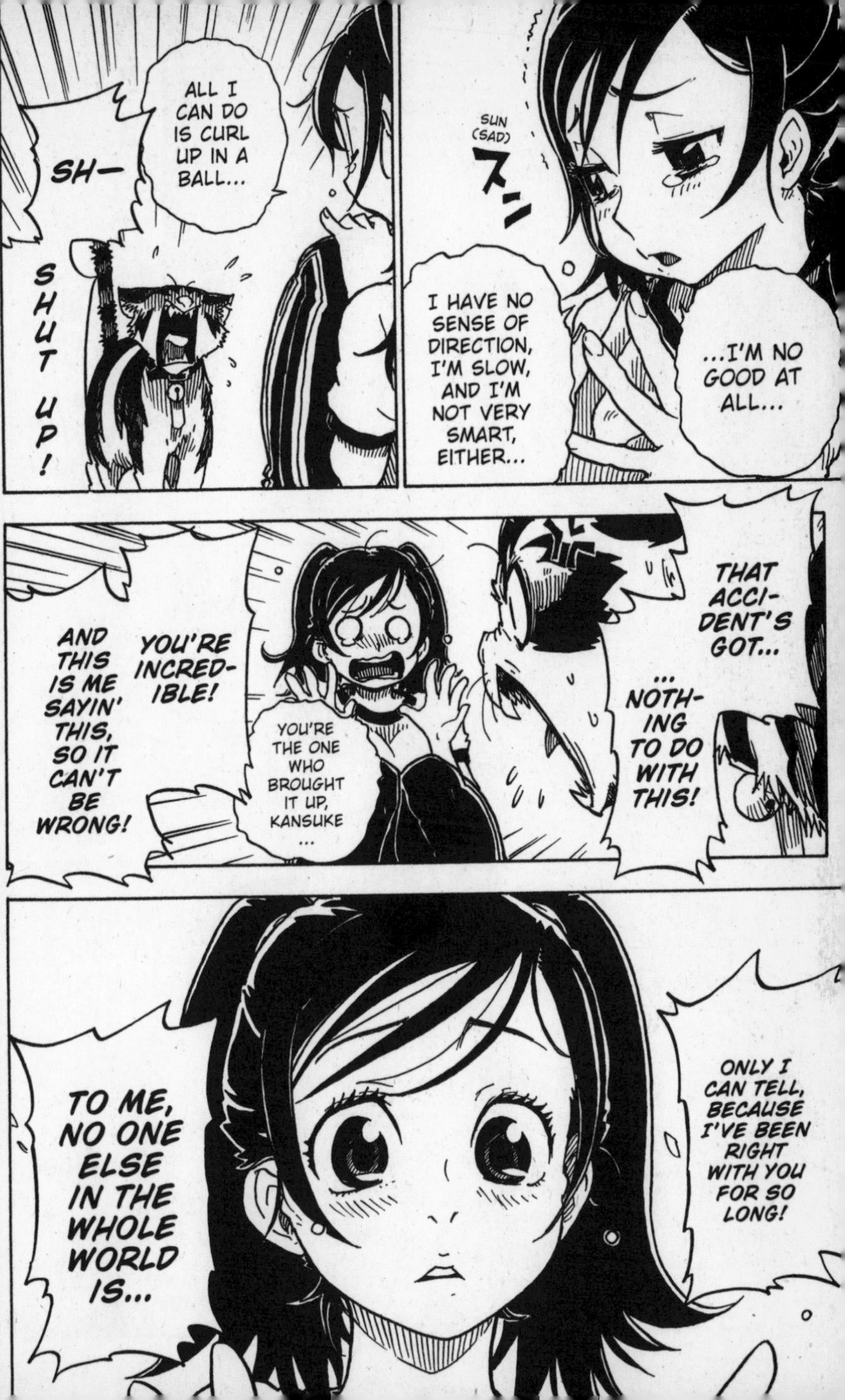
SUN (SAD)
I HAVE NO SENSE OF DIRECTION, I'M SLOW, AND I'M NOT VERY SMART, EITHER...
...I'M NO GOOD AT ALL...
ALL I CAN DO IS CURL UP IN A BALL...
SH—
SHUT UP!
THAT ACCIDENT'S GOT...
...NOTHING TO DO WITH THIS!
YOU'RE THE ONE WHO BROUGHT IT UP, KANSUKE...
YOU'RE INCREDIBLE!
AND THIS IS ME SAYIN' THIS, SO IT CAN'T BE WRONG!
ONLY I CAN TELL, BECAUSE I'VE BEEN RIGHT WITH YOU FOR SO LONG!
TO ME, NO ONE ELSE IN THE WHOLE WORLD IS...

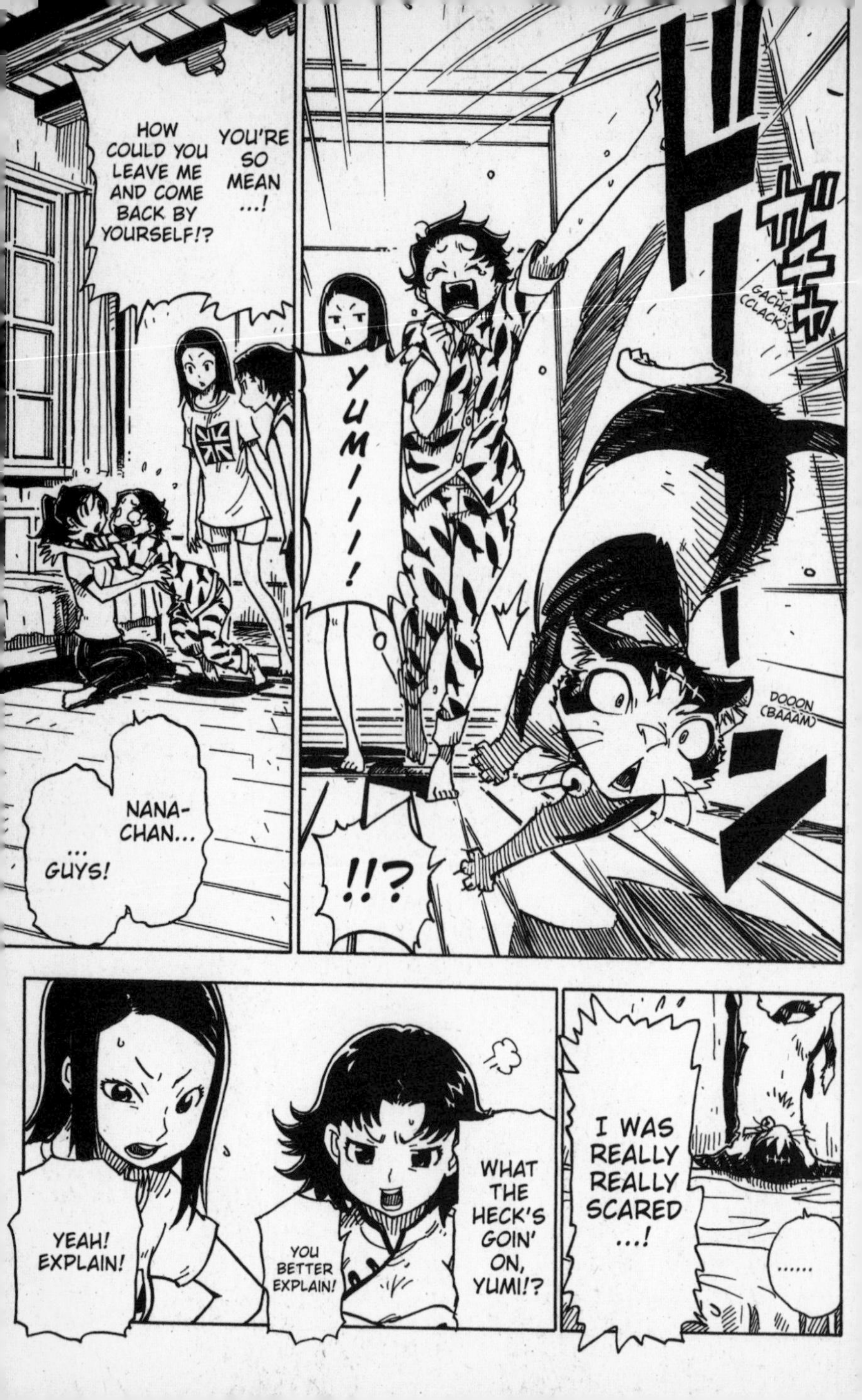
GACHA (CLACK)
YUMI!!!!!
DOOON (BAAAM)
!!?
YOU'RE SO MEAN ...!
HOW COULD YOU LEAVE ME AND COME BACK BY YOURSELF!?
NANA-CHAN...
... GUYS!
I WAS REALLY REALLY SCARED ...!
......
WHAT THE HECK'S GOIN' ON, YUMI!?
YOU BETTER EXPLAIN!
YEAH! EXPLAIN!

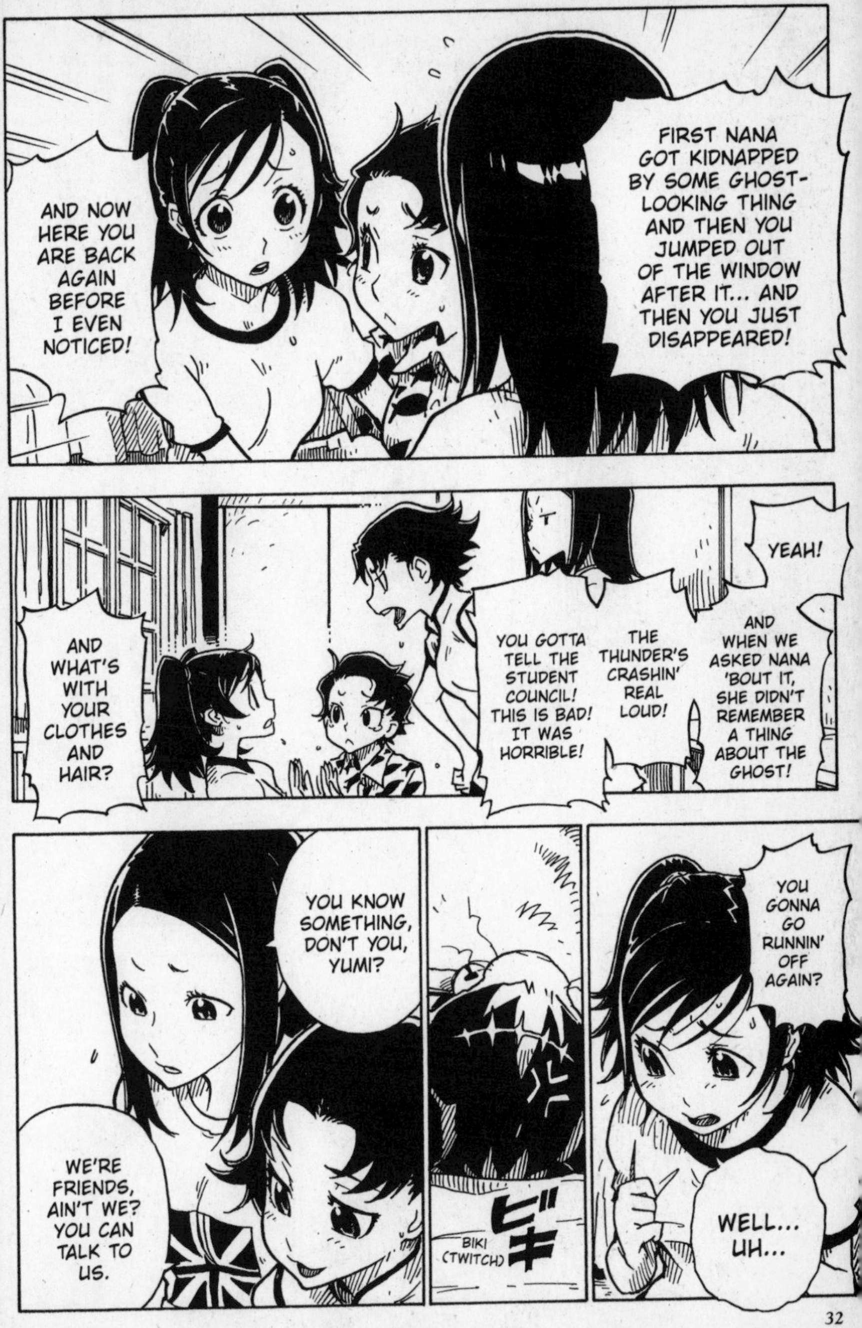
FIRST NANA GOT KIDNAPPED BY SOME GHOST-LOOKING THING AND THEN YOU JUMPED OUT OF THE WINDOW AFTER IT... AND THEN YOU JUST DISAPPEARED!
AND NOW HERE YOU ARE BACK AGAIN BEFORE I EVEN NOTICED!
YEAH!
AND WHEN WE ASKED NANA 'BOUT IT, SHE DIDN'T REMEMBER A THING ABOUT THE GHOST!
THE THUNDER'S CRASHIN' REAL LOUD!
YOU GOTTA TELL THE STUDENT COUNCIL! THIS IS BAD! IT WAS HORRIBLE!
AND WHAT'S WITH YOUR CLOTHES AND HAIR?
YOU GONNA GO RUNNIN' OFF AGAIN?
WELL... UH...
ビキ
BIKI (TWITCH)
YOU KNOW SOMETHING, DON'T YOU, YUMI?
WE'RE FRIENDS, AIN'T WE? YOU CAN TALK TO US.

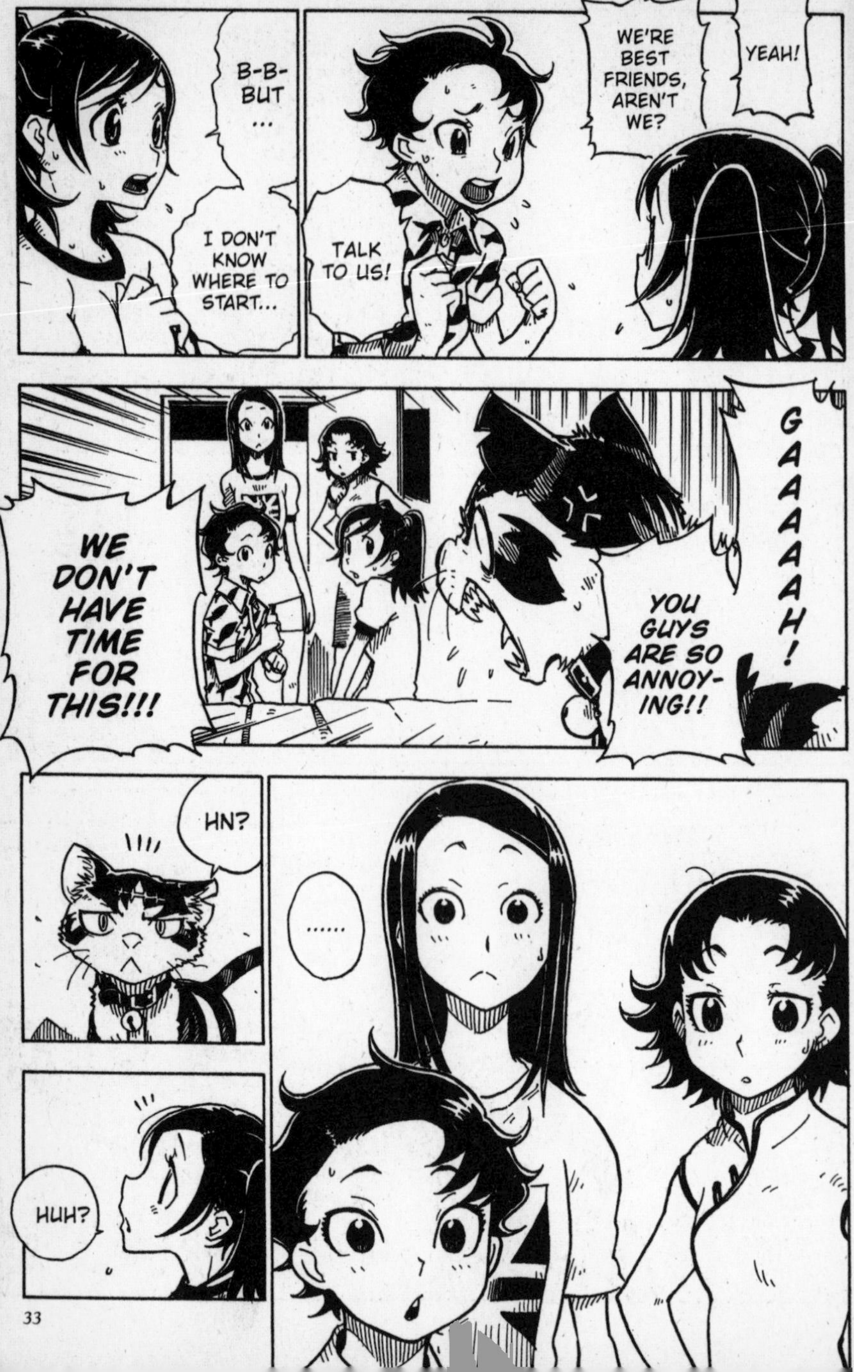
YEAH!
WE'RE BEST FRIENDS, AREN'T WE?
TALK TO US!
B-B-BUT ...
I DON'T KNOW WHERE TO START...
GAAAAAAH!
YOU GUYS ARE SO ANNOY-ING!!
WE DON'T HAVE TIME FOR THIS!!!
......
HN?
HUH?

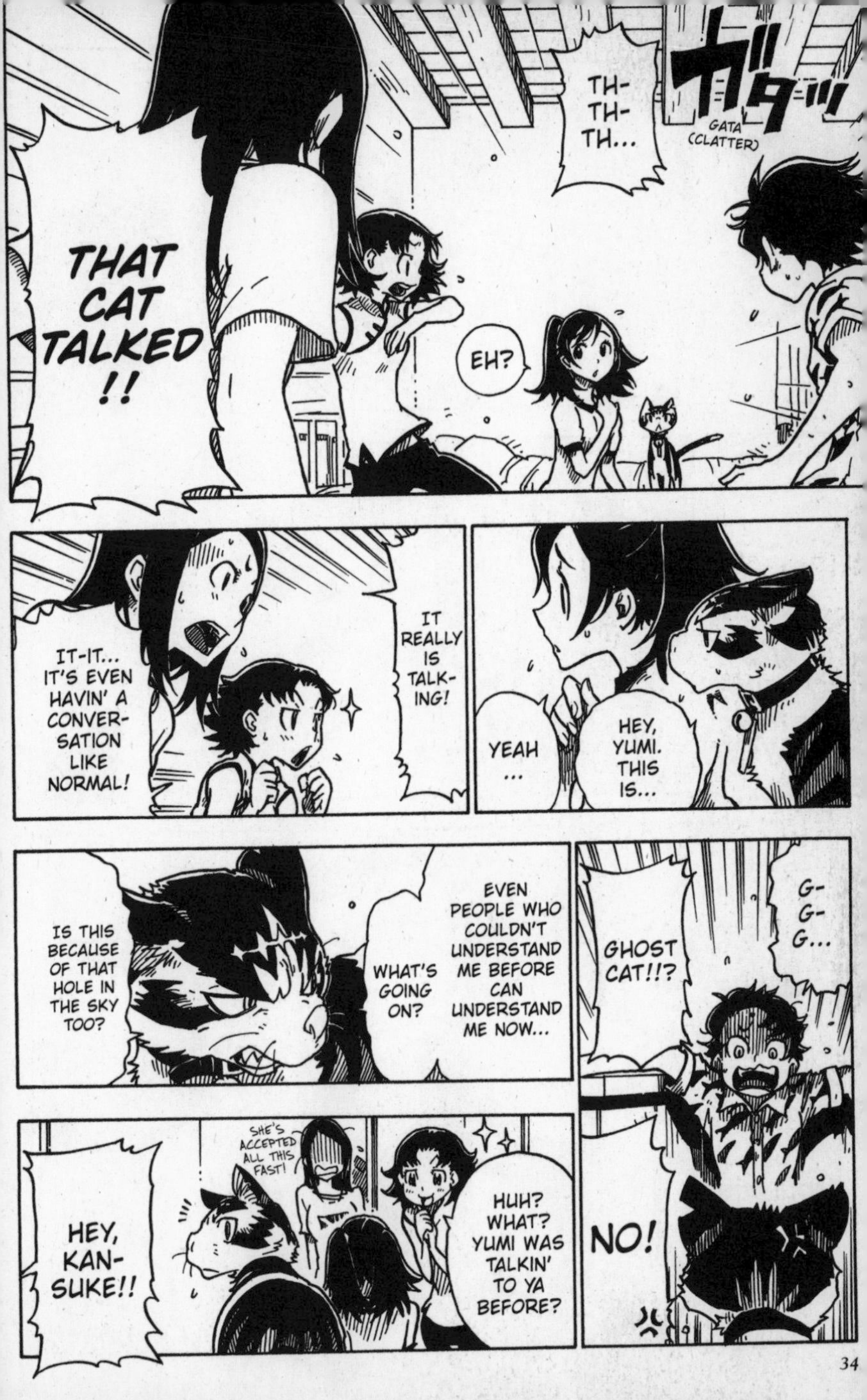
GATA (CLATTER)
TH- TH- TH...
EH?
THAT CAT TALKED!!
HEY, YUMI. THIS IS...
YEAH...
IT REALLY IS TALKING!
IT-IT... IT'S EVEN HAVIN' A CONVERSATION LIKE NORMAL!
G-G-G...
GHOST CAT!!?
NO!
EVEN PEOPLE WHO COULDN'T UNDERSTAND ME BEFORE CAN UNDERSTAND ME NOW...
WHAT'S GOING ON?
IS THIS BECAUSE OF THAT HOLE IN THE SKY TOO?
HUH? WHAT? YUMI WAS TALKIN' TO YA BEFORE?
SHE'S ACCEPTED ALL THIS FAST!
HEY, KANSUKE!!

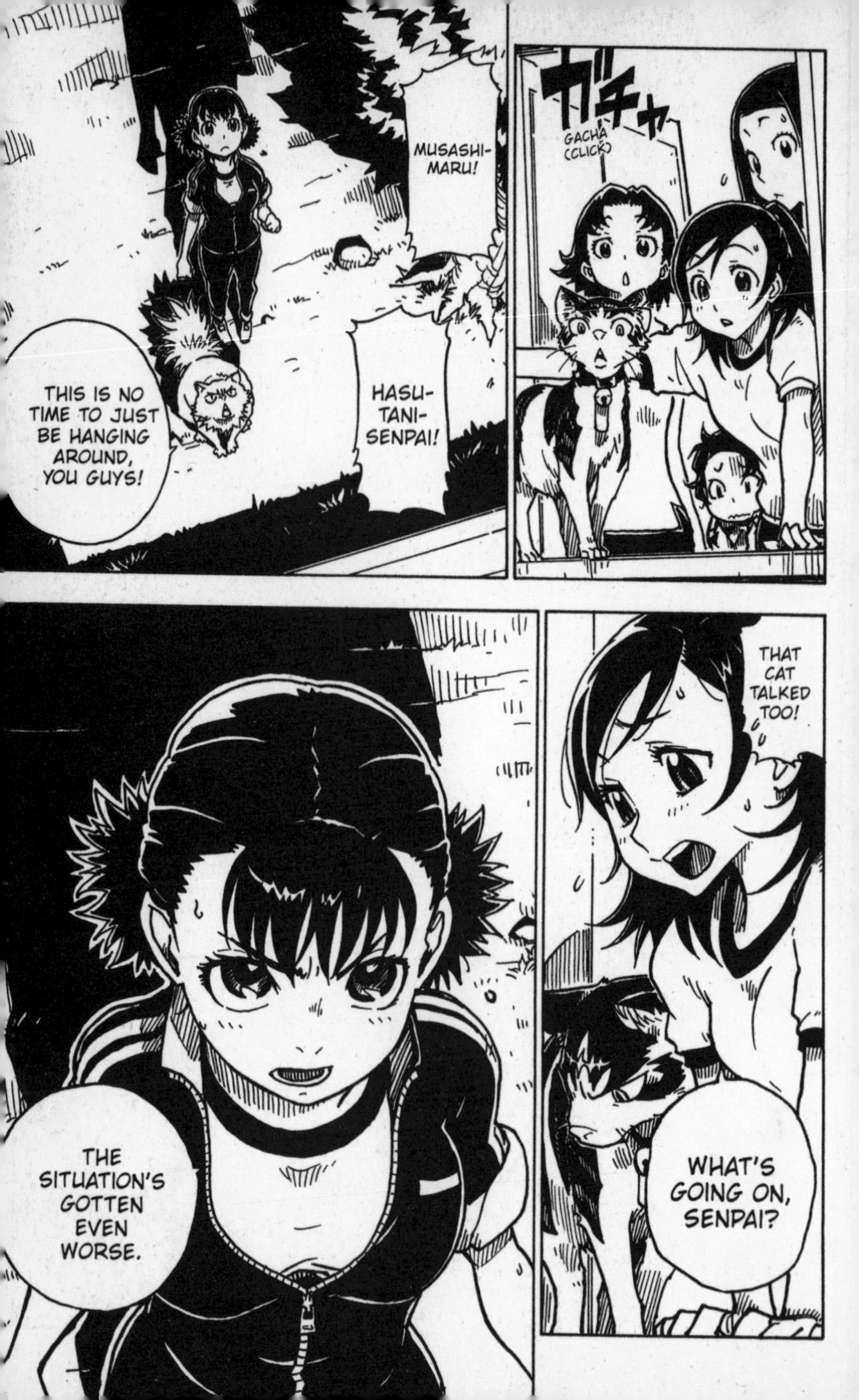
ガチャ
GACHA (CLICK)
MUSASHI-MARU!
HASU-TANI-SENPAI!
THIS IS NO TIME TO JUST BE HANGING AROUND, YOU GUYS!
THAT CAT TALKED TOO!
WHAT'S GOING ON, SENPAI?
THE SITUATION'S GOTTEN EVEN WORSE.

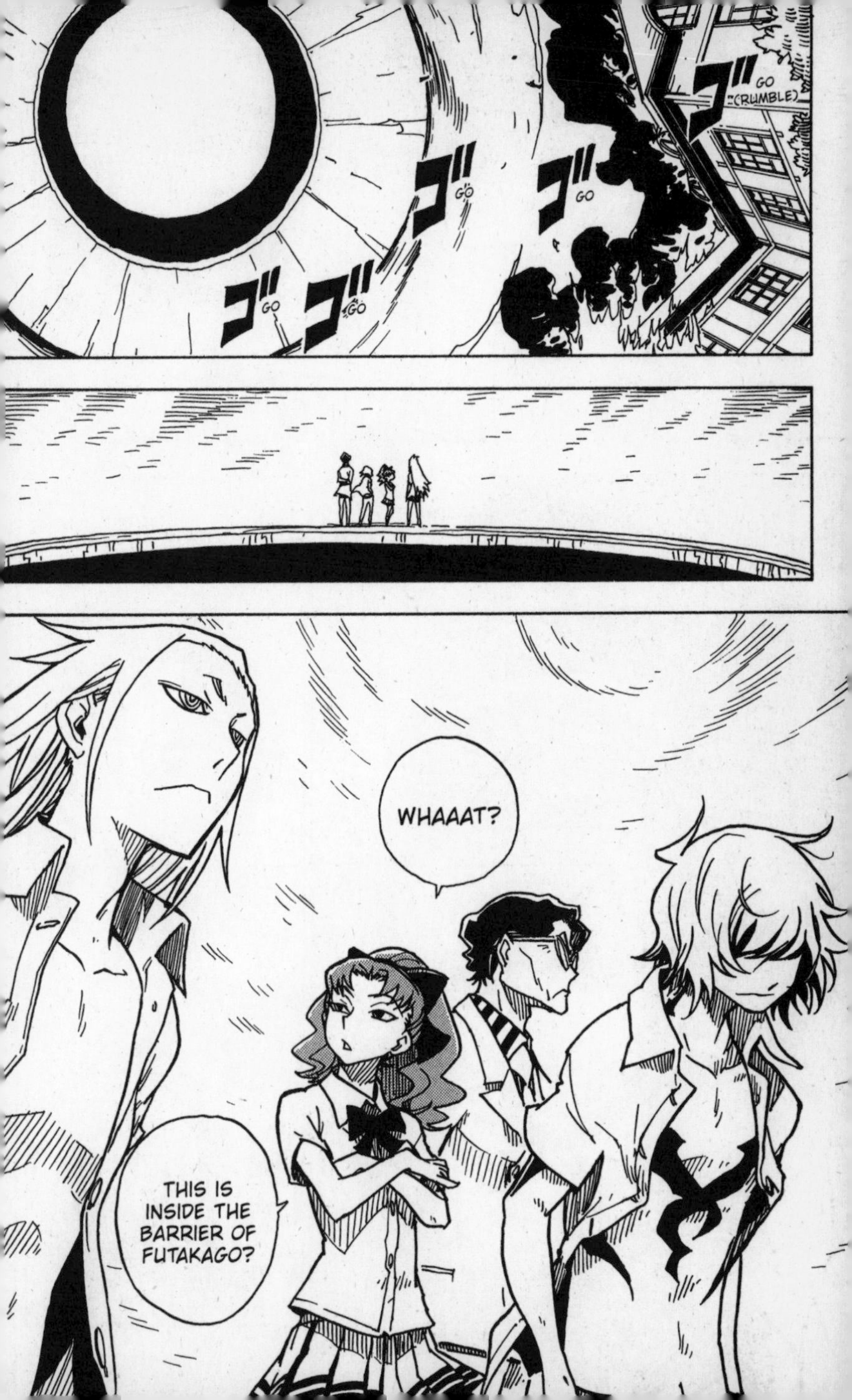
GO (CRUMBLE)
GO
GO
GO
GO
WHAAAT?
THIS IS INSIDE THE BARRIER OF FUTAKAGO?

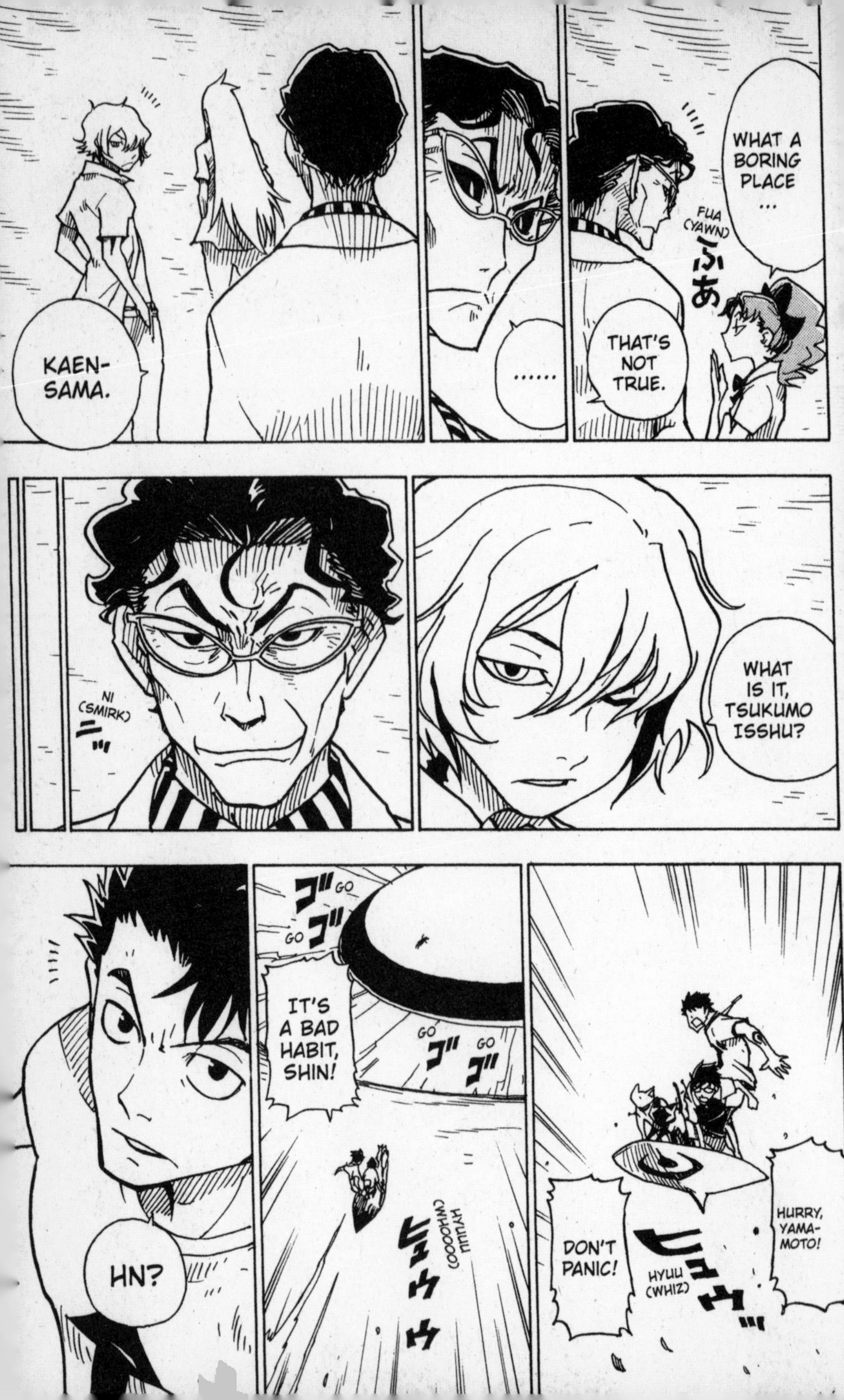
WHAT A BORING PLACE ...
FUA (YAWN) ふあ
THAT'S NOT TRUE.
......
KAEN-SAMA.
WHAT IS IT, TSUKUMO ISSHU?
NI (SMIRK) ニッ
HURRY, YAMAMOTO!
HYUU (WHIZ) ヒュウ
DON'T PANIC!
ゴ GO ゴ GO
IT'S A BAD HABIT, SHIN!
GO ゴ GO ゴ
HYUUU (WHOOOO) ヒュウウ
HN?

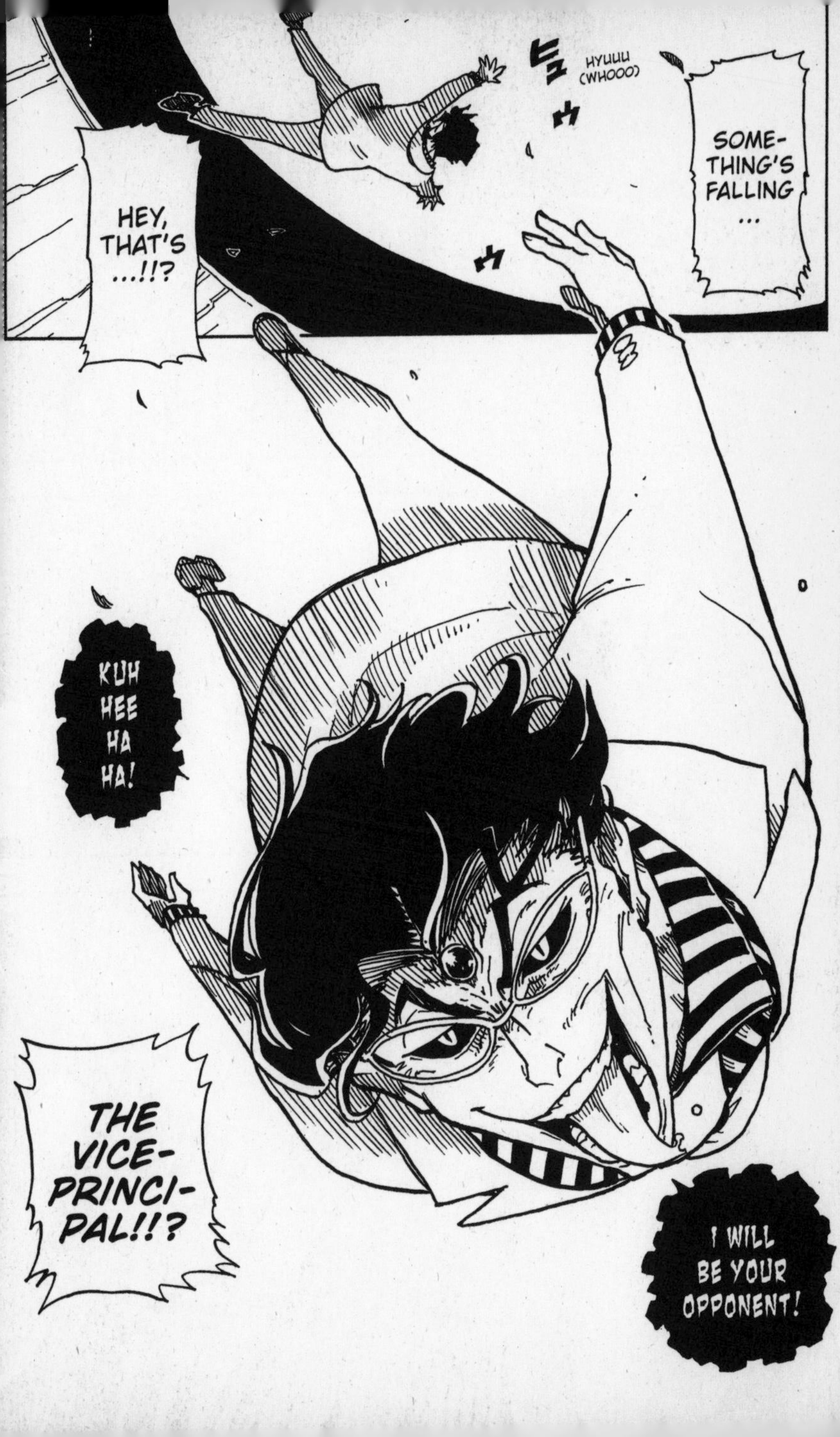
SOME-THING'S FALLING ...
HYUUU (WHOOO)
HEY, THAT'S ...!!?
KUH HEE HA HA!
THE VICE-PRINCIPAL!!?
I WILL BE YOUR OPPONENT!

CHAPTER 19
DECISIVE BATTLE

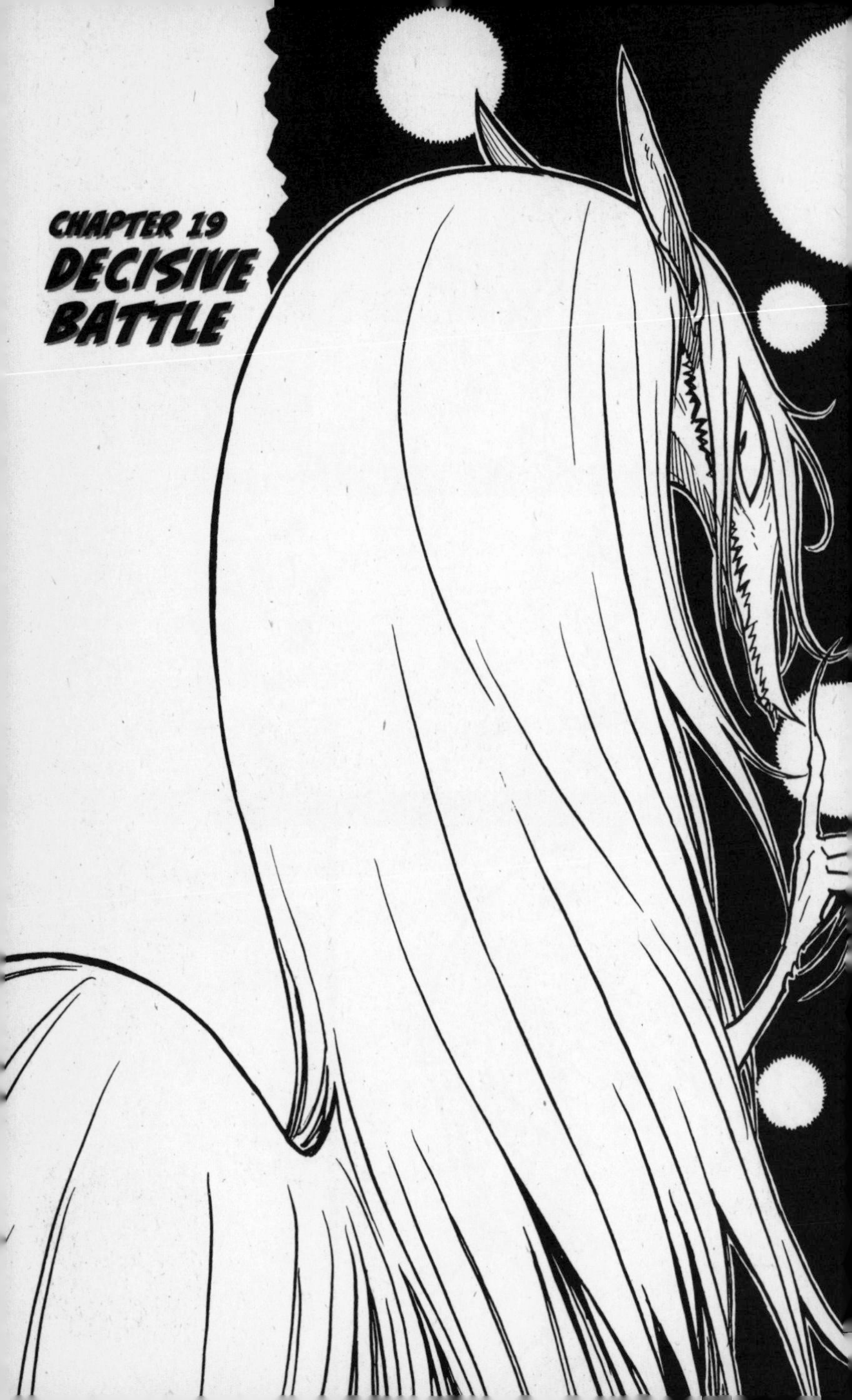

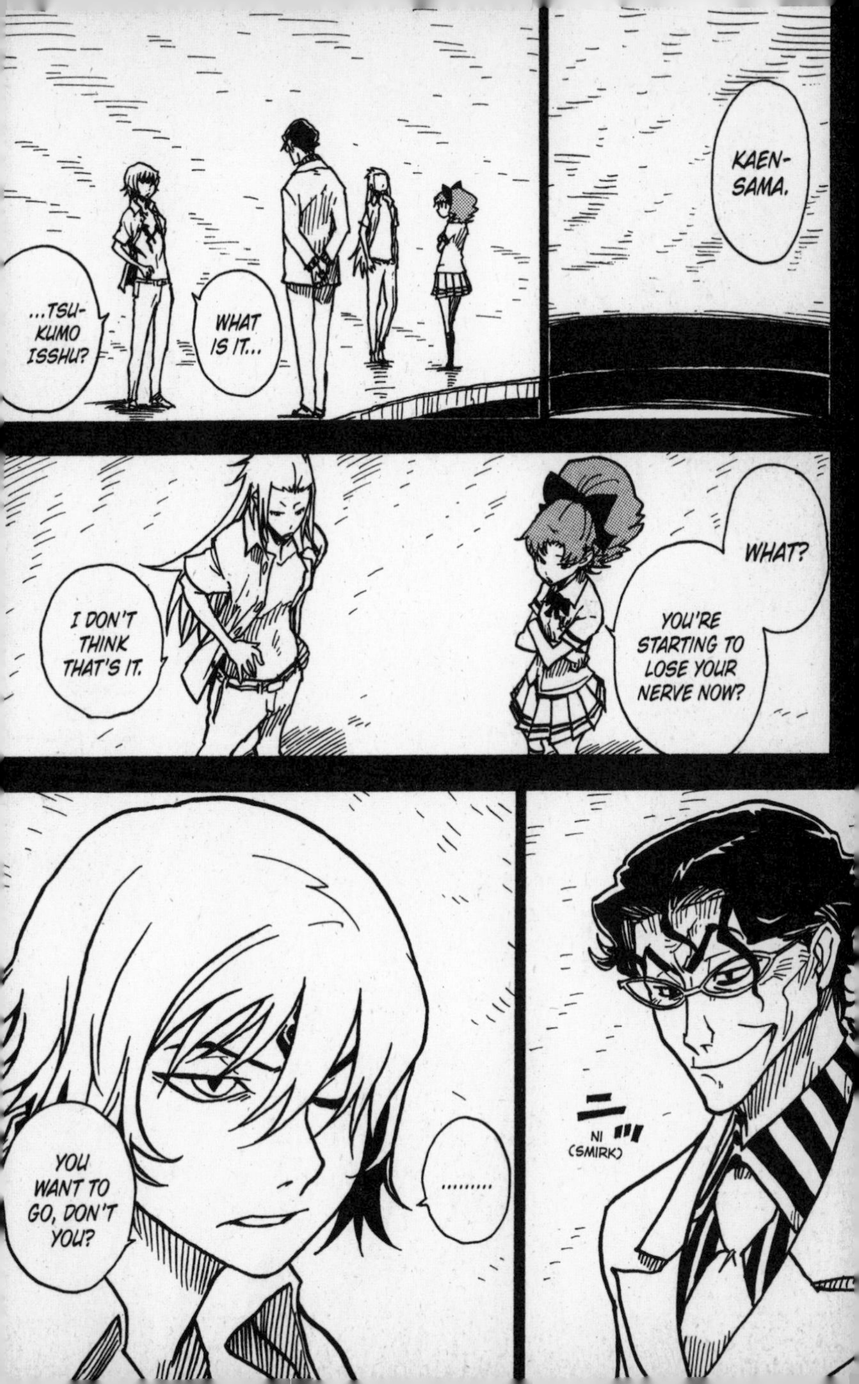
KAEN-SAMA.
WHAT IS IT...
...TSU-KUMO ISSHU?
WHAT?
YOU'RE STARTING TO LOSE YOUR NERVE NOW?
I DON'T THINK THAT'S IT.
NI (SMIRK)
....
YOU WANT TO GO, DON'T YOU?

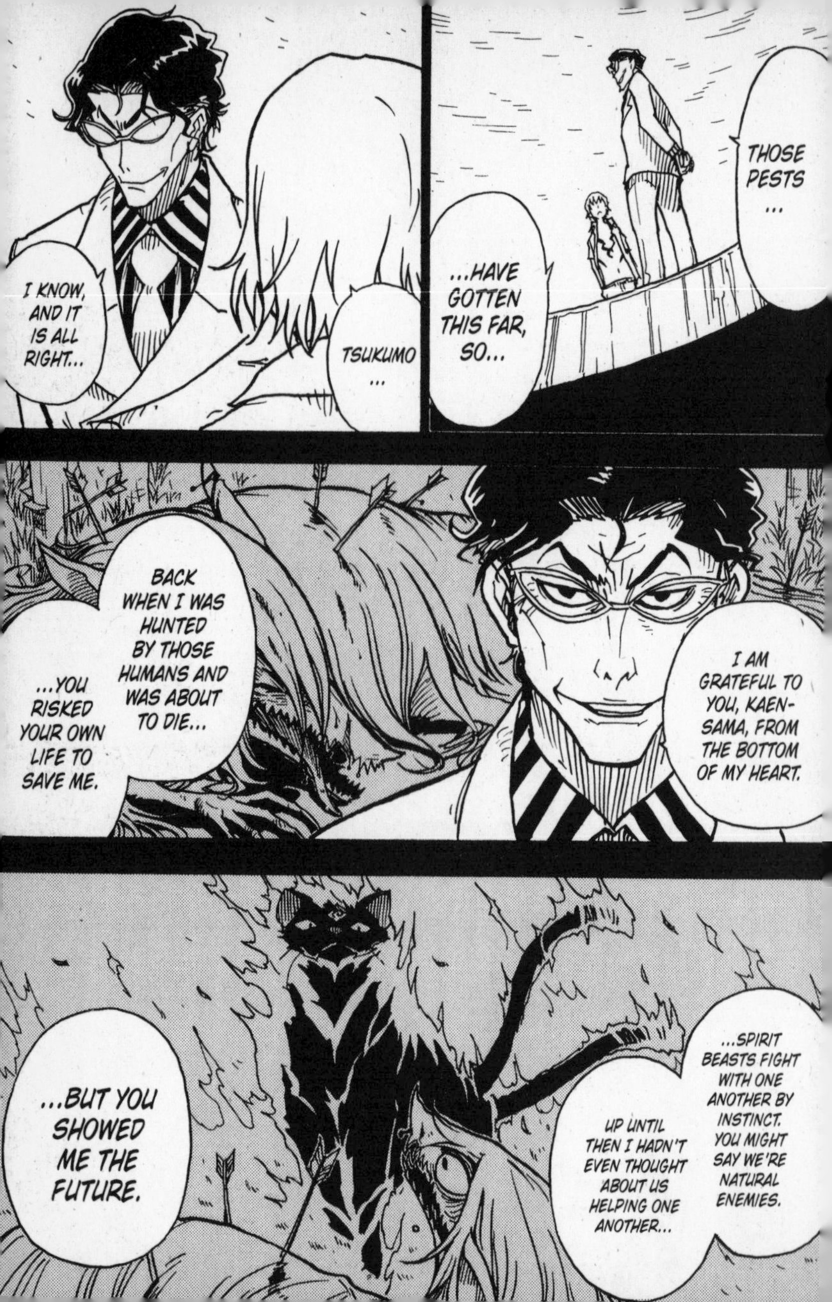
THOSE PESTS...
...HAVE GOTTEN THIS FAR, SO...
TSUKUMO...
I KNOW, AND IT IS ALL RIGHT...
I AM GRATEFUL TO YOU, KAEN-SAMA, FROM THE BOTTOM OF MY HEART.
BACK WHEN I WAS HUNTED BY THOSE HUMANS AND WAS ABOUT TO DIE...
...YOU RISKED YOUR OWN LIFE TO SAVE ME.
...SPIRIT BEASTS FIGHT WITH ONE ANOTHER BY INSTINCT. YOU MIGHT SAY WE'RE NATURAL ENEMIES.
UP UNTIL THEN I HADN'T EVEN THOUGHT ABOUT US HELPING ONE ANOTHER...
...BUT YOU SHOWED ME THE FUTURE.

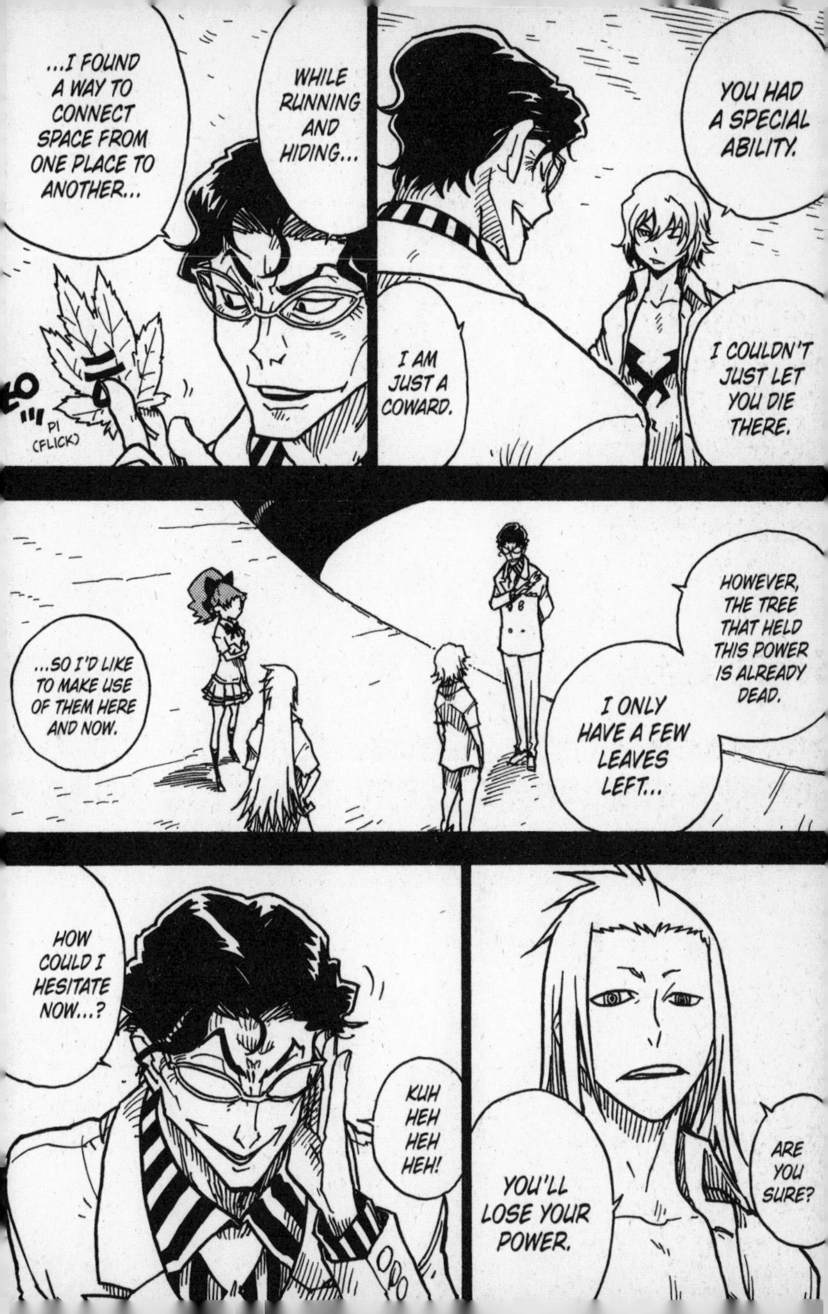
YOU HAD A SPECIAL ABILITY.
I COULDN'T JUST LET YOU DIE THERE.
I AM JUST A COWARD.
WHILE RUNNING AND HIDING...
...I FOUND A WAY TO CONNECT SPACE FROM ONE PLACE TO ANOTHER...
PI (FLICK)
HOWEVER, THE TREE THAT HELD THIS POWER IS ALREADY DEAD.
I ONLY HAVE A FEW LEAVES LEFT...
...SO I'D LIKE TO MAKE USE OF THEM HERE AND NOW.
ARE YOU SURE?
YOU'LL LOSE YOUR POWER.
KUH HEH HEH HEH!
HOW COULD I HESITATE NOW...?

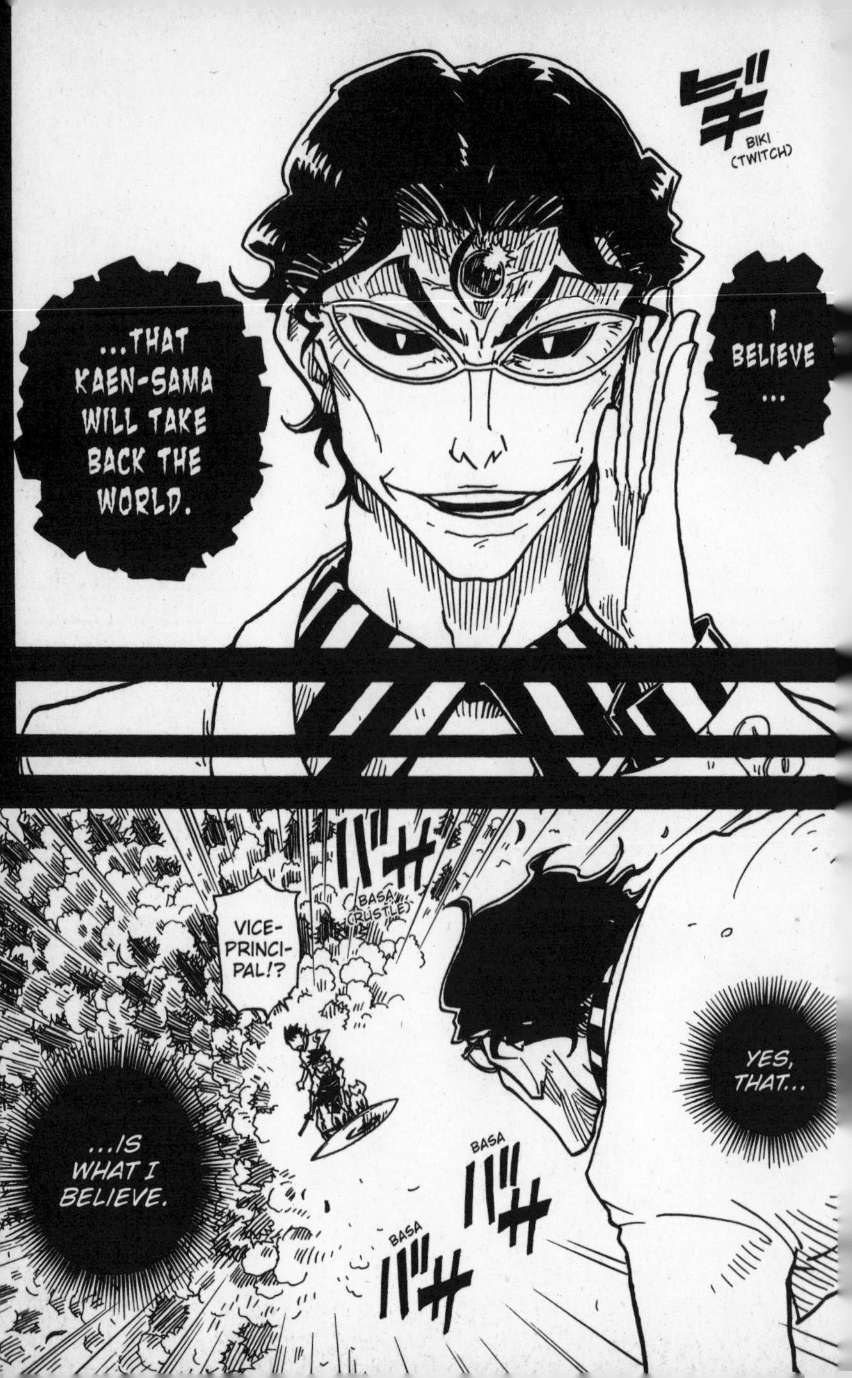
BIKI (TWITCH)
I BELIEVE ...
...THAT KAEN-SAMA WILL TAKE BACK THE WORLD.
BASA (RUSTLE)
VICE-PRINCIPAL!?
YES, THAT...
BASA
BASA
...IS WHAT I BELIEVE.

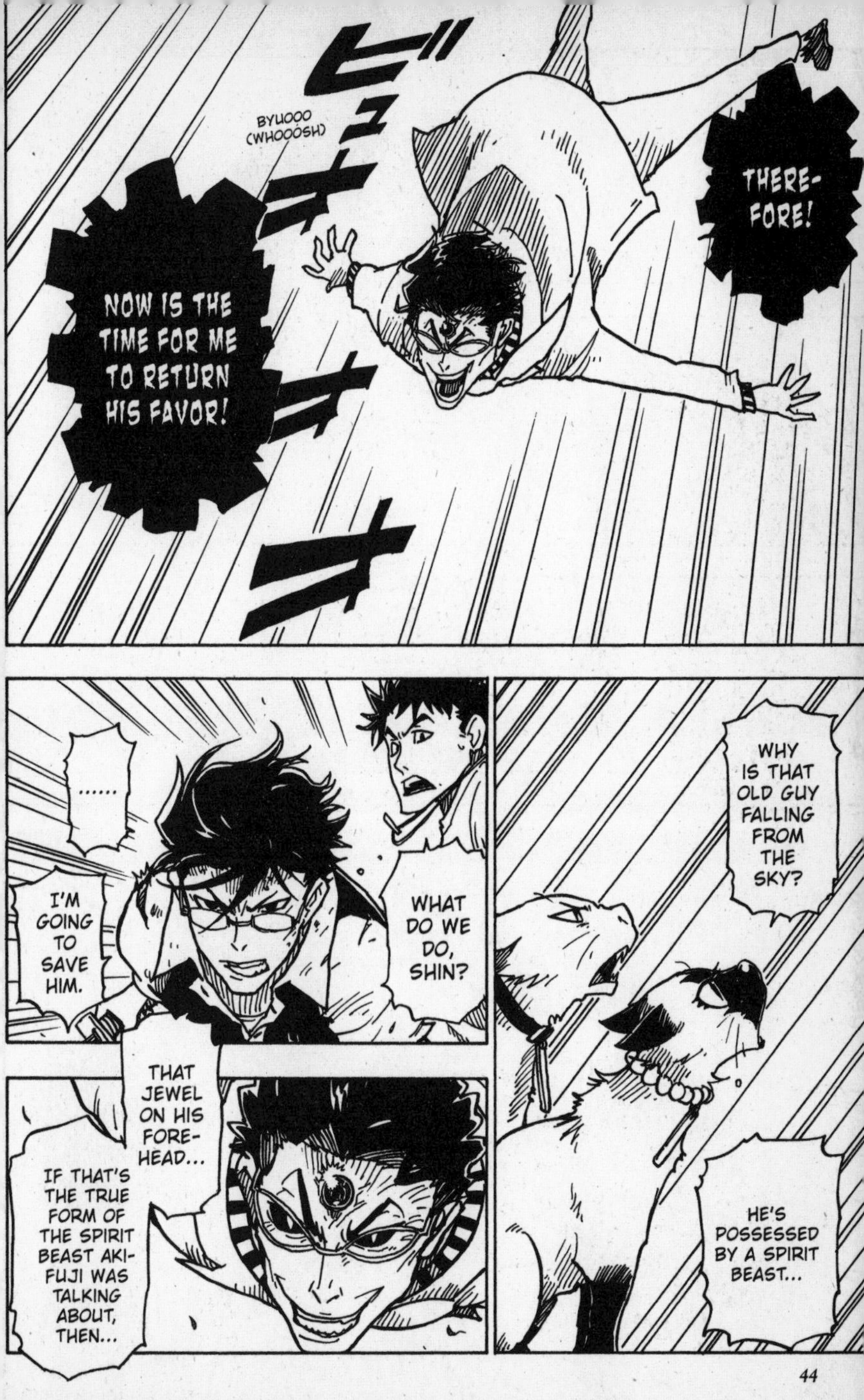
THERE-FORE!
BYUOOO (WHOOOSH)
NOW IS THE TIME FOR ME TO RETURN HIS FAVOR!
WHY IS THAT OLD GUY FALLING FROM THE SKY?
HE'S POSSESSED BY A SPIRIT BEAST...
WHAT DO WE DO, SHIN?
......
I'M GOING TO SAVE HIM.
THAT JEWEL ON HIS FORE-HEAD...
IF THAT'S THE TRUE FORM OF THE SPIRIT BEAST AKI-FUJI WAS TALKING ABOUT, THEN...

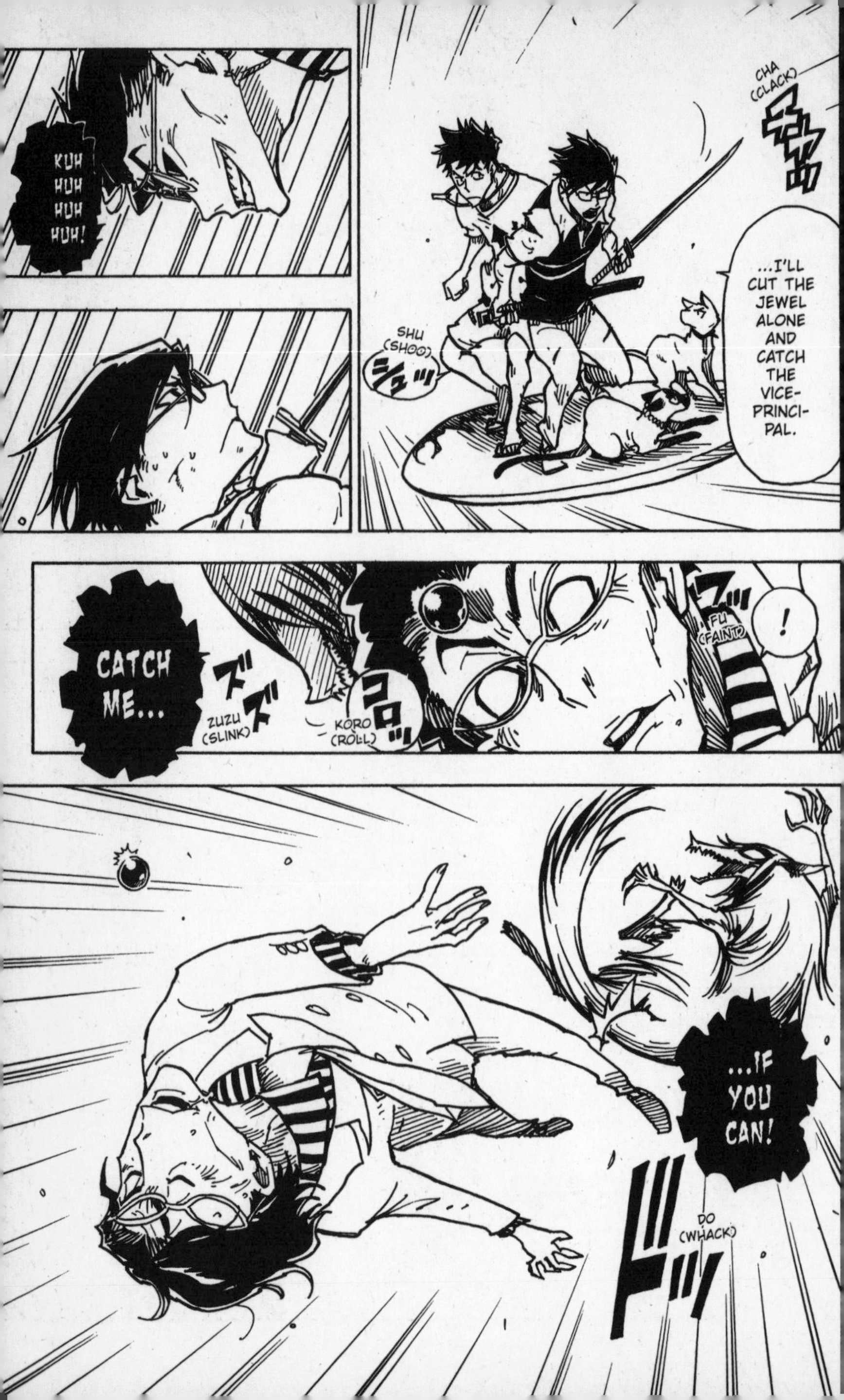
CHA (CLACK)
...I'LL CUT THE JEWEL ALONE AND CATCH THE VICE-PRINCIPAL.
SHU (SHOO)
KUH HUH HUH HUH!
!
FU (FAINT)
KORO (ROLL)
ZUZU (SLINK)
CATCH ME...
...IF YOU CAN!
DO (WHACK)

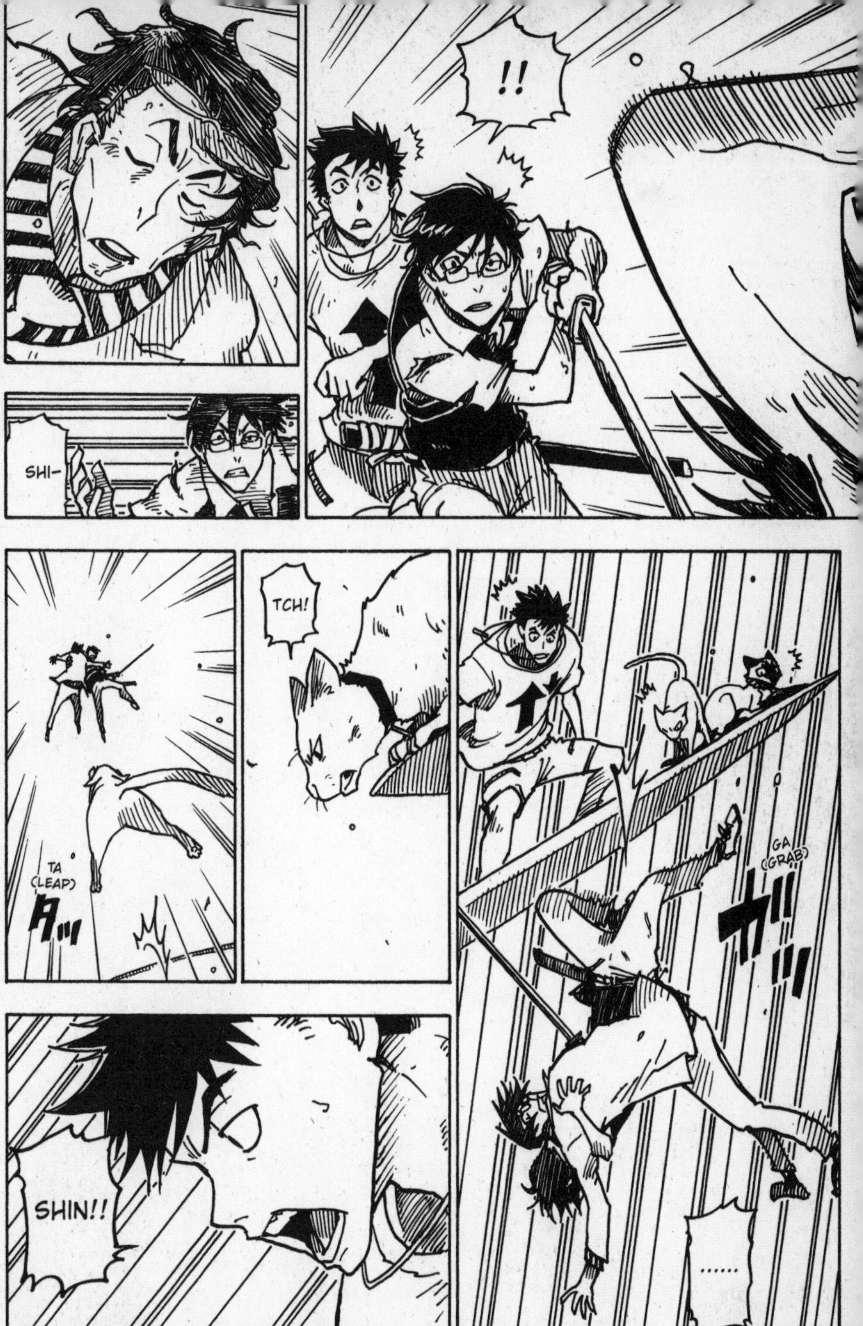
!!
SHI-
GA (GRAB)
......
TCH!
TA (LEAP)
SHIN!!

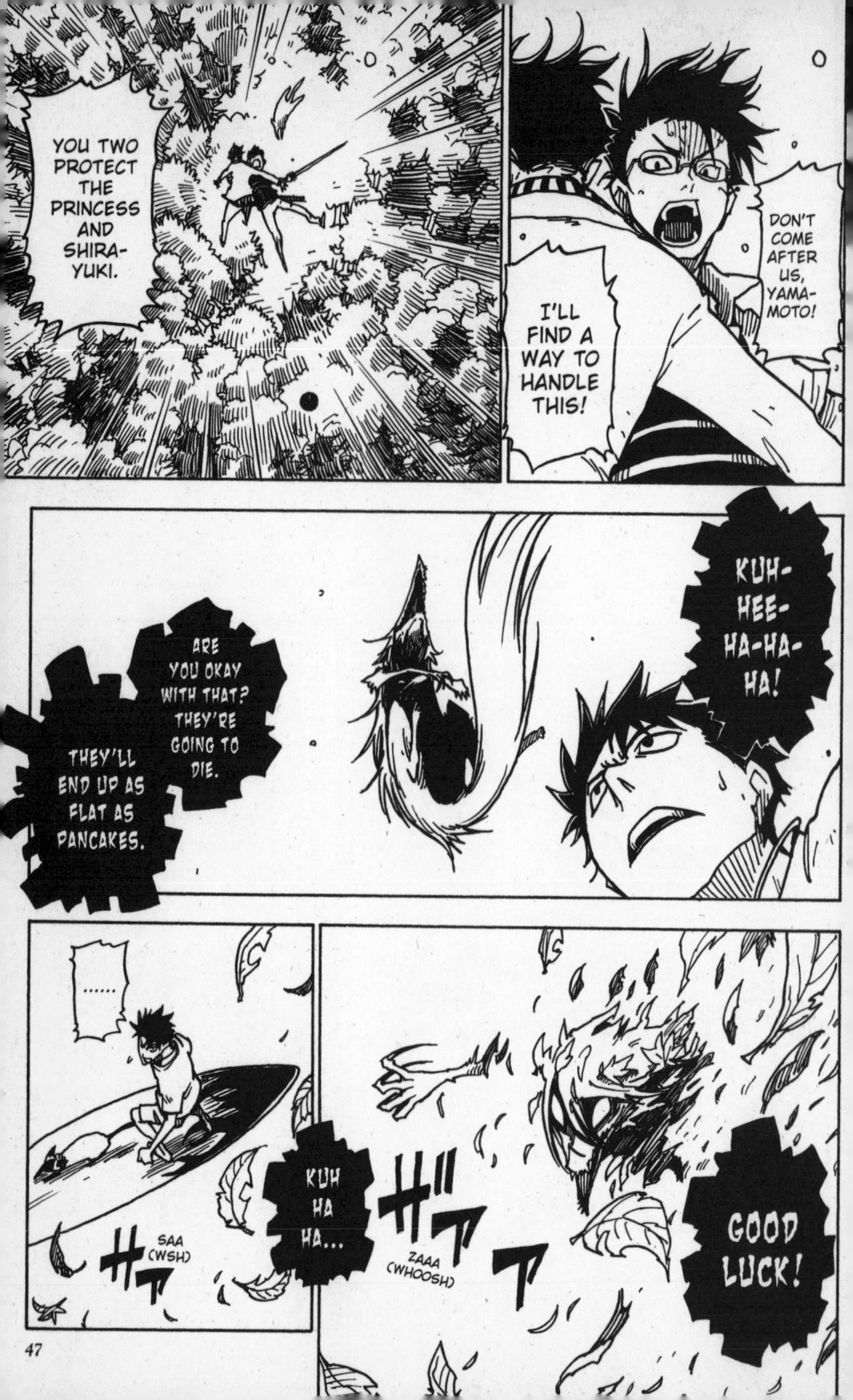
DON'T COME AFTER US, YAMAMOTO!
I'LL FIND A WAY TO HANDLE THIS!
YOU TWO PROTECT THE PRINCESS AND SHIRAYUKI.
KUH-HEE-HA-HA-HA!
ARE YOU OKAY WITH THAT? THEY'RE GOING TO DIE.
THEY'LL END UP AS FLAT AS PANCAKES.
GOOD LUCK!
ZAAA (WHOOSH)
KUH HA HA...
......
SAA (WSH)

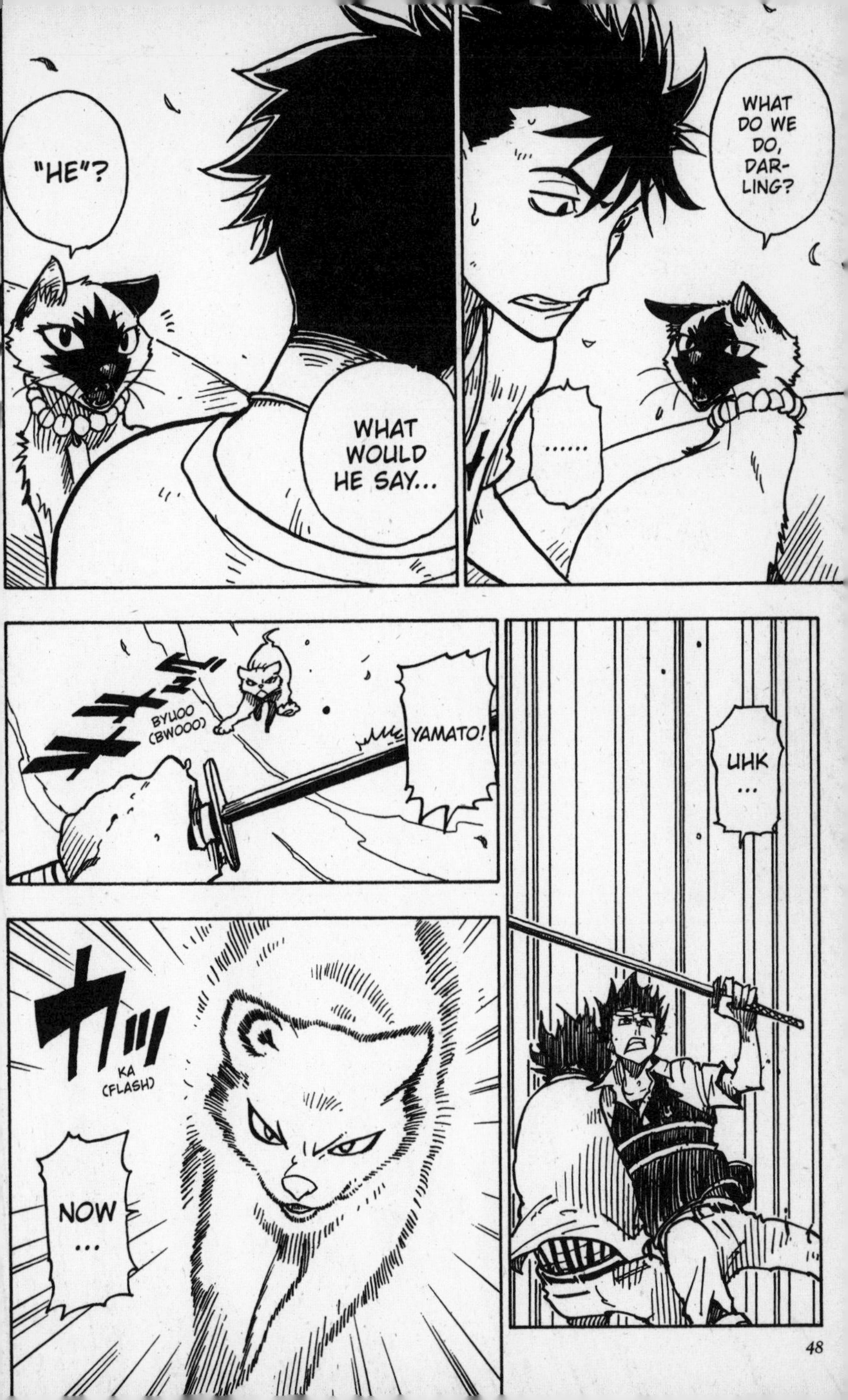
WHAT DO WE DO, DARLING?
......
WHAT WOULD HE SAY...
"HE"?
UHK ...
YAMATO!
BYUOO (BWOOO)
KA (FLASH)
NOW ...

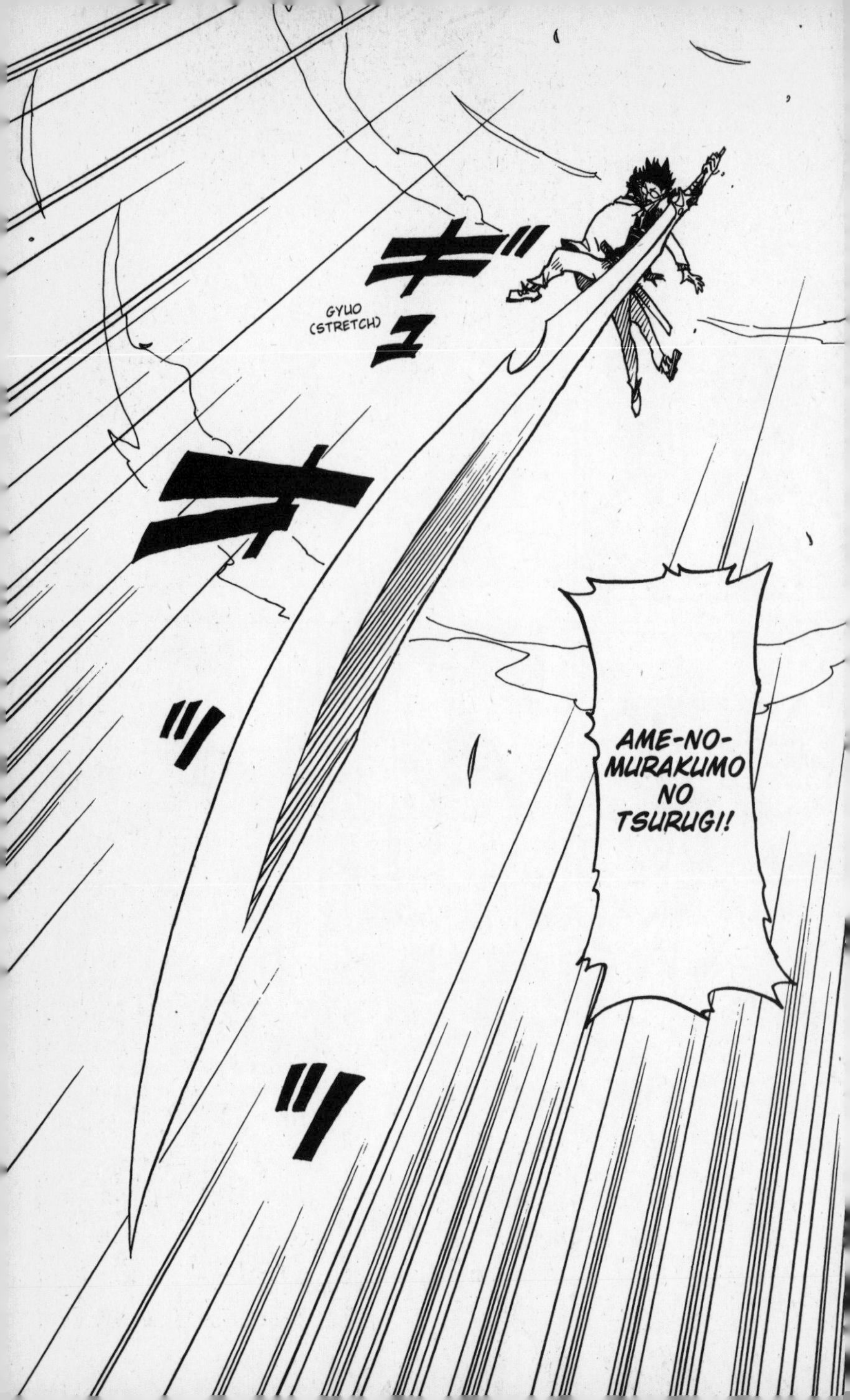
GYUO (STRETCH)
AME-NO-MURAKUMO NO TSURUGI!

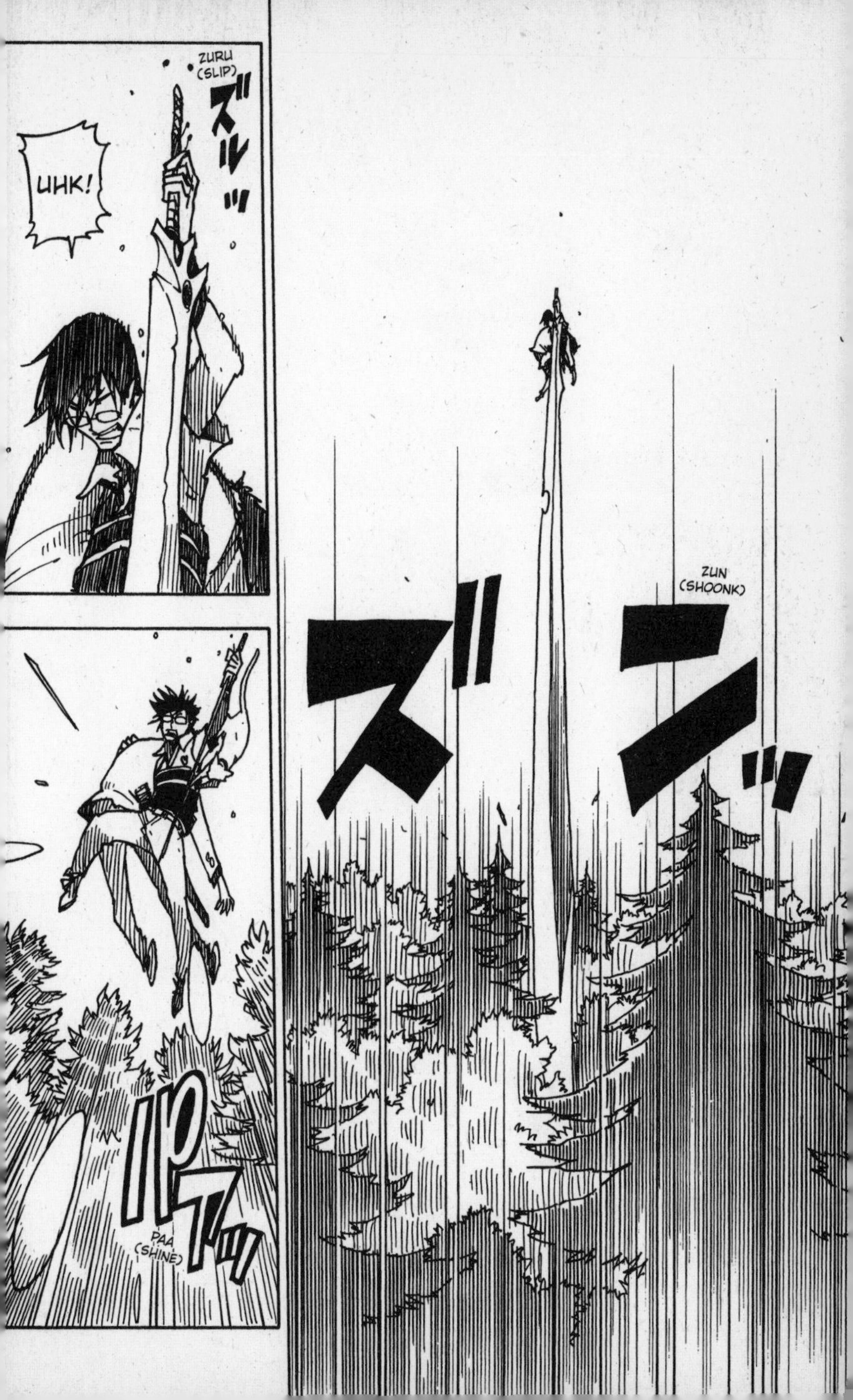
ZUN
(SHOONK)
ZURU
(SLIP)
UHK!
PAA
(SHINE)

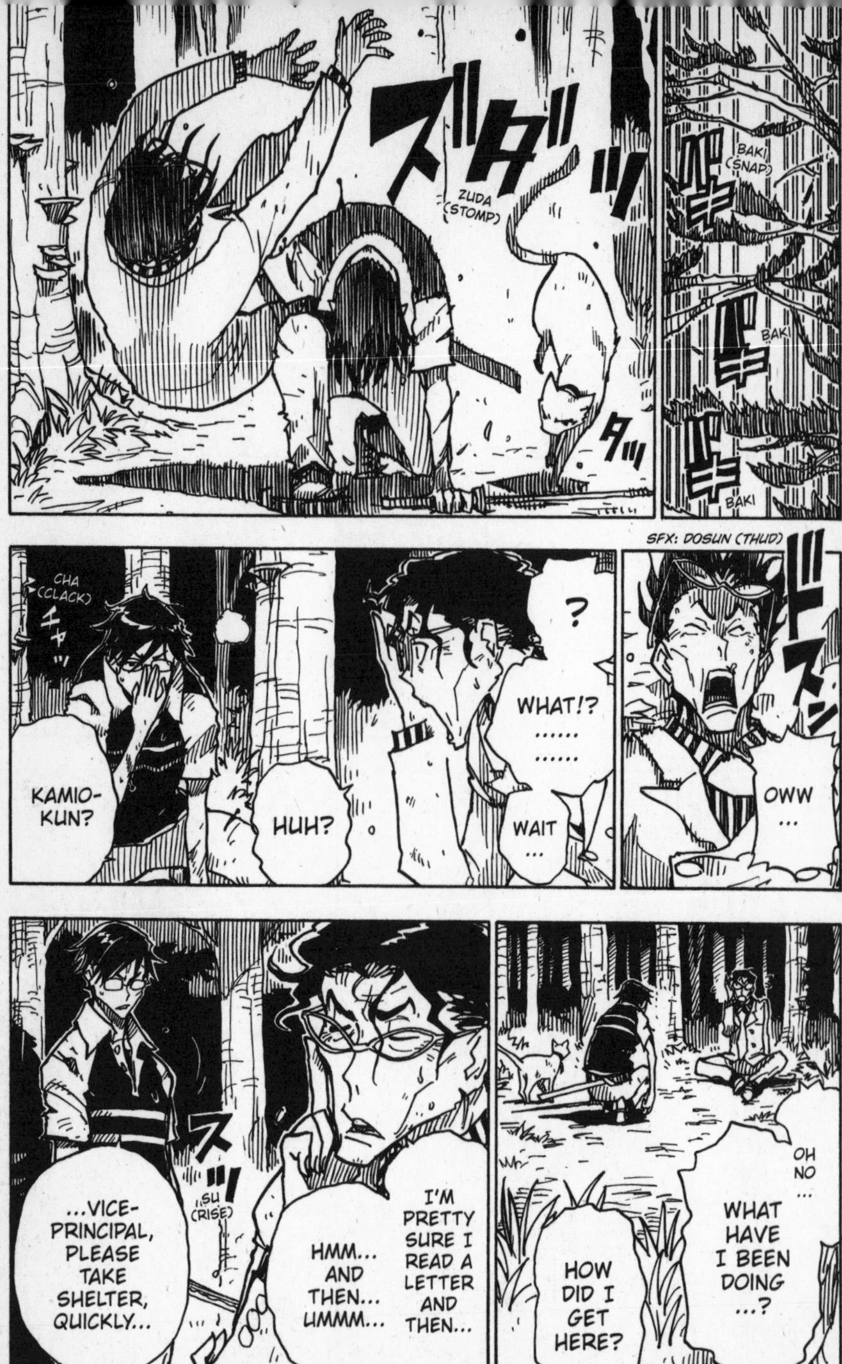
BAKI (SNAP)
BAKI
BAKI
ZUDA (STOMP)
SFX: DOSUN (THUD)
OWW ...
?
WHAT!? ....
WAIT ...
HUH?
CHA (CLACK)
KAMIO-KUN?
OH NO ...
WHAT HAVE I BEEN DOING ...?
HOW DID I GET HERE?
I'M PRETTY SURE I READ A LETTER AND THEN...
HMM... AND THEN... UMMM...
SU (RISE)
...VICE-PRINCIPAL, PLEASE TAKE SHELTER, QUICKLY...

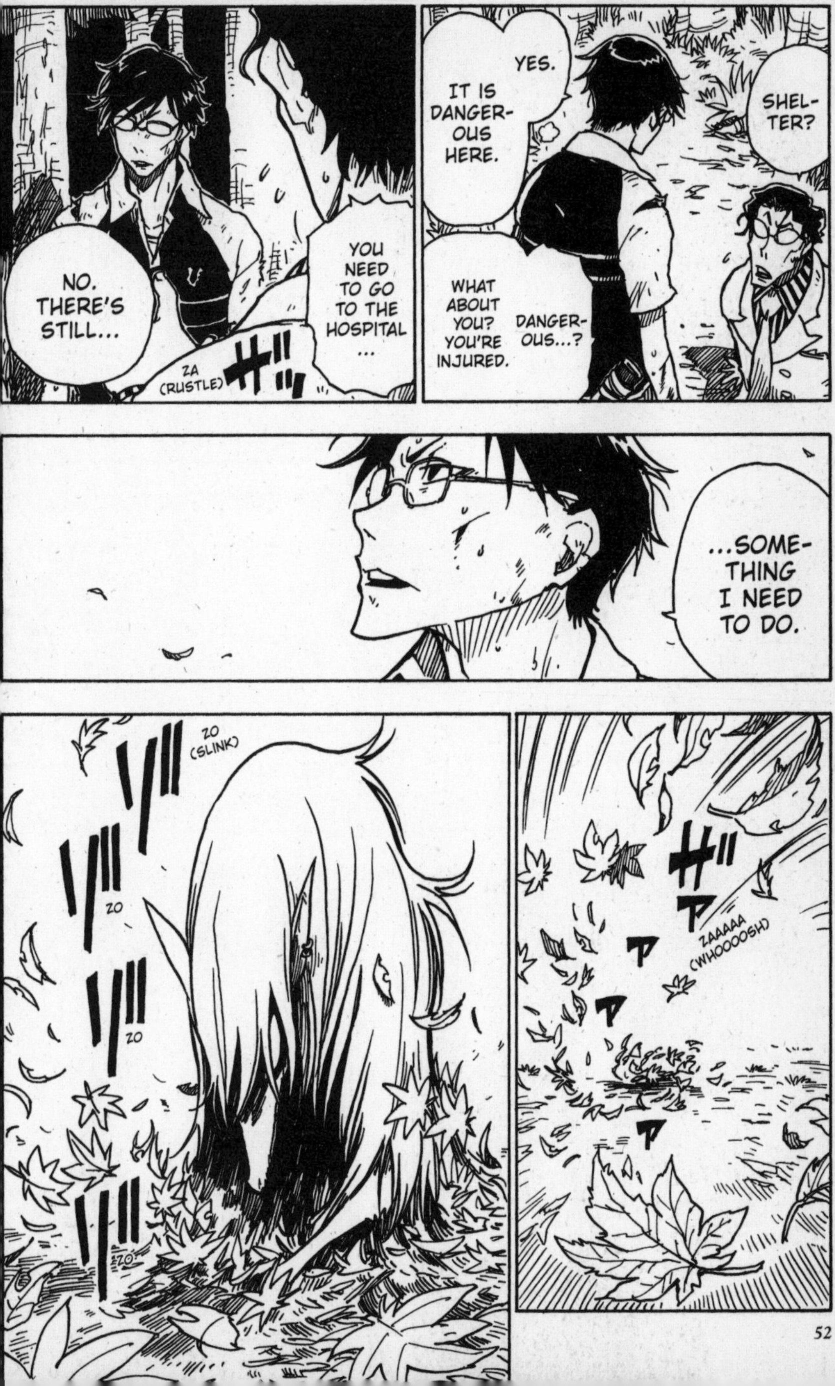
SHEL-TER?
YES.
IT IS DANGER-OUS HERE.
DANGER-OUS...?
WHAT ABOUT YOU? YOU'RE INJURED.
YOU NEED TO GO TO THE HOSPITAL ...
ZA (RUSTLE)
NO. THERE'S STILL...
...SOME-THING I NEED TO DO.
ZAAAAA (WHOOOOSH)
ZO (SLINK)
ZO
ZO
ZO

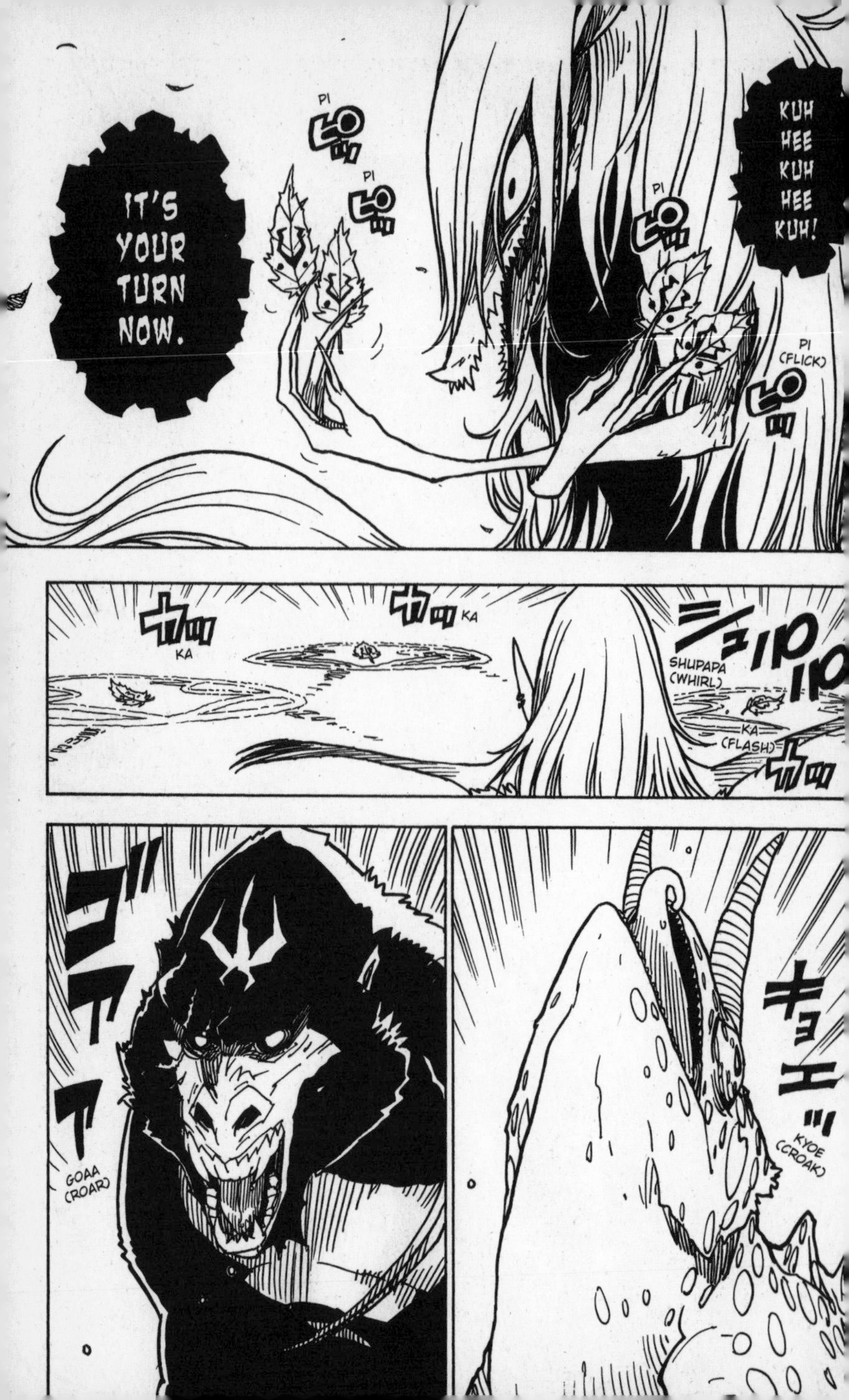
KUH HEE KUH HEE KUH!
PI
PI (FLICK)
PI
PI
IT'S YOUR TURN NOW.
SHUPAPA (WHIRL)
KA (FLASH)
KA
KA
KYOE (CROAK)
GOAA (ROAR)

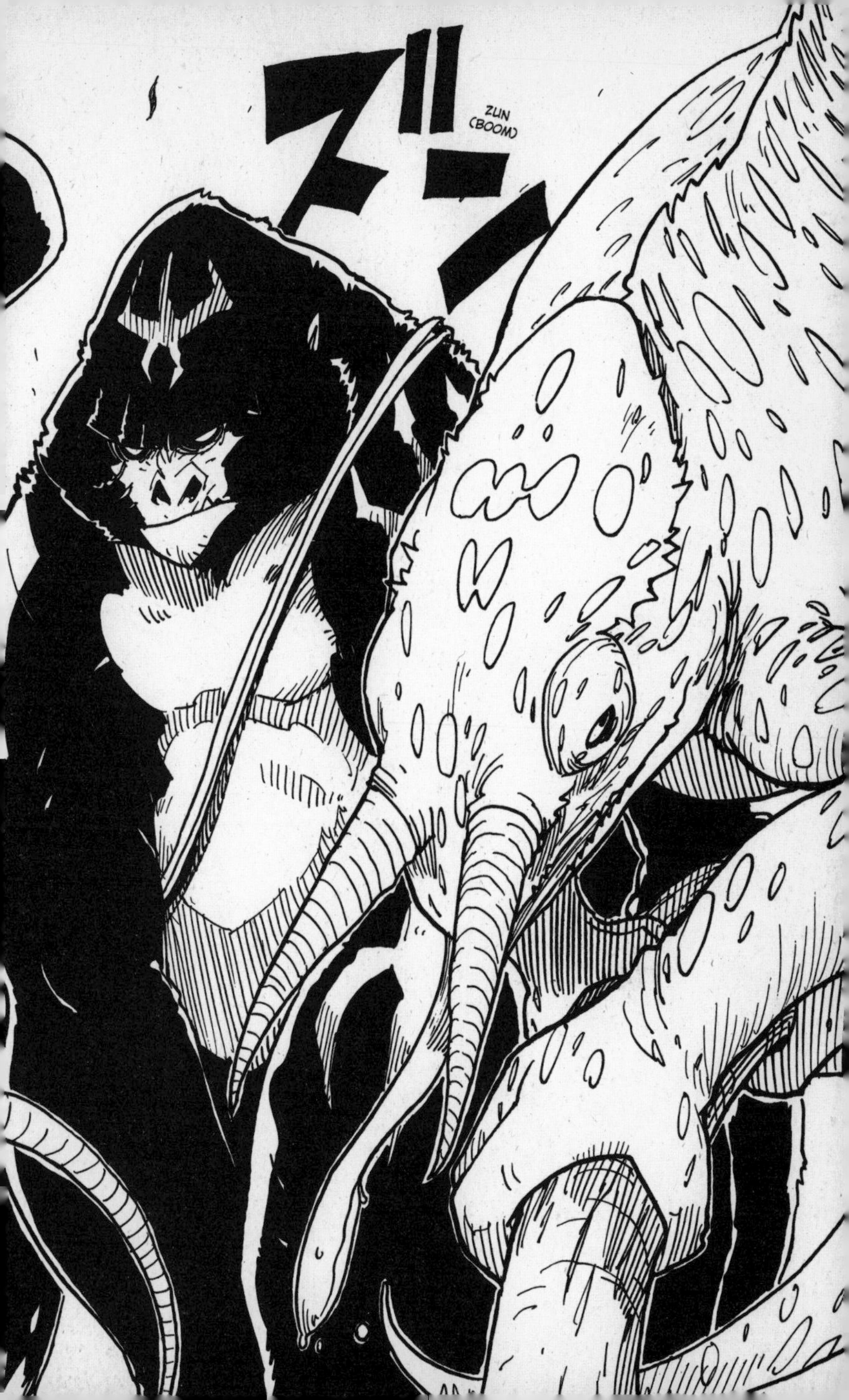
ズーン
ZUN
(BOOM)

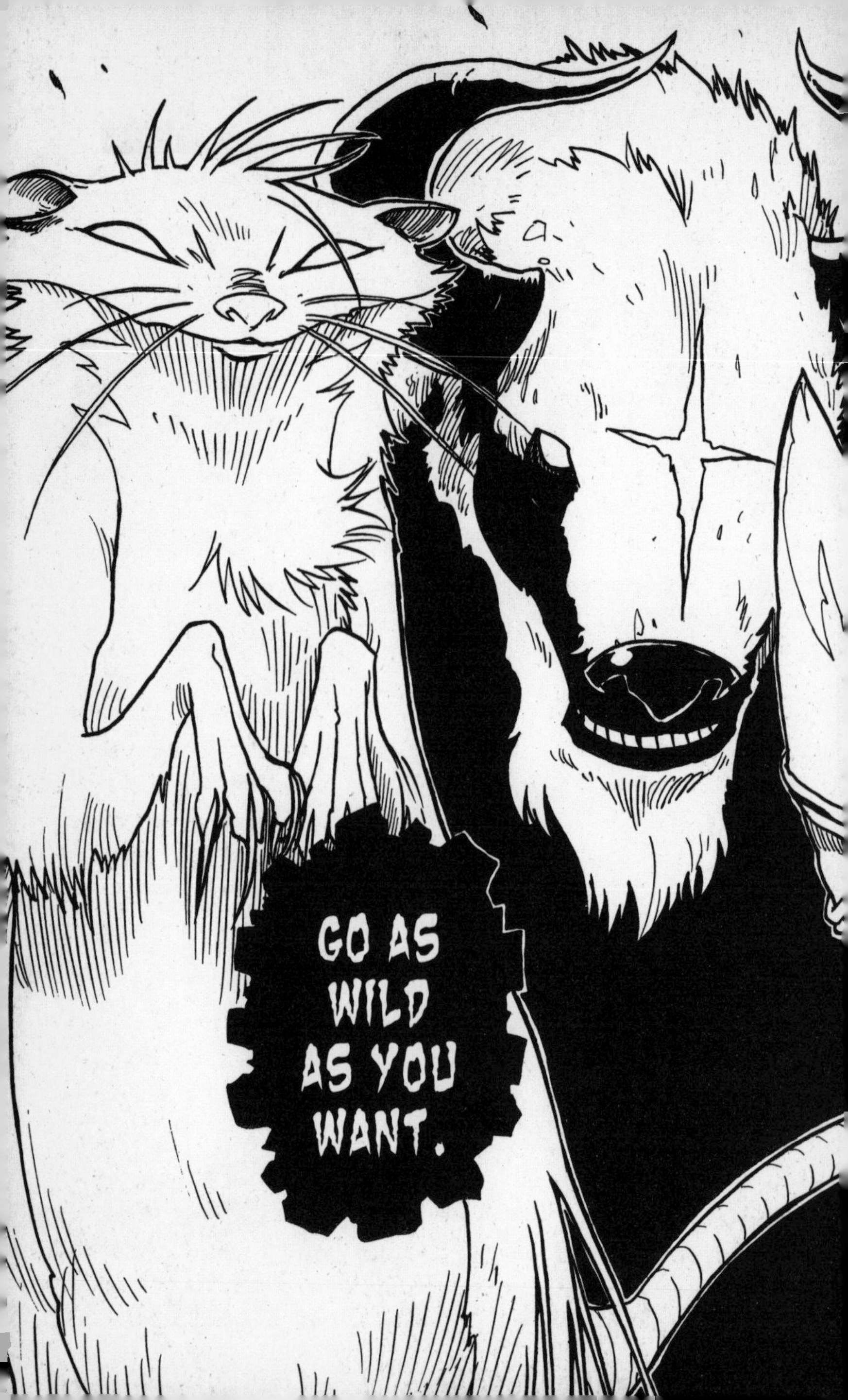
GO AS WILD AS YOU WANT.

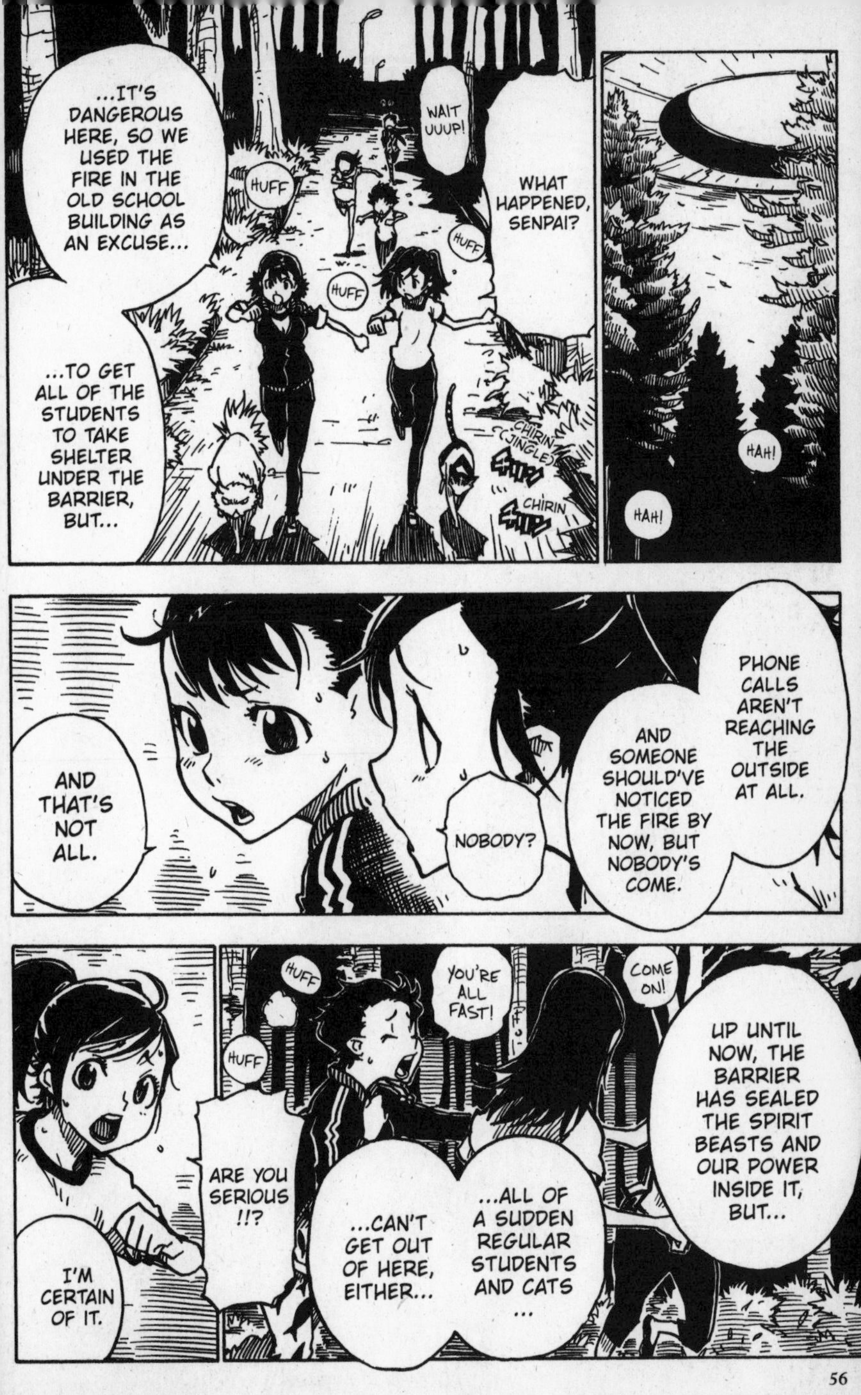
HAH!
HAH!
WAIT UUUP!
WHAT HAPPENED, SENPAI?
HUFF
HUFF
HUFF
...IT'S DANGEROUS HERE, SO WE USED THE FIRE IN THE OLD SCHOOL BUILDING AS AN EXCUSE...
CHIRIN (JINGLE)
CHIRIN
...TO GET ALL OF THE STUDENTS TO TAKE SHELTER UNDER THE BARRIER, BUT...
PHONE CALLS AREN'T REACHING THE OUTSIDE AT ALL.
AND SOMEONE SHOULD'VE NOTICED THE FIRE BY NOW, BUT NOBODY'S COME.
NOBODY?
AND THAT'S NOT ALL.
COME ON!
UP UNTIL NOW, THE BARRIER HAS SEALED THE SPIRIT BEASTS AND OUR POWER INSIDE IT, BUT...
YOU'RE ALL FAST!
HUFF
HUFF
...ALL OF A SUDDEN REGULAR STUDENTS AND CATS ...
...CAN'T GET OUT OF HERE, EITHER...
ARE YOU SERIOUS!!?
I'M CERTAIN OF IT.

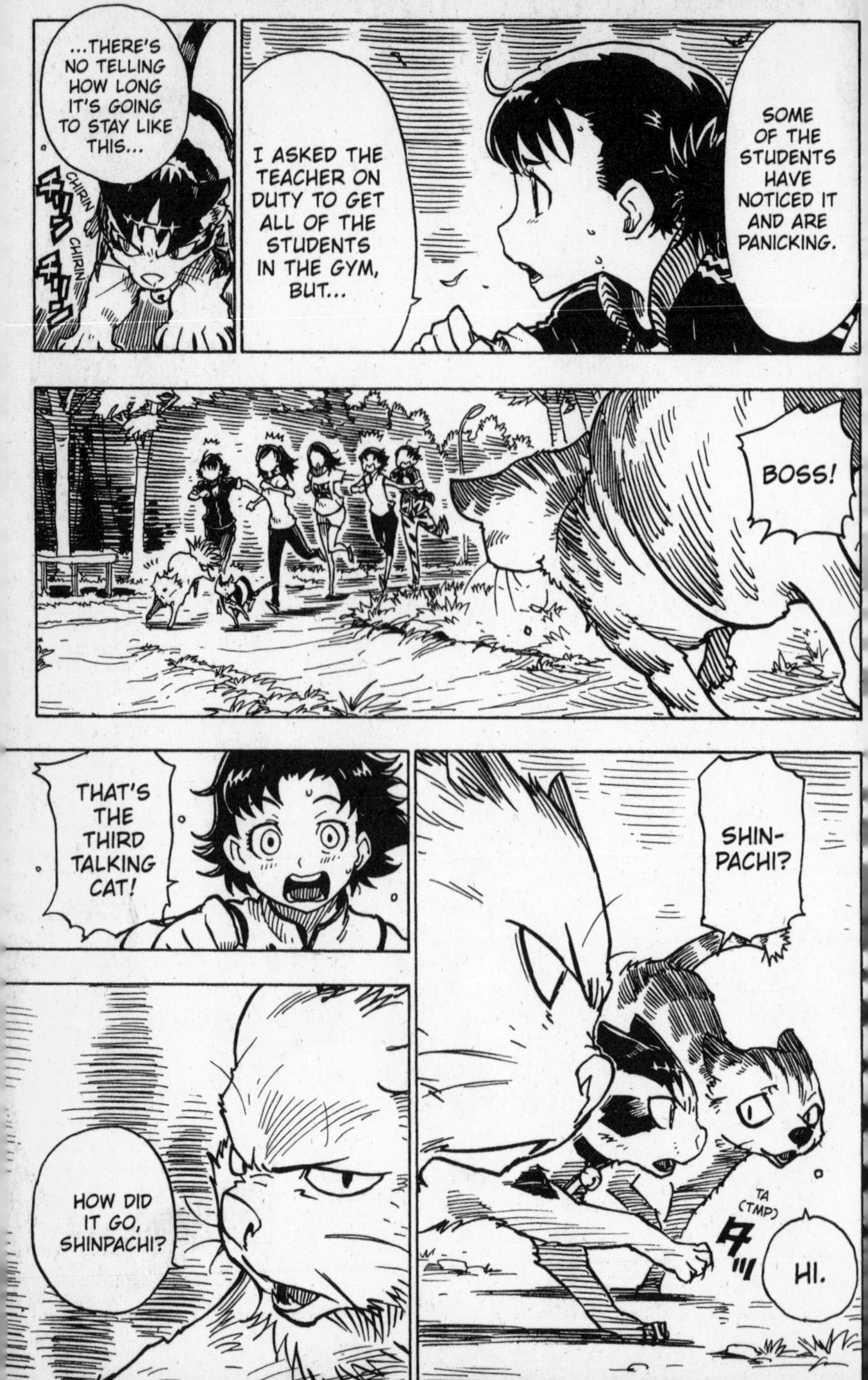
SOME OF THE STUDENTS HAVE NOTICED IT AND ARE PANICKING.
I ASKED THE TEACHER ON DUTY TO GET ALL OF THE STUDENTS IN THE GYM, BUT...
...THERE'S NO TELLING HOW LONG IT'S GOING TO STAY LIKE THIS...
CHIRIN
CHIRIN
BOSS!
SHIN-PACHI?
TA (TMP)
HI.
THAT'S THE THIRD TALKING CAT!
HOW DID IT GO, SHINPACHI?

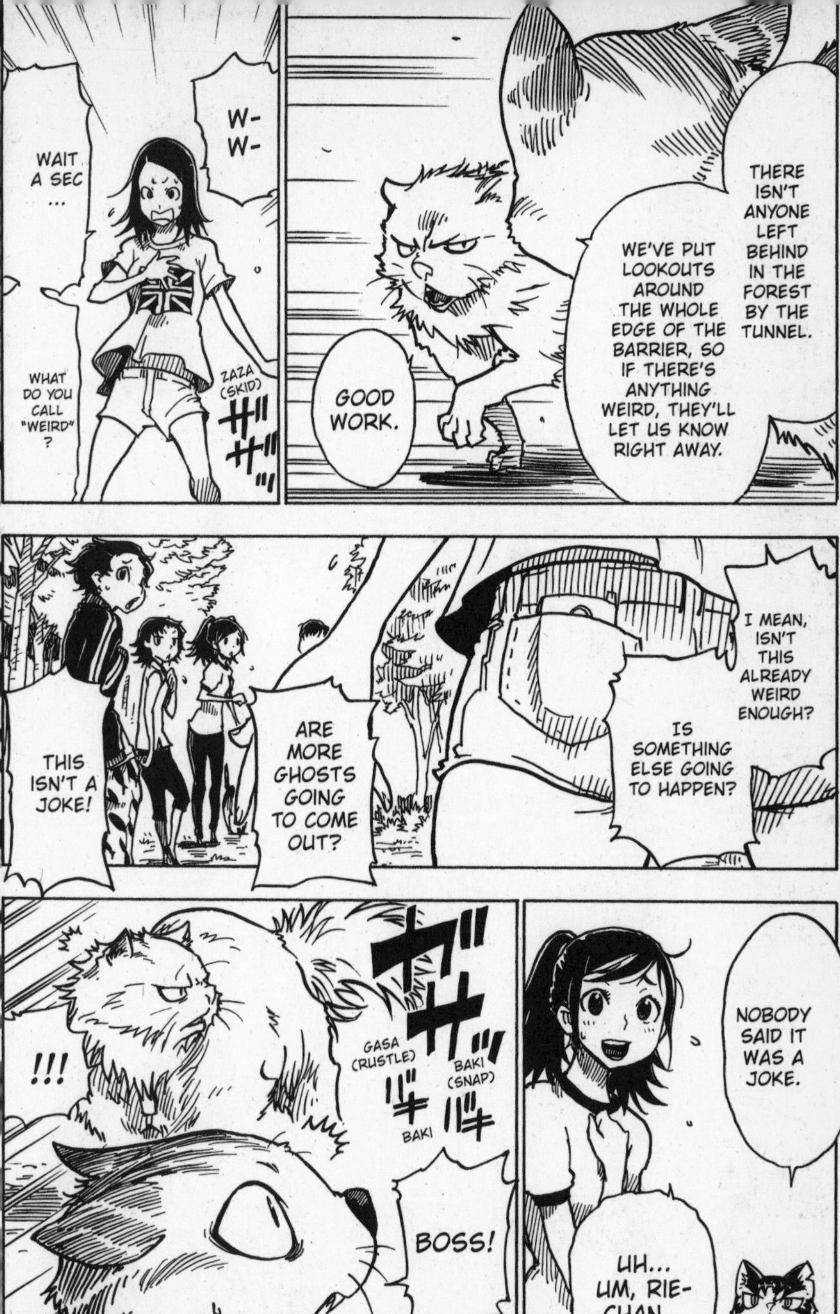
THERE ISN'T ANYONE LEFT BEHIND IN THE FOREST BY THE TUNNEL.
WE'VE PUT LOOKOUTS AROUND THE WHOLE EDGE OF THE BARRIER, SO IF THERE'S ANYTHING WEIRD, THEY'LL LET US KNOW RIGHT AWAY.
GOOD WORK.
W- W-
WAIT A SEC ...
ZAZA (SKID)
WHAT DO YOU CALL "WEIRD" ?
I MEAN, ISN'T THIS ALREADY WEIRD ENOUGH?
IS SOMETHING ELSE GOING TO HAPPEN?
ARE MORE GHOSTS GOING TO COME OUT?
THIS ISN'T A JOKE!
NOBODY SAID IT WAS A JOKE.
UH... UM, RIE-CHAN...
GASA (RUSTLE)
BAKI (SNAP)
BAKI
BOSS!
!!!

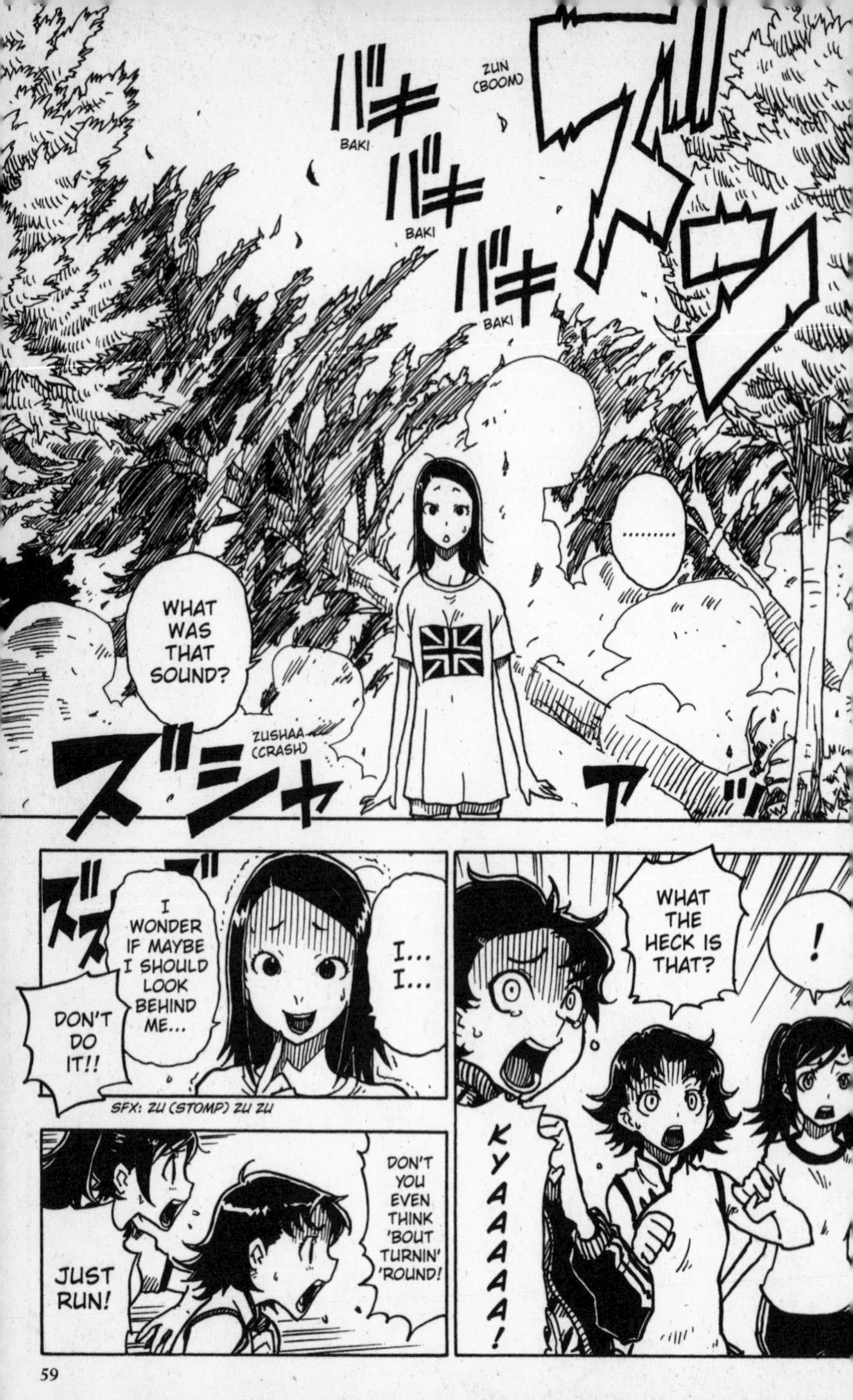
ZUN (BOOM)
BAKI
BAKI
BAKI
....
WHAT WAS THAT SOUND?
ZUSHAA (CRASH)
!
WHAT THE HECK IS THAT?
KYAAAAAA!
I... I...
I WONDER IF MAYBE I SHOULD LOOK BEHIND ME...
DON'T DO IT!!
SFX: ZU (STOMP) ZU ZU
DON'T YOU EVEN THINK 'BOUT TURNIN' 'ROUND!
JUST RUN!

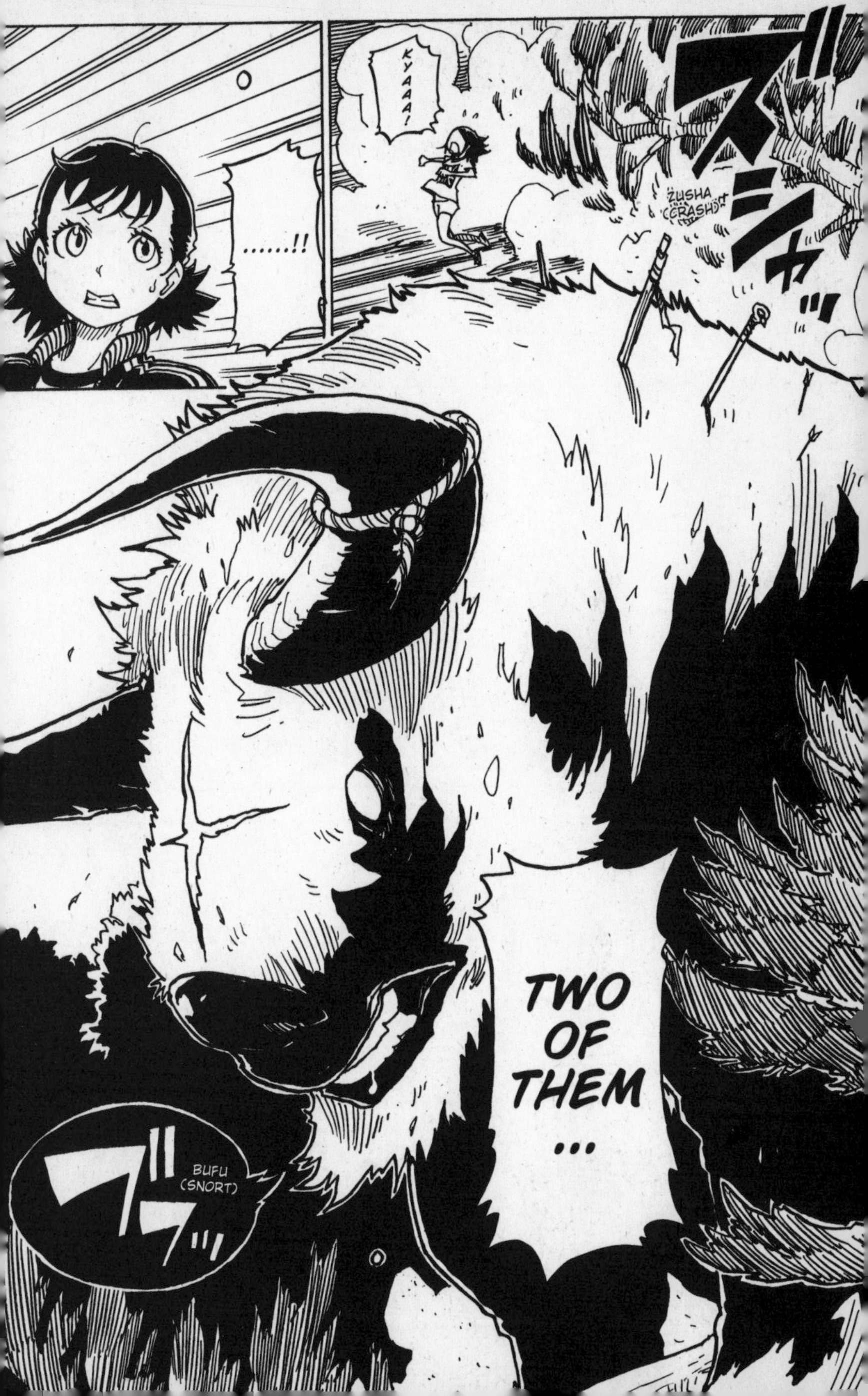

KYAAA!
ズシャッ
ZUSHA (CRASH)!!
......!!
TWO OF THEM ...
ブフッ
BUFU (SNORT)

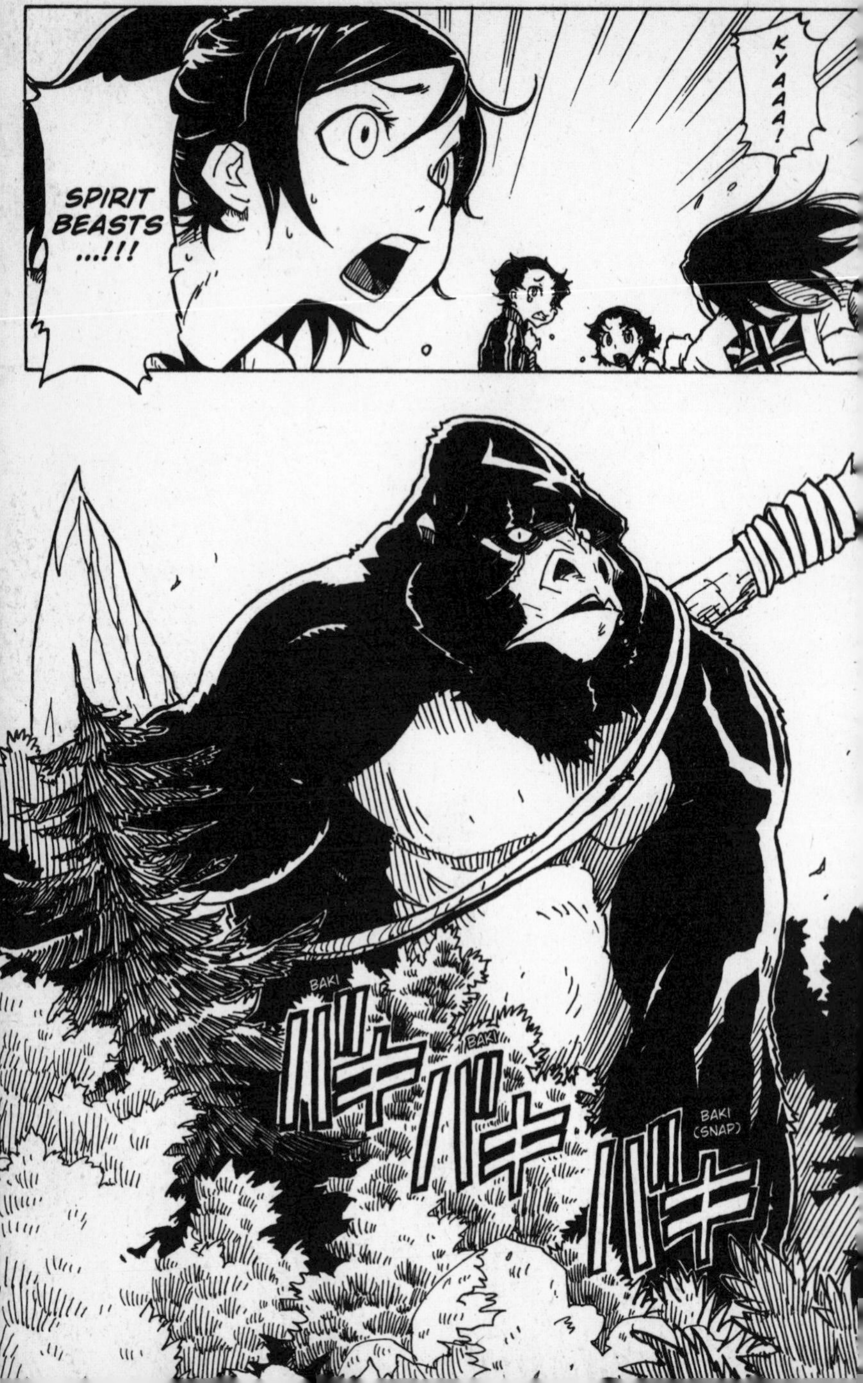
KYAAA!
SPIRIT BEASTS ...!!!
バキ
BAKI (SNAP)
バキ
BAKI
バキ
BAKI

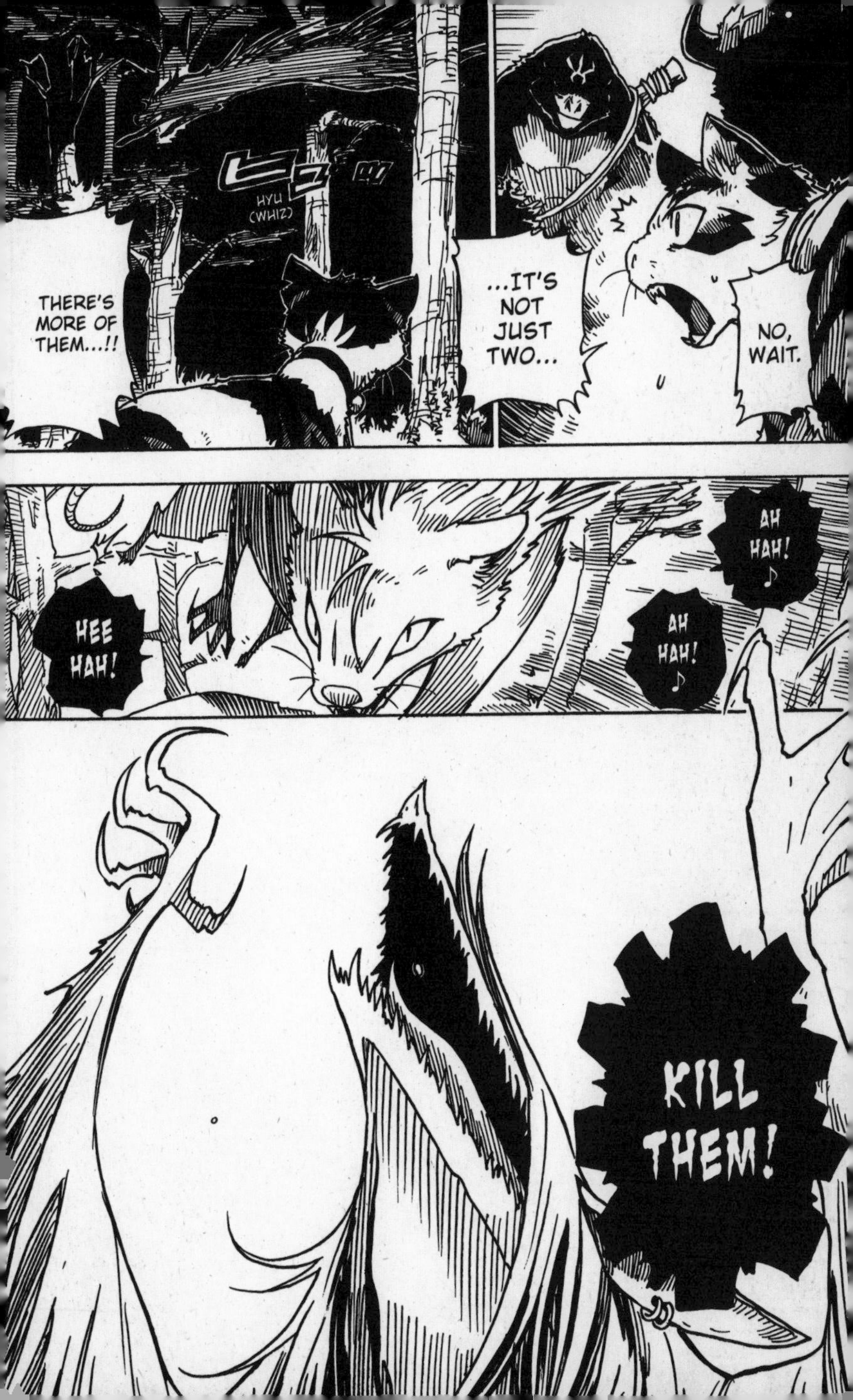
NO, WAIT.
...IT'S NOT JUST TWO...
HYU (WHIZ)
THERE'S MORE OF THEM...!!
AH HAH! ♪
AH HAH! ♪
HEE HAH!
KILL THEM!

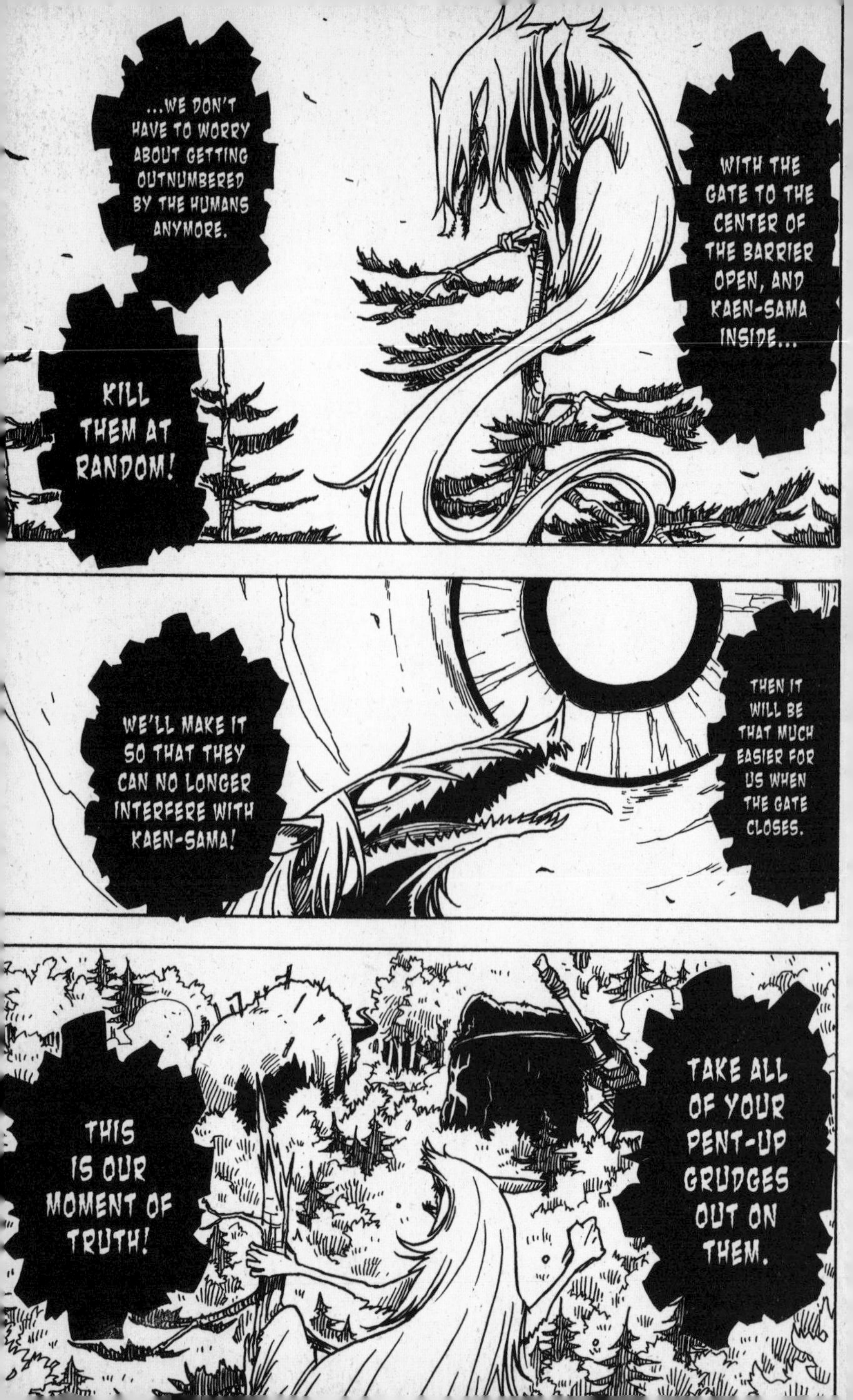

WITH THE GATE TO THE CENTER OF THE BARRIER OPEN, AND KAEN-SAMA INSIDE...
...WE DON'T HAVE TO WORRY ABOUT GETTING OUTNUMBERED BY THE HUMANS ANYMORE.
KILL THEM AT RANDOM!
THEN IT WILL BE THAT MUCH EASIER FOR US WHEN THE GATE CLOSES.
WE'LL MAKE IT SO THAT THEY CAN NO LONGER INTERFERE WITH KAEN-SAMA!
TAKE ALL OF YOUR PENT-UP GRUDGES OUT ON THEM.
THIS IS OUR MOMENT OF TRUTH!

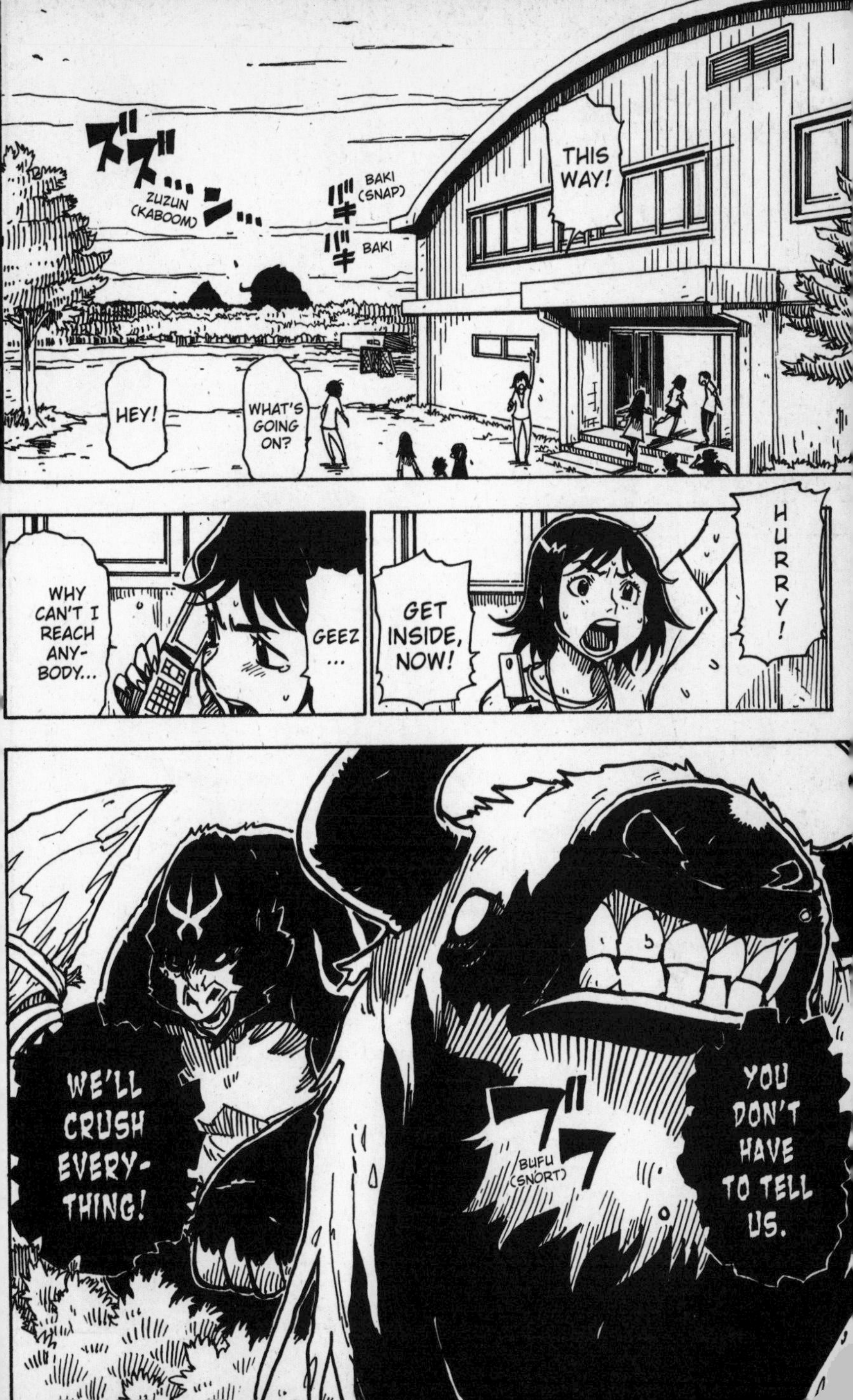
THIS WAY!
BAKI (SNAP)
BAKI
ZUZUN (KABOOM)
WHAT'S GOING ON?
HEY!
HURRY!
GET INSIDE, NOW!
GEEZ...
WHY CAN'T I REACH ANY-BODY...
YOU DON'T HAVE TO TELL US.
BUFU (SNORT)
WE'LL CRUSH EVERY-THING!

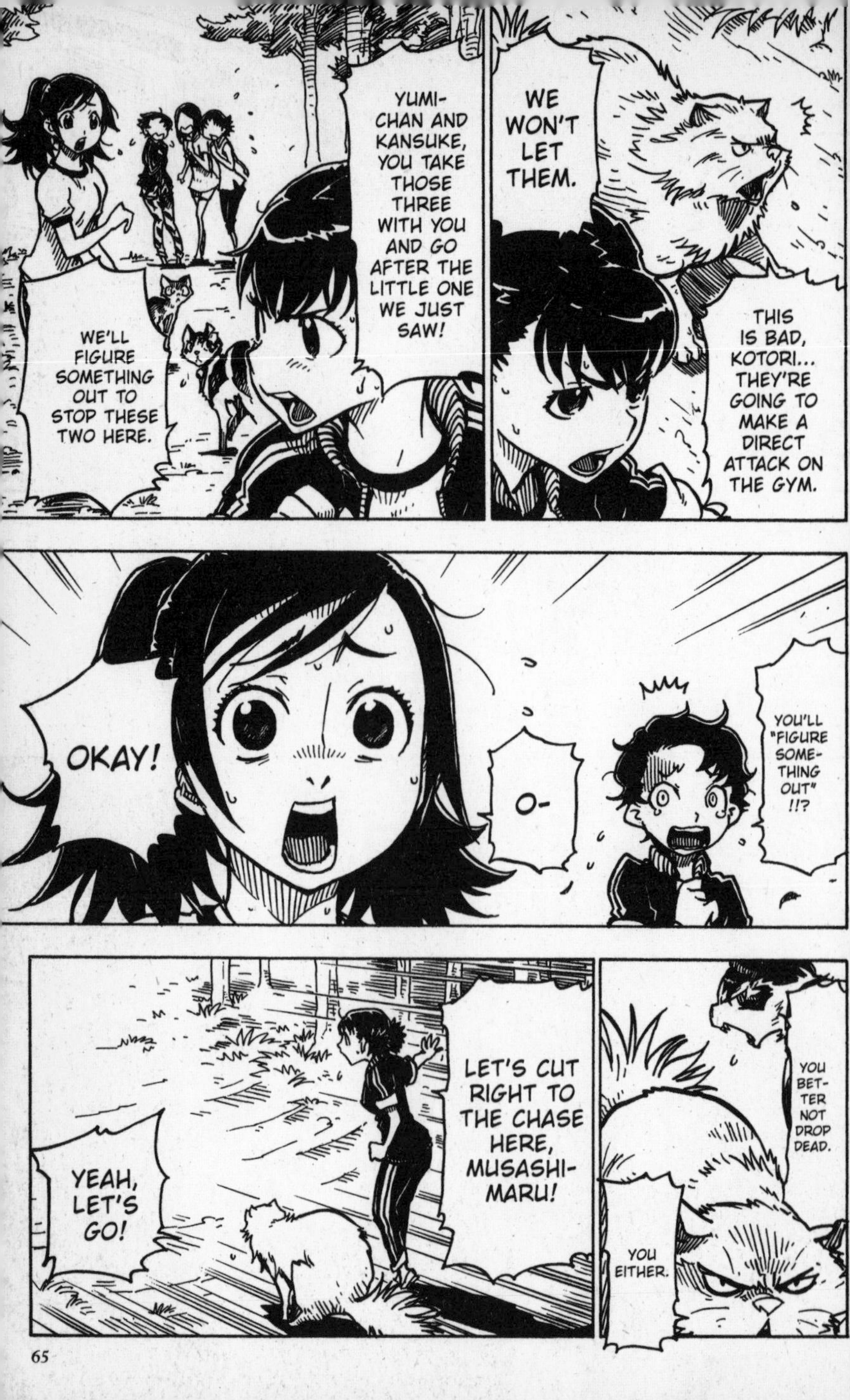
THIS IS BAD, KOTORI... THEY'RE GOING TO MAKE A DIRECT ATTACK ON THE GYM.
WE WON'T LET THEM.
YUMI-CHAN AND KANSUKE, YOU TAKE THOSE THREE WITH YOU AND GO AFTER THE LITTLE ONE WE JUST SAW!
WE'LL FIGURE SOMETHING OUT TO STOP THESE TWO HERE.
YOU'LL "FIGURE SOME-THING OUT" !!?
O-
OKAY!
YOU BET-TER NOT DROP DEAD.
YOU EITHER.
LET'S CUT RIGHT TO THE CHASE HERE, MUSASHI-MARU!
YEAH, LET'S GO!

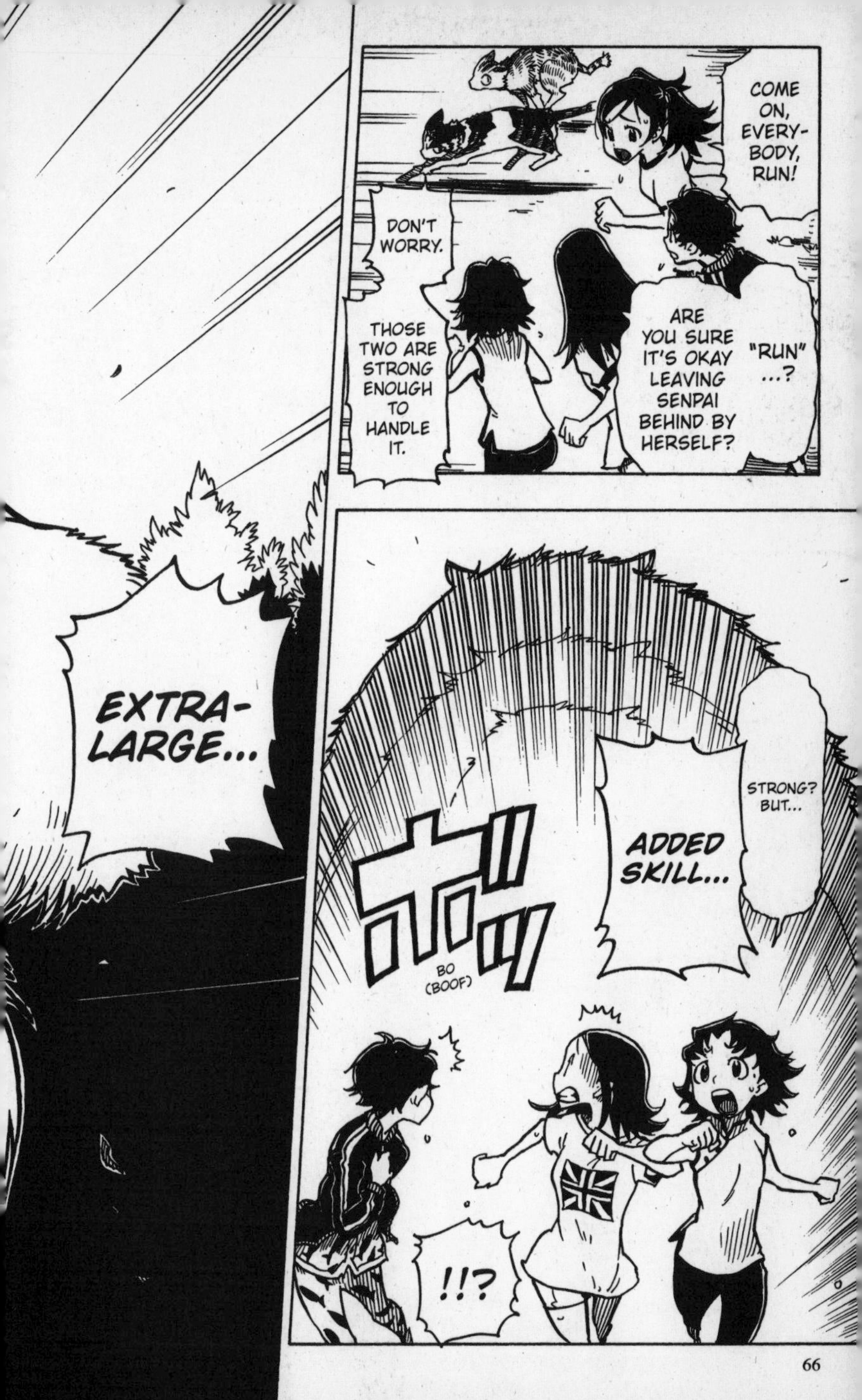
COME ON, EVERYBODY, RUN!
"RUN" ...?
ARE YOU SURE IT'S OKAY LEAVING SENPAI BEHIND BY HERSELF?
DON'T WORRY.
THOSE TWO ARE STRONG ENOUGH TO HANDLE IT.
STRONG? BUT...
ADDED SKILL...
ボッ
BO (BOOF)
!!?
EXTRA-LARGE...

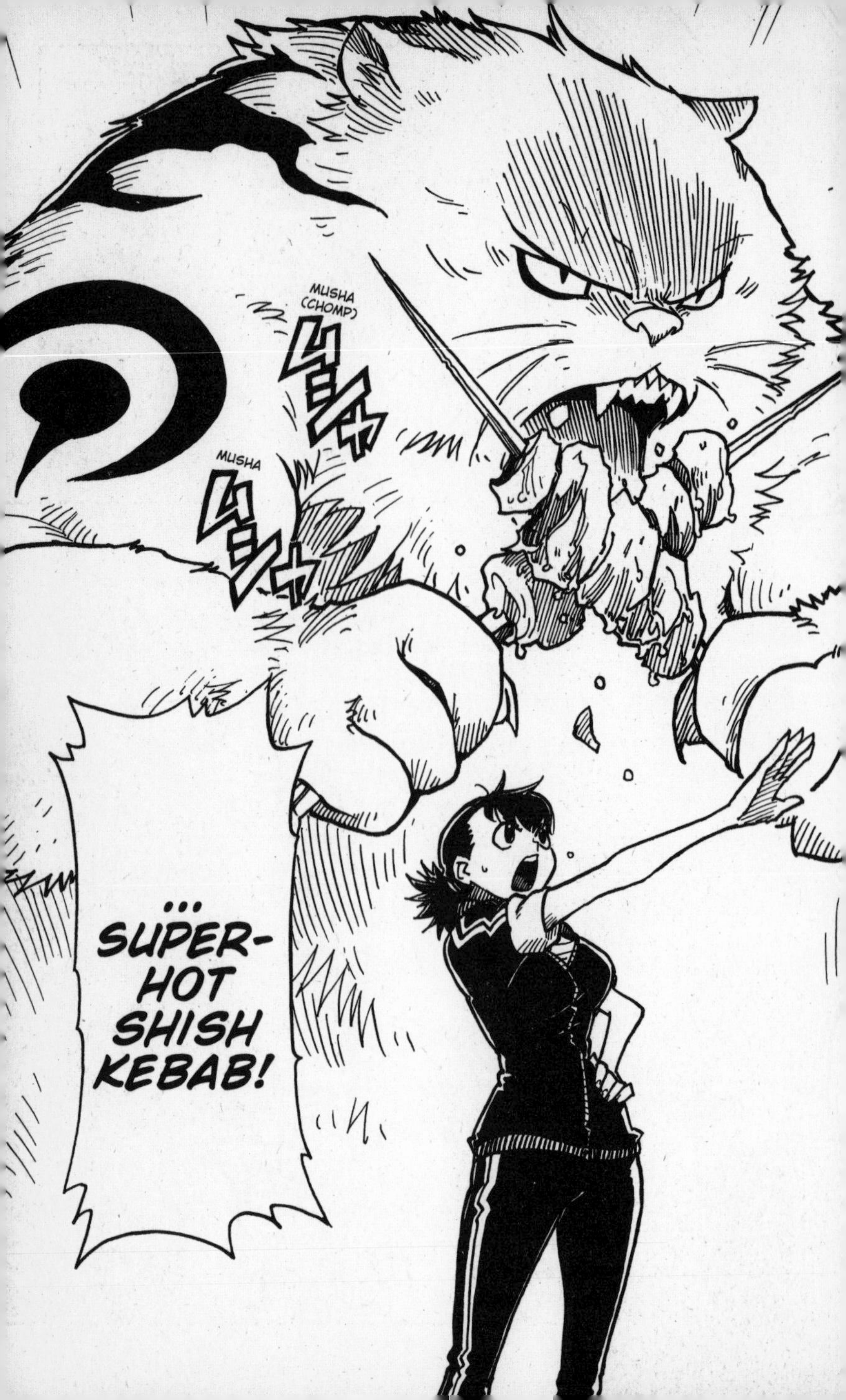
MUSHA (CHOMP)
MUSHA
... SUPER-HOT SHISH KEBAB!

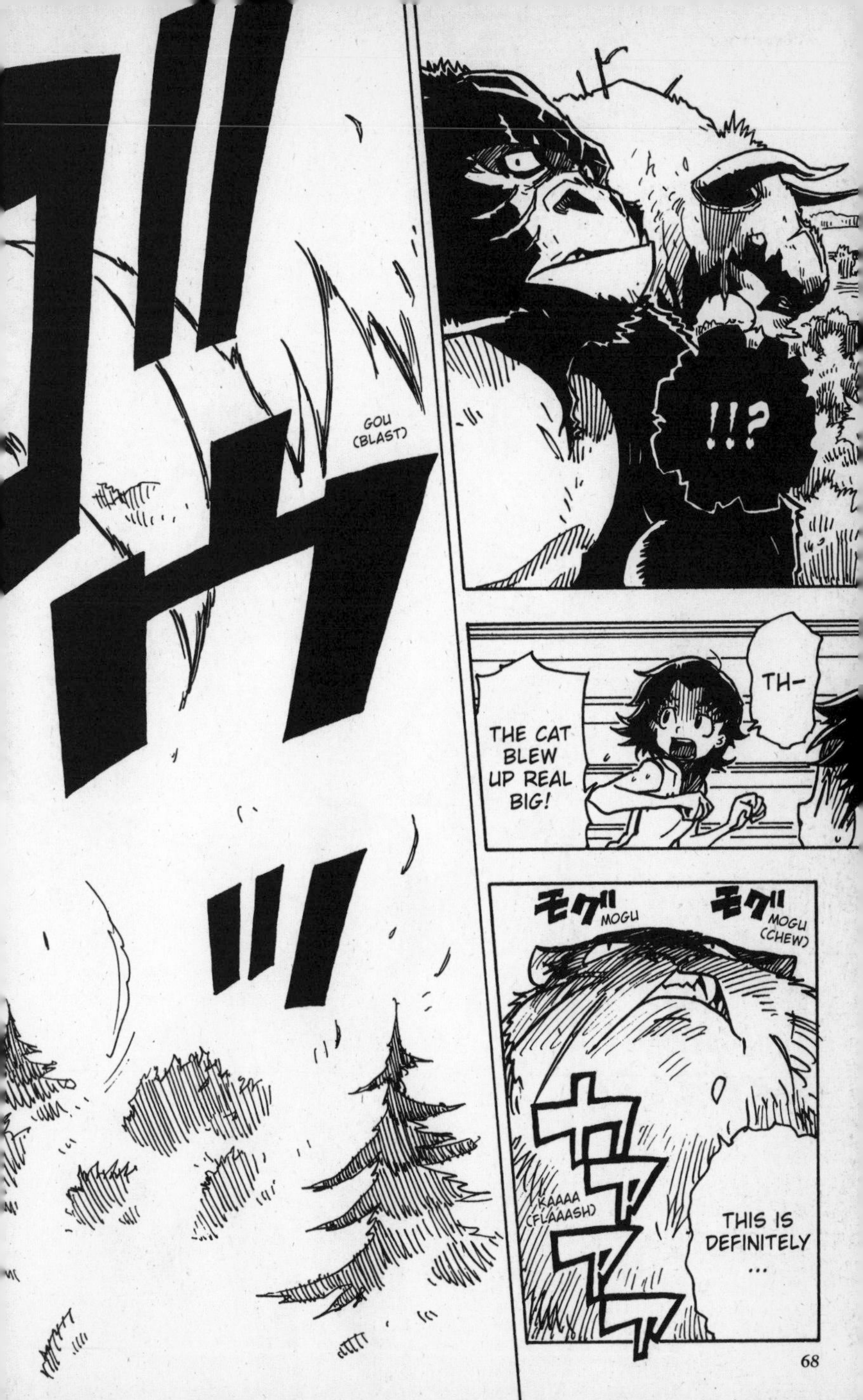
!!?
TH-
THE CAT BLEW UP REAL BIG!
モグ MOGU
モグ MOGU (CHEW)
KAAAA (FLAAASH)
THIS IS DEFINITELY ...
GOU (BLAST)

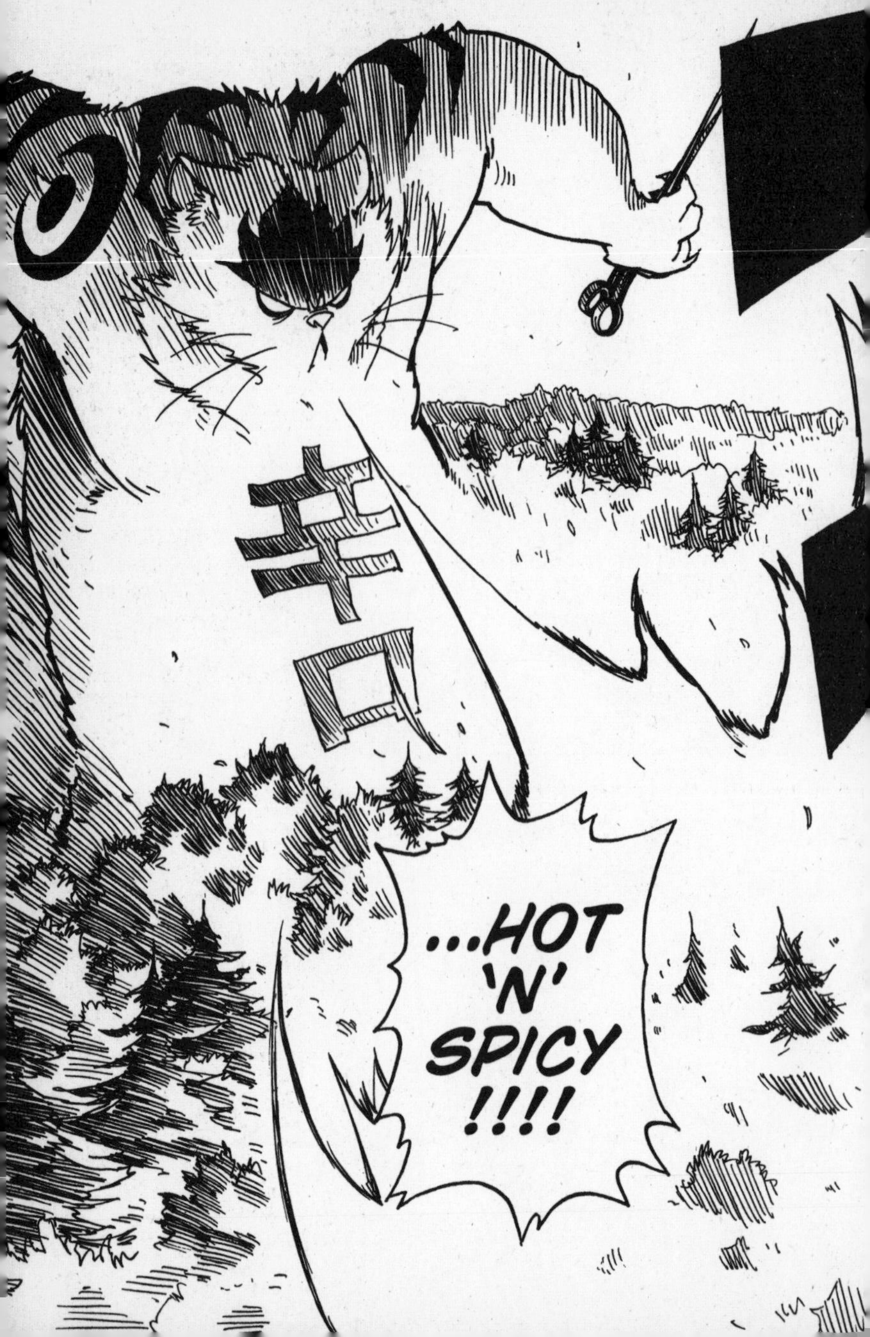
辛口
...HOT 'N' SPICY !!!!

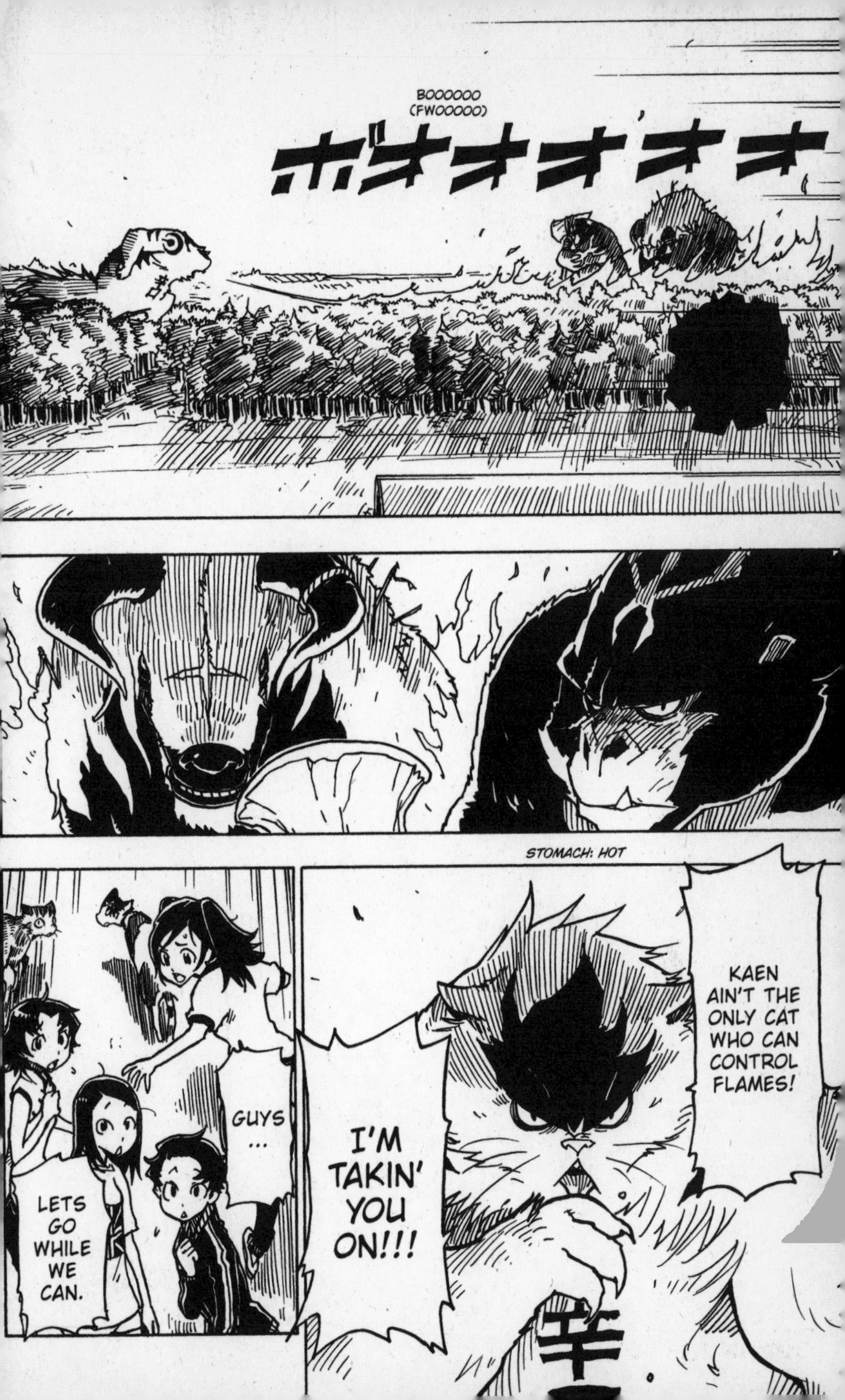
BOOOOOO
(FWOOOOO)
ボオオオオオ
STOMACH: HOT
KAEN AIN'T THE ONLY CAT WHO CAN CONTROL FLAMES!
I'M TAKIN' YOU ON!!!
GUYS ...
LETS GO WHILE WE CAN.

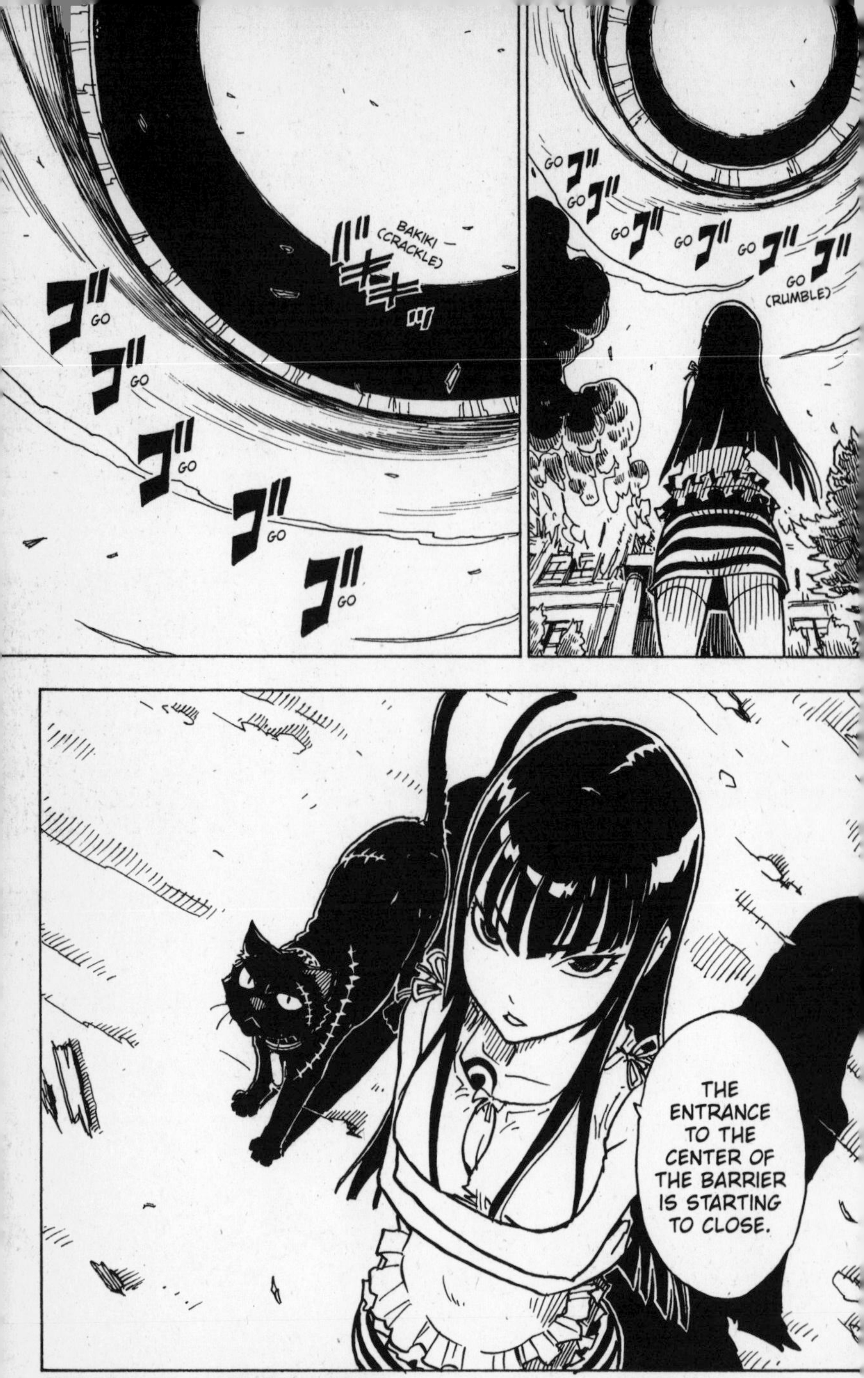
GO
GO
GO
GO
GO
GO (RUMBLE)
BAKIKI (CRACKLE)
GO
GO
GO
GO
GO
THE ENTRANCE TO THE CENTER OF THE BARRIER IS STARTING TO CLOSE.

CHAPTER 20 • SNOW COUNTRY

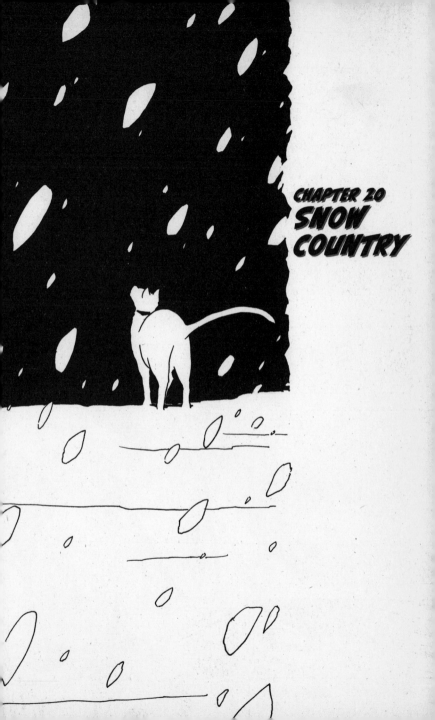

CHAPTER 20
SNOW COUNTRY

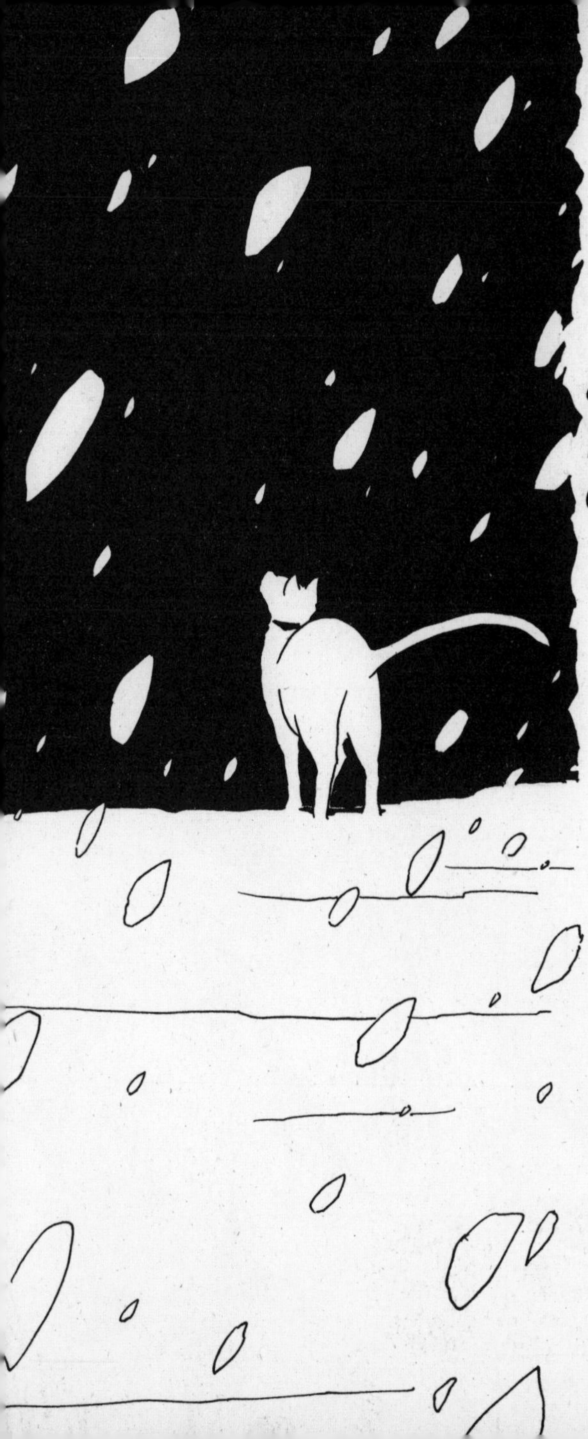

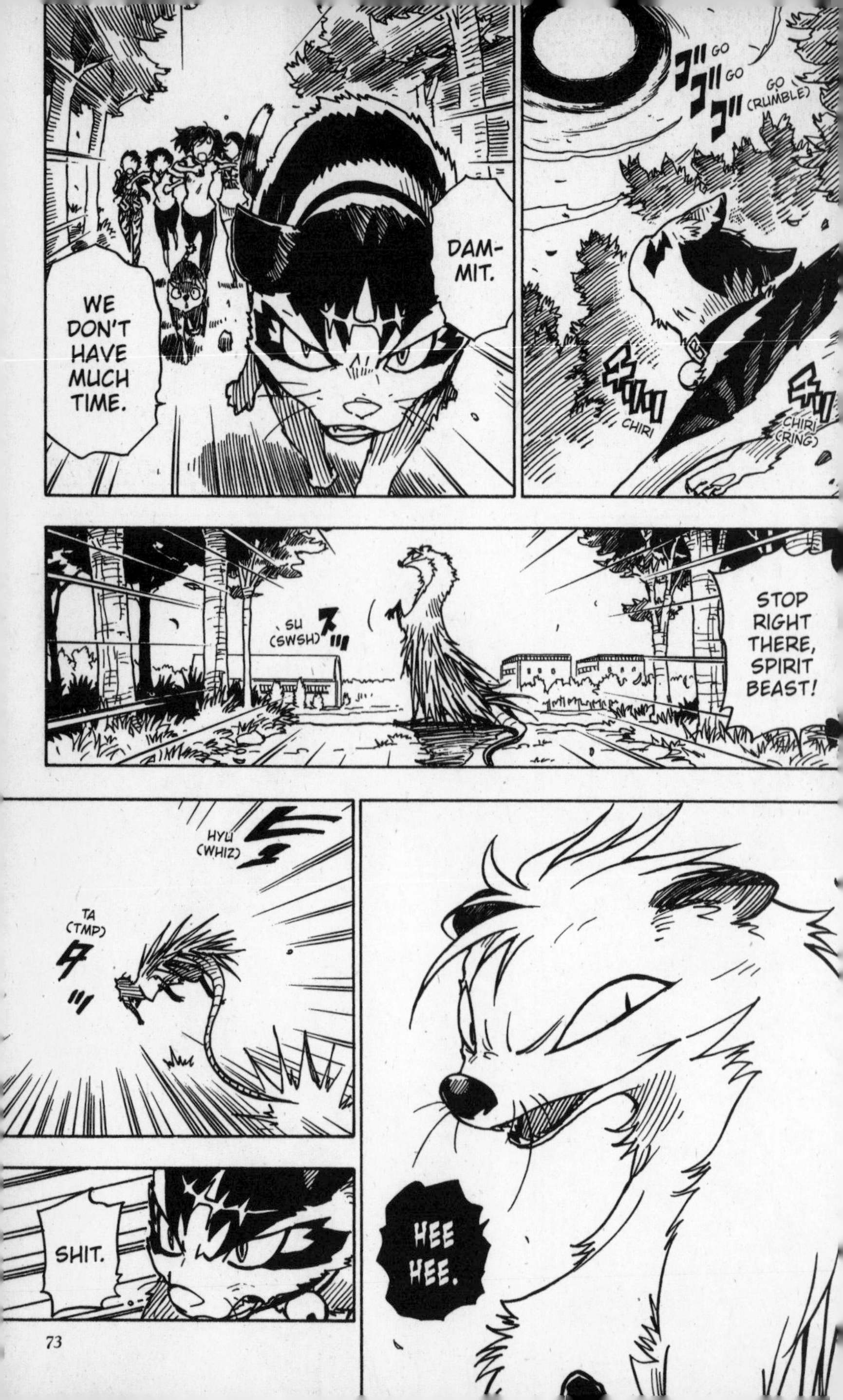
GO
GO
GO (RUMBLE)
CHIRI
CHIRI (RING)
DAM-MIT.
WE DON'T HAVE MUCH TIME.
STOP RIGHT THERE, SPIRIT BEAST!
SU (SWSH)
HEE HEE.
HYU (WHIZ)
TA (TMP)
SHIT.

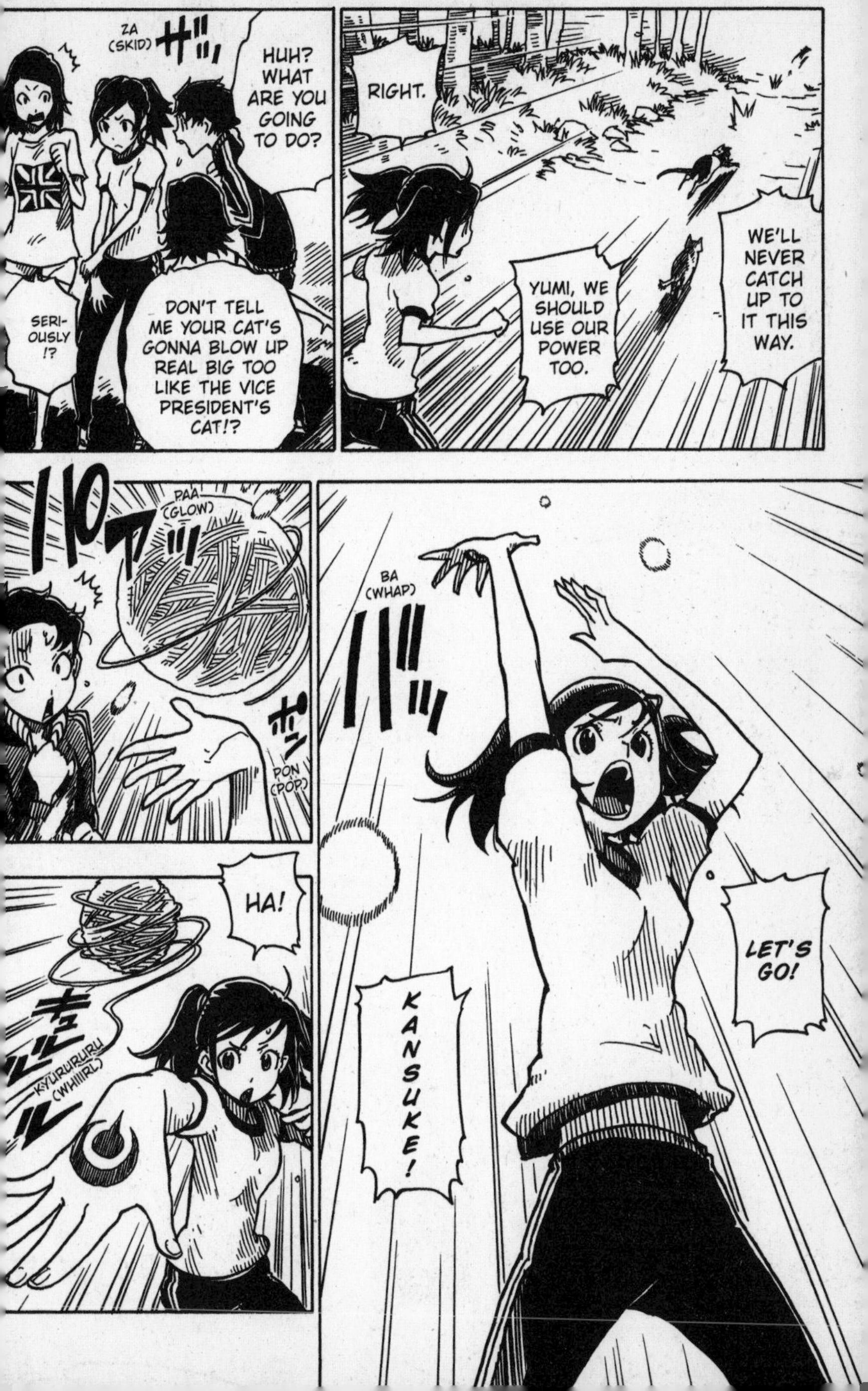
WE'LL NEVER CATCH UP TO IT THIS WAY.
YUMI, WE SHOULD USE OUR POWER TOO.
RIGHT.
ZA (SKID)
HUH? WHAT ARE YOU GOING TO DO?
DON'T TELL ME YOUR CAT'S GONNA BLOW UP REAL BIG TOO LIKE THE VICE PRESIDENT'S CAT!?
SERI-OUSLY!?
BA (WHAP)
KANSUKE!
LET'S GO!
PAA (GLOW)
PON (POP)
HA!
KYURURURU (WHIIRL)

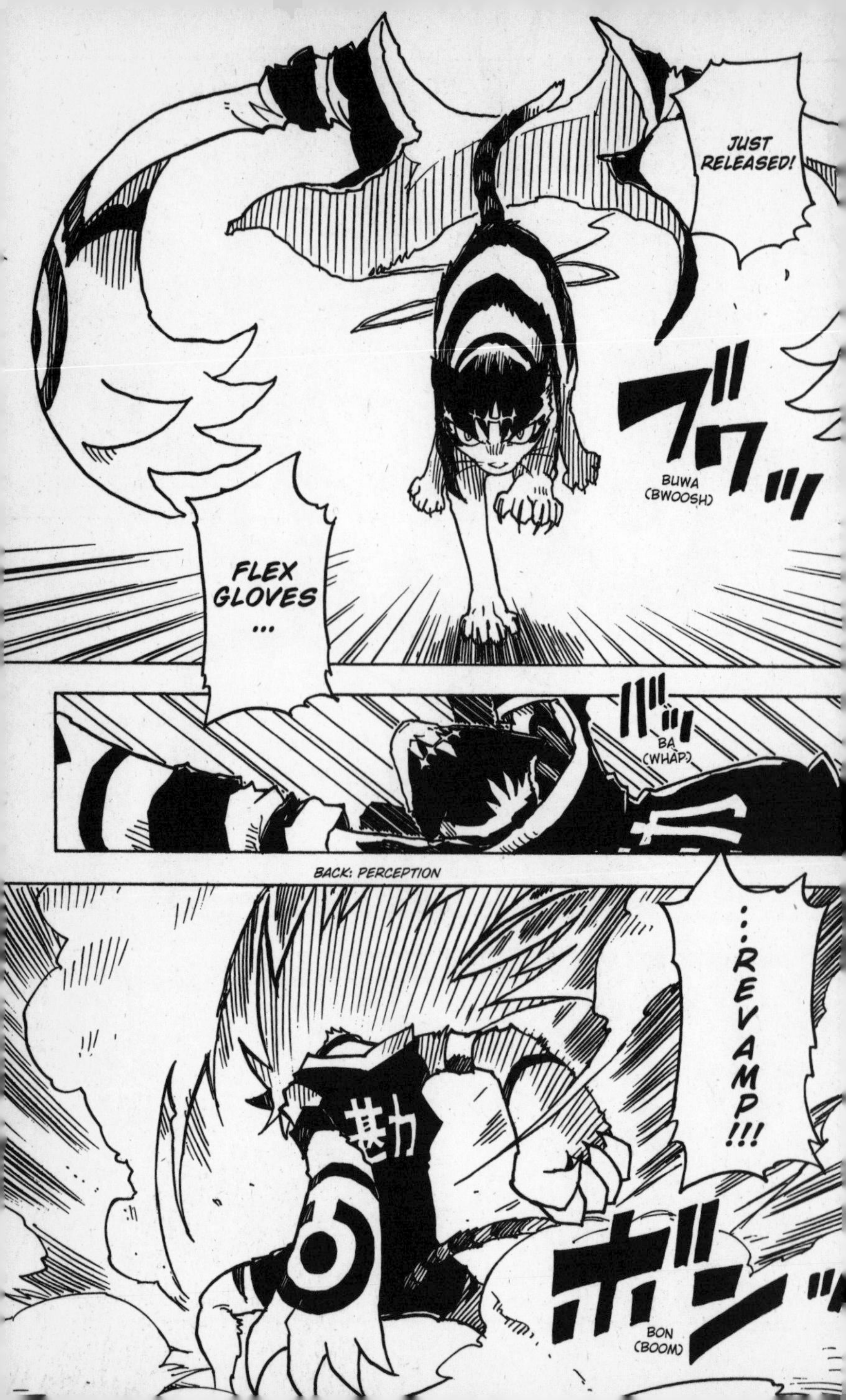
JUST RELEASED!
BUWA (BWOOSH)
FLEX GLOVES ...
BA (WHAP)
BACK: PERCEPTION
...REVAMP!!!
BON (BOOM)

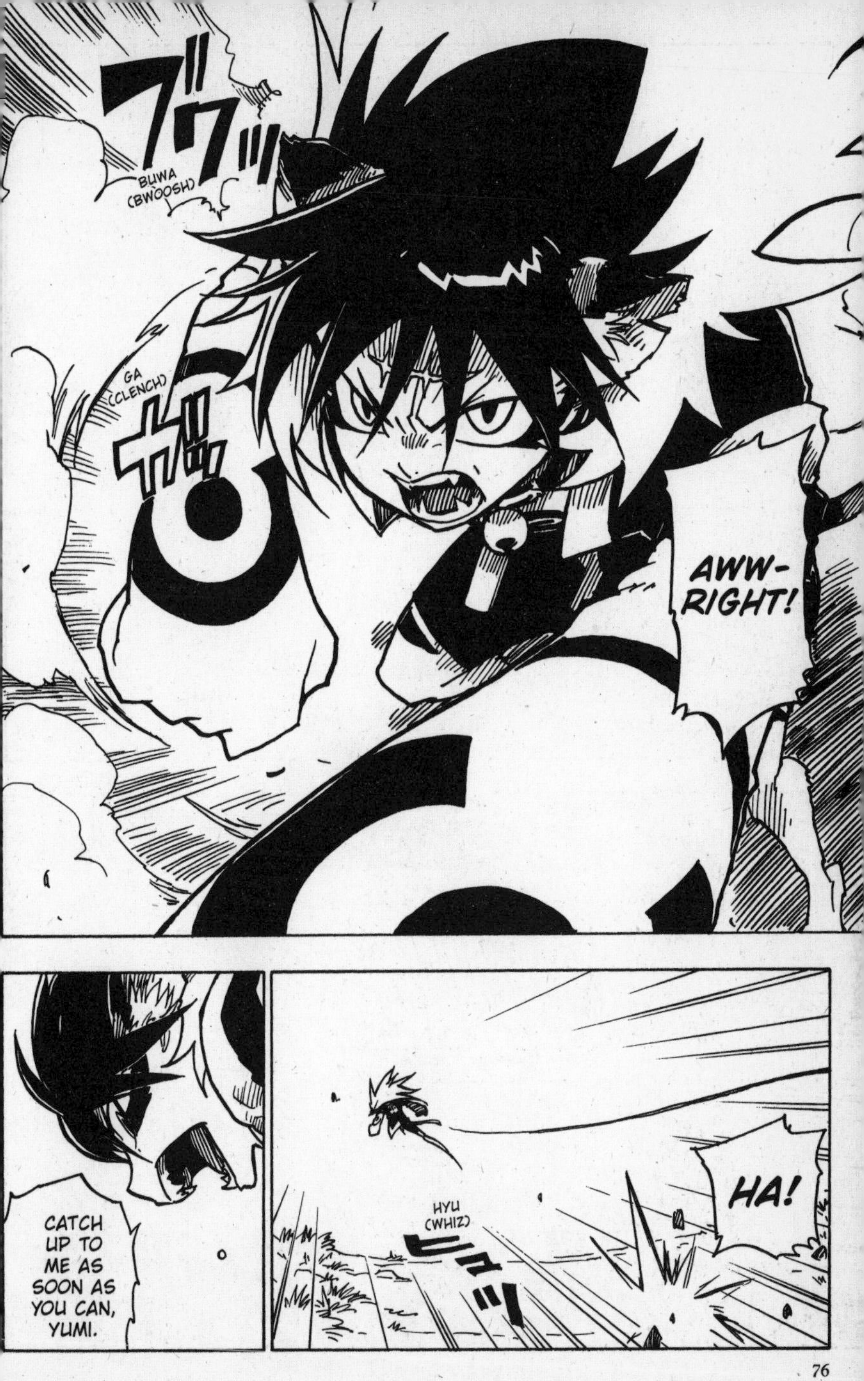
BUWA (BWOOSH)
GA (CLENCH)
AWW-RIGHT!
HA!
HYU (WHIZ)
CATCH UP TO ME AS SOON AS YOU CAN, YUMI.

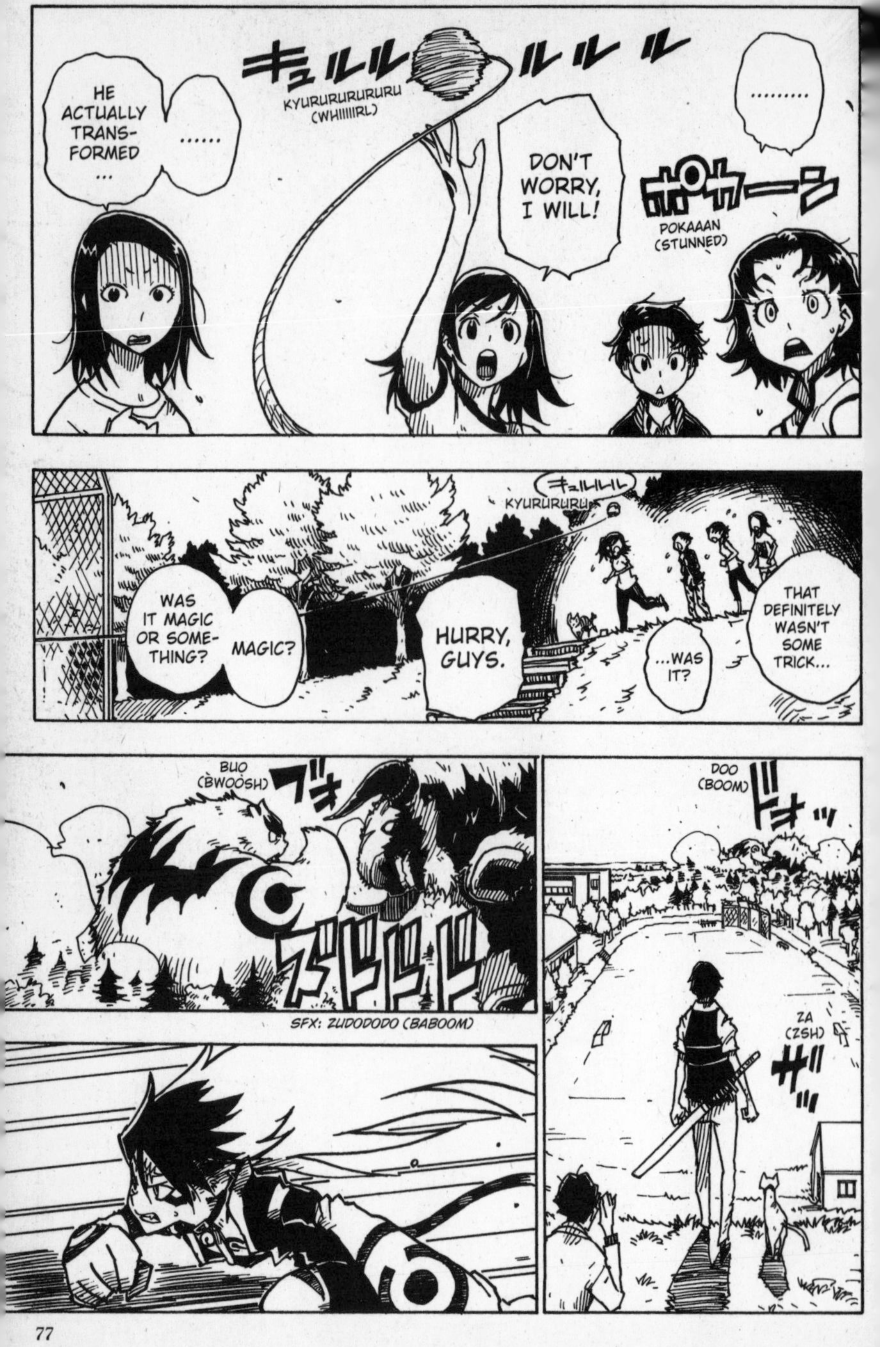
....
POKAAAN (STUNNED)
DON'T WORRY, I WILL!
KYURURURURURU (WHIIIIIRL)
......
HE ACTUALLY TRANS-FORMED ...
KYURURURU
THAT DEFINITELY WASN'T SOME TRICK...
...WAS IT?
HURRY, GUYS.
MAGIC?
WAS IT MAGIC OR SOME-THING?
DOO (BOOM)
ZA (ZSH)
BUO (BWOOSH)
SFX: ZUDODODO (BABOOM)

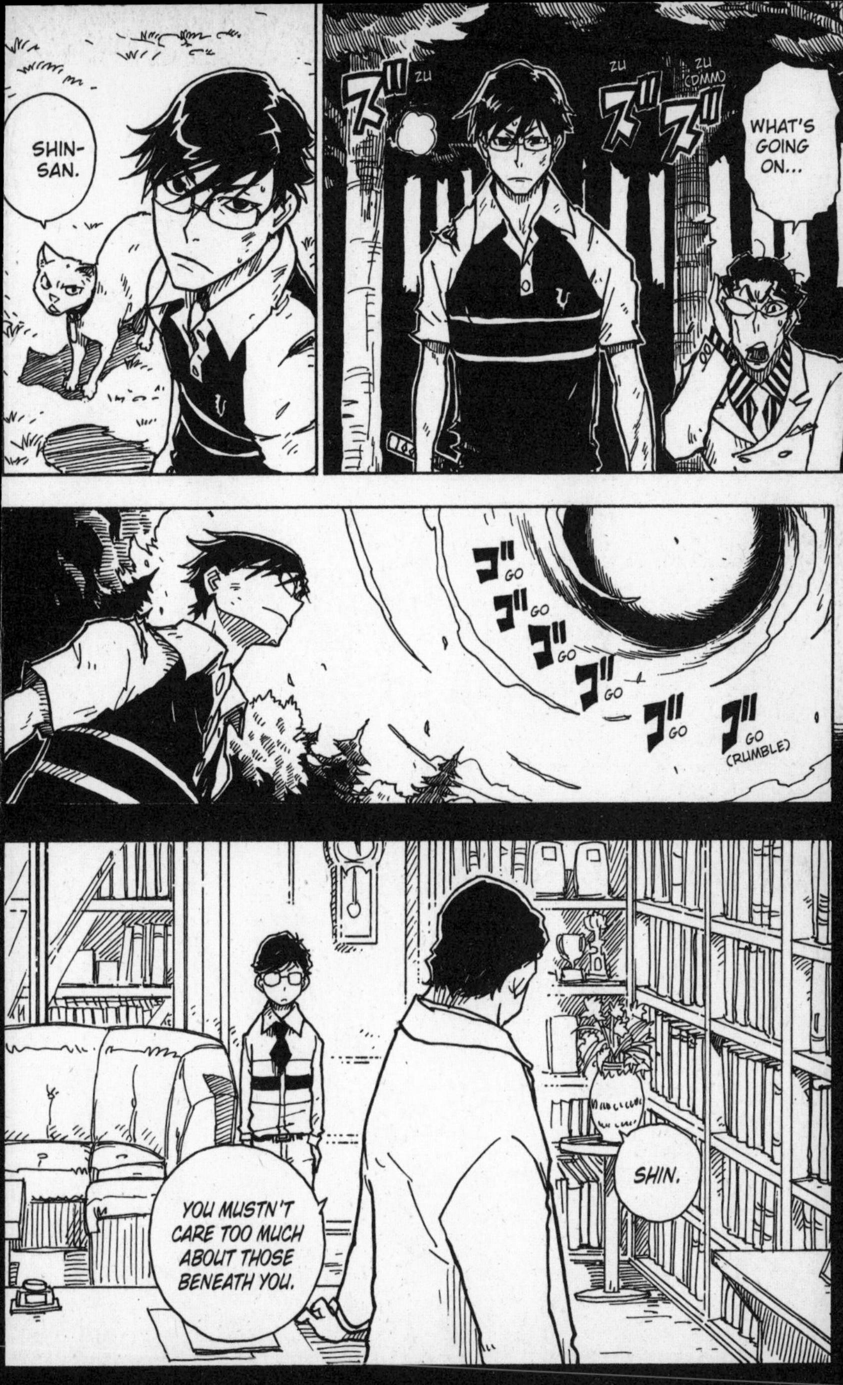

WHAT'S GOING ON...
ズ ZU
ズ ZU
ズ ZU (DMM)
SHIN-SAN.
ゴ GO
ゴ GO
ゴ GO
ゴ GO
ゴ GO
ゴ GO (RUMBLE)
SHIN.
YOU MUSTN'T CARE TOO MUCH ABOUT THOSE BENEATH YOU.

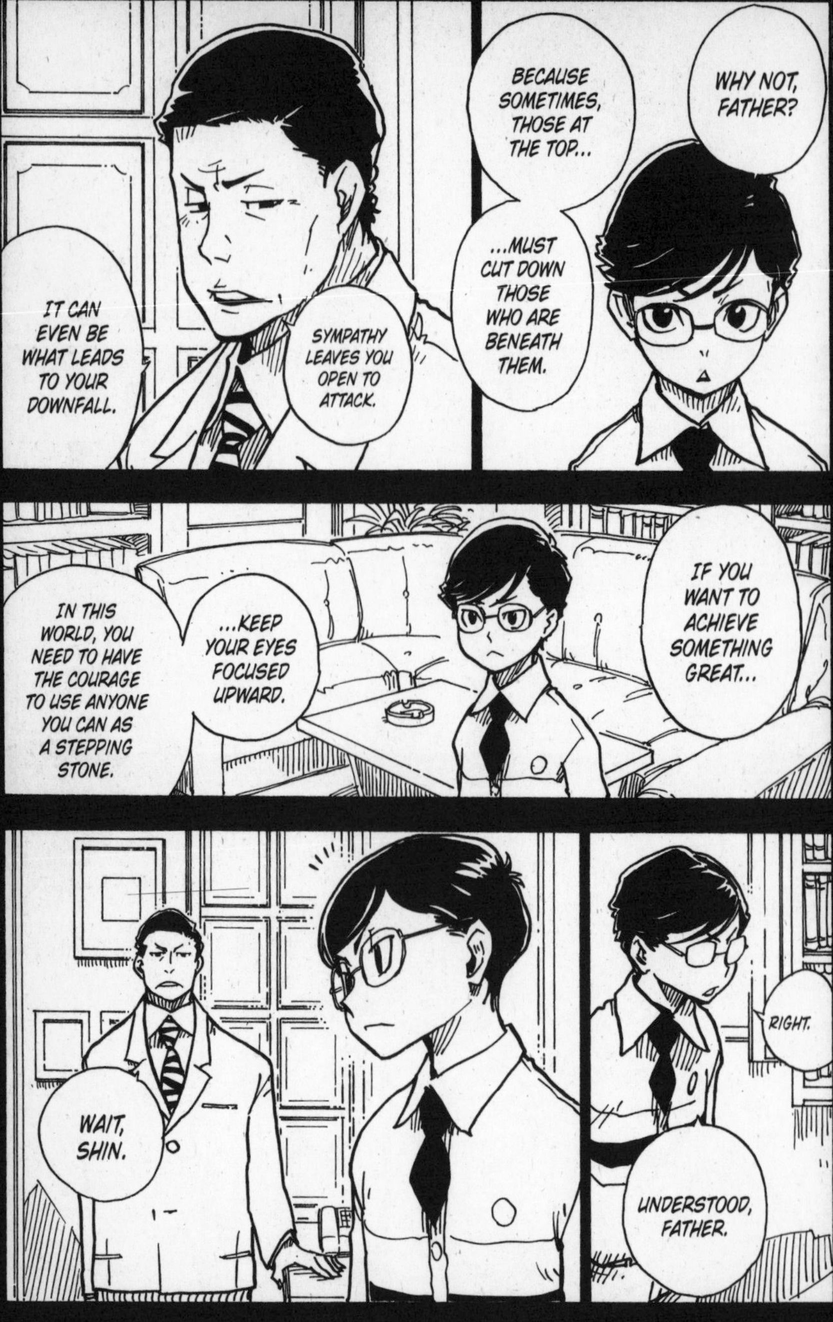
WHY NOT, FATHER?
BECAUSE SOMETIMES, THOSE AT THE TOP...
...MUST CUT DOWN THOSE WHO ARE BENEATH THEM.
SYMPATHY LEAVES YOU OPEN TO ATTACK.
IT CAN EVEN BE WHAT LEADS TO YOUR DOWNFALL.
IF YOU WANT TO ACHIEVE SOMETHING GREAT...
...KEEP YOUR EYES FOCUSED UPWARD.
IN THIS WORLD, YOU NEED TO HAVE THE COURAGE TO USE ANYONE YOU CAN AS A STEPPING STONE.
RIGHT.
UNDERSTOOD, FATHER.
WAIT, SHIN.

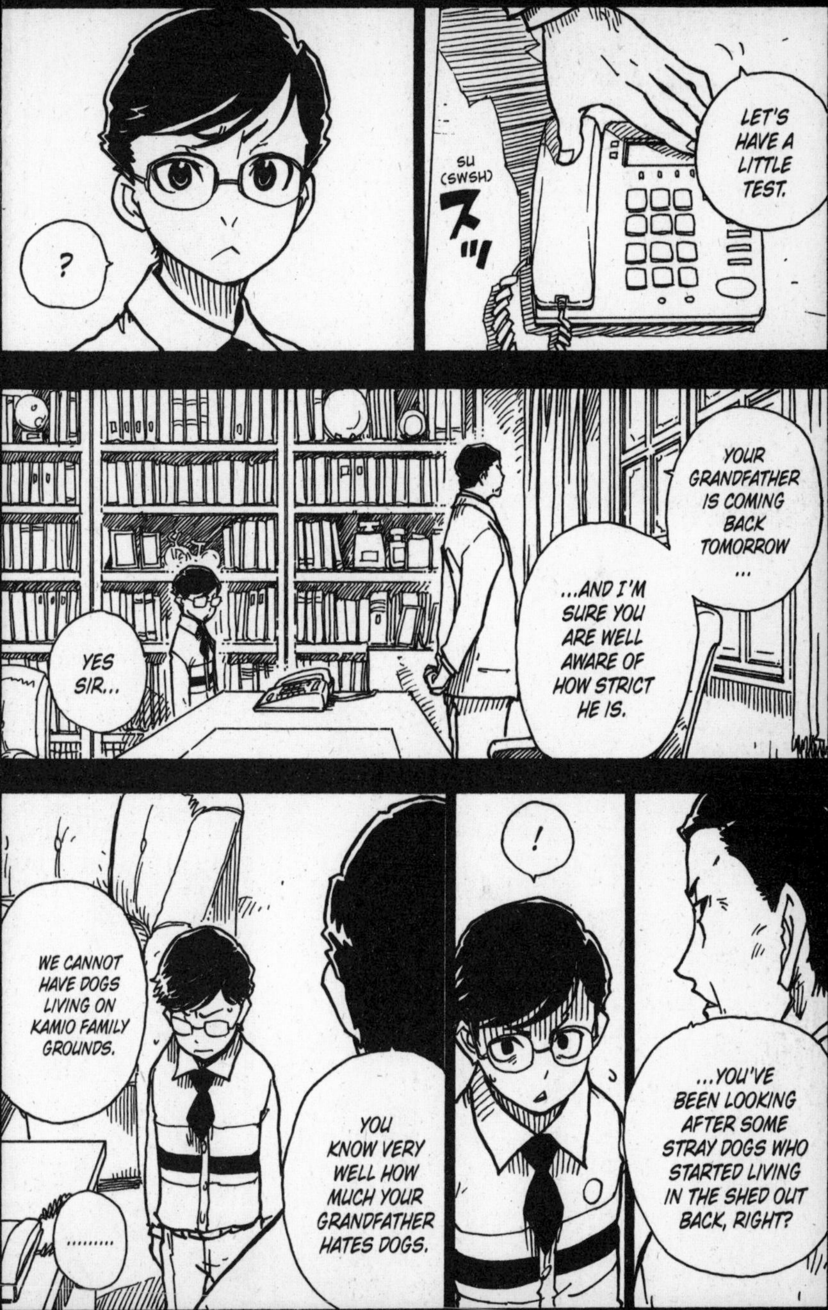
LET'S HAVE A LITTLE TEST.
SU (SWSH)
ズッ
?
YOUR GRANDFATHER IS COMING BACK TOMORROW ...
...AND I'M SURE YOU ARE WELL AWARE OF HOW STRICT HE IS.
YES SIR...
...YOU'VE BEEN LOOKING AFTER SOME STRAY DOGS WHO STARTED LIVING IN THE SHED OUT BACK, RIGHT?
!
YOU KNOW VERY WELL HOW MUCH YOUR GRANDFATHER HATES DOGS.
WE CANNOT HAVE DOGS LIVING ON KAMIO FAMILY GROUNDS.
....

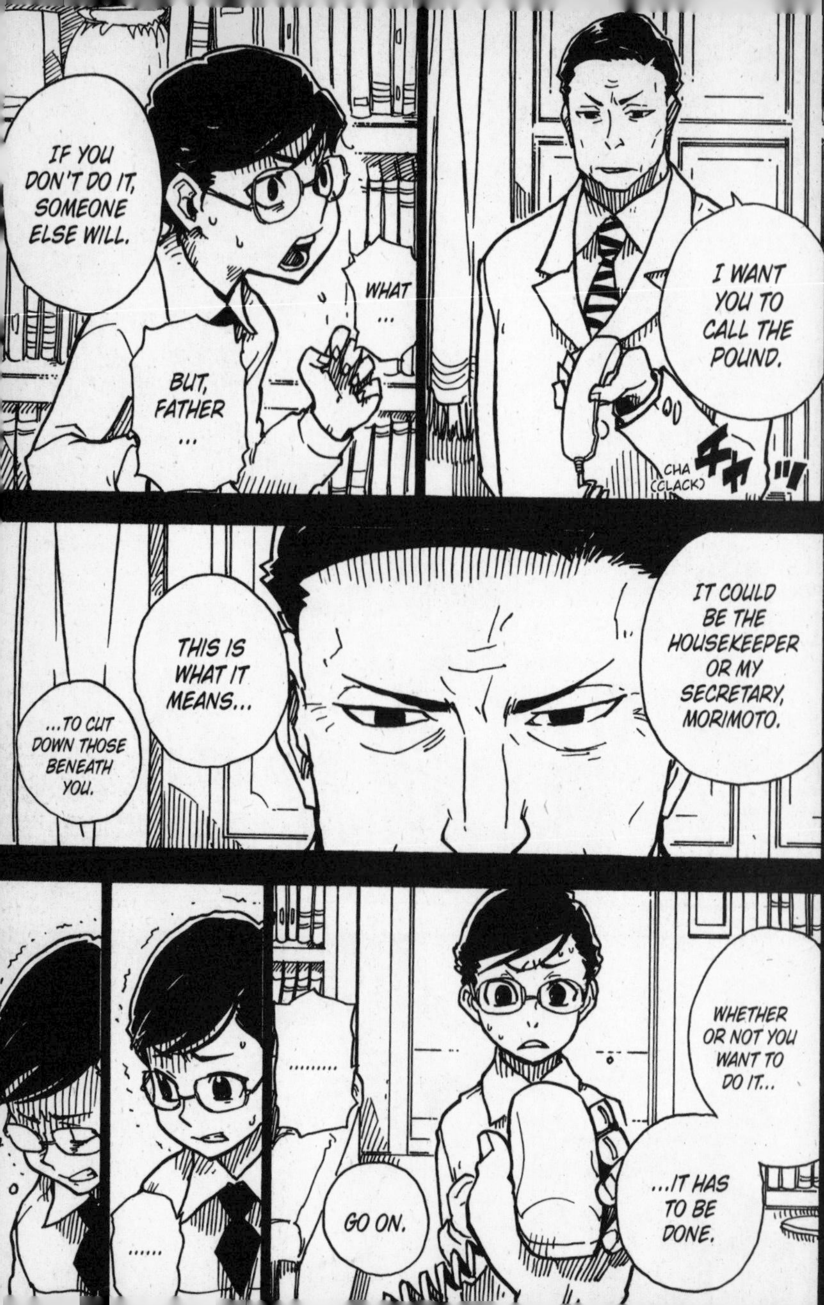
I WANT YOU TO CALL THE POUND.
CHA (CLACK)
WHAT ...
BUT, FATHER ...
IF YOU DON'T DO IT, SOMEONE ELSE WILL.
IT COULD BE THE HOUSEKEEPER OR MY SECRETARY, MORIMOTO.
THIS IS WHAT IT MEANS...
...TO CUT DOWN THOSE BENEATH YOU.
WHETHER OR NOT YOU WANT TO DO IT...
...IT HAS TO BE DONE.
GO ON.
....
......

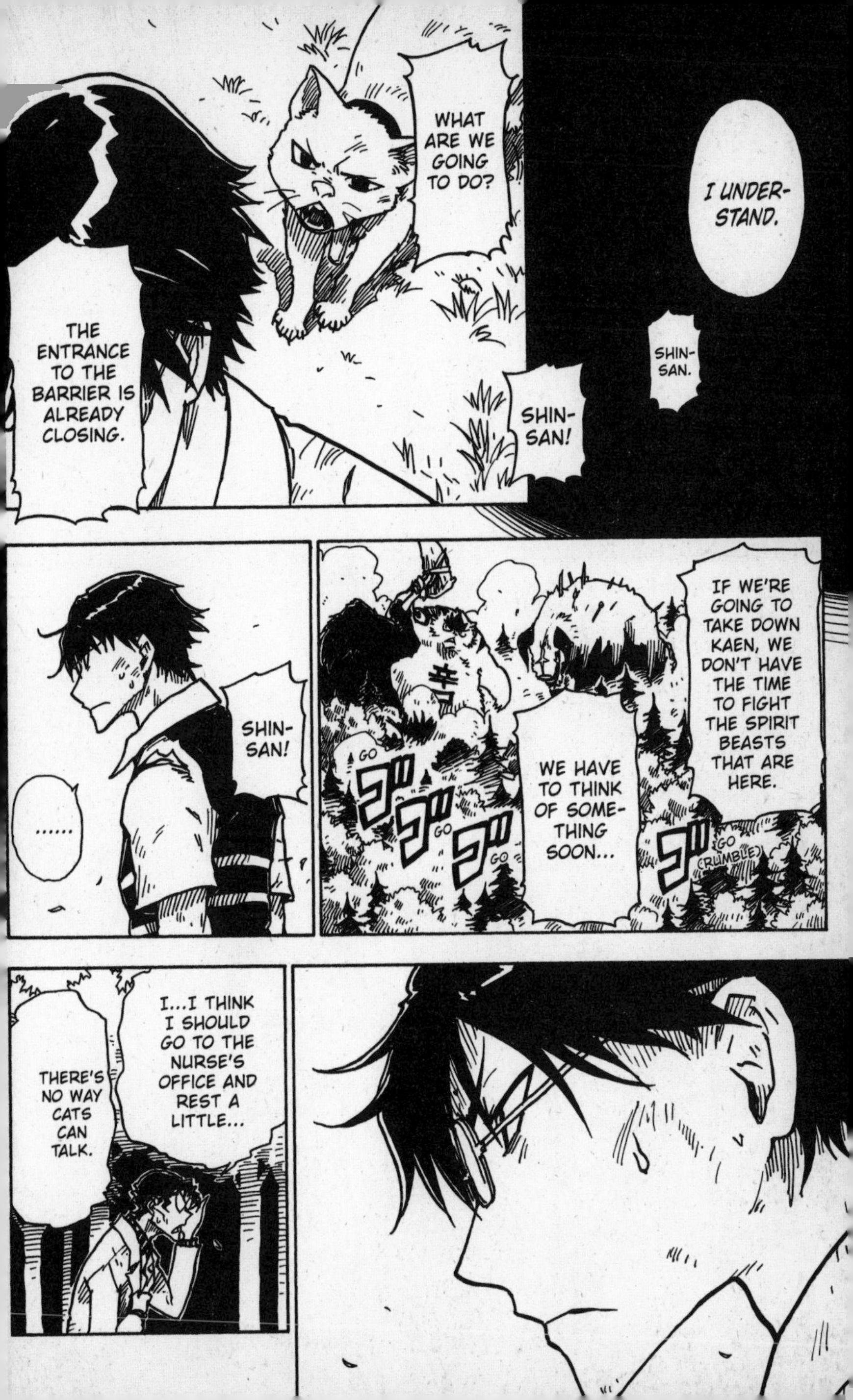
I UNDER-STAND.
SHIN-SAN.
WHAT ARE WE GOING TO DO?
SHIN-SAN!
THE ENTRANCE TO THE BARRIER IS ALREADY CLOSING.
IF WE'RE GOING TO TAKE DOWN KAEN, WE DON'T HAVE THE TIME TO FIGHT THE SPIRIT BEASTS THAT ARE HERE.
GO (RUMBLE)
WE HAVE TO THINK OF SOME-THING SOON...
GO
GO
GO
SHIN-SAN!
......
I...I THINK I SHOULD GO TO THE NURSE'S OFFICE AND REST A LITTLE...
THERE'S NO WAY CATS CAN TALK.

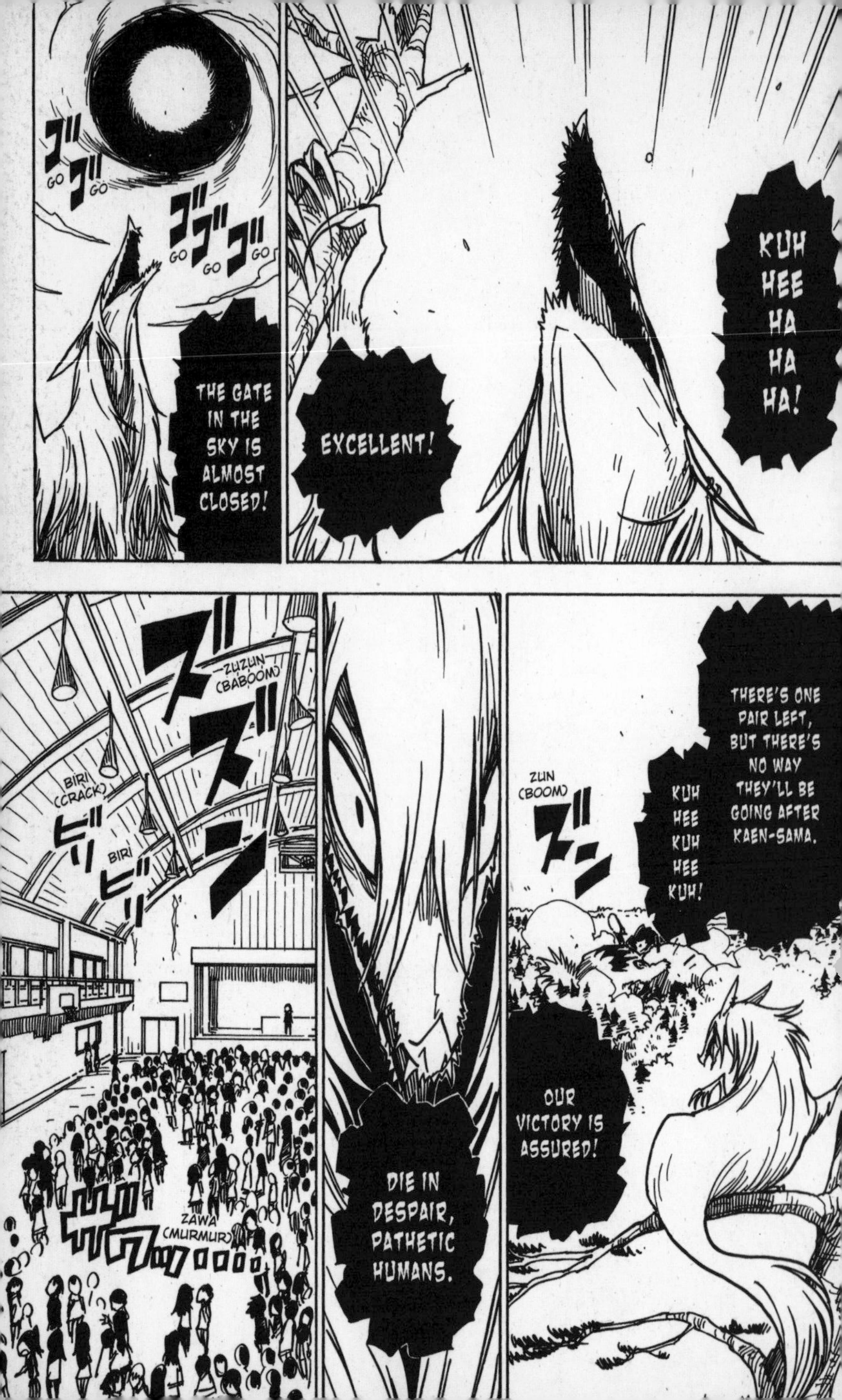
KUH HEE HA HA HA!
EXCELLENT!
GO GO GO GO GO
THE GATE IN THE SKY IS ALMOST CLOSED!
THERE'S ONE PAIR LEFT, BUT THERE'S NO WAY THEY'LL BE GOING AFTER KAEN-SAMA.
KUH HEE KUH HEE KUH!
ZUN (BOOM)
OUR VICTORY IS ASSURED!
DIE IN DESPAIR, PATHETIC HUMANS.
ZUZUN (BABOOM)
BIRI (CRACK)
BIRI
ZAWA (MURMUR)

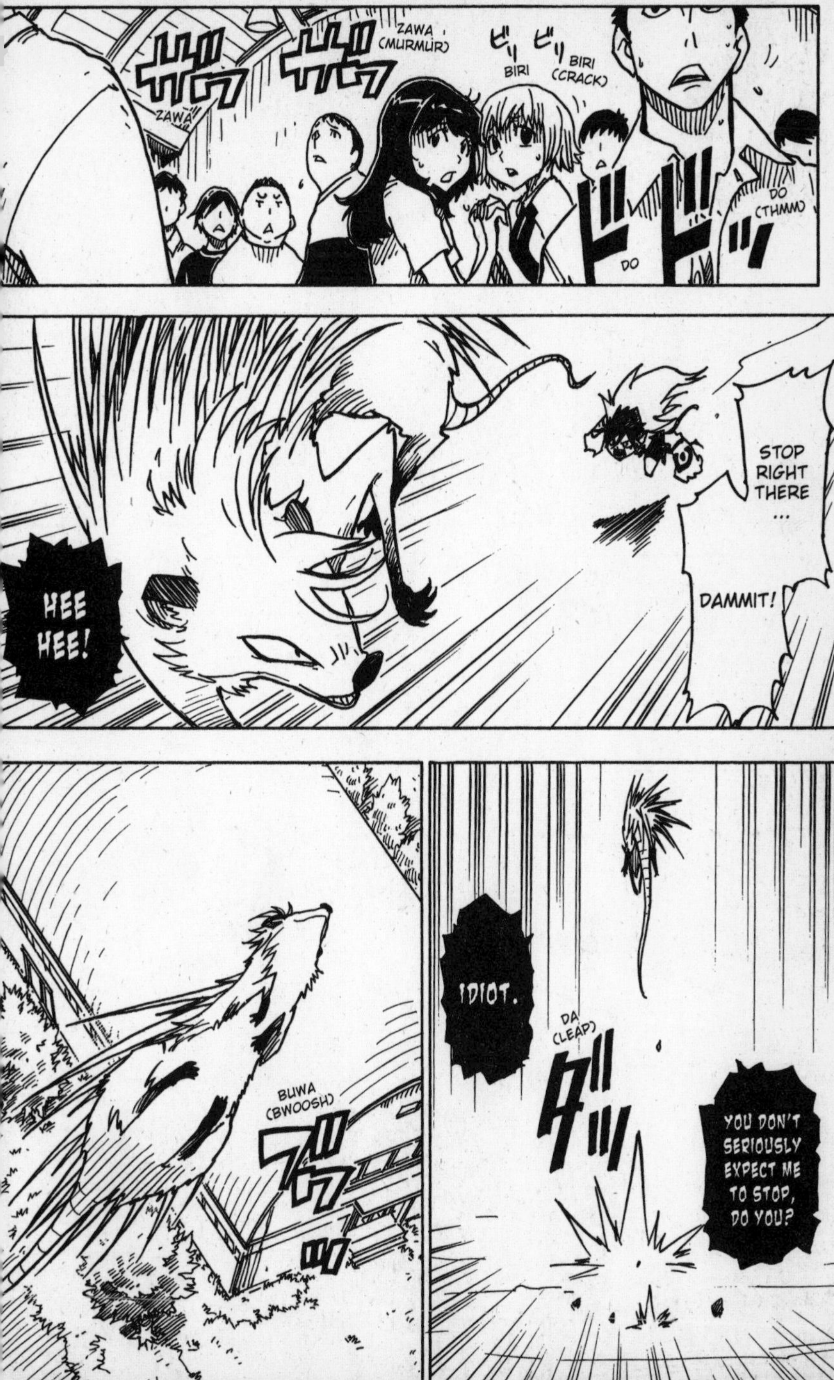
ビリ ビリ
BIRI
BIRI (CRACK)
ZAWA (MURMUR)
ZAWA
DO (THMM)
DO
STOP RIGHT THERE...
DAMMIT!
HEE HEE!
IDIOT.
DA (LEAP)
YOU DON'T SERIOUSLY EXPECT ME TO STOP, DO YOU?
BUWA (BWOOSH)

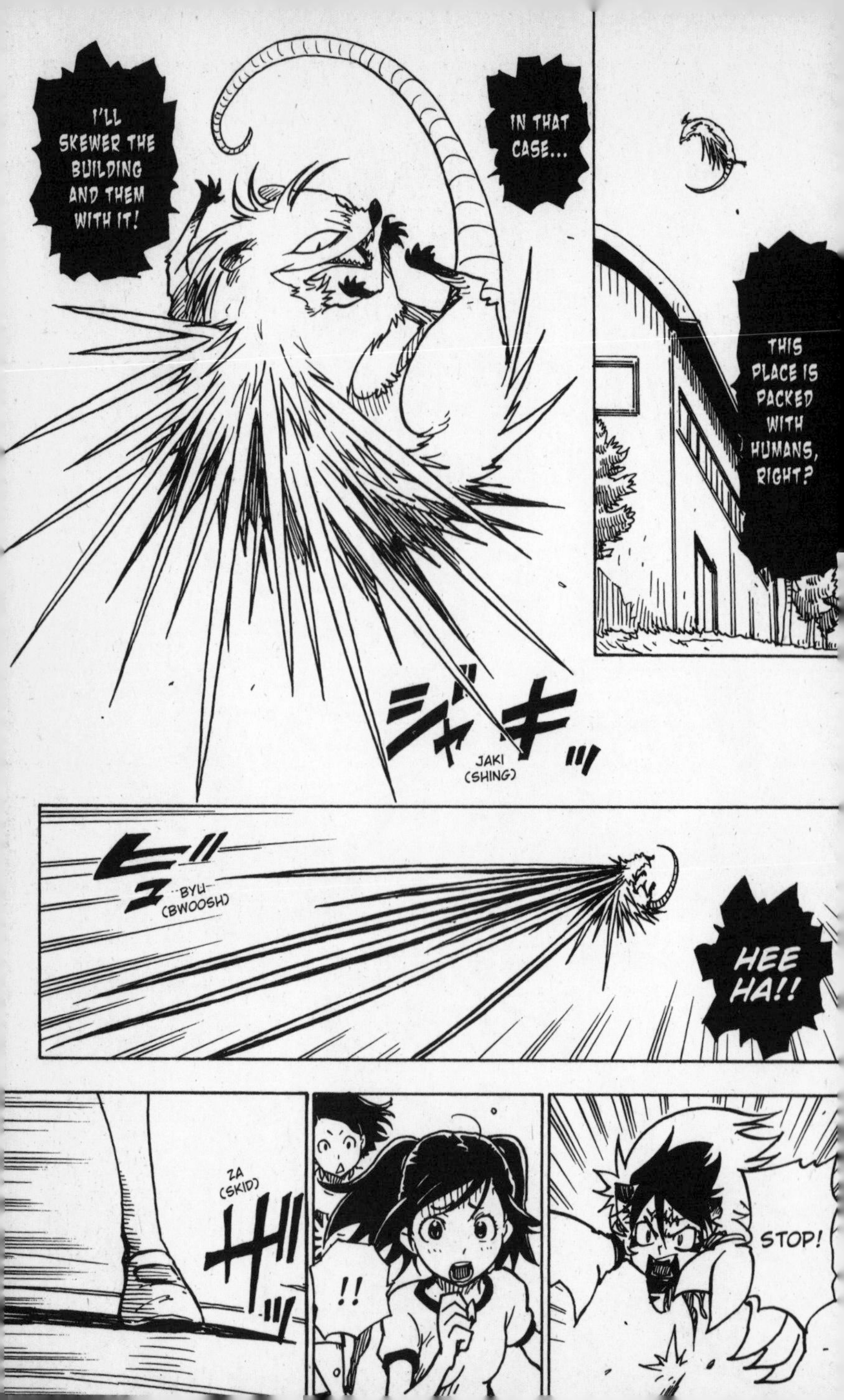

THIS PLACE IS PACKED WITH HUMANS, RIGHT?
IN THAT CASE...
I'LL SKEWER THE BUILDING AND THEM WITH IT!
JAKI (SHING)
HEE HA!!
BYU (BWOOSH)
STOP!
!!
ZA (SKID)

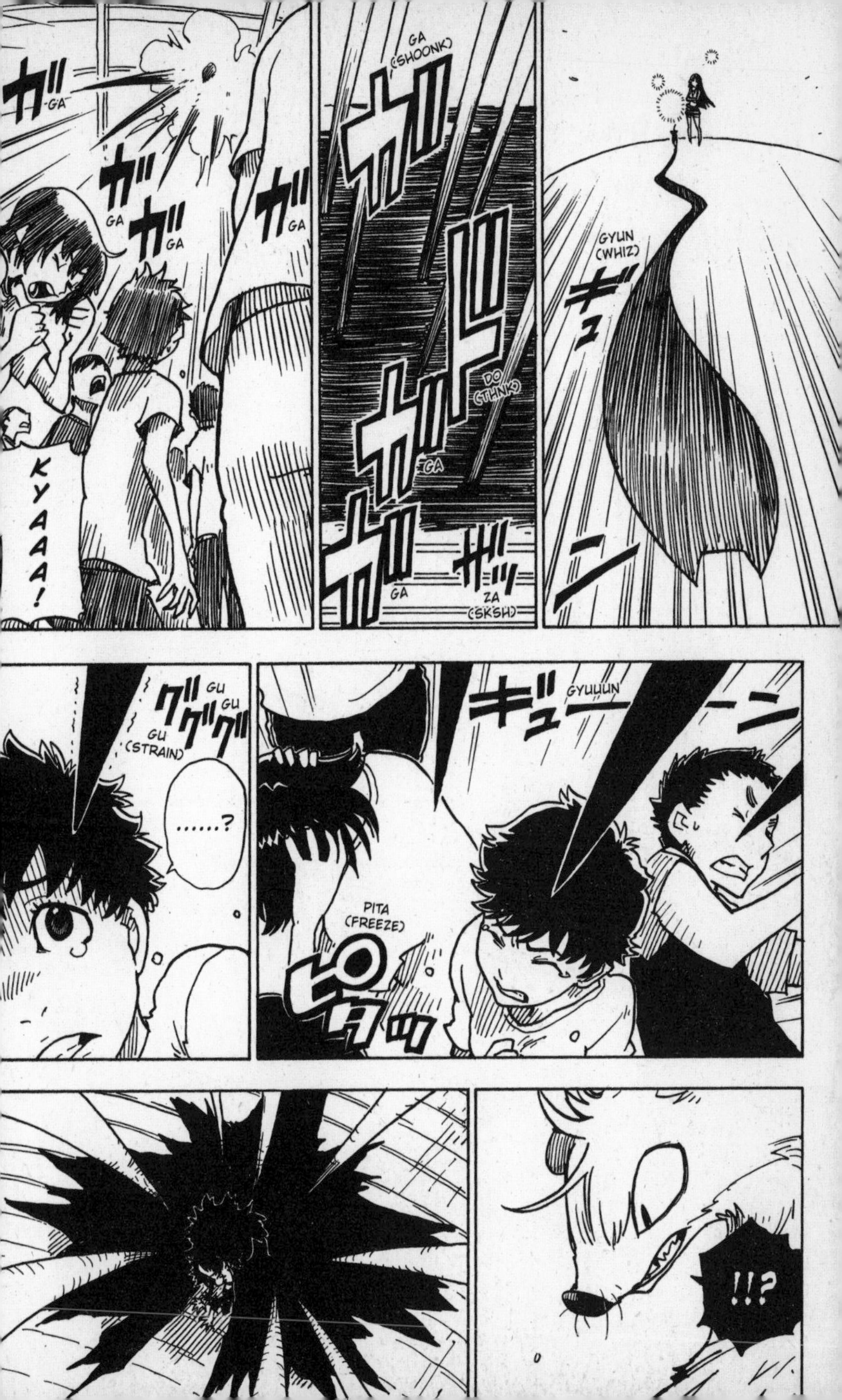
ギュン
GYUN (WHIZ)
ガッ
GA (SHOONK)
ドッ
DO (THNK)
ガッ
GA
ガッ
GA
ザッ
ZA (SKSH)
ガ
GA
ガ
GA
ガ
GA
ガ
GA
KYAAAA!
ギューーン
GYUUUN
ピタッ
PITA (FREEZE)
グググ
GU GU GU (STRAIN)
......?
!!?

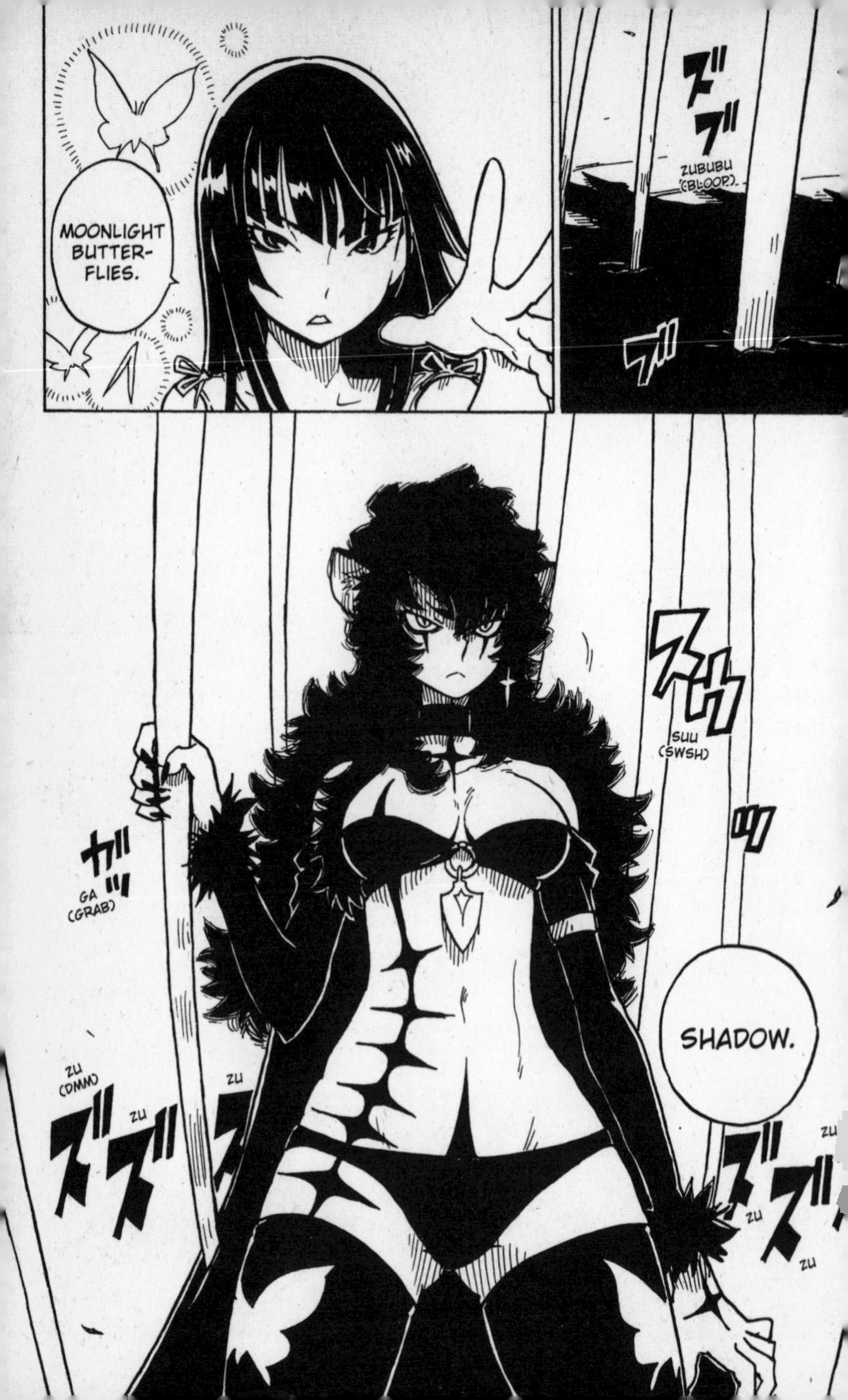
ZUBUBU (BLOOP)
MOONLIGHT BUTTER-FLIES.
SUU (SWSH)
SHADOW.
ZU ZU ZU
GA ZU (GRAB)
ZU (DMM) ZU ZU

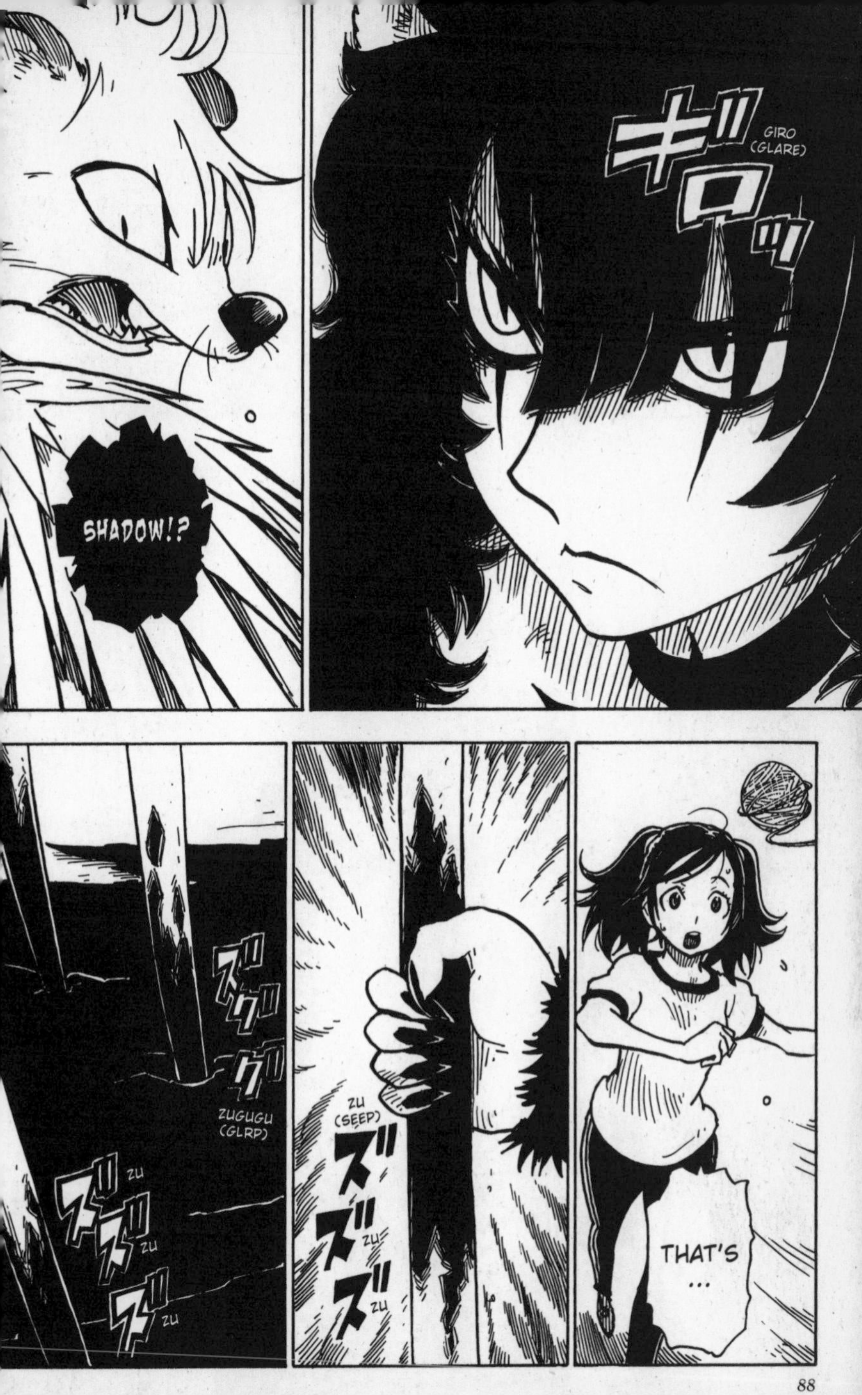
GIRO (GLARE)
SHADOW!?
THAT'S ...
ZU (SEEP)
ZU
ZU
ZUGUGU (GLRP)
ZU
ZU
ZU

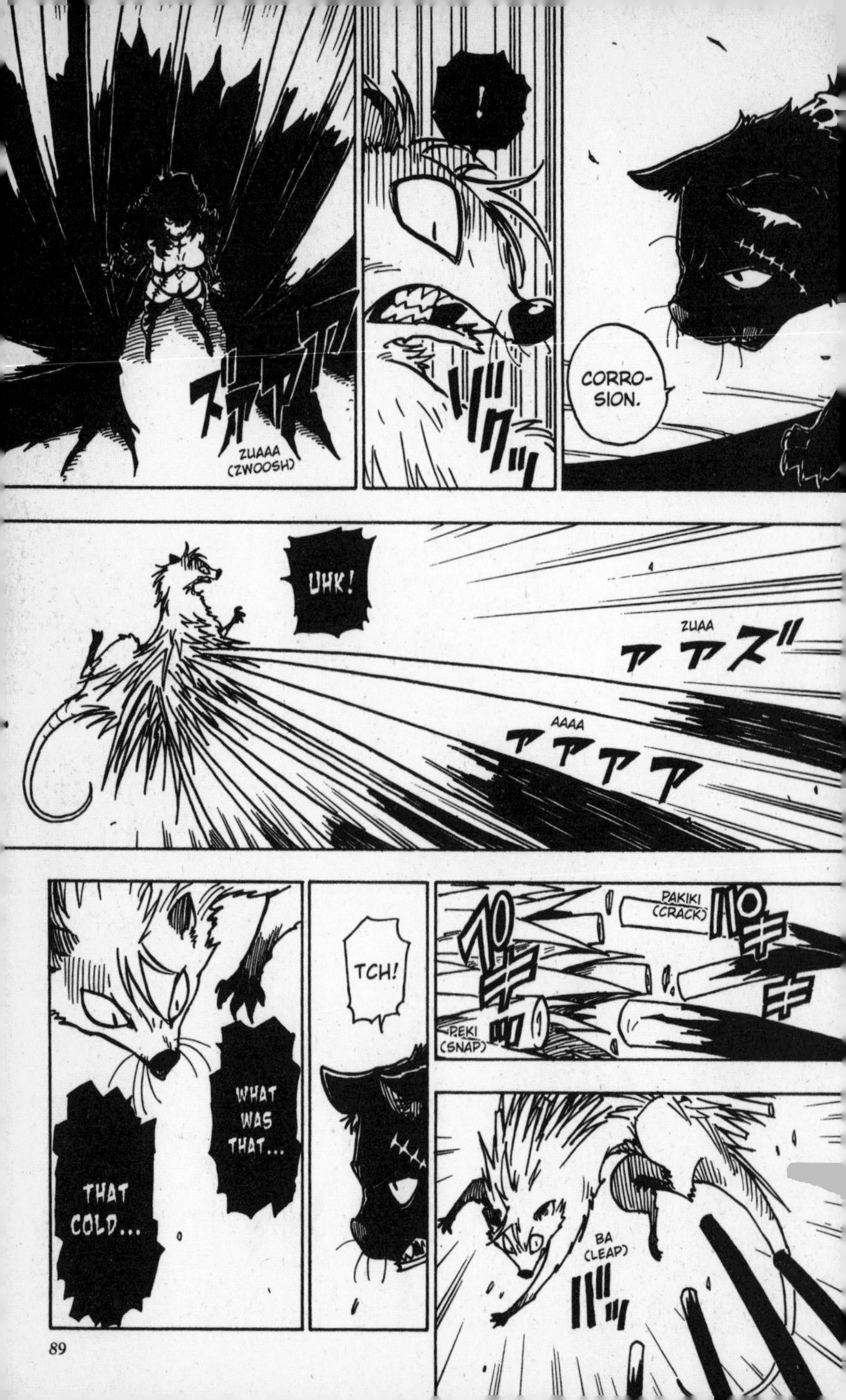
CORRO-SION.
!
ZUAAA (ZWOOSH)
UHK!
ZUAA
AAAA
PAKIKI (CRACK)
P.EKI (SNAP)
BA (LEAP)
TCH!
WHAT WAS THAT...
THAT COLD...

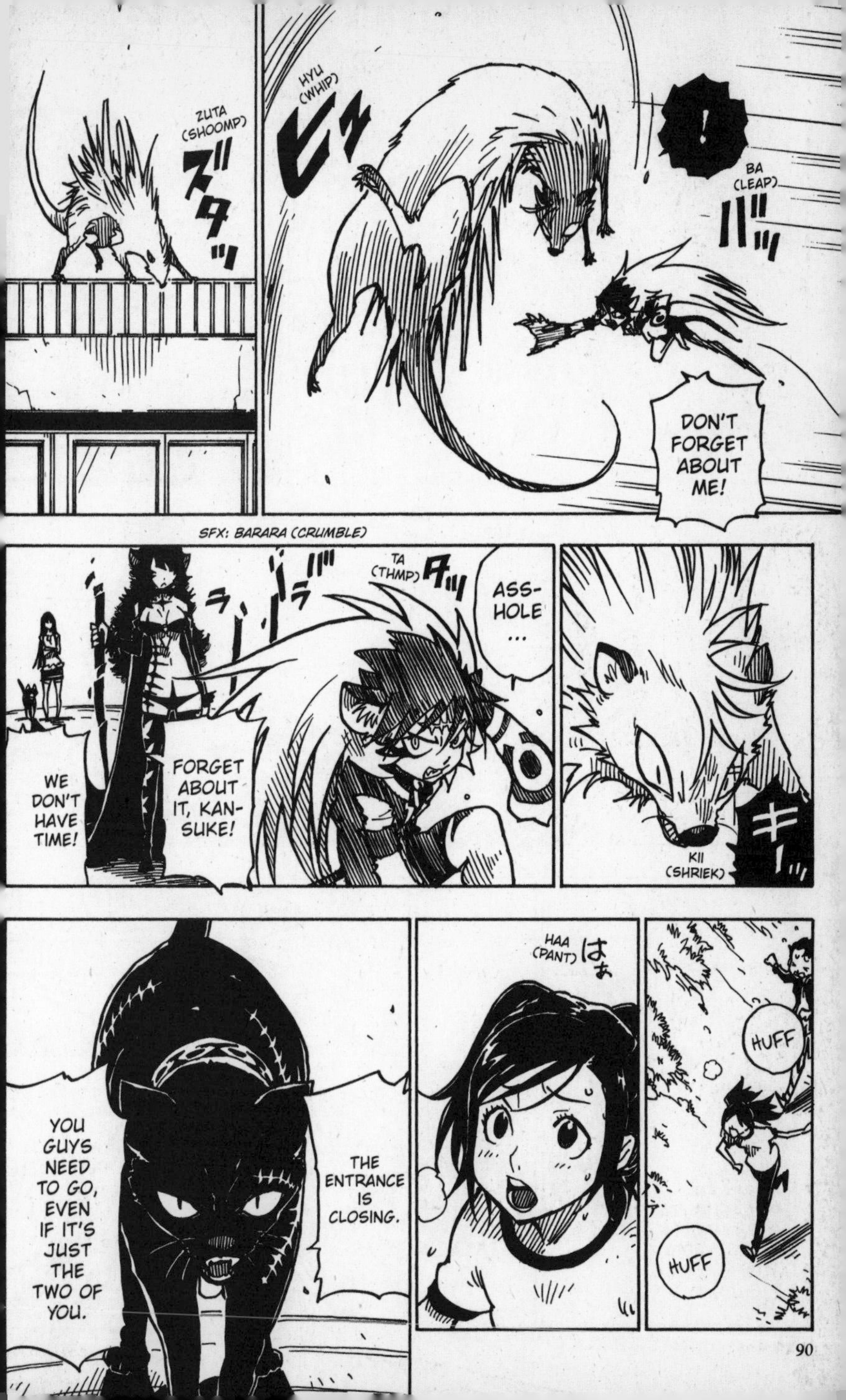
!
BA (LEAP)
DON'T FORGET ABOUT ME!
HYU (WHIP)
ZUTA (SHOOMP)
SFX: BARARA (CRUMBLE)
KII (SHRIEK)
ASS-HOLE ...
TA (THMP)
FORGET ABOUT IT, KAN-SUKE!
WE DON'T HAVE TIME!
HUFF
HUFF
HAA (PANT)
THE ENTRANCE IS CLOSING.
YOU GUYS NEED TO GO, EVEN IF IT'S JUST THE TWO OF YOU.

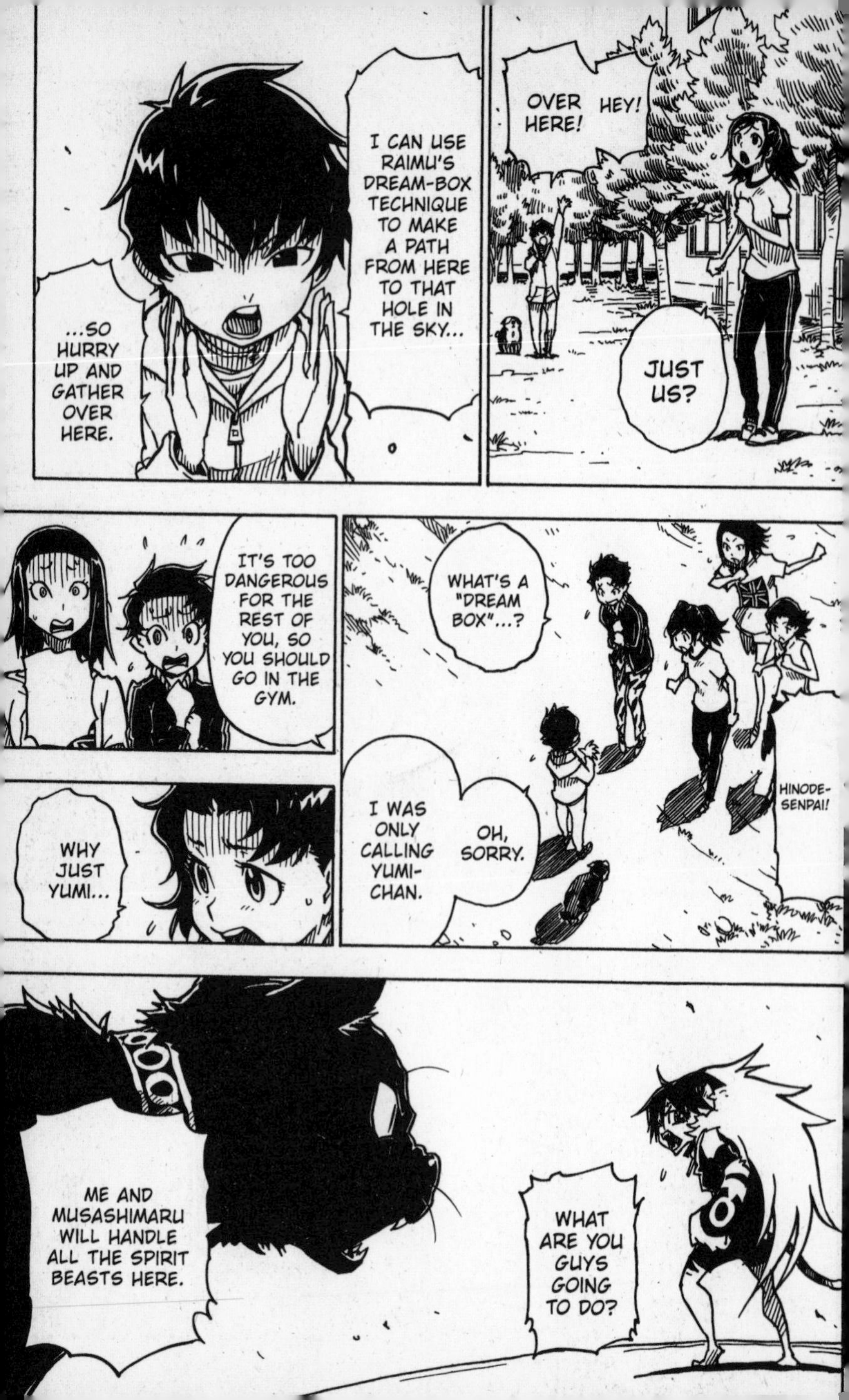
HEY!
OVER HERE!
JUST US?
I CAN USE RAIMU'S DREAM-BOX TECHNIQUE TO MAKE A PATH FROM HERE TO THAT HOLE IN THE SKY...
...SO HURRY UP AND GATHER OVER HERE.
WHAT'S A "DREAM BOX"...?
HINODE-SENPAI!
OH, SORRY.
I WAS ONLY CALLING YUMI-CHAN.
IT'S TOO DANGEROUS FOR THE REST OF YOU, SO YOU SHOULD GO IN THE GYM.
WHY JUST YUMI...
WHAT ARE YOU GUYS GOING TO DO?
ME AND MUSASHIMARU WILL HANDLE ALL THE SPIRIT BEASTS HERE.

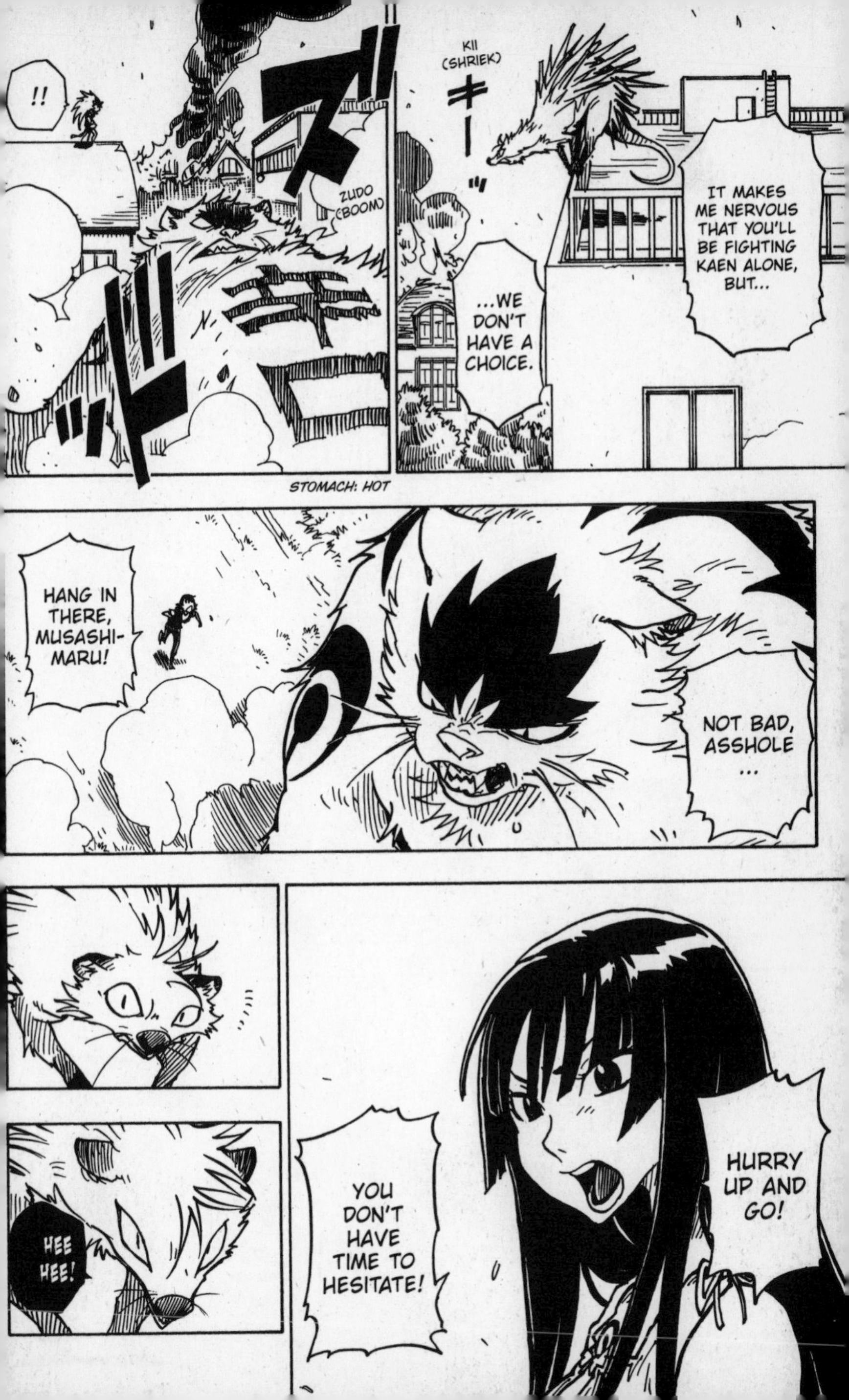
KII (SHRIEK)
IT MAKES ME NERVOUS THAT YOU'LL BE FIGHTING KAEN ALONE, BUT...
...WE DON'T HAVE A CHOICE.
ZUDO (BOOM)
!!
STOMACH: HOT
NOT BAD, ASSHOLE ...
HANG IN THERE, MUSASHI-MARU!
HURRY UP AND GO!
YOU DON'T HAVE TIME TO HESITATE!
HEE HEE!

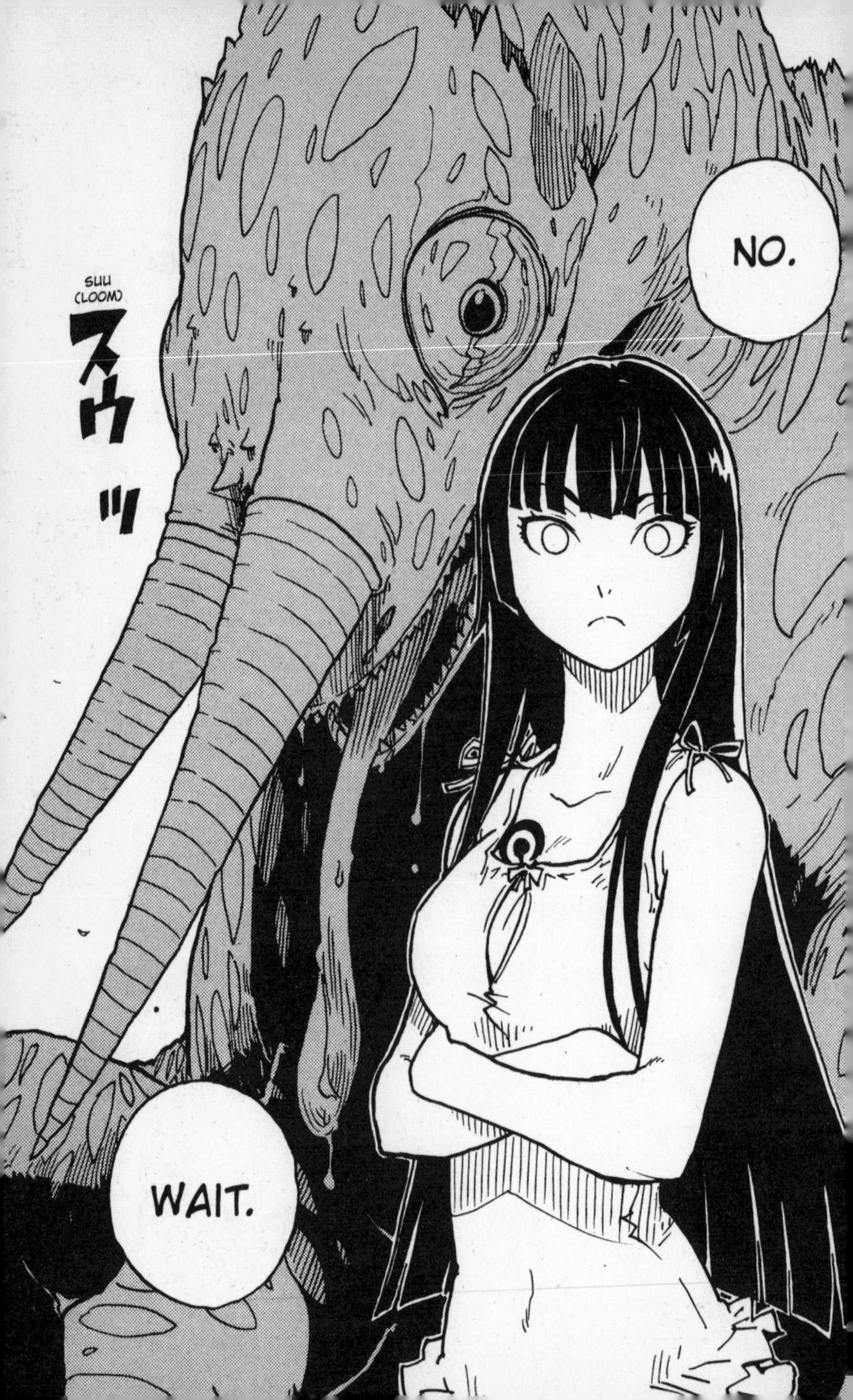
NO.
SUU (LOOM)
スゥッ
WAIT.

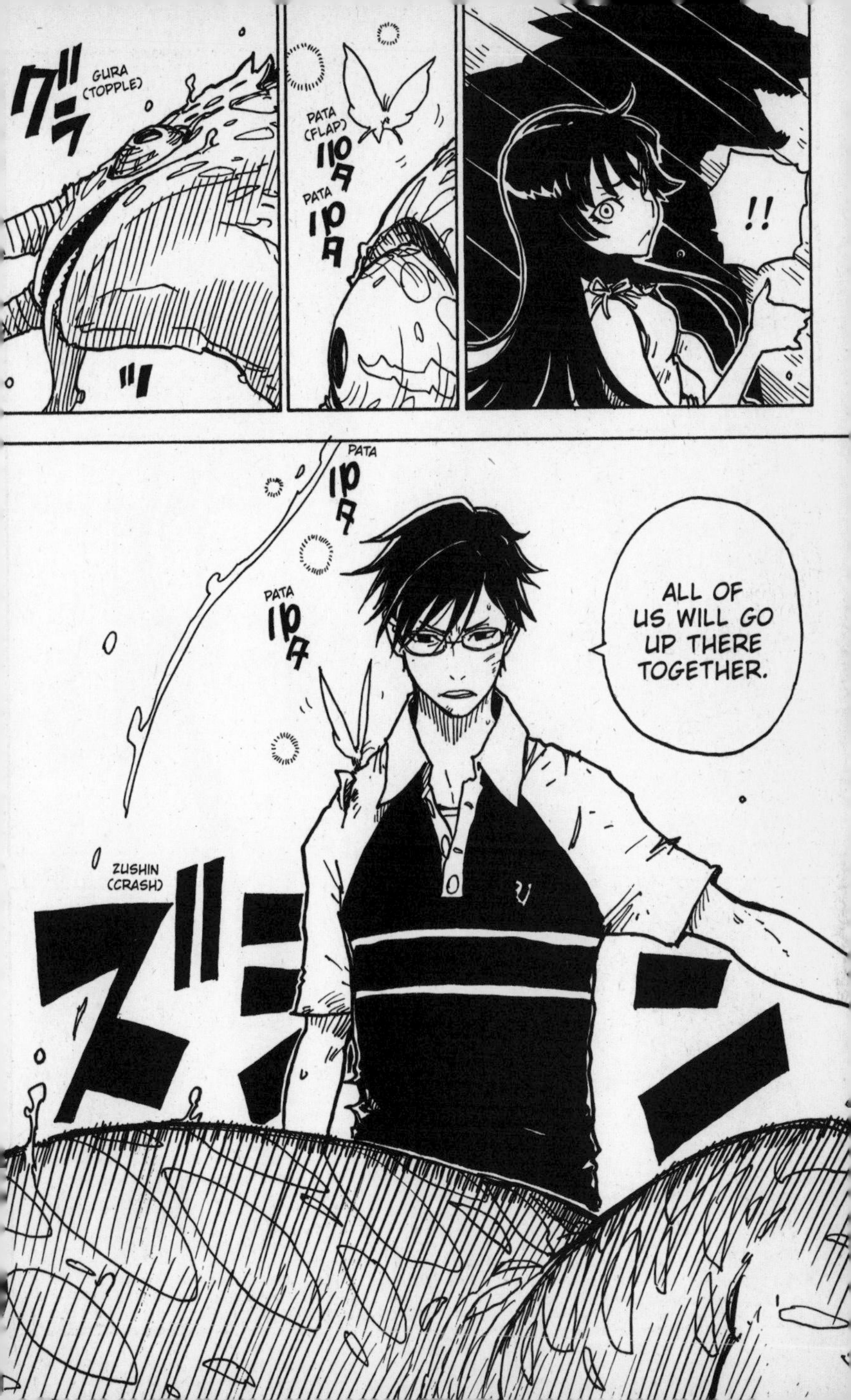
!!
PATA (FLAP)
パタ
PATA
パタ
GURA (TOPPLE)
グラ
ッ
PATA
パタ
PATA
パタ
ALL OF US WILL GO UP THERE TOGETHER.
ZUSHIN (CRASH)
ズシン

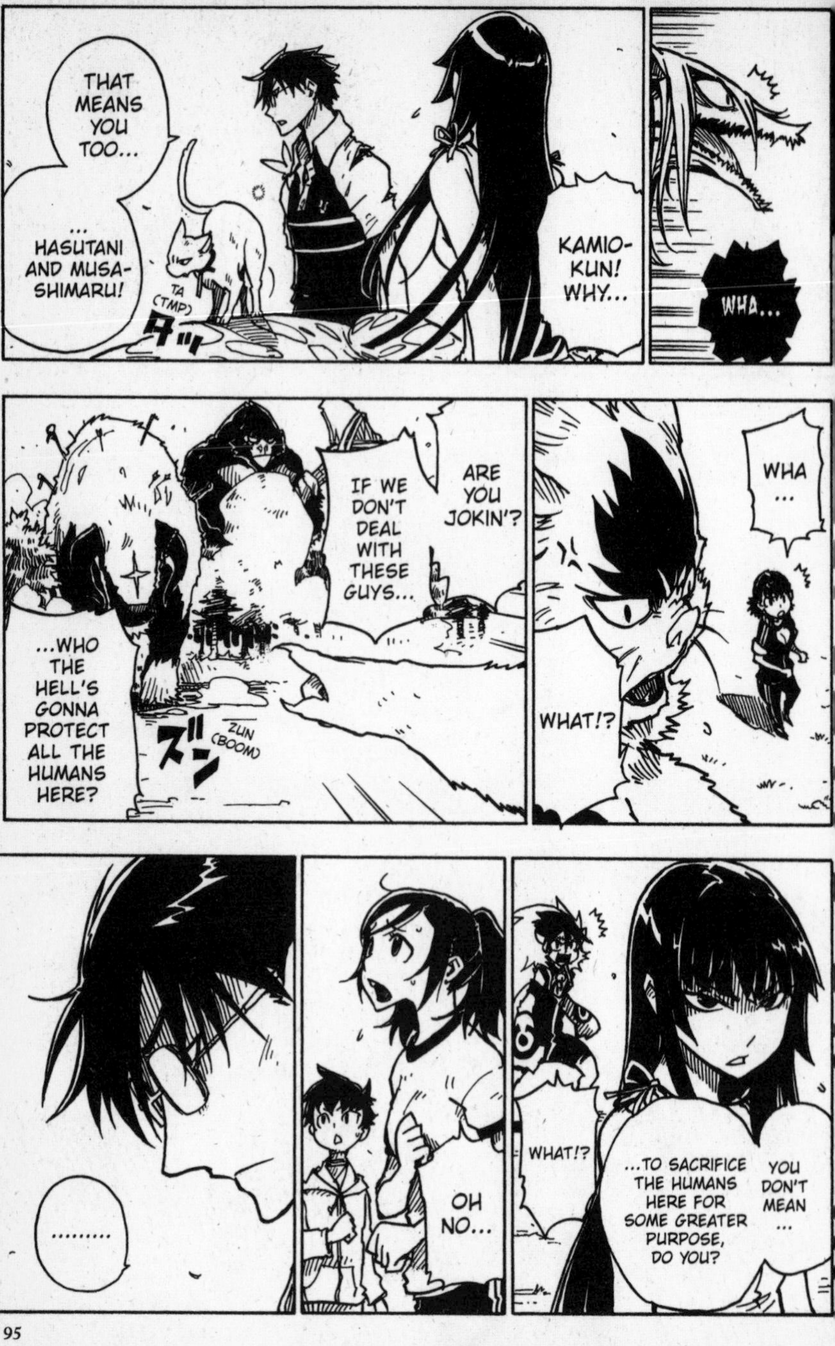
WHA...
KAMIO-KUN! WHY...
THAT MEANS YOU TOO...
...HASUTANI AND MUSA-SHIMARU!
TA (TMP)
WHA ...
WHAT!?
ARE YOU JOKIN'?
IF WE DON'T DEAL WITH THESE GUYS...
...WHO THE HELL'S GONNA PROTECT ALL THE HUMANS HERE?
ZUN (BOOM)
YOU DON'T MEAN ...
...TO SACRIFICE THE HUMANS HERE FOR SOME GREATER PURPOSE, DO YOU?
WHAT!?
OH NO...
....

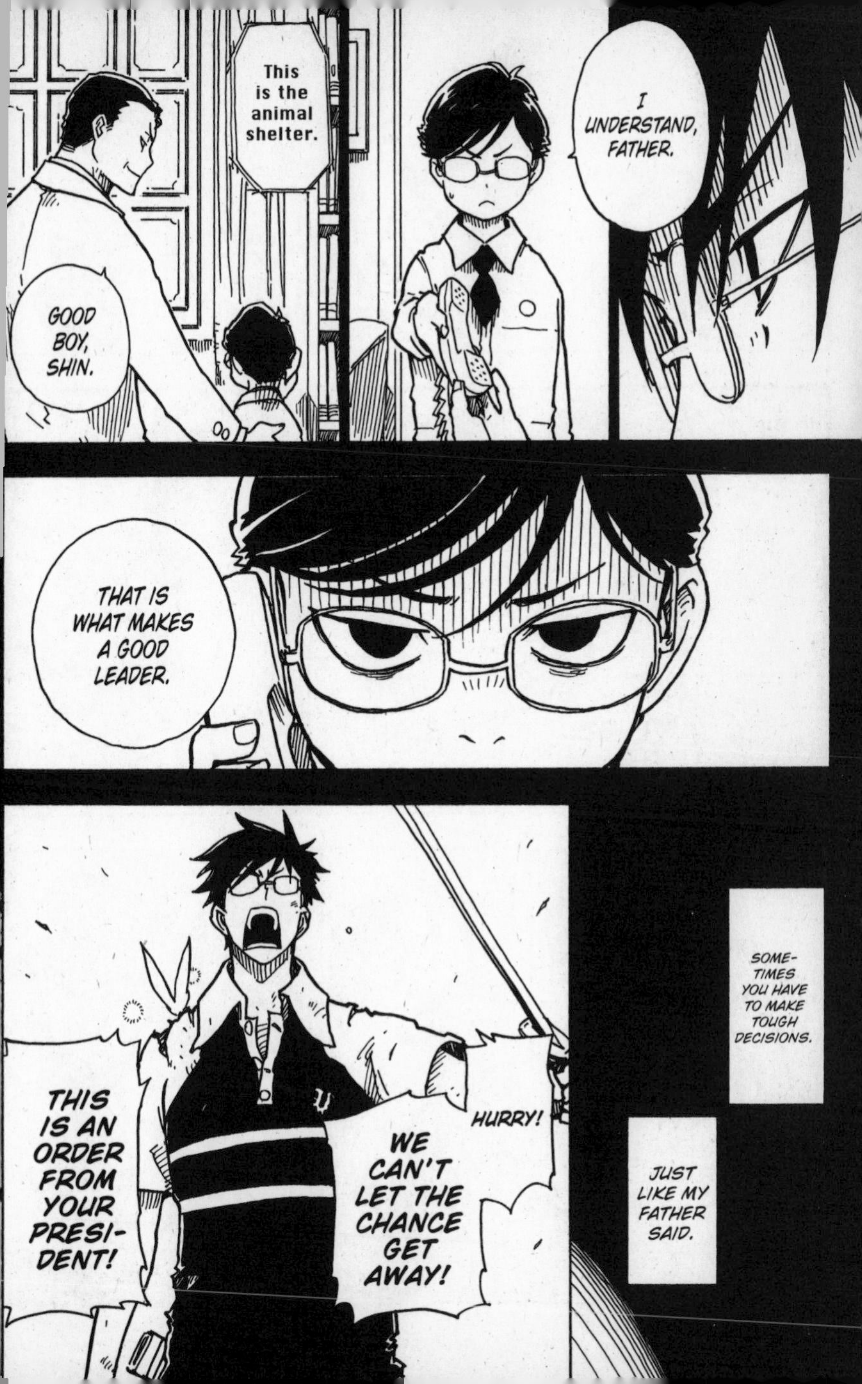
I UNDERSTAND, FATHER.
This is the animal shelter.
GOOD BOY, SHIN.
THAT IS WHAT MAKES A GOOD LEADER.
SOME-TIMES YOU HAVE TO MAKE TOUGH DECISIONS.
JUST LIKE MY FATHER SAID.
HURRY!
WE CAN'T LET THE CHANCE GET AWAY!
THIS IS AN ORDER FROM YOUR PRESI-DENT!

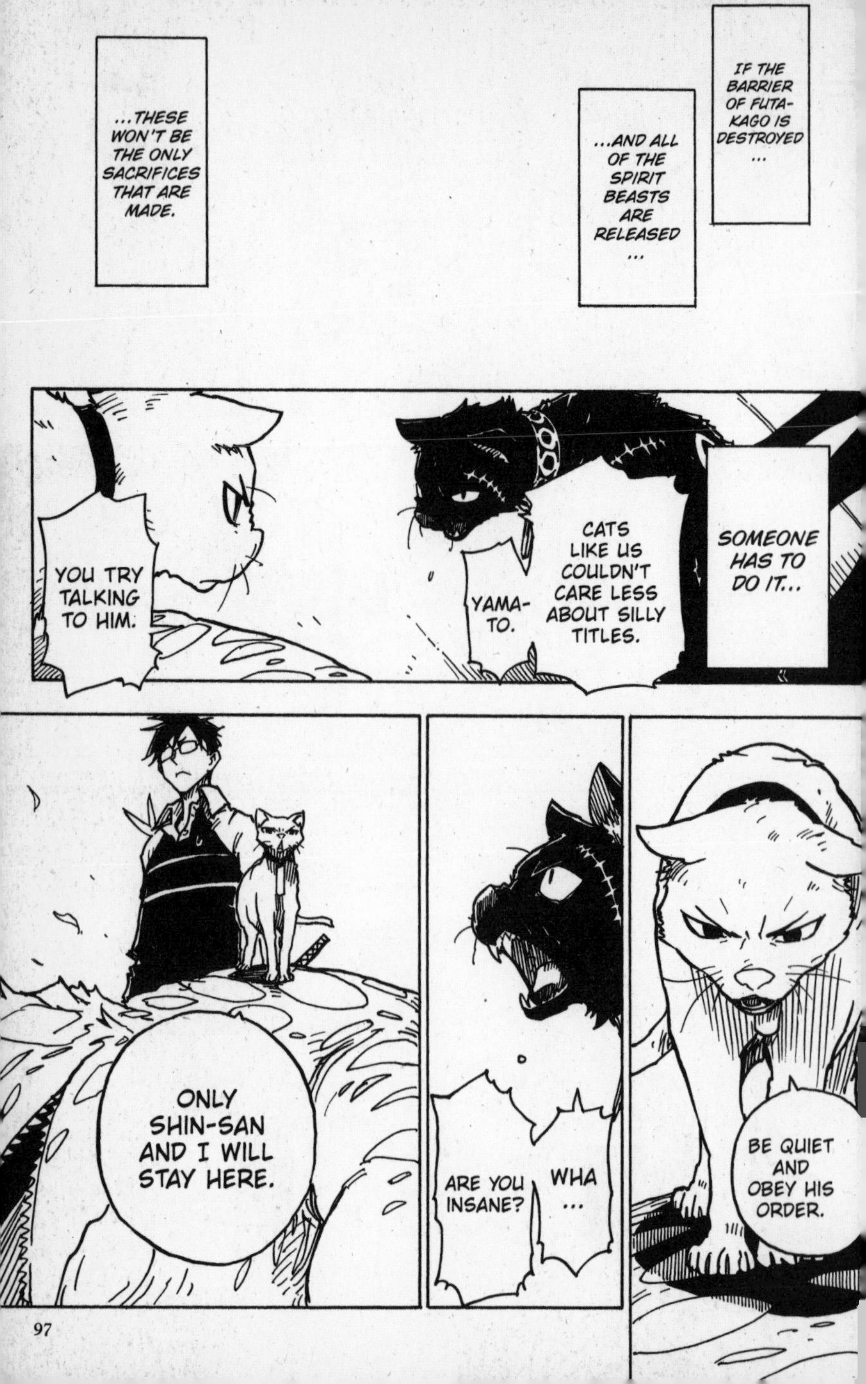
IF THE BARRIER OF FUTA-KAGO IS DESTROYED...
...AND ALL OF THE SPIRIT BEASTS ARE RELEASED...
...THESE WON'T BE THE ONLY SACRIFICES THAT ARE MADE.
SOMEONE HAS TO DO IT...
CATS LIKE US COULDN'T CARE LESS ABOUT SILLY TITLES.
YAMA-TO.
YOU TRY TALKING TO HIM.
BE QUIET AND OBEY HIS ORDER.
WHA...
ARE YOU INSANE?
ONLY SHIN-SAN AND I WILL STAY HERE.

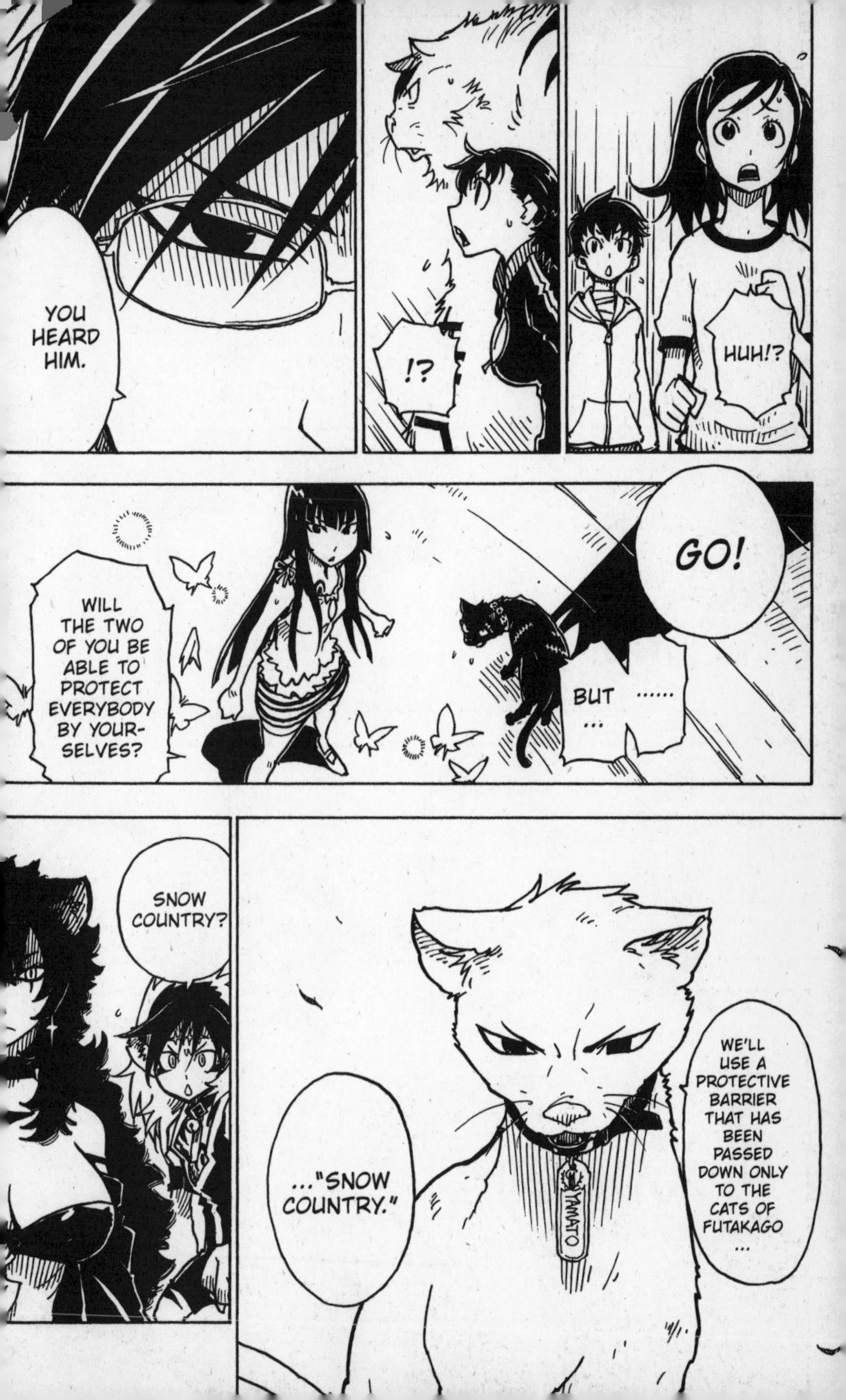
HUH!?
!?
YOU HEARD HIM.
GO!
BUT ... .
WILL THE TWO OF YOU BE ABLE TO PROTECT EVERYBODY BY YOURSELVES?
WE'LL USE A PROTECTIVE BARRIER THAT HAS BEEN PASSED DOWN ONLY TO THE CATS OF FUTAKAGO ...
..."SNOW COUNTRY."
YAMATO
SNOW COUNTRY?

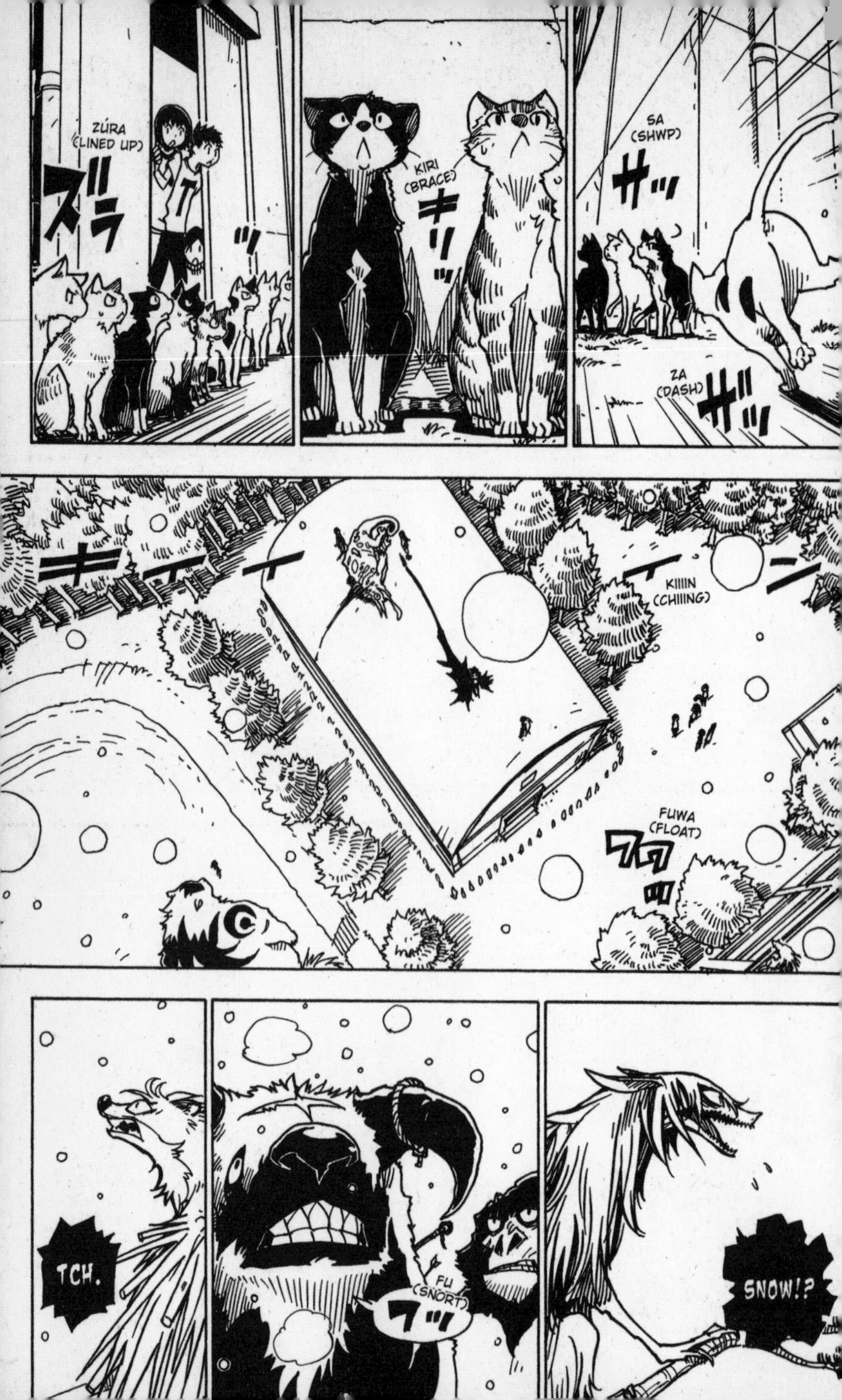
SA (SHWP)
サッ
ZA (DASH)
ザッ
KIRI (BRACE)
キリッ
ZÚRA (LINED UP)
ズラ
KIIIN (CHIIING)
キィーーン
FUWA (FLOAT)
フワ
SNOW!?
FU (SNORT)
フッ
TCH.

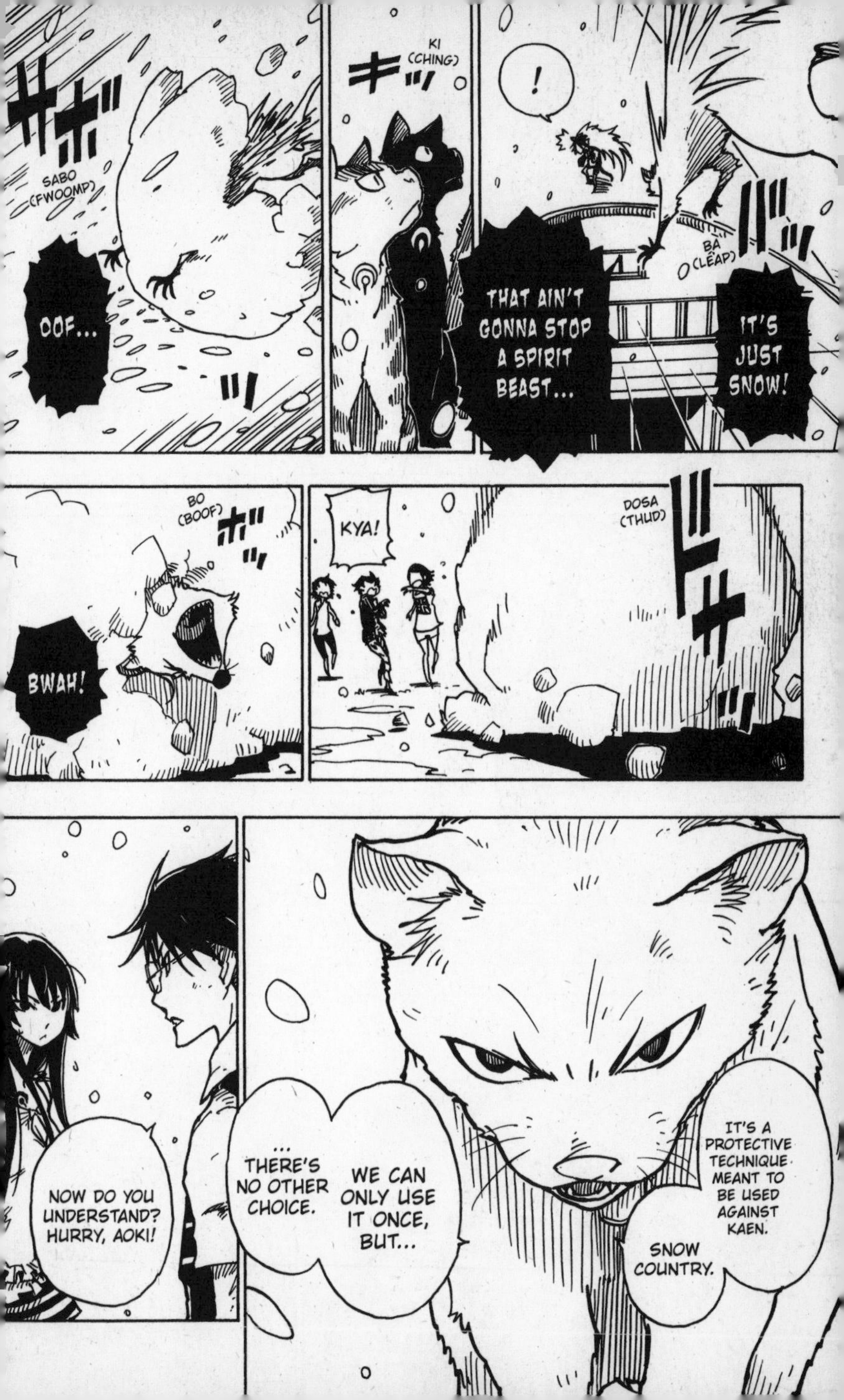
!
BA (LEAP)
IT'S JUST SNOW!
THAT AIN'T GONNA STOP A SPIRIT BEAST...
KI (CHING)
SABO (FWOOMP)
OOF...
DOSA (THUD)
KYA!
BO (BOOF)
BWAH!
IT'S A PROTECTIVE TECHNIQUE MEANT TO BE USED AGAINST KAEN.
SNOW COUNTRY.
WE CAN ONLY USE IT ONCE, BUT...
... THERE'S NO OTHER CHOICE.
NOW DO YOU UNDERSTAND? HURRY, AOKI!

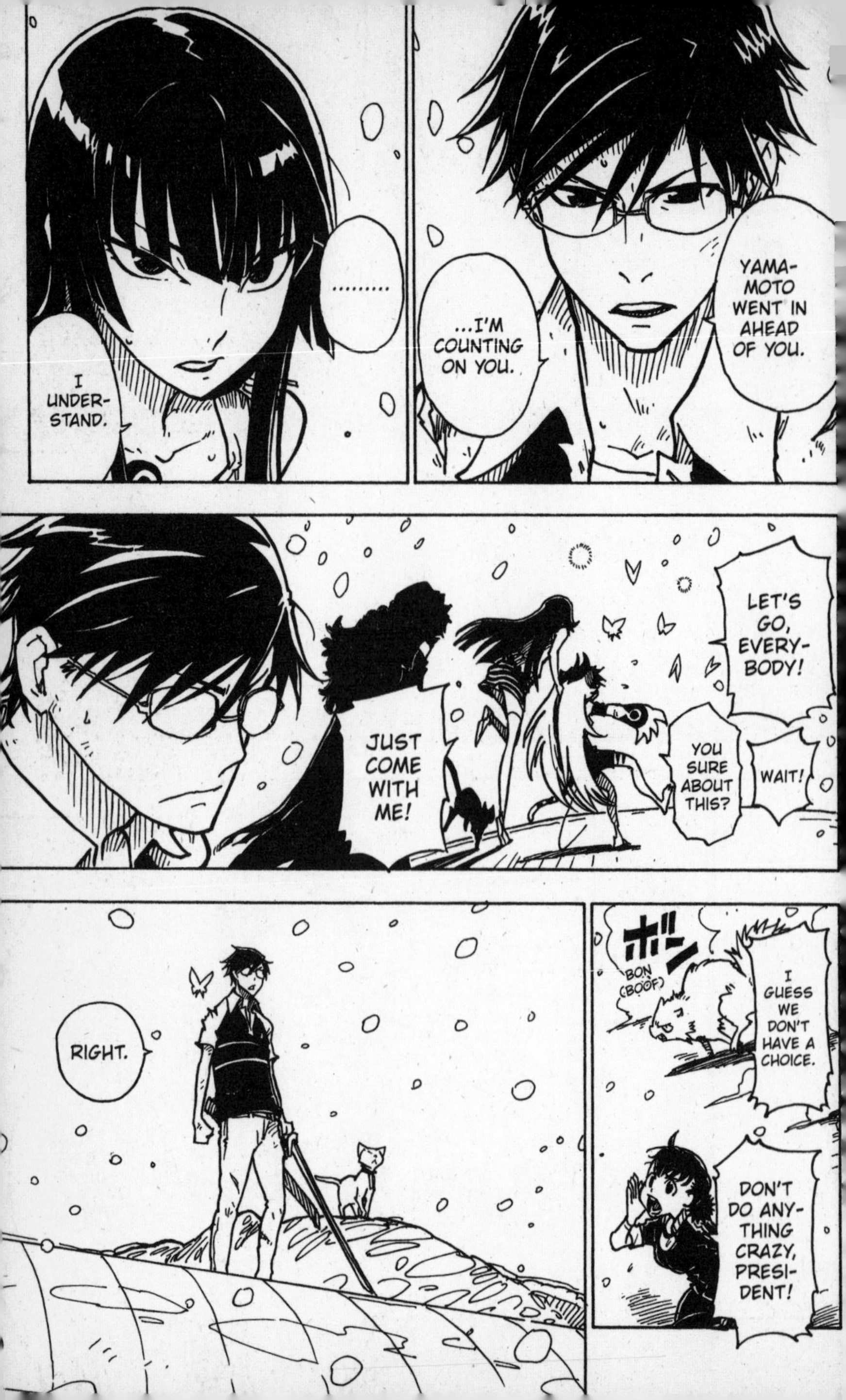
YAMAMOTO WENT IN AHEAD OF YOU.
...I'M COUNTING ON YOU.
....
I UNDERSTAND.
LET'S GO, EVERYBODY!
WAIT!
YOU SURE ABOUT THIS?
JUST COME WITH ME!
ボン
BON (BOOF)
I GUESS WE DON'T HAVE A CHOICE.
DON'T DO ANYTHING CRAZY, PRESIDENT!
RIGHT.

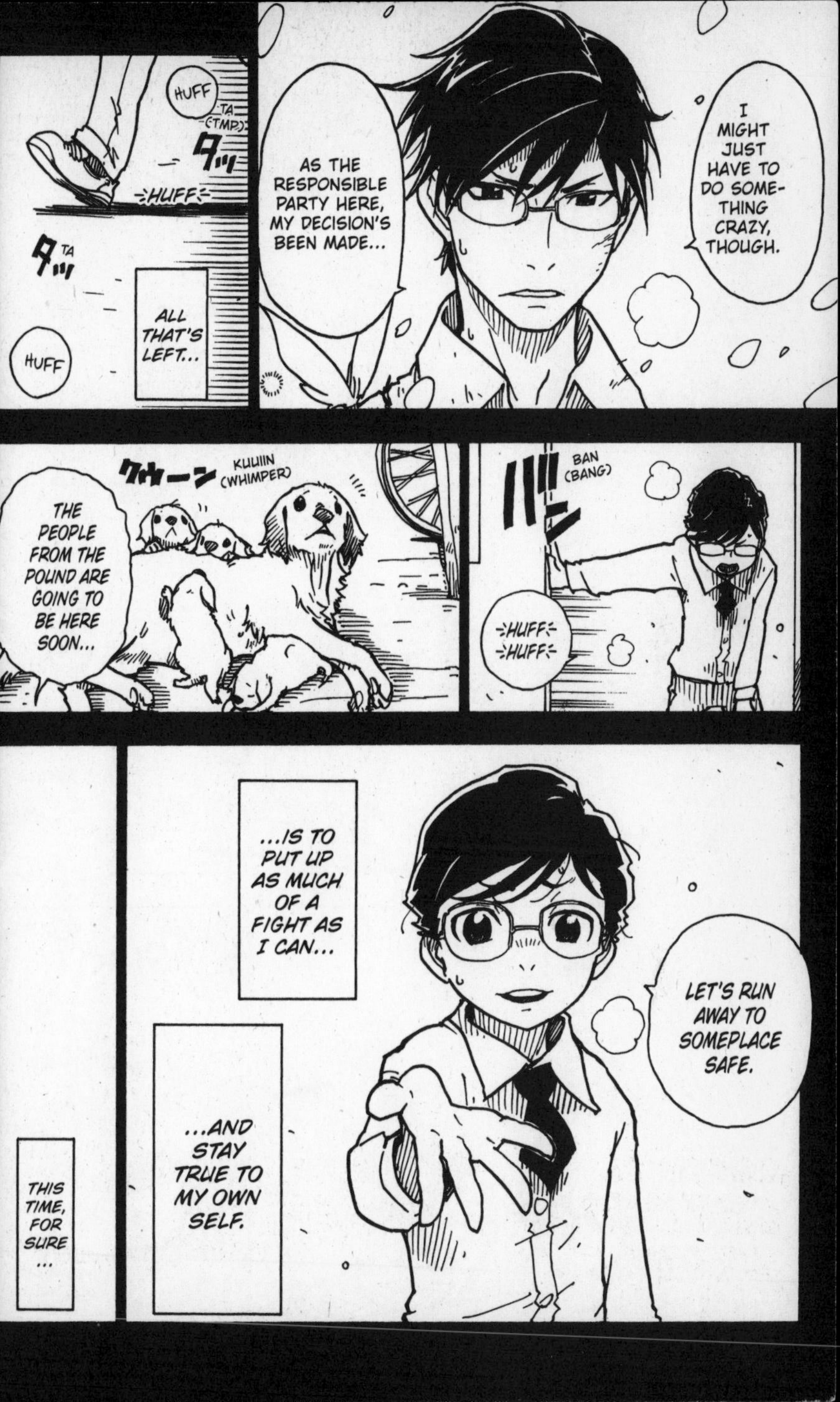
I MIGHT JUST HAVE TO DO SOME-THING CRAZY, THOUGH.
AS THE RESPONSIBLE PARTY HERE, MY DECISION'S BEEN MADE...
HUFF
TA (TMP)
HUFF
TA
ALL THAT'S LEFT...
HUFF
BAN (BANG)
HUFF HUFF
KUUIIN (WHIMPER)
THE PEOPLE FROM THE POUND ARE GOING TO BE HERE SOON...
LET'S RUN AWAY TO SOMEPLACE SAFE.
...IS TO PUT UP AS MUCH OF A FIGHT AS I CAN...
...AND STAY TRUE TO MY OWN SELF.
THIS TIME, FOR SURE...

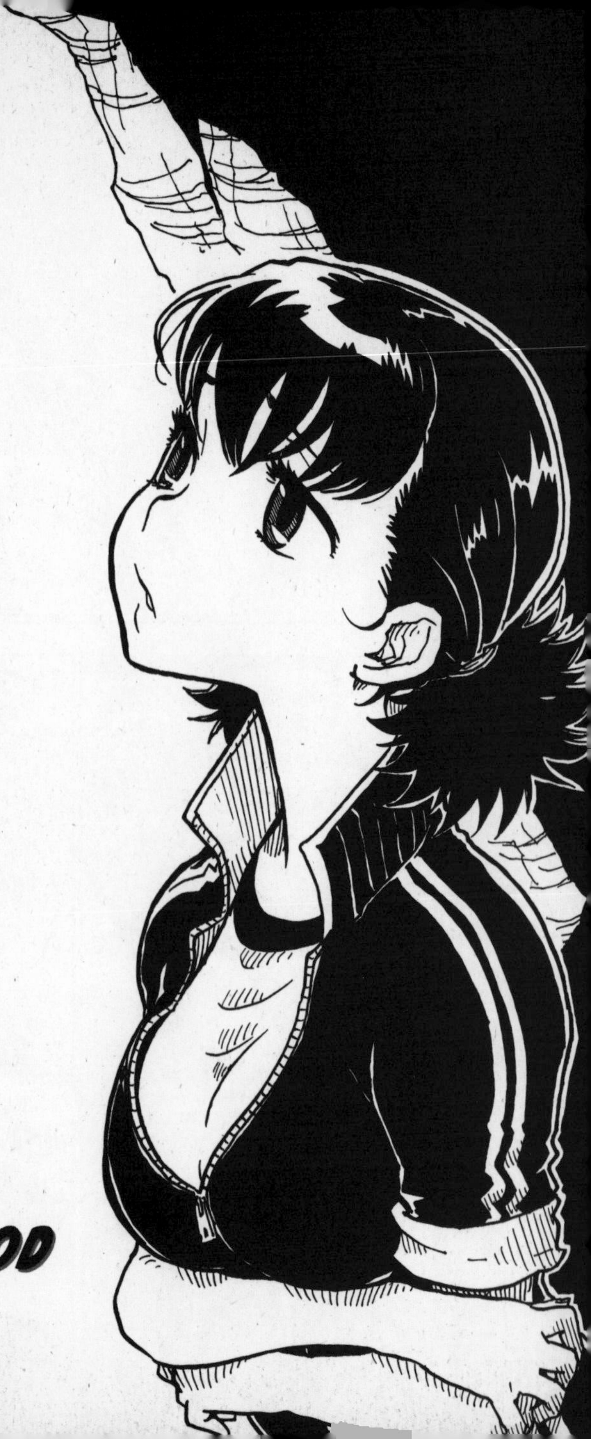

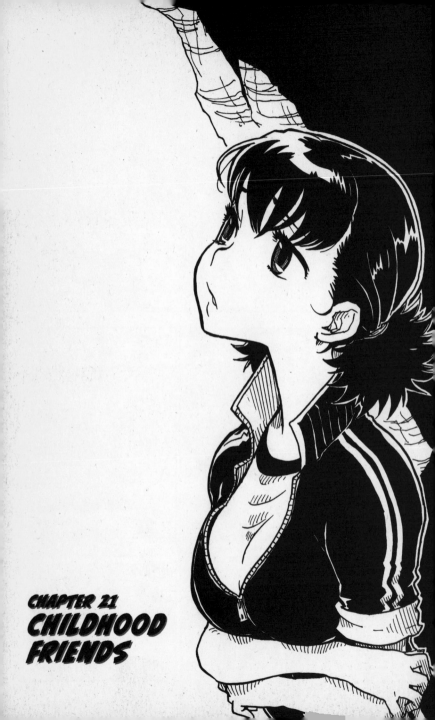

CHAPTER 21
CHILDHOOD FRIENDS

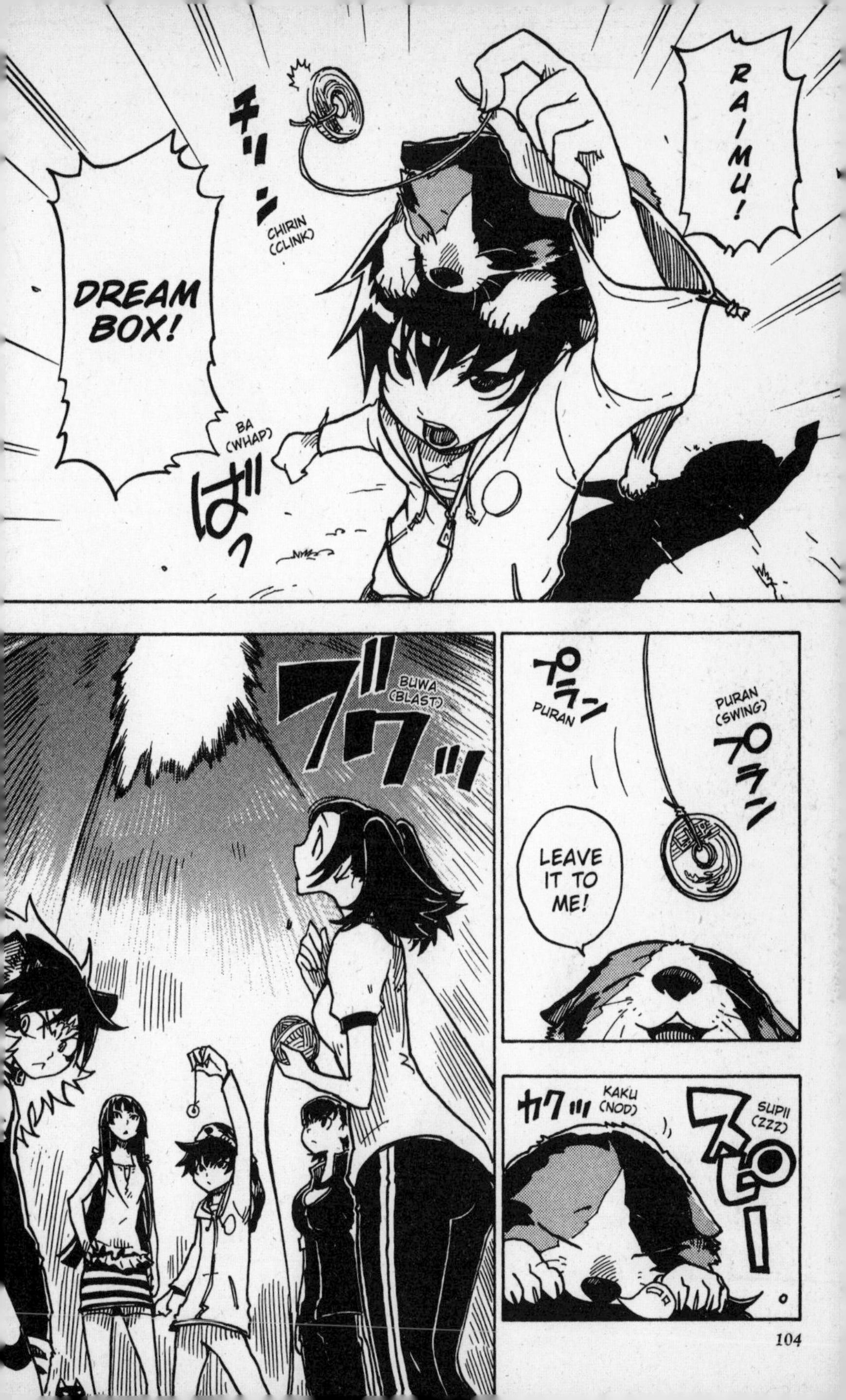
RAIMU!
チリン
CHIRIN (CLINK)
DREAM BOX!
BA (WHAP)
ばっ
PURAN (SWING)
プラン
PURAN
プラン
LEAVE IT TO ME!
KAKU (NOD)
カクッ
SUPII (ZZZ)
スピー。
BUWA (BLAST)
ブワッ

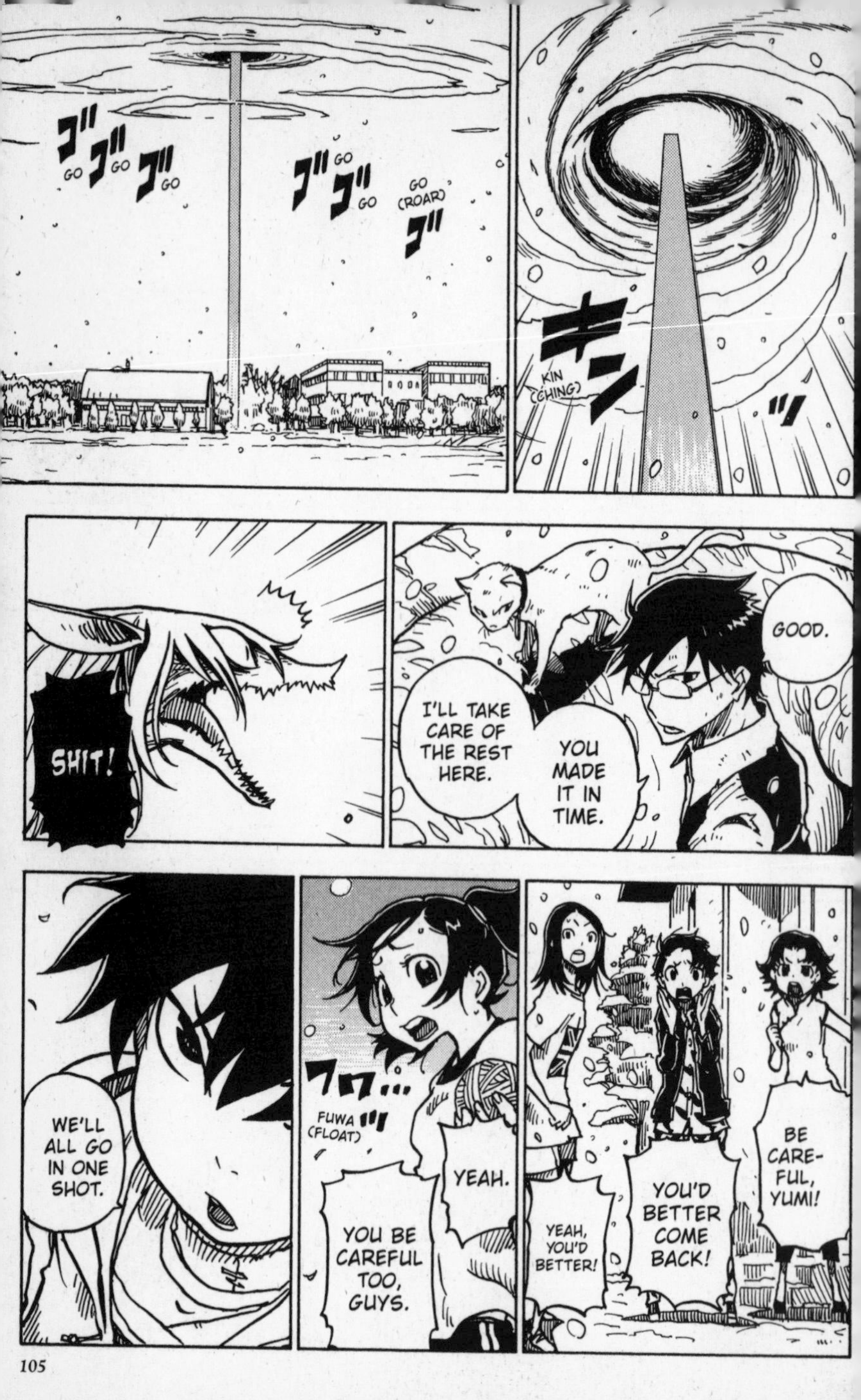
KIN (CHING)
GO GO GO GO GO
GO (ROAR)
GOOD.
YOU MADE IT IN TIME.
I'LL TAKE CARE OF THE REST HERE.
SHIT!
BE CARE-FUL, YUMI!
YOU'D BETTER COME BACK!
YEAH, YOU'D BETTER!
FUWA (FLOAT)
YEAH.
YOU BE CAREFUL TOO, GUYS.
WE'LL ALL GO IN ONE SHOT.

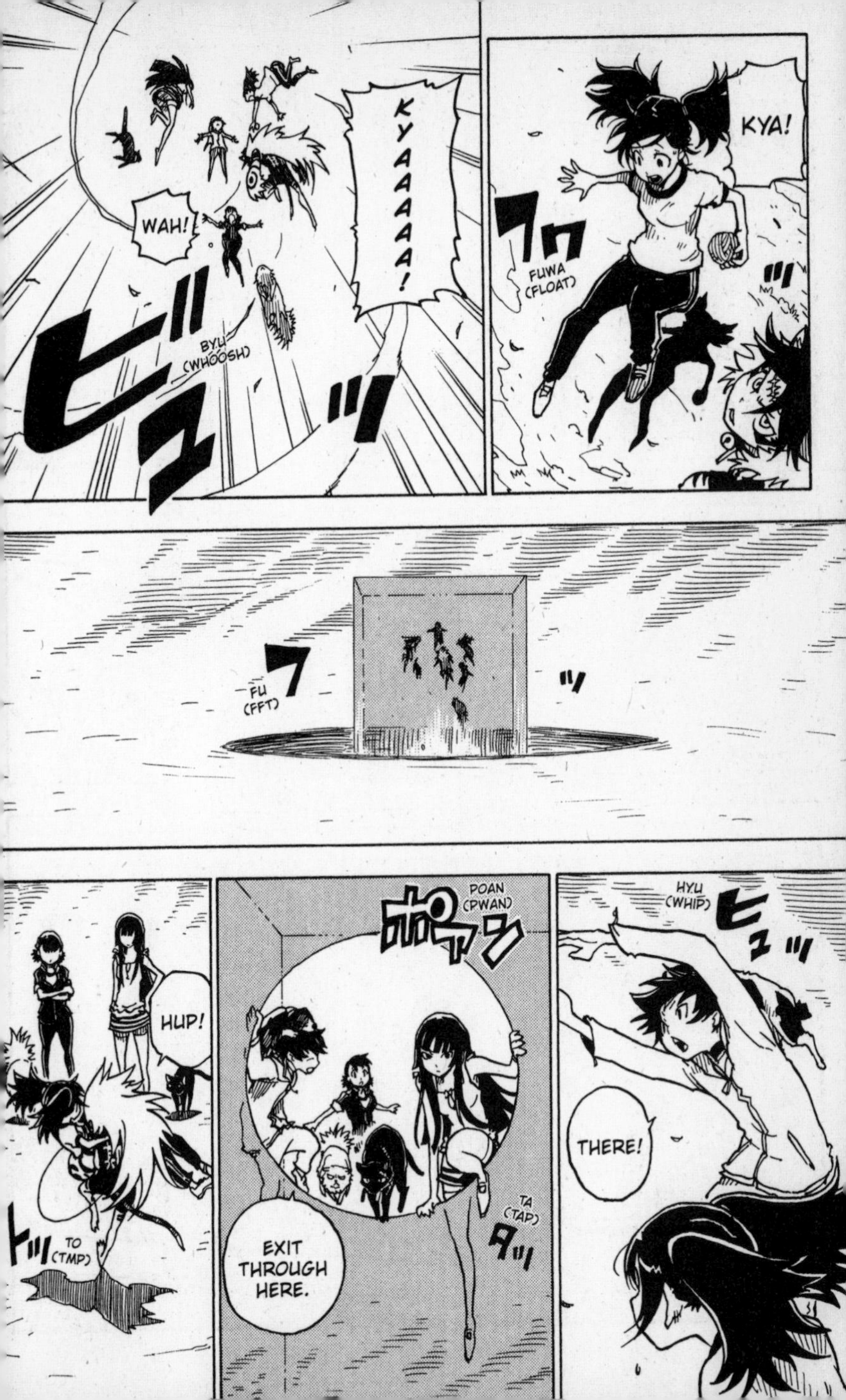

KYA!
FUWA (FLOAT)
KYAAAAAA!
WAH!
BYU (WHOOSH)
FU (FFT)
HYU (WHIP)
THERE!
POAN (PWAN)
EXIT THROUGH HERE.
TA (TAP)
HUP!
TO (TMP)

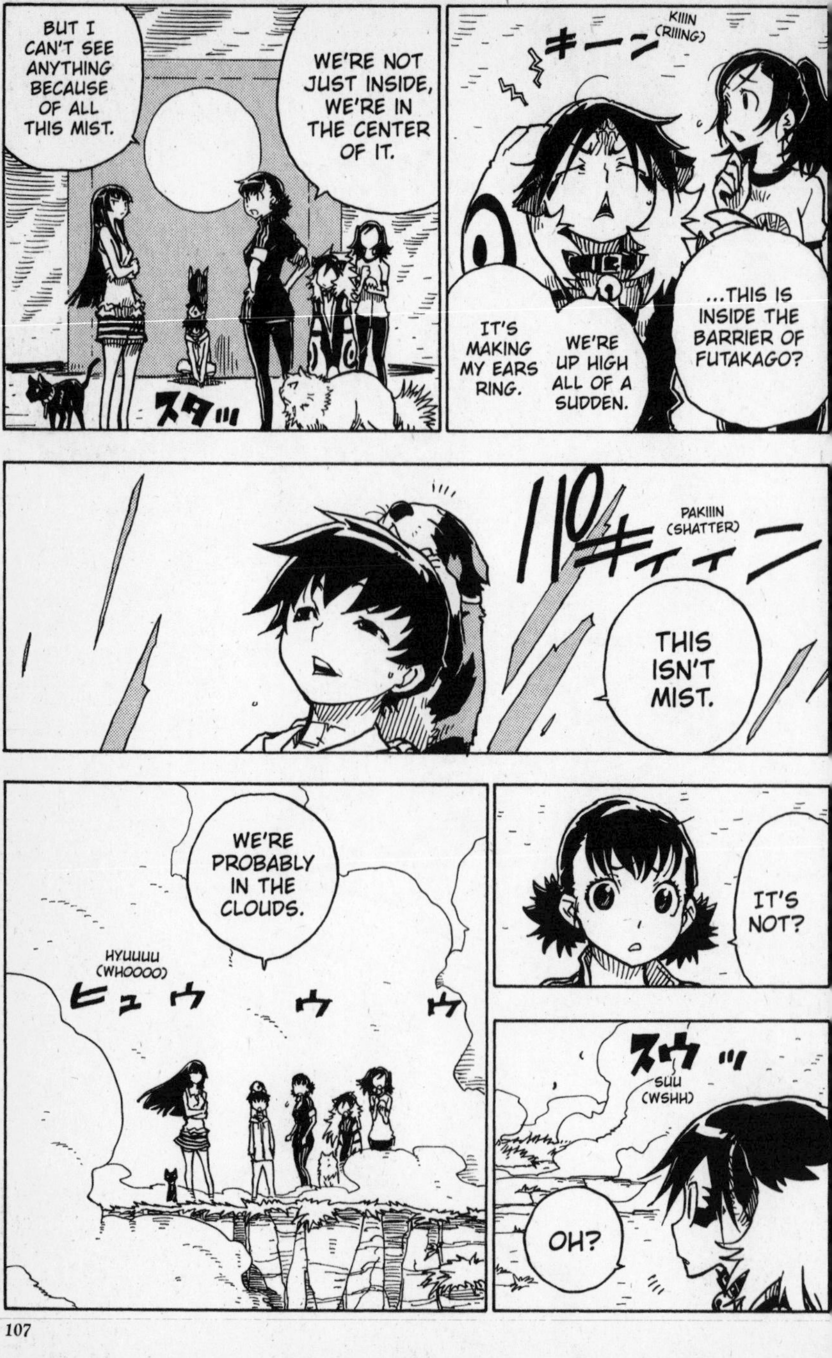
KIIN (RIIING)
...THIS IS INSIDE THE BARRIER OF FUTAKAGO?
WE'RE UP HIGH ALL OF A SUDDEN.
IT'S MAKING MY EARS RING.
WE'RE NOT JUST INSIDE, WE'RE IN THE CENTER OF IT.
BUT I CAN'T SEE ANYTHING BECAUSE OF ALL THIS MIST.
PAKIIIN (SHATTER)
THIS ISN'T MIST.
IT'S NOT?
SUU (WSHH)
OH?
WE'RE PROBABLY IN THE CLOUDS.
HYUUUU (WHOOOO)

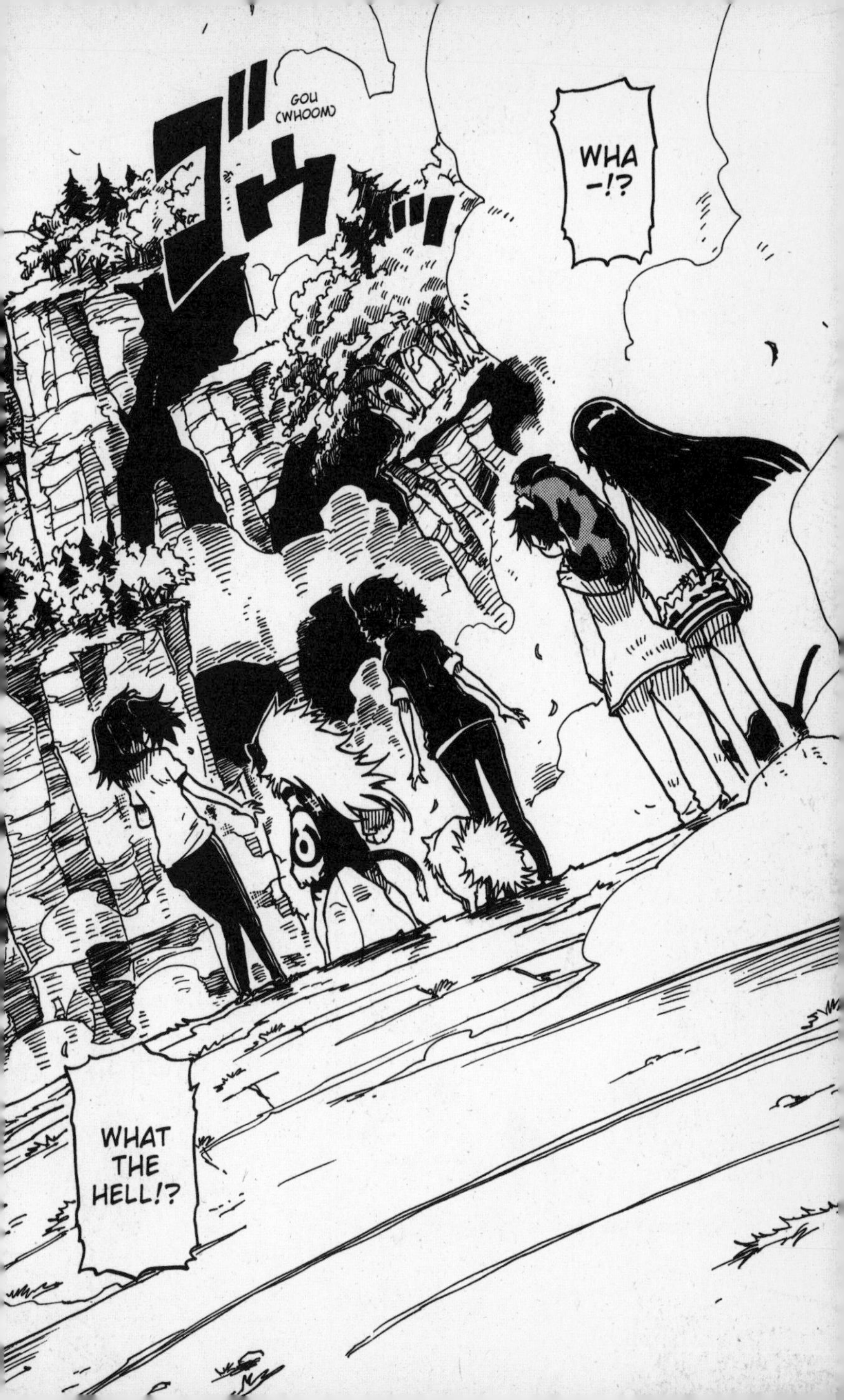
WHA
-!?
GOU
(WHOOM)
WHAT
THE
HELL!?

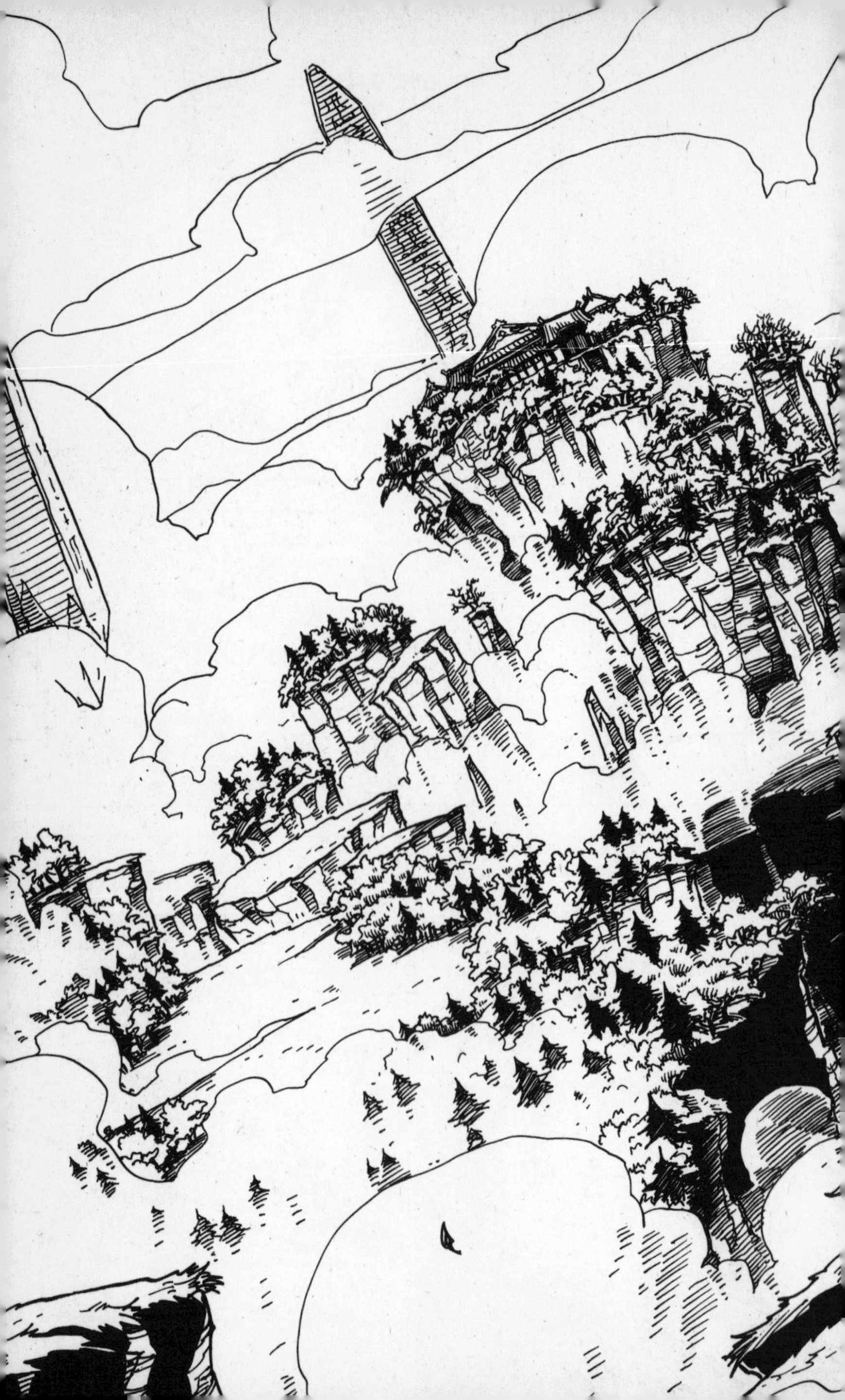

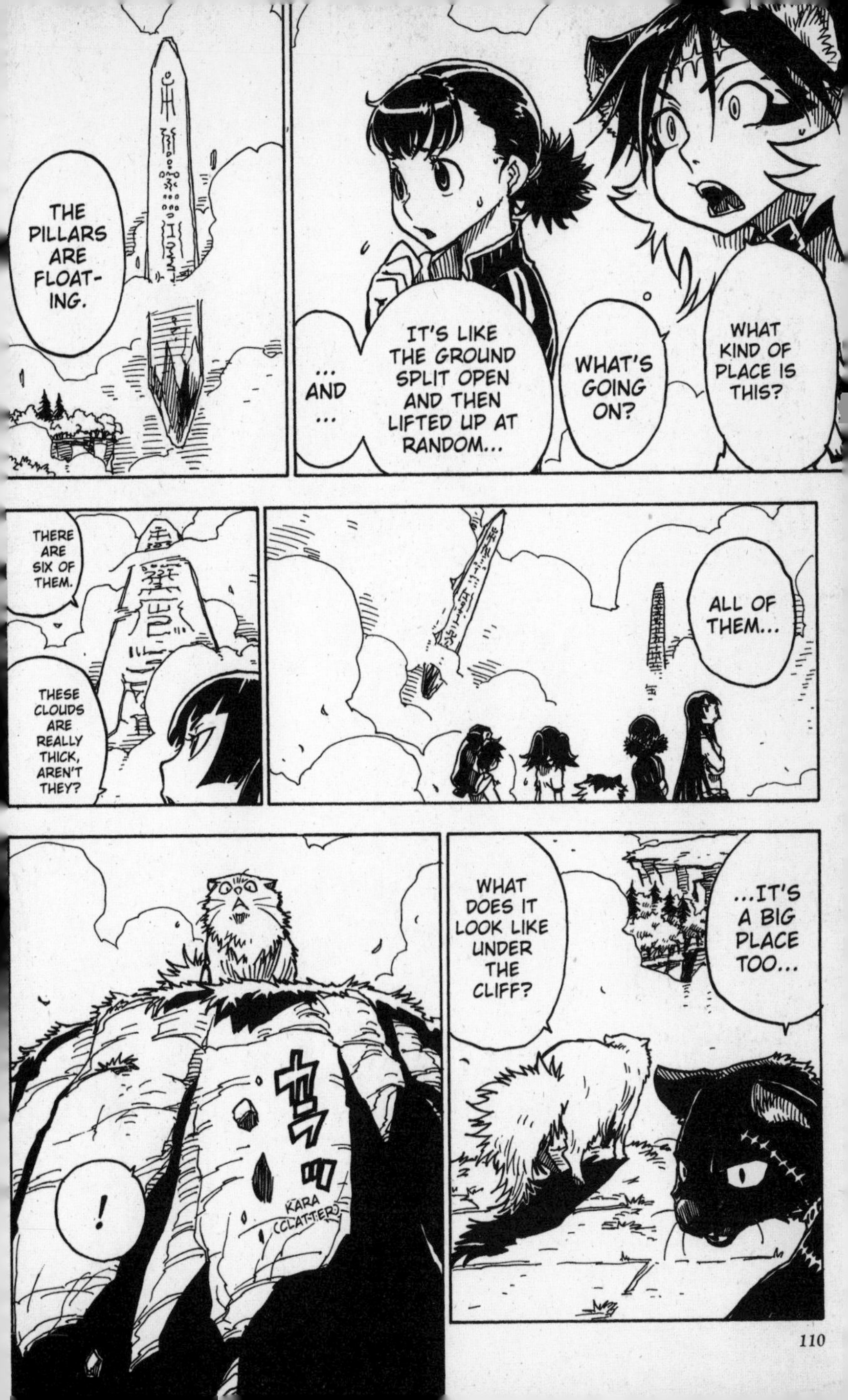
WHAT KIND OF PLACE IS THIS?
WHAT'S GOING ON?
IT'S LIKE THE GROUND SPLIT OPEN AND THEN LIFTED UP AT RANDOM...
...AND...
THE PILLARS ARE FLOAT-ING.
ALL OF THEM...
THERE ARE SIX OF THEM.
THESE CLOUDS ARE REALLY THICK, AREN'T THEY?
...IT'S A BIG PLACE TOO...
WHAT DOES IT LOOK LIKE UNDER THE CLIFF?
!
KARA (CLATTER)

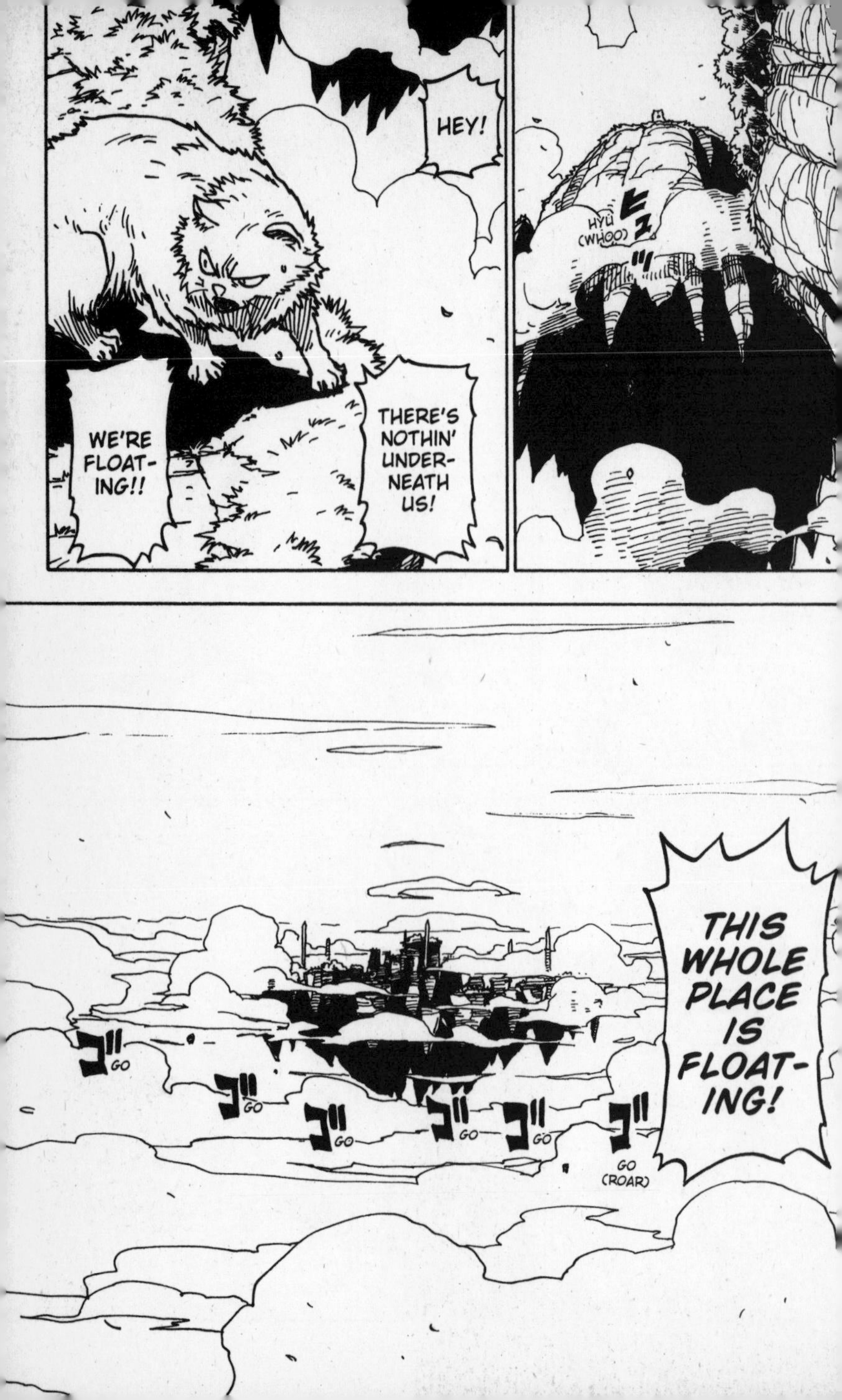
ヒュ
HYU (WHOO)
HEY!
THERE'S NOTHIN' UNDER-NEATH US!
WE'RE FLOAT-ING!!
THIS WHOLE PLACE IS FLOAT-ING!
ゴ GO (ROAR)
ゴ GO
ゴ GO
ゴ GO
ゴ GO
ゴ GO

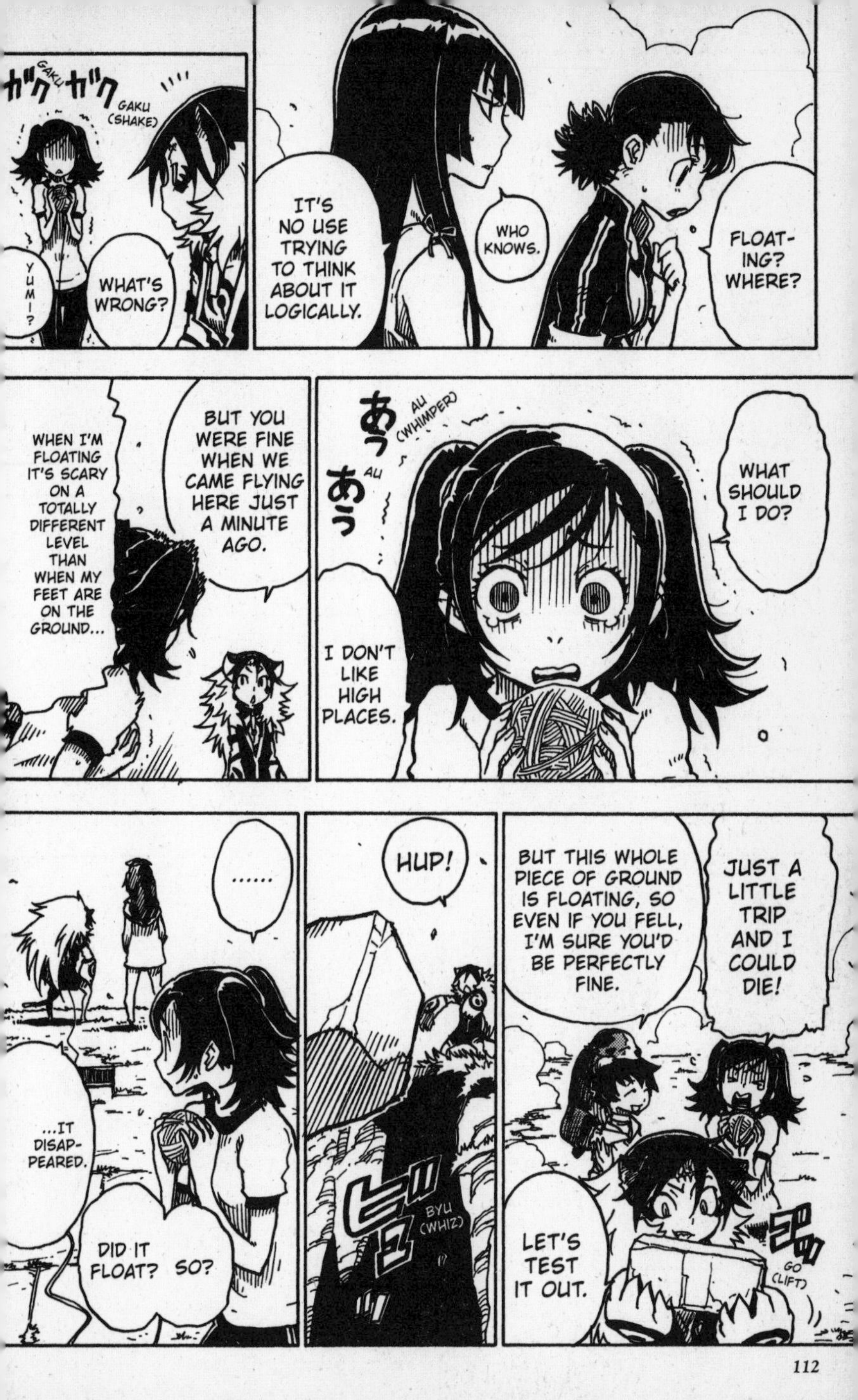
FLOATING? WHERE?
WHO KNOWS.
IT'S NO USE TRYING TO THINK ABOUT IT LOGICALLY.
ガク ガク
GAKU
GAKU (SHAKE)
WHAT'S WRONG?
YUMI?
あう
AU (WHIMPER)
あう
AU
WHAT SHOULD I DO?
I DON'T LIKE HIGH PLACES.
BUT YOU WERE FINE WHEN WE CAME FLYING HERE JUST A MINUTE AGO.
WHEN I'M FLOATING IT'S SCARY ON A TOTALLY DIFFERENT LEVEL THAN WHEN MY FEET ARE ON THE GROUND...
JUST A LITTLE TRIP AND I COULD DIE!
BUT THIS WHOLE PIECE OF GROUND IS FLOATING, SO EVEN IF YOU FELL, I'M SURE YOU'D BE PERFECTLY FINE.
LET'S TEST IT OUT.
ゴッ
GO (LIFT)
HUP!
ビュ
BYU (WHIZ)
......
SO?
DID IT FLOAT?
...IT DISAPPEARED.

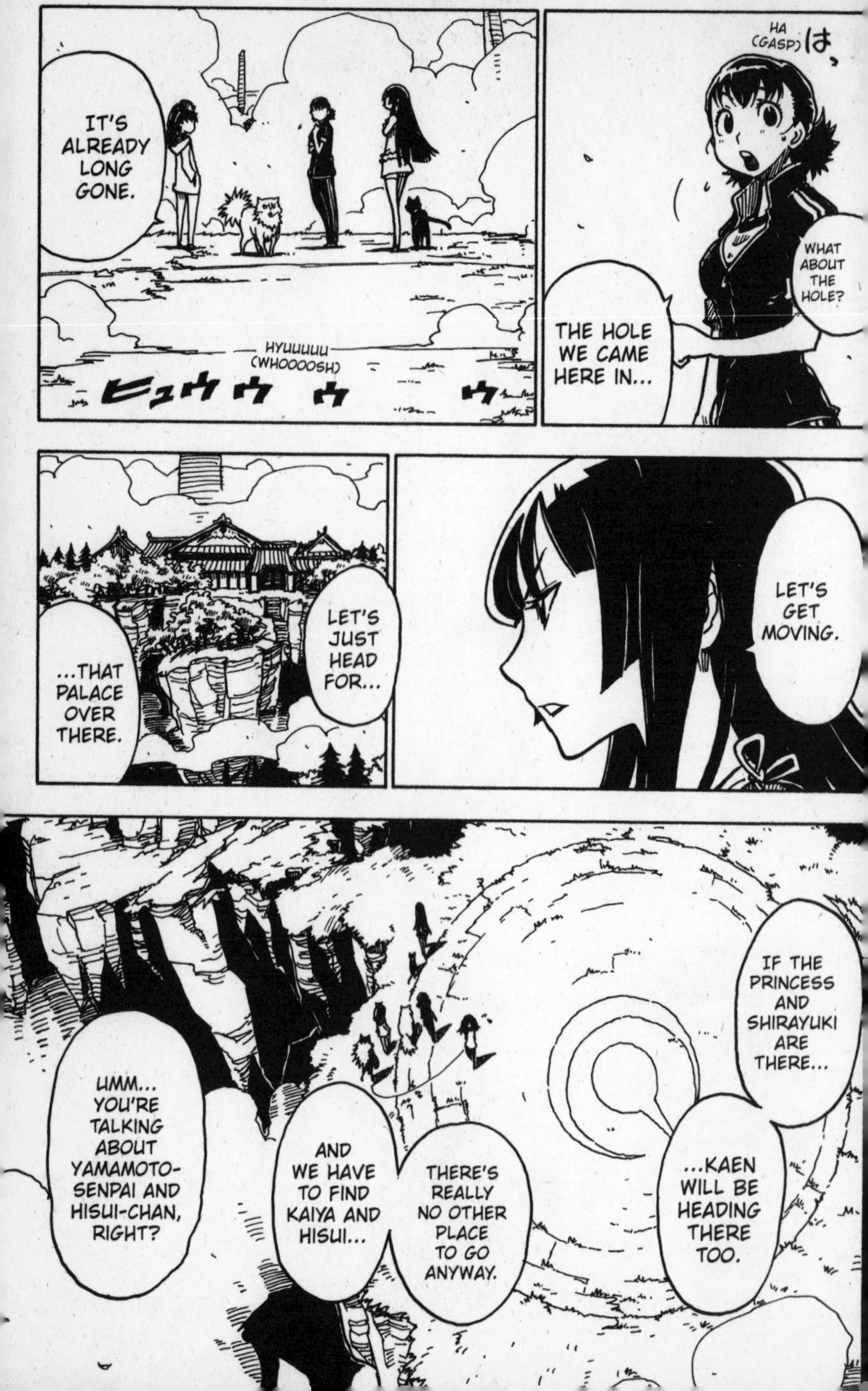
HA (GASP) は
WHAT ABOUT THE HOLE?
THE HOLE WE CAME HERE IN...
IT'S ALREADY LONG GONE.
HYUUUUU (WHOOOOSH)
ヒュウウ ウ ウ
LET'S GET MOVING.
LET'S JUST HEAD FOR...
...THAT PALACE OVER THERE.
IF THE PRINCESS AND SHIRAYUKI ARE THERE...
...KAEN WILL BE HEADING THERE TOO.
THERE'S REALLY NO OTHER PLACE TO GO ANYWAY.
AND WE HAVE TO FIND KAIYA AND HISUI...
UMM... YOU'RE TALKING ABOUT YAMAMOTO-SENPAI AND HISUI-CHAN, RIGHT?

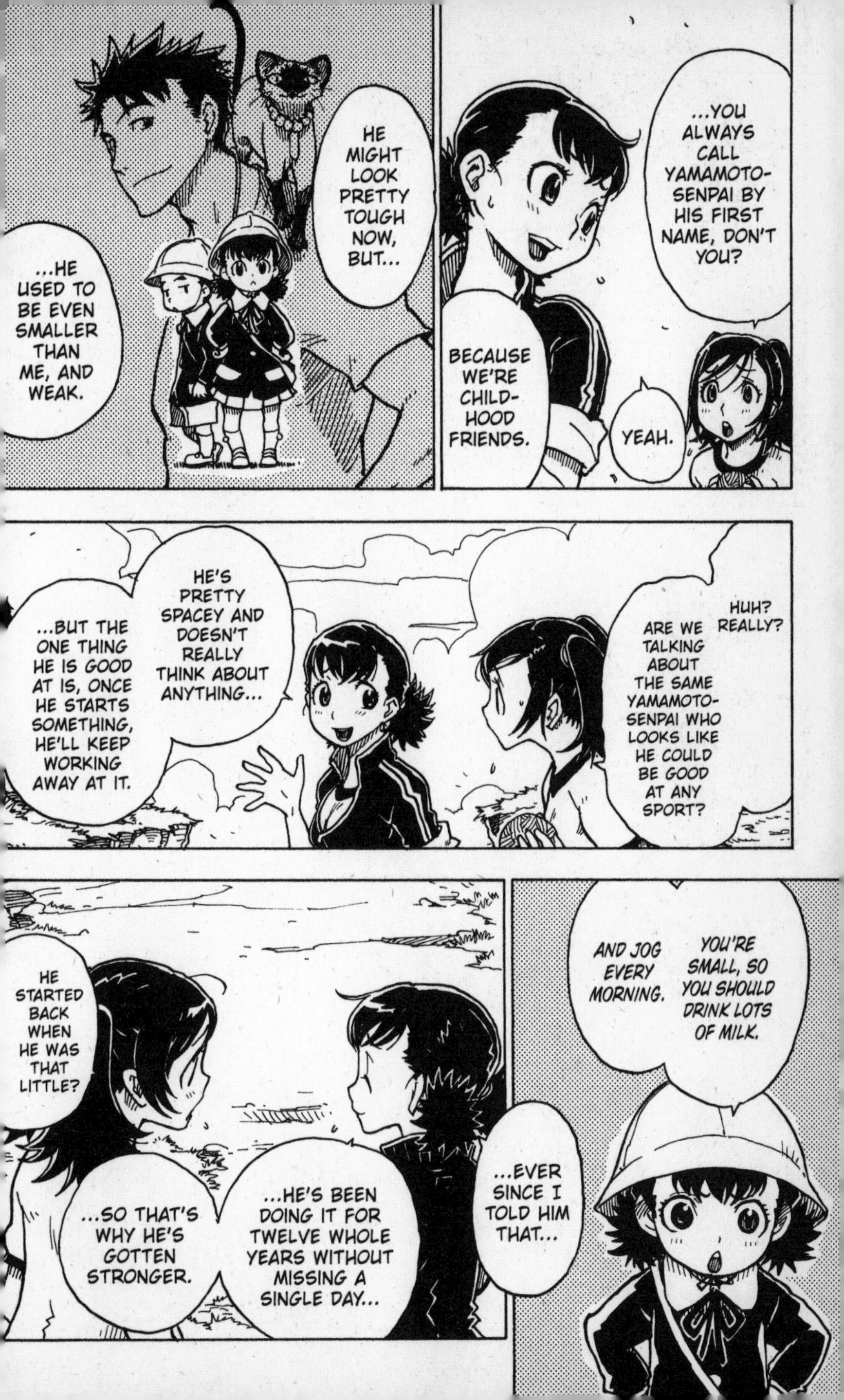
...YOU ALWAYS CALL YAMAMOTO-SENPAI BY HIS FIRST NAME, DON'T YOU?
YEAH.
BECAUSE WE'RE CHILD-HOOD FRIENDS.
HE MIGHT LOOK PRETTY TOUGH NOW, BUT...
...HE USED TO BE EVEN SMALLER THAN ME, AND WEAK.
HUH? REALLY?
ARE WE TALKING ABOUT THE SAME YAMAMOTO-SENPAI WHO LOOKS LIKE HE COULD BE GOOD AT ANY SPORT?
HE'S PRETTY SPACEY AND DOESN'T REALLY THINK ABOUT ANYTHING...
...BUT THE ONE THING HE IS GOOD AT IS, ONCE HE STARTS SOMETHING, HE'LL KEEP WORKING AWAY AT IT.
YOU'RE SMALL, SO YOU SHOULD DRINK LOTS OF MILK.
AND JOG EVERY MORNING.
...EVER SINCE I TOLD HIM THAT...
...HE'S BEEN DOING IT FOR TWELVE WHOLE YEARS WITHOUT MISSING A SINGLE DAY...
...SO THAT'S WHY HE'S GOTTEN STRONGER.
HE STARTED BACK WHEN HE WAS THAT LITTLE?

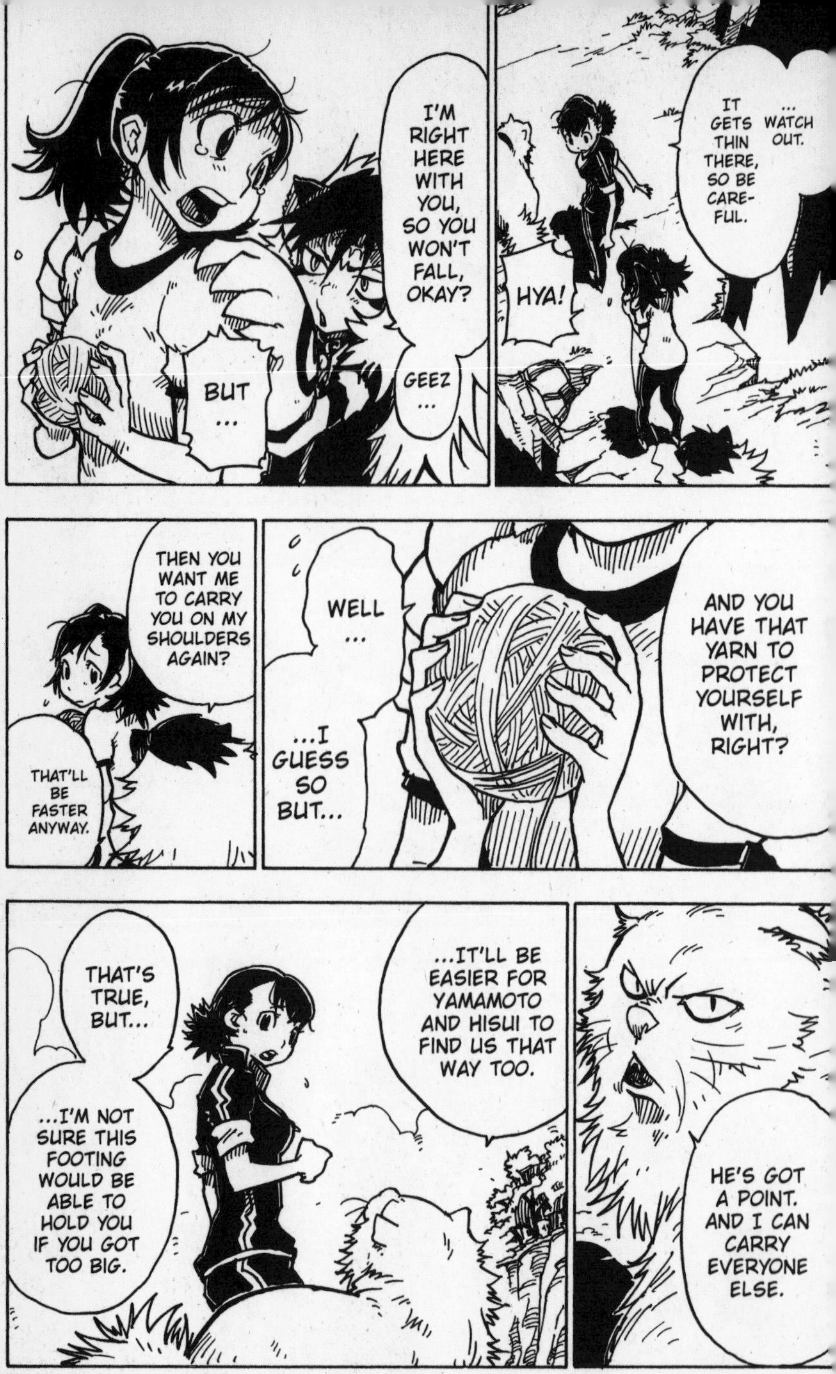
...WATCH OUT.
IT GETS THIN THERE, SO BE CARE-FUL.
HYA!
I'M RIGHT HERE WITH YOU, SO YOU WON'T FALL, OKAY?
GEEZ ...
BUT ...
AND YOU HAVE THAT YARN TO PROTECT YOURSELF WITH, RIGHT?
WELL ...
...I GUESS SO BUT...
THEN YOU WANT ME TO CARRY YOU ON MY SHOULDERS AGAIN?
THAT'LL BE FASTER ANYWAY.
HE'S GOT A POINT. AND I CAN CARRY EVERYONE ELSE.
...IT'LL BE EASIER FOR YAMAMOTO AND HISUI TO FIND US THAT WAY TOO.
THAT'S TRUE, BUT...
...I'M NOT SURE THIS FOOTING WOULD BE ABLE TO HOLD YOU IF YOU GOT TOO BIG.

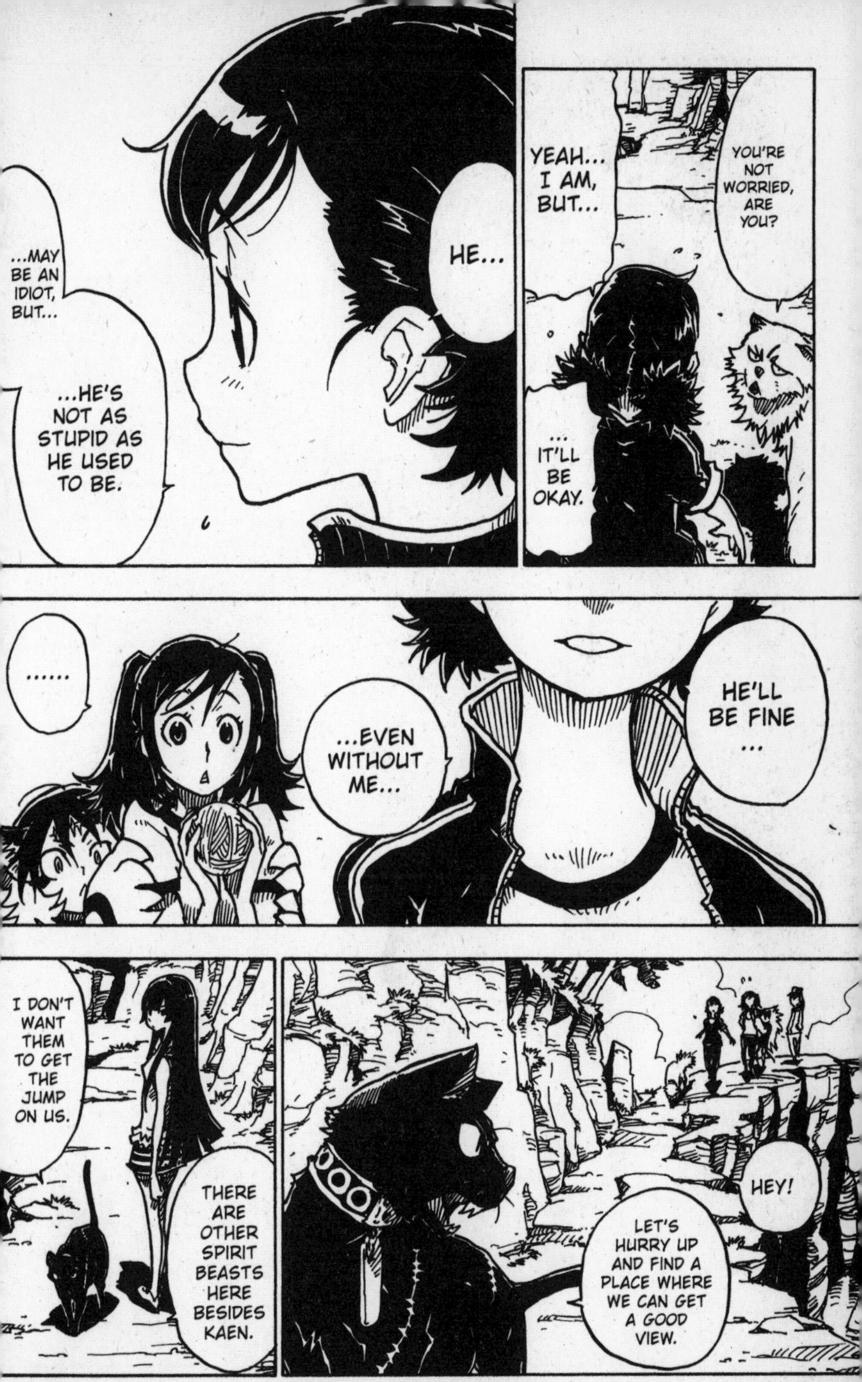
YOU'RE NOT WORRIED, ARE YOU?
YEAH... I AM, BUT...
...IT'LL BE OKAY.
HE...
...MAY BE AN IDIOT, BUT...
...HE'S NOT AS STUPID AS HE USED TO BE.
HE'LL BE FINE ...
...EVEN WITHOUT ME...
......
HEY!
LET'S HURRY UP AND FIND A PLACE WHERE WE CAN GET A GOOD VIEW.
THERE ARE OTHER SPIRIT BEASTS HERE BESIDES KAEN.
I DON'T WANT THEM TO GET THE JUMP ON US.

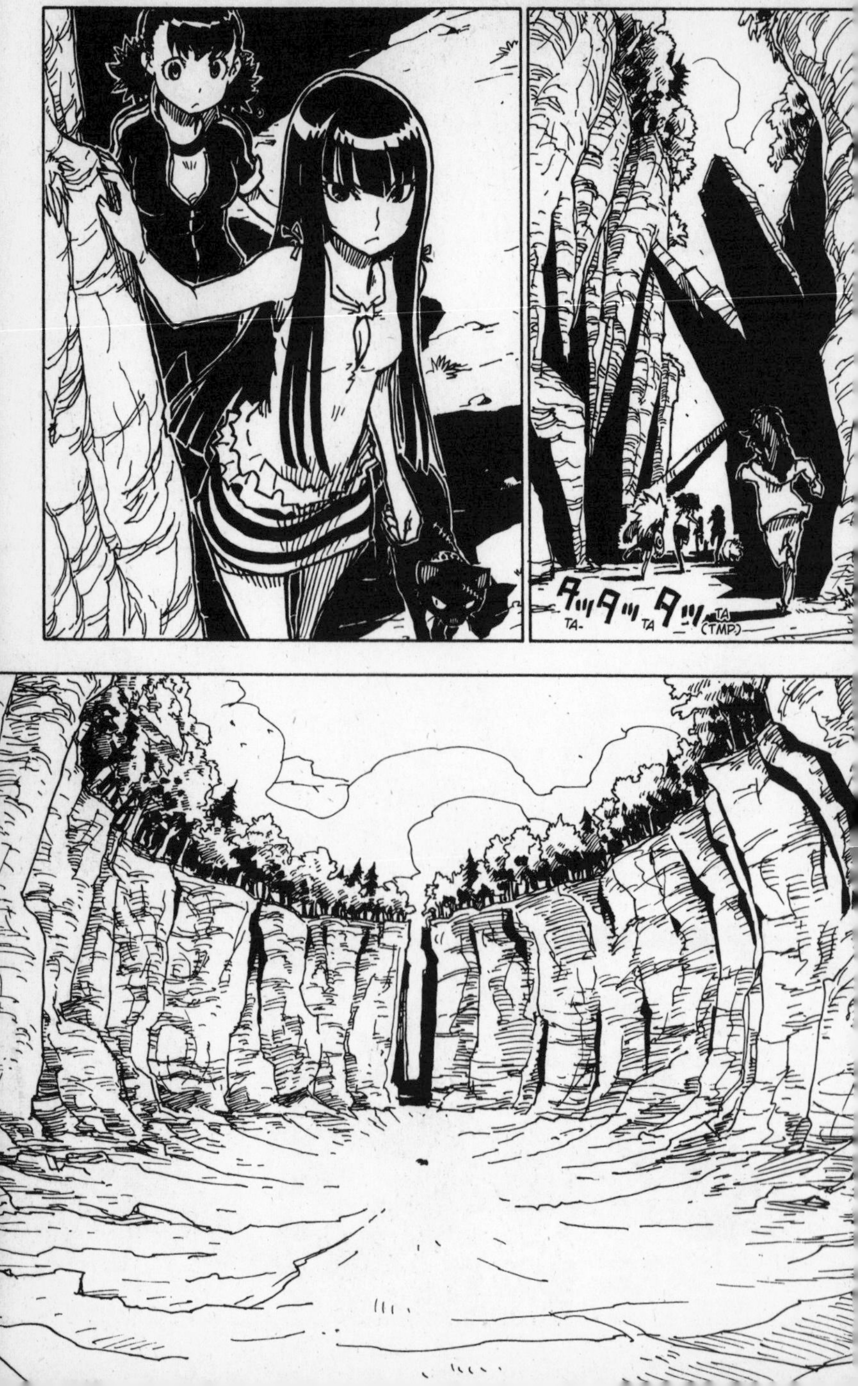

タッタッタッ
TA-
TA
TA
(TMP)

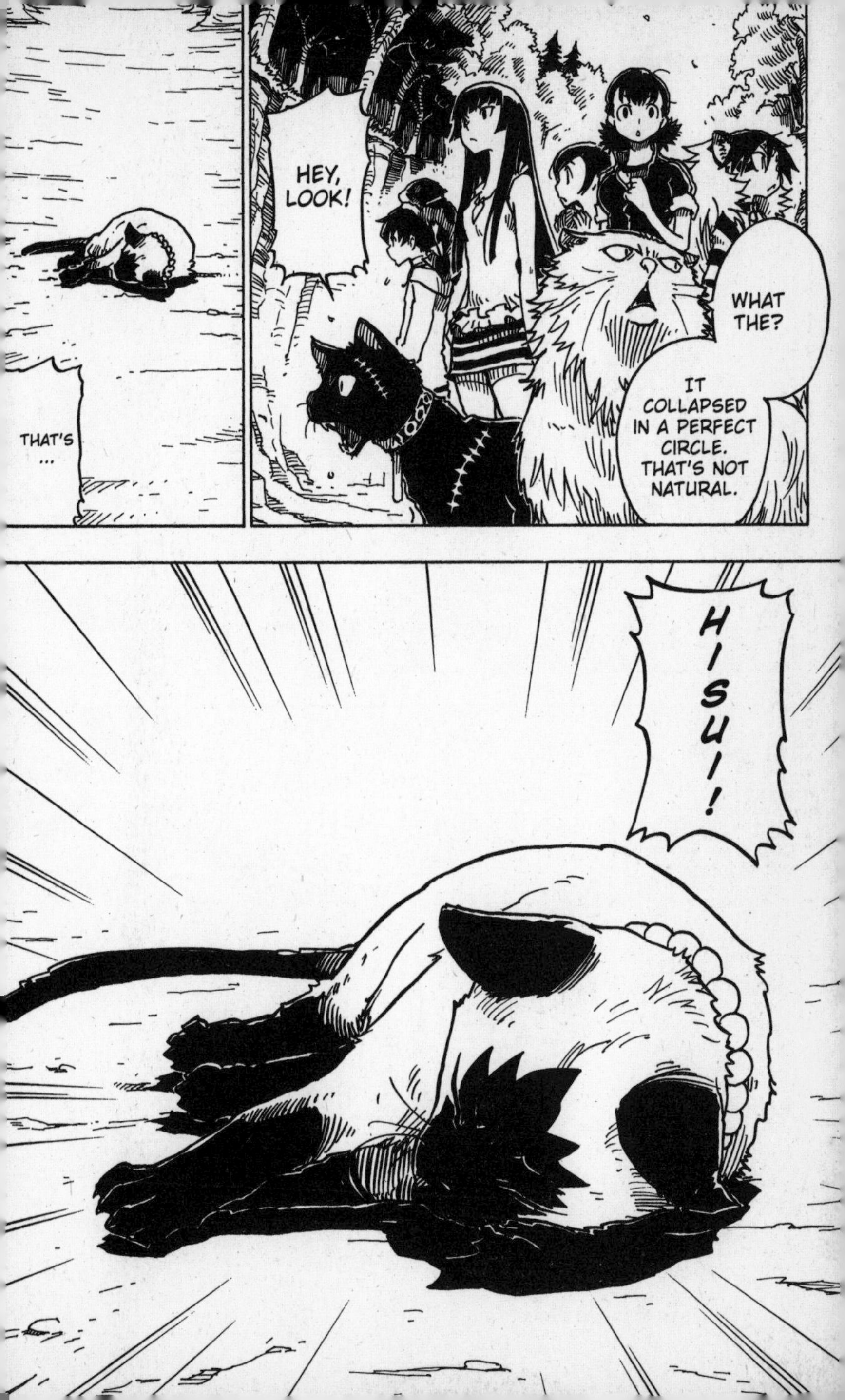
HEY, LOOK!
WHAT THE?
IT COLLAPSED IN A PERFECT CIRCLE. THAT'S NOT NATURAL.
THAT'S ...
HISUI!

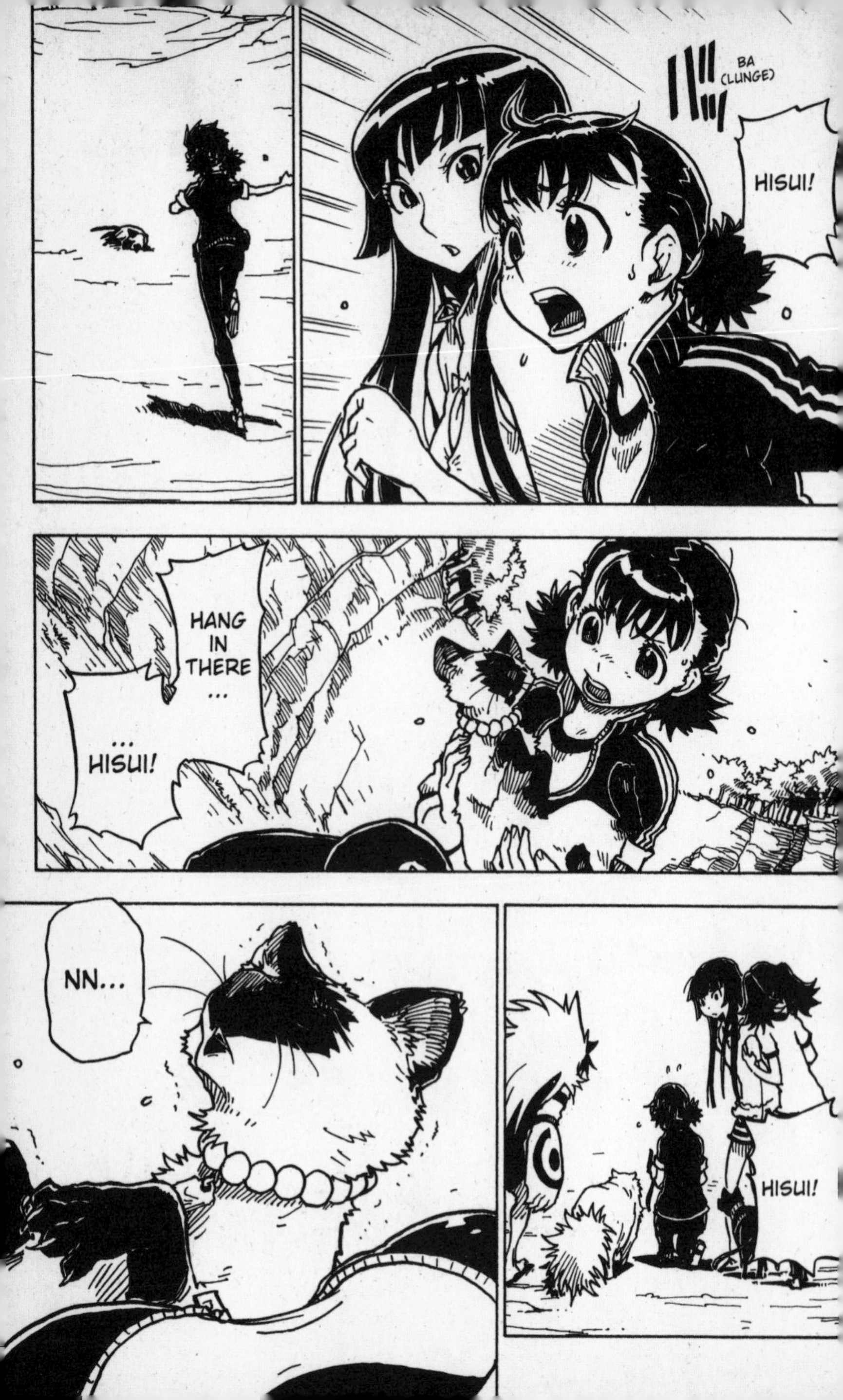
BA
(LUNGE)
HISUI!
HANG IN THERE...
...HISUI!
HISUI!
NN...

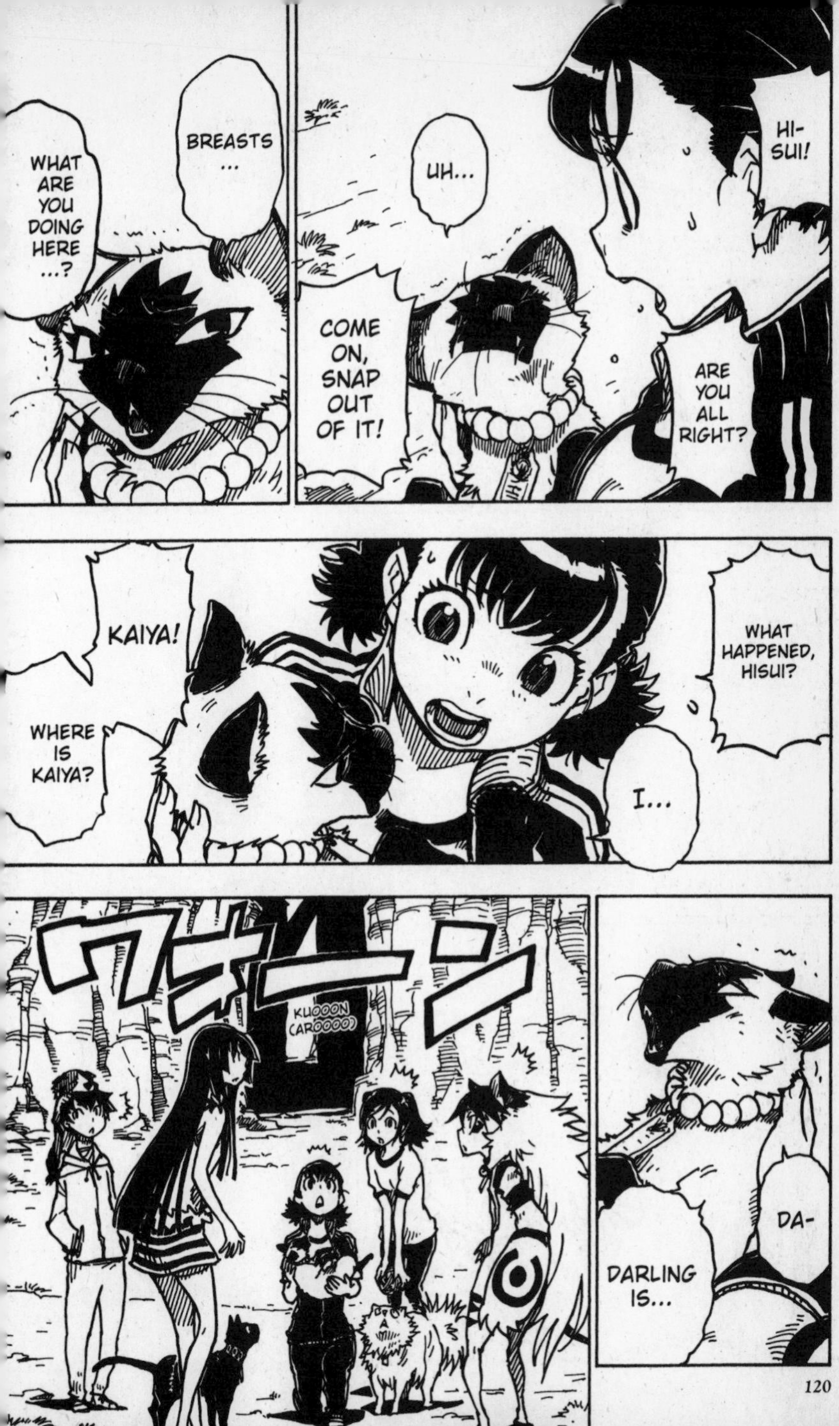
HI-SUI!
ARE YOU ALL RIGHT?
UH...
COME ON, SNAP OUT OF IT!
BREASTS ...
WHAT ARE YOU DOING HERE ...?
WHAT HAPPENED, HISUI?
I...
KAIYA!
WHERE IS KAIYA?
DA-
DARLING IS...
ワオーン
KUOOON (AROOOOO)

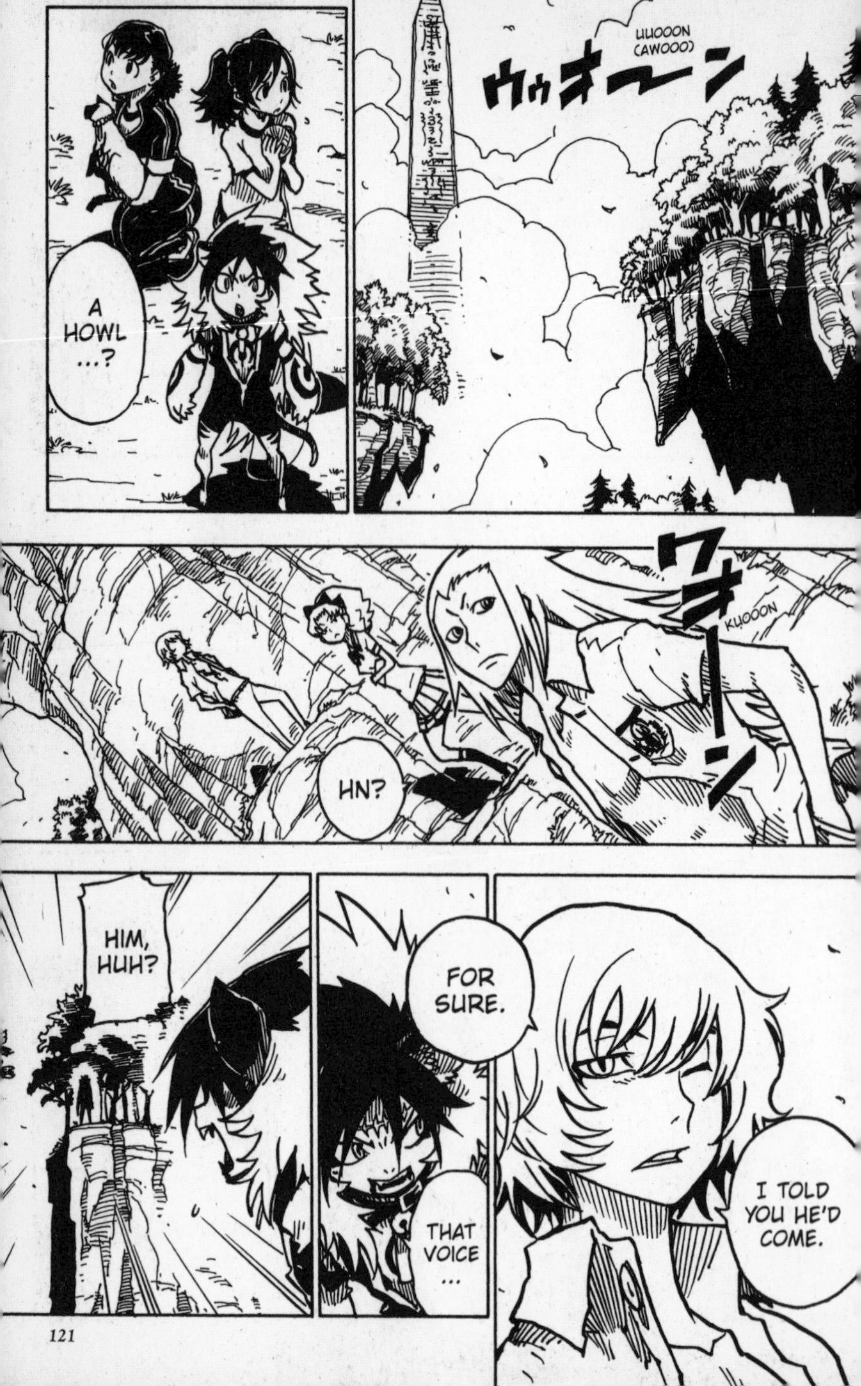

UUOOON (AWOOO)
ウゥオーーン
A HOWL ...?
KUOOON
ワオーーン
HN?
I TOLD YOU HE'D COME.
FOR SURE.
THAT VOICE ...
HIM, HUH?

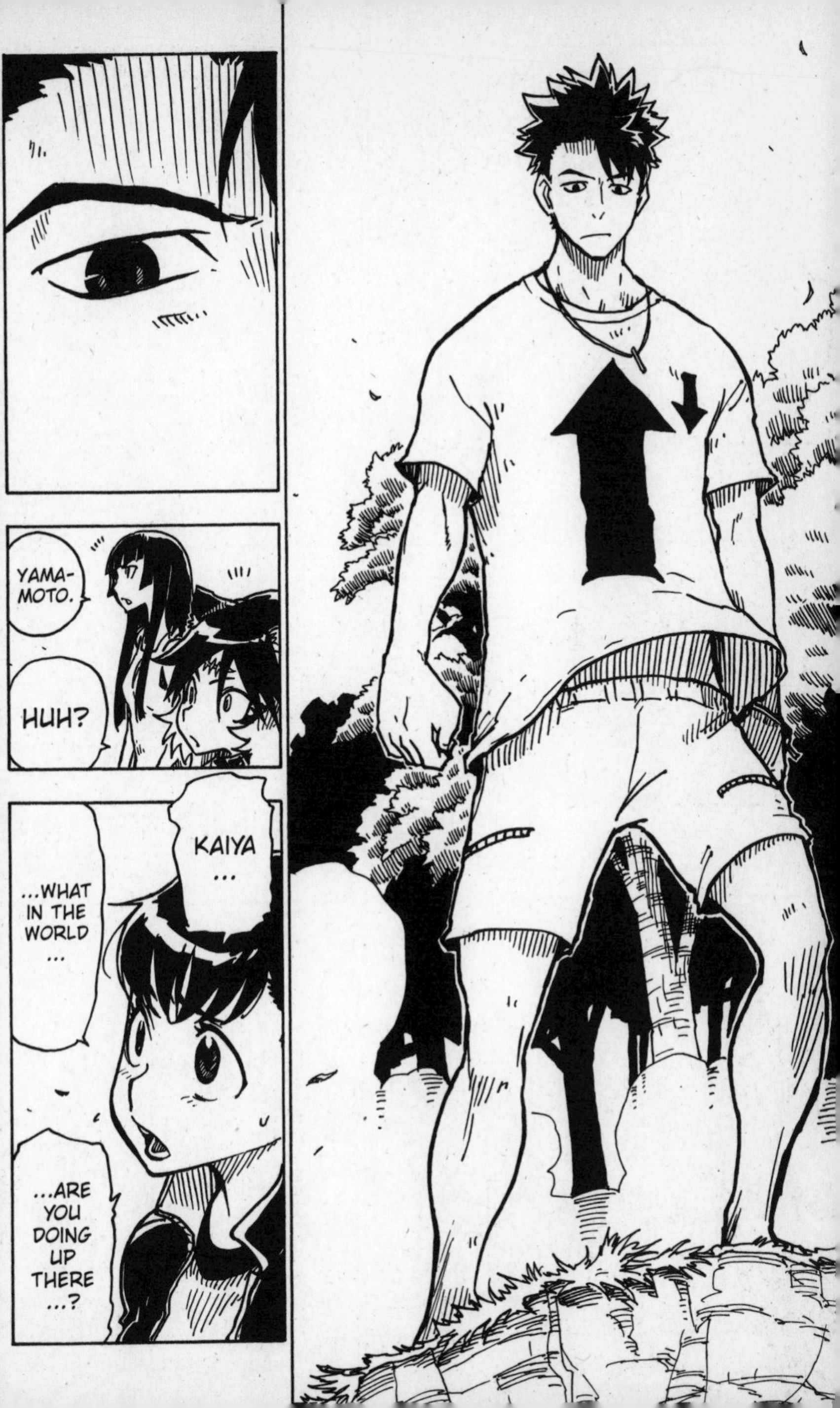
YAMA-MOTO.
HUH?
KAIYA ...
...WHAT IN THE WORLD ...
...ARE YOU DOING UP THERE ...?

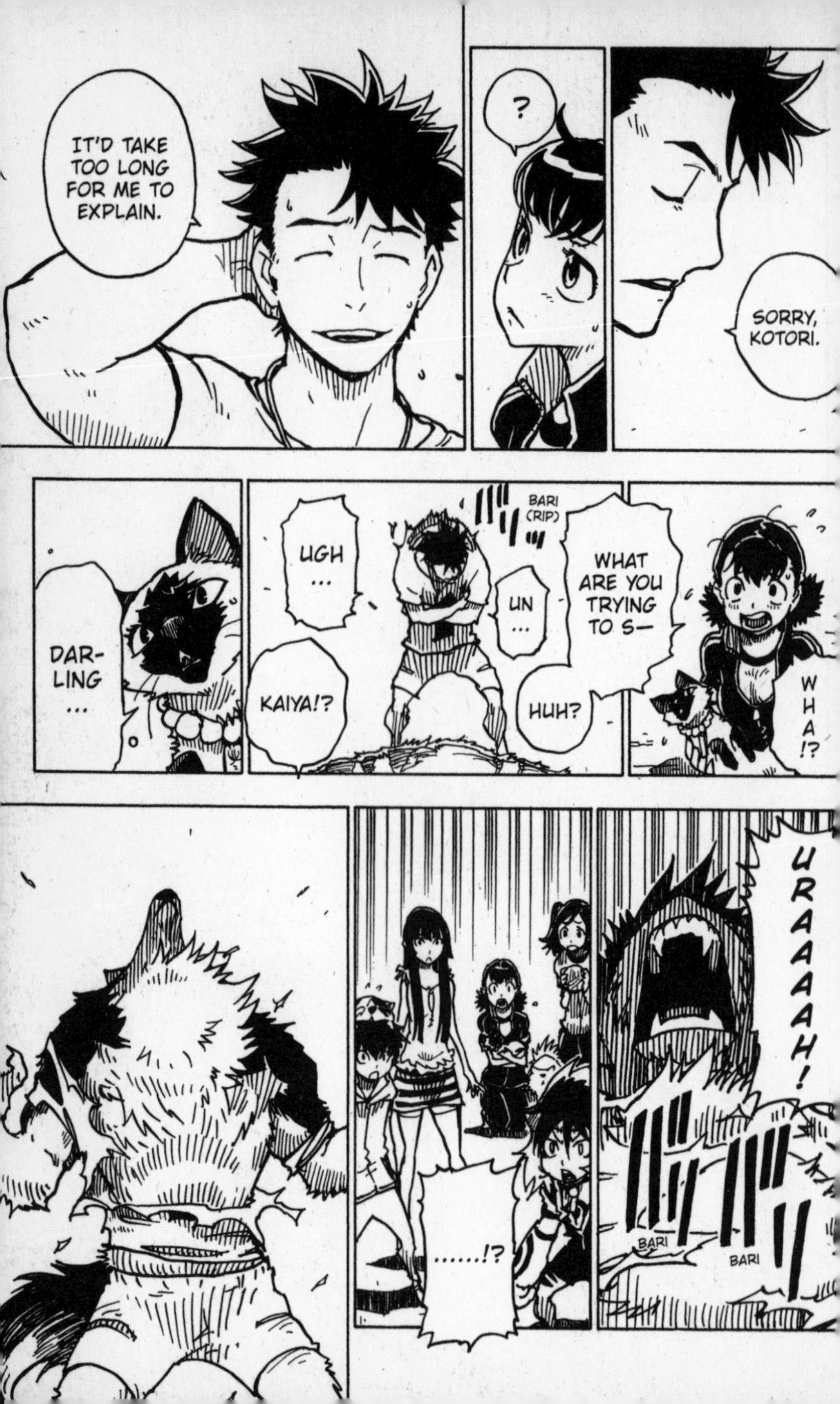
SORRY, KOTORI.
?
IT'D TAKE TOO LONG FOR ME TO EXPLAIN.
WHAT ARE YOU TRYING TO S—
WHA!?
BARI (RIP)
UN...
HUH?
UGH...
KAIYA!?
DAR-LING...
URAAAAAH!
BARI
BARI
......!?

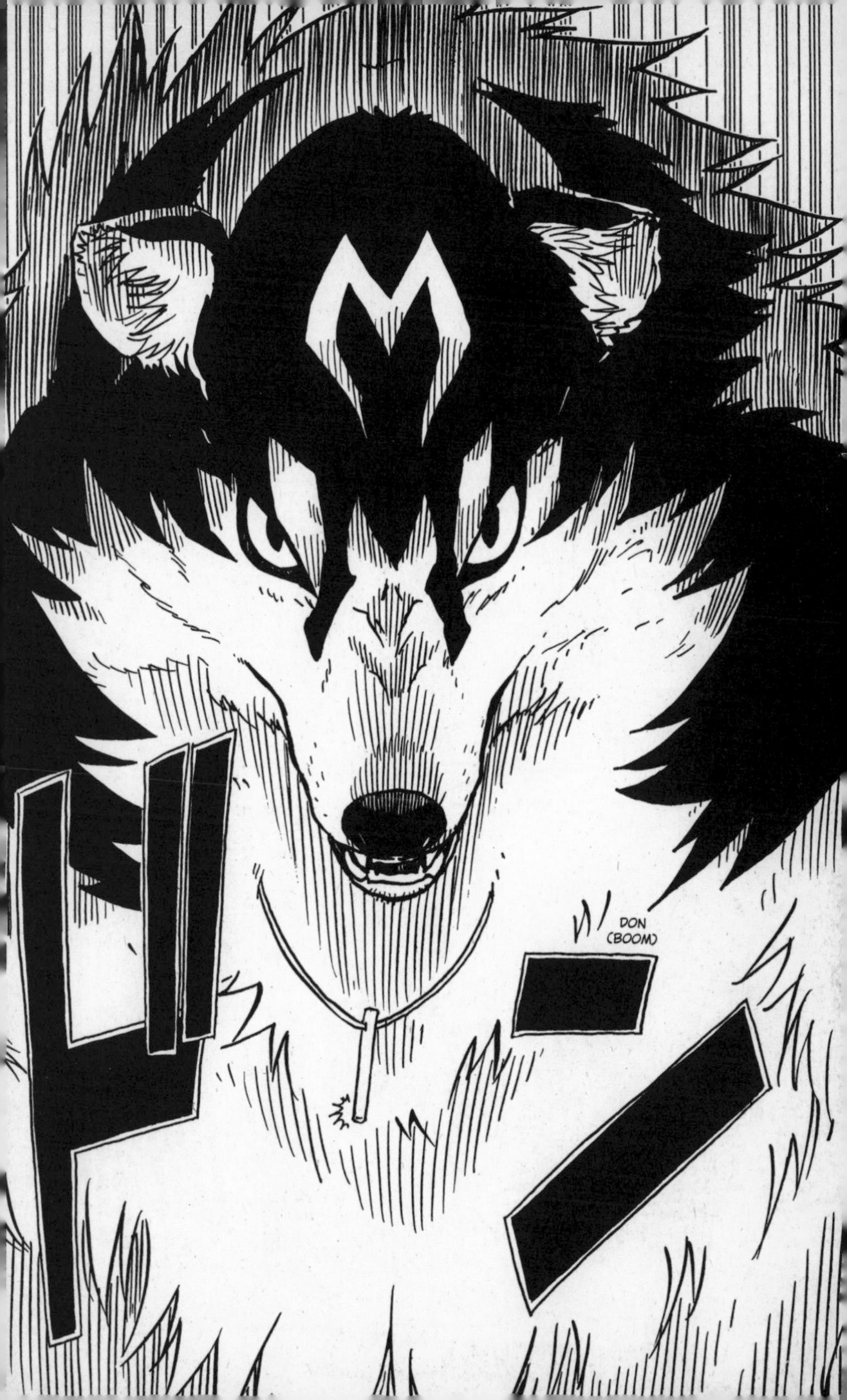
DON
(BOOM)

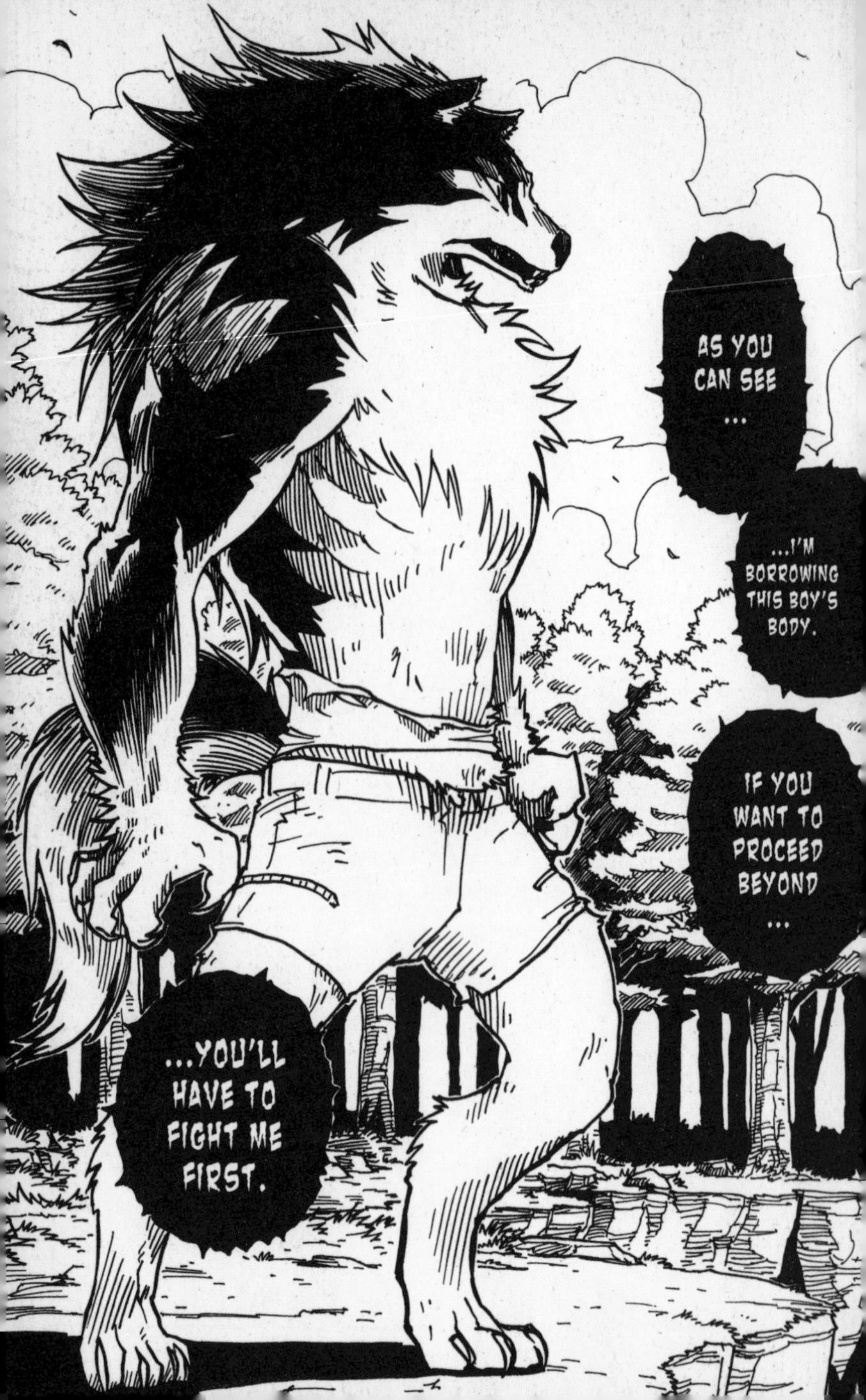
AS YOU CAN SEE ...
...I'M BORROWING THIS BOY'S BODY.
IF YOU WANT TO PROCEED BEYOND ...
...YOU'LL HAVE TO FIGHT ME FIRST.

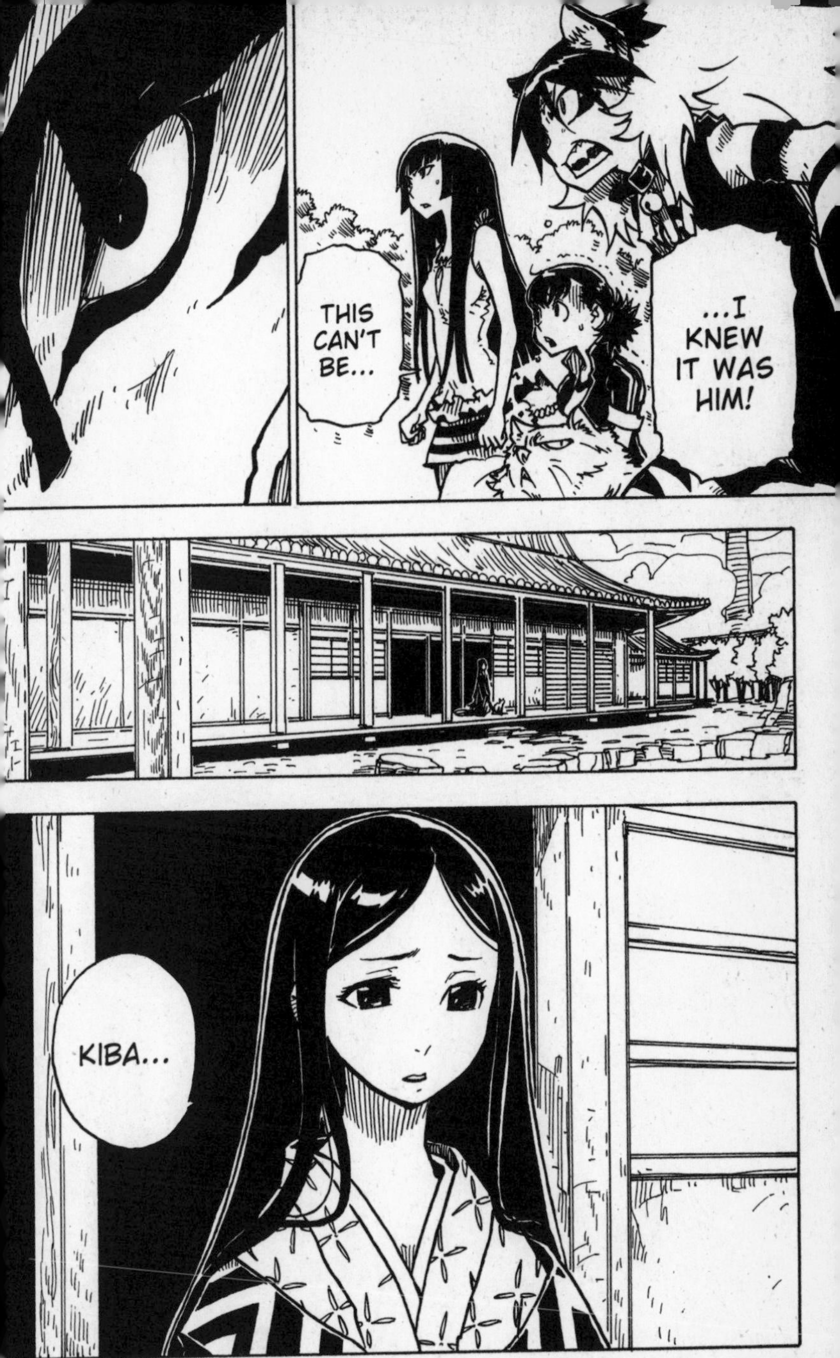
...I KNEW IT WAS HIM!
THIS CAN'T BE...
KIBA...

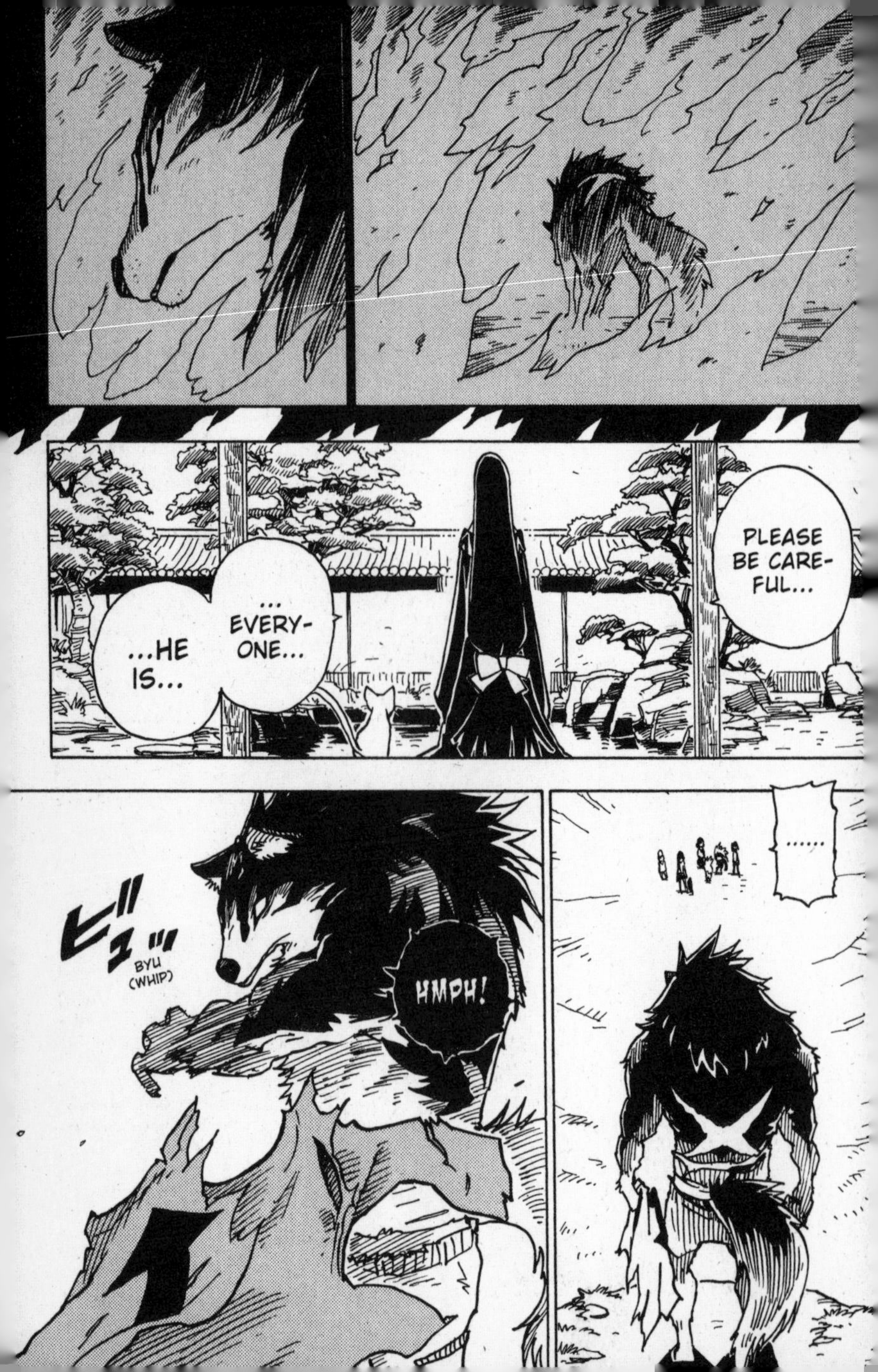
PLEASE BE CARE-FUL...
... EVERY-ONE...
...HE IS...
......
HMPH!
BYU (WHIP)

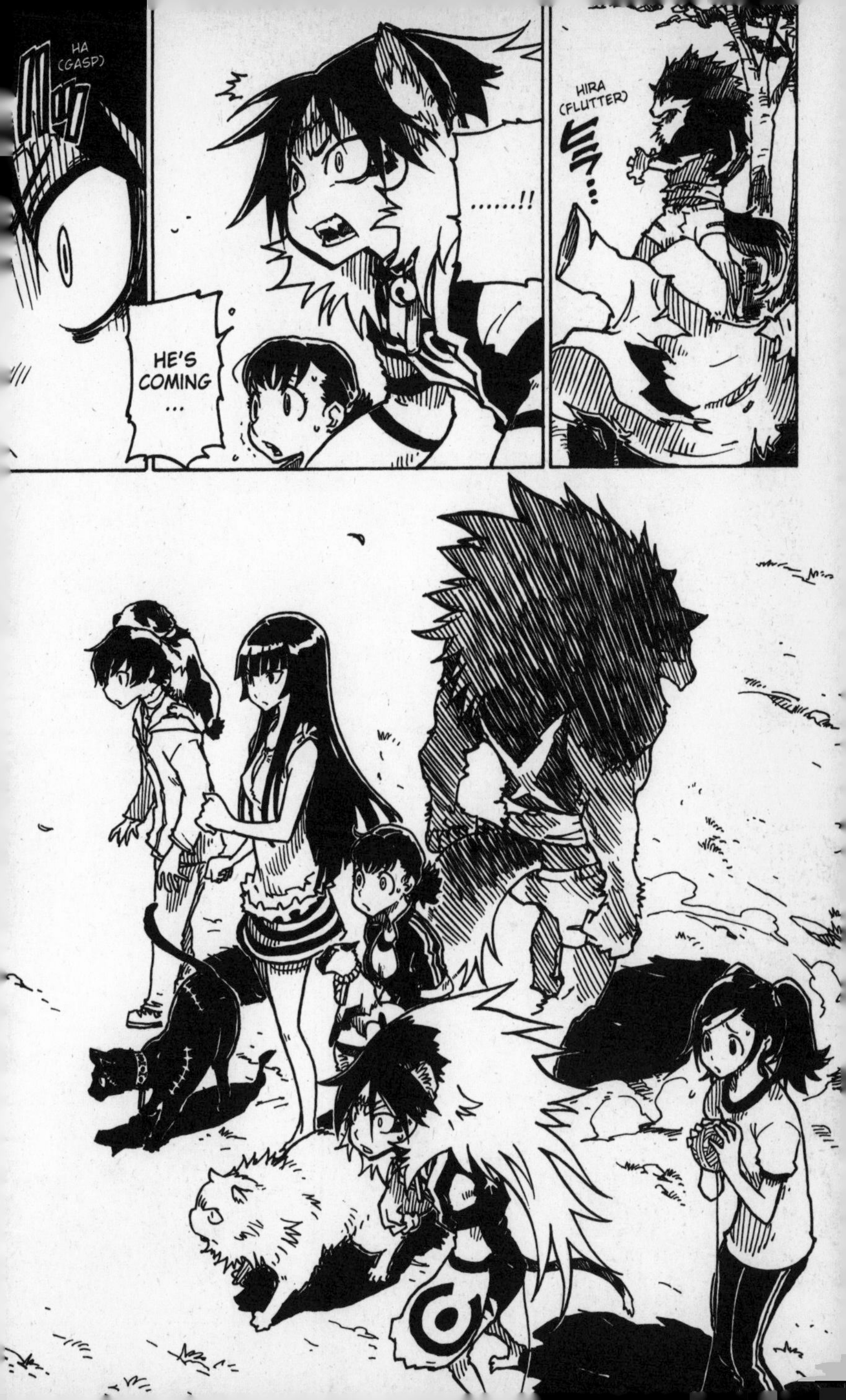
HIRA (FLUTTER)
......!!
HE'S COMING ...
HA (GASP)

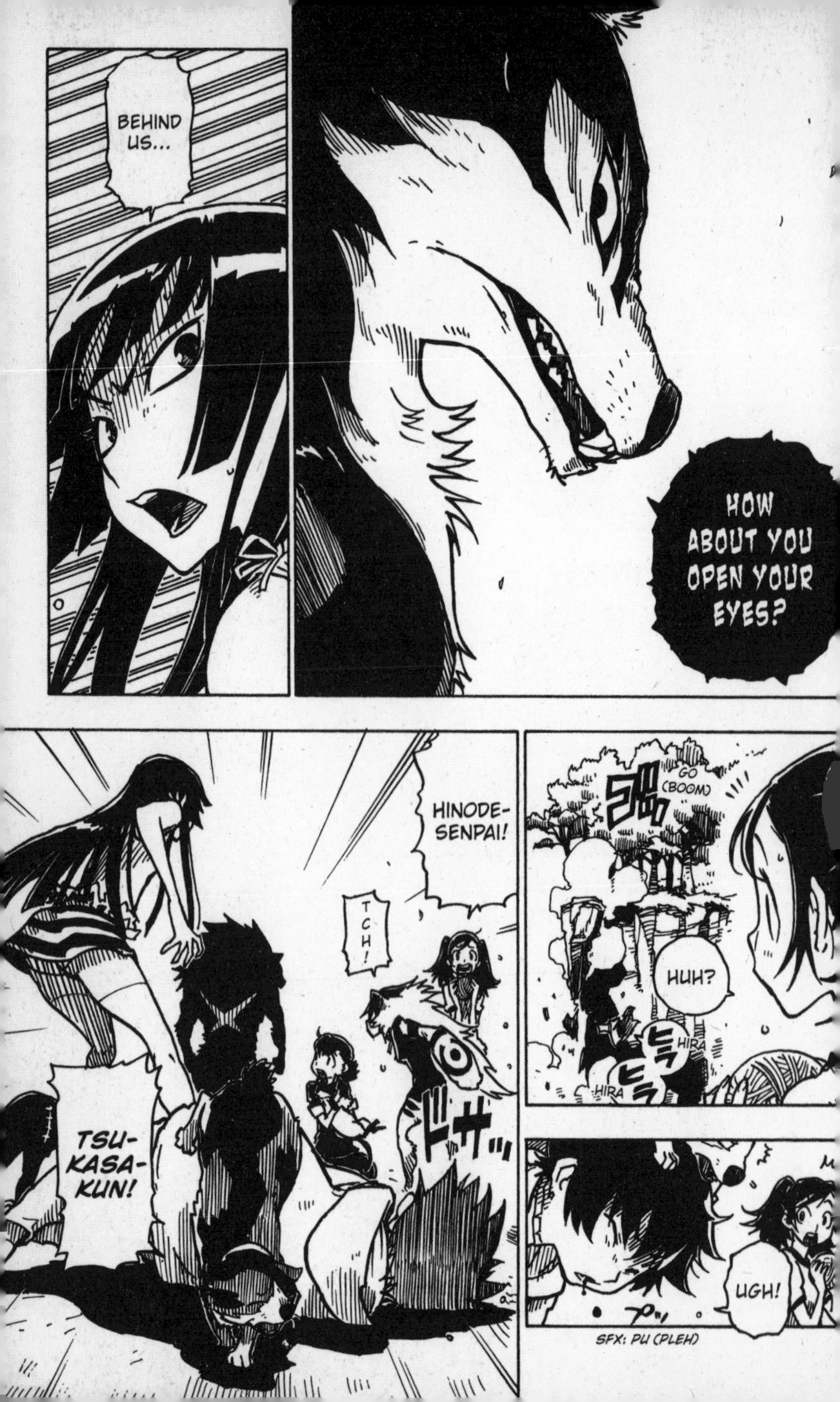
HOW ABOUT YOU OPEN YOUR EYES?
BEHIND US...
GO (BOOM)
HUH?
HIRA
HIRA
UGH!
SFX: PU (PLEH)
HINODE-SENPAI!
TCH!
TSU-KASA-KUN!

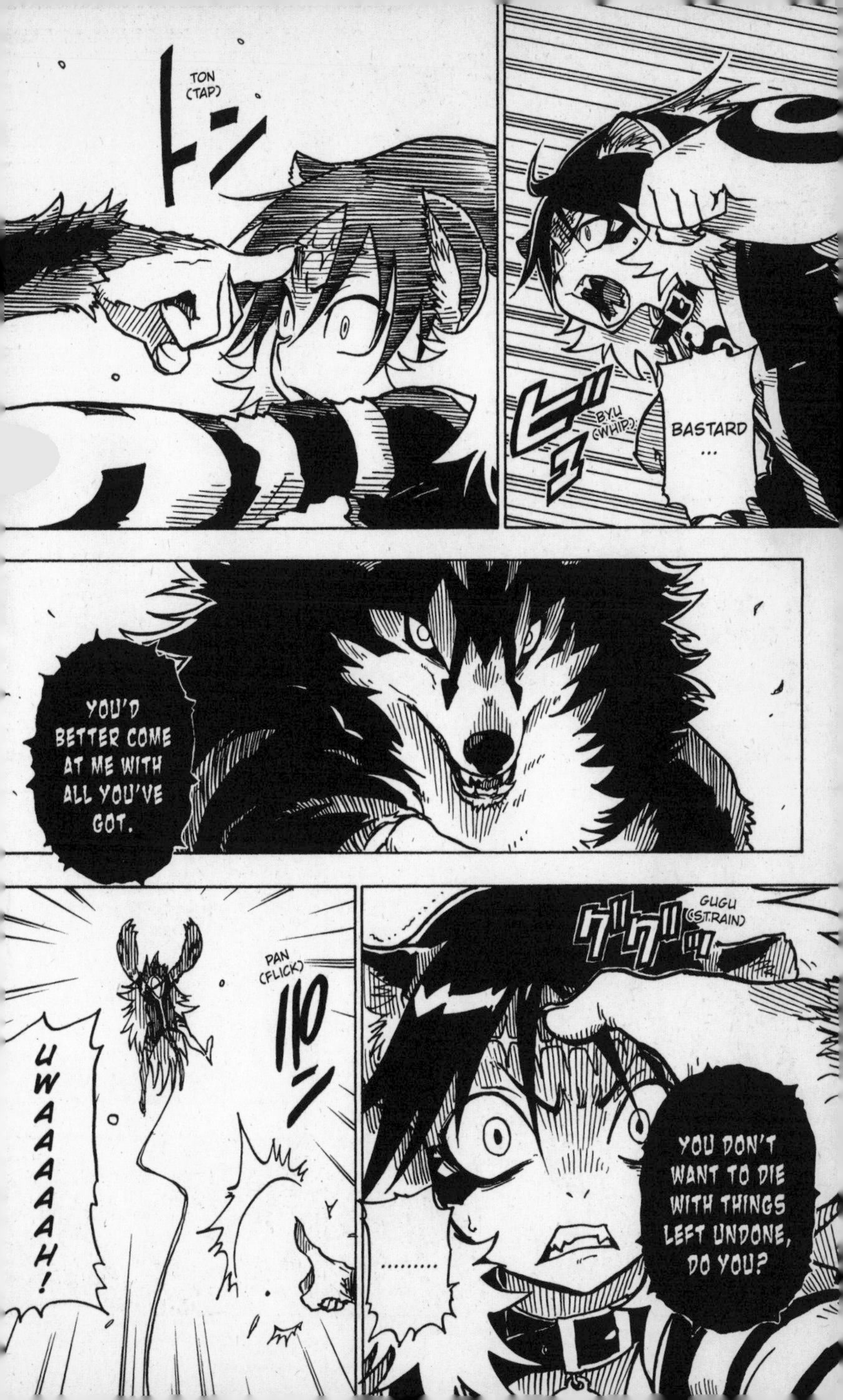

BYU (WHIP)
BASTARD ...
TON (TAP)
YOU'D BETTER COME AT ME WITH ALL YOU'VE GOT.
GUGU (STRAIN)
YOU DON'T WANT TO DIE WITH THINGS LEFT UNDONE, DO YOU?
....
PAN (FLICK)
UWAAAAAAAH!

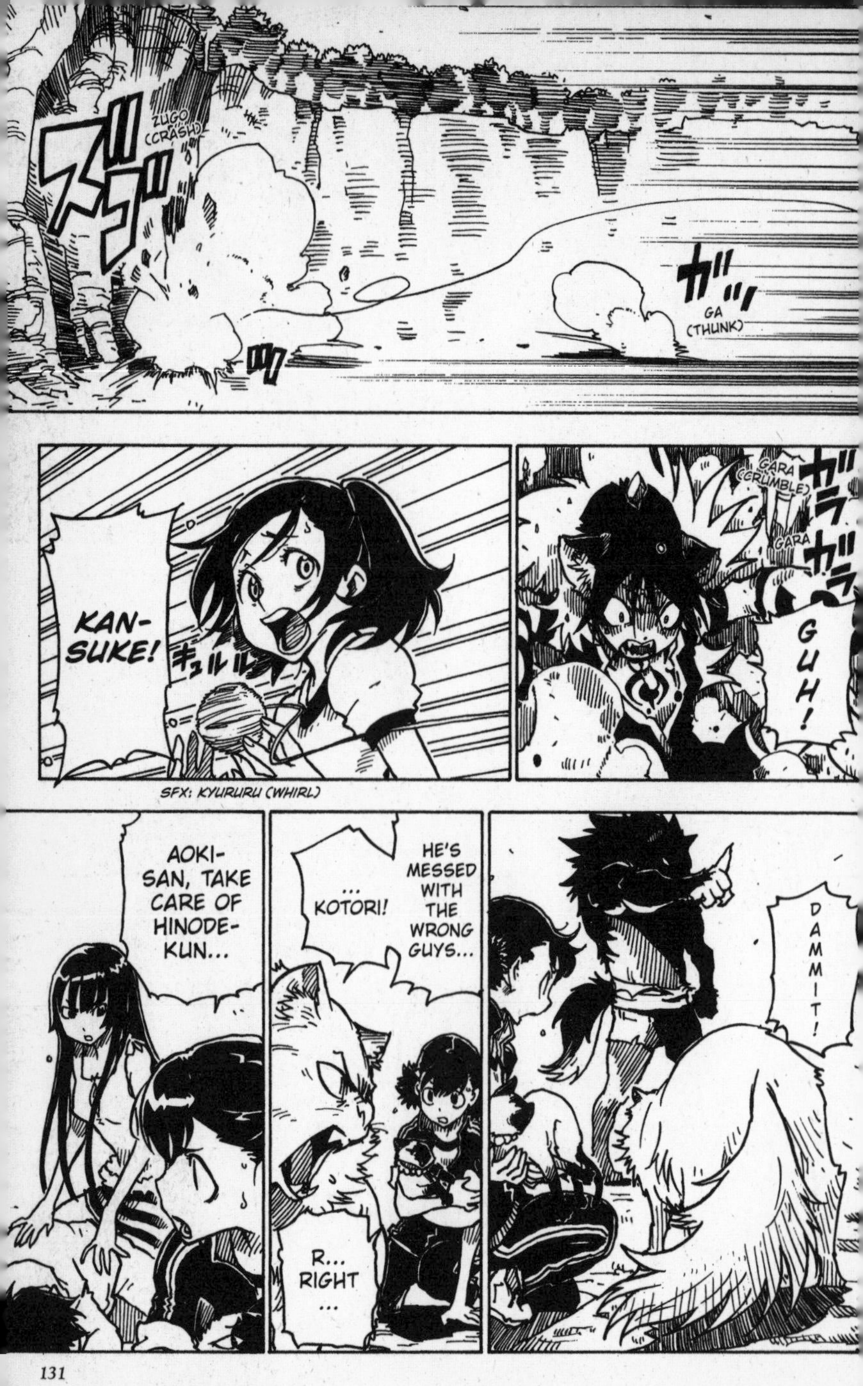
ZUGO (CRASH)
GA (THUNK)
GARA (CRUMBLE)
GARA
GUH!
KAN-SUKE!
SFX: KYURURU (WHIRL)
DAMMIT!
HE'S MESSED WITH THE WRONG GUYS...
... KOTORI!
R... RIGHT ...
AOKI-SAN, TAKE CARE OF HINODE-KUN...

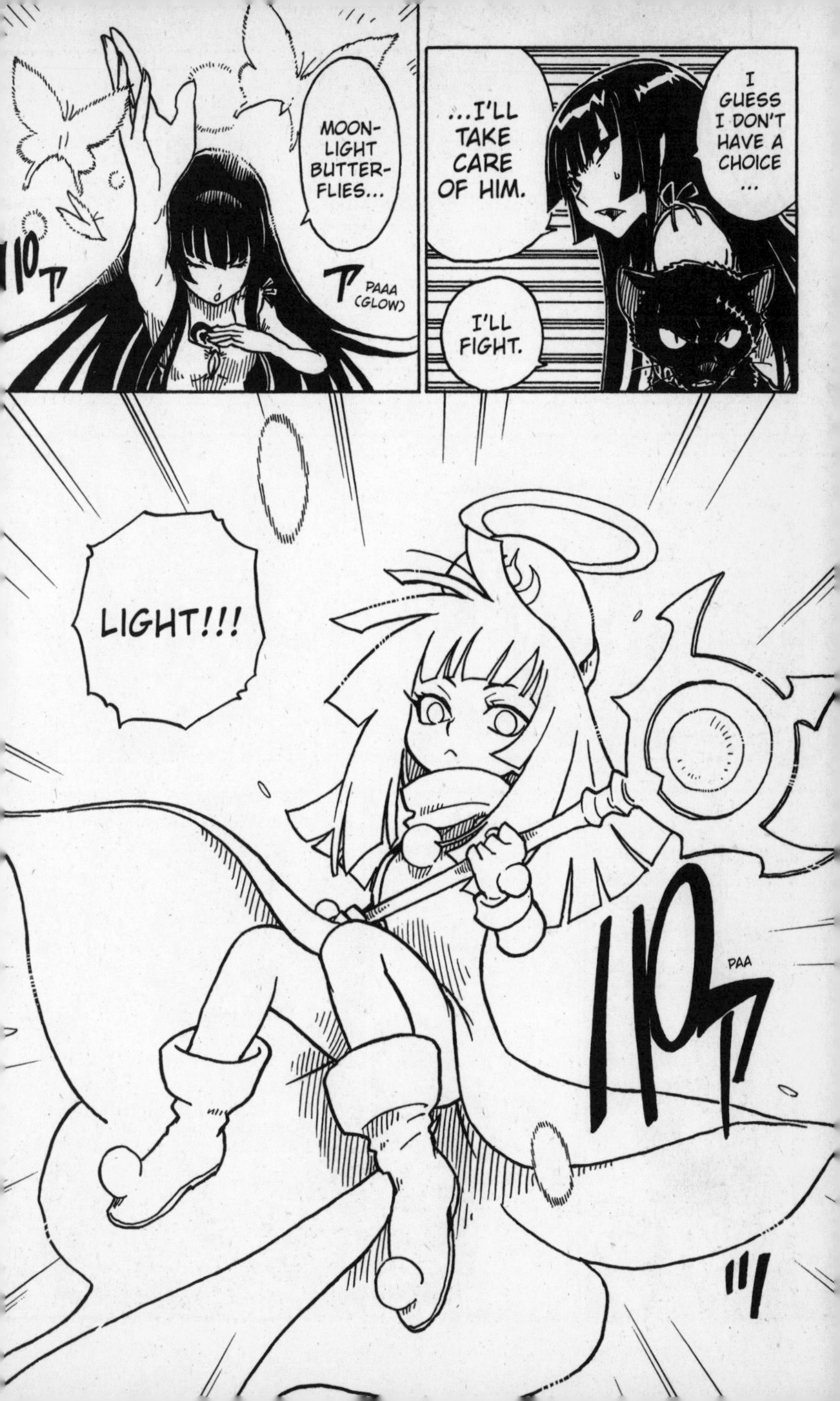
I GUESS I DON'T HAVE A CHOICE ...
...I'LL TAKE CARE OF HIM.
I'LL FIGHT.
MOON-LIGHT BUTTER-FLIES...
PAAA (GLOW)
LIGHT!!!
PAA

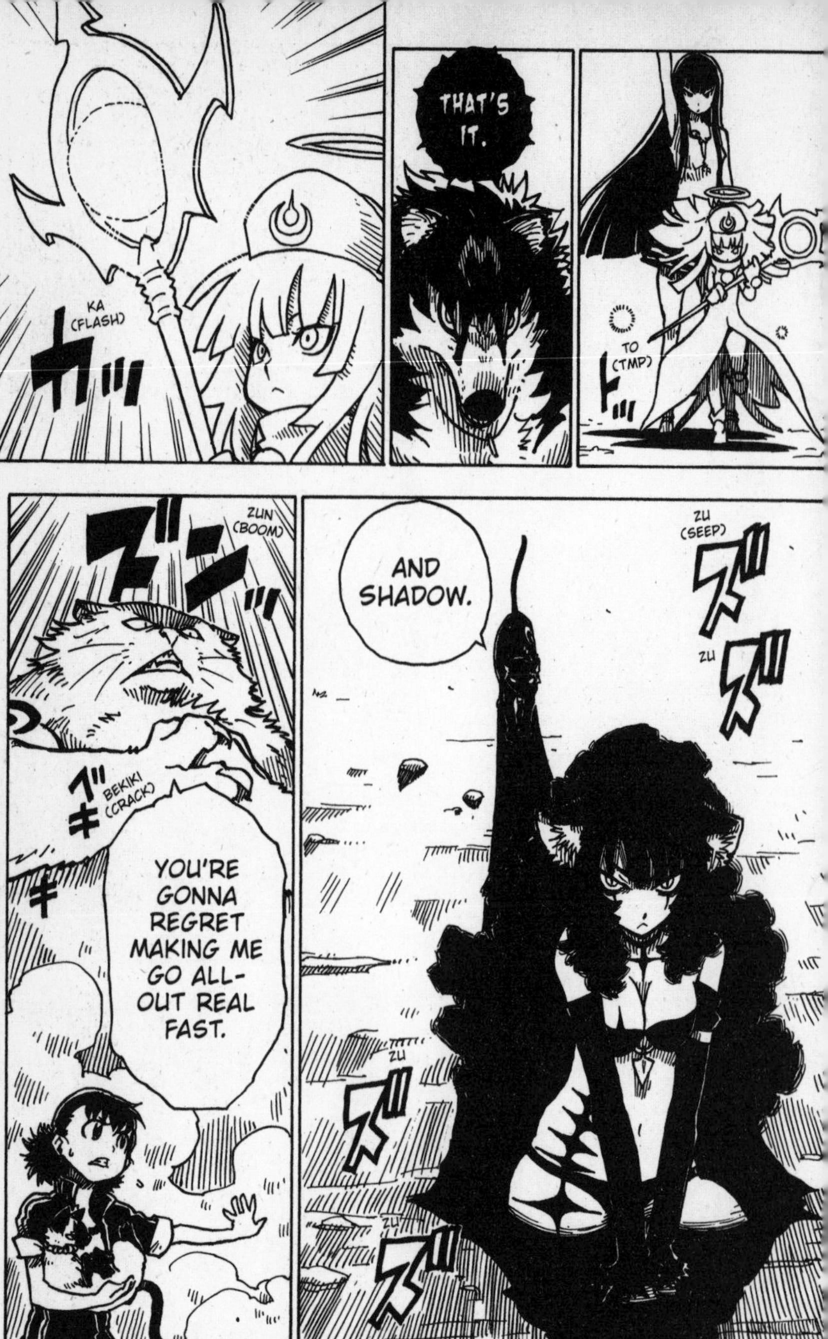
TO
(TMP)
THAT'S IT.
KA
(FLASH)
AND SHADOW.
ZU
(SEEP)
ZU
ZU
ZU
ZUN
(BOOM)
BEKIKI
(CRACK)
YOU'RE GONNA REGRET MAKING ME GO ALL-OUT REAL FAST.

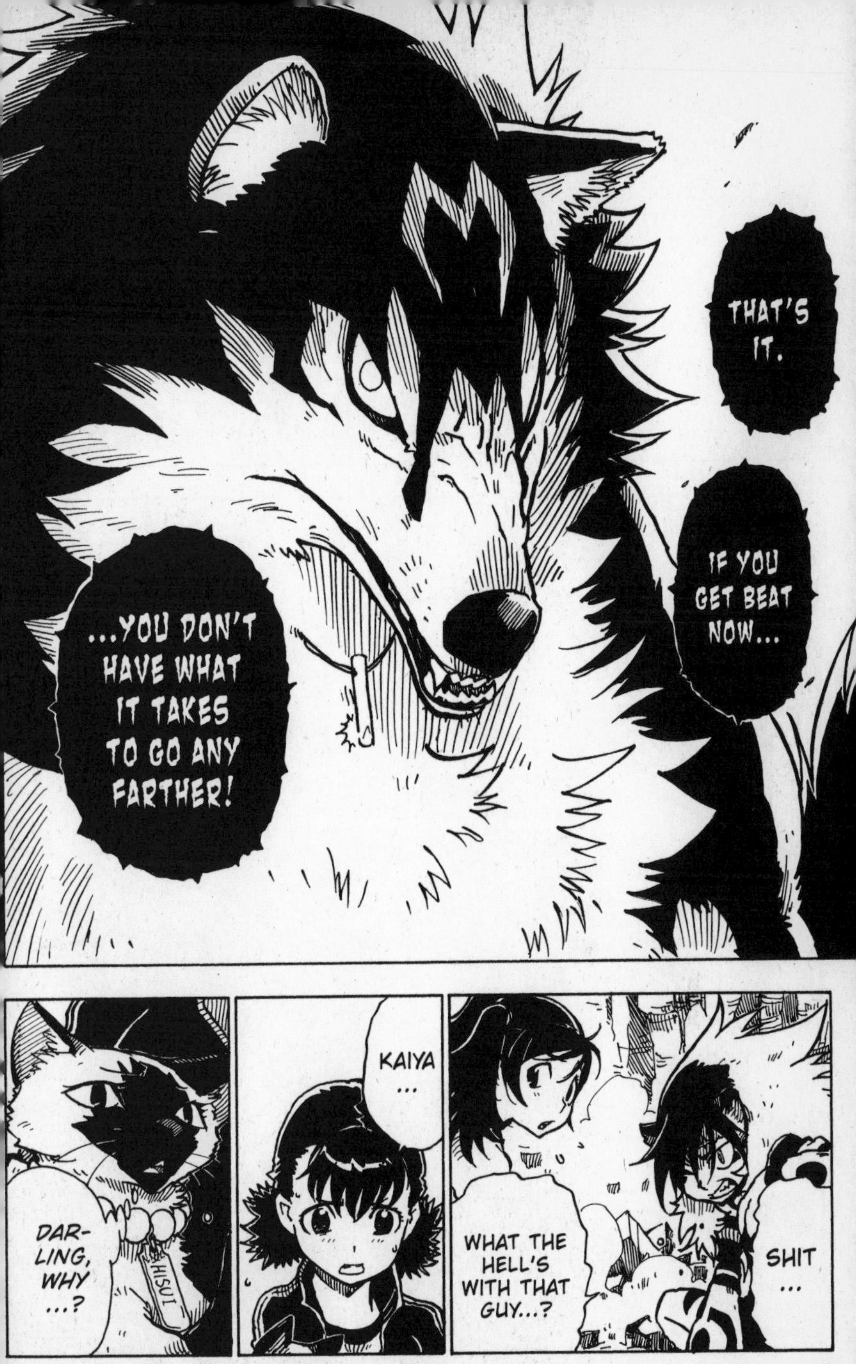
THAT'S IT.
IF YOU GET BEAT NOW...
...YOU DON'T HAVE WHAT IT TAKES TO GO ANY FARTHER!
SHIT ...
WHAT THE HELL'S WITH THAT GUY...?
KAIYA ...
DAR-LING, WHY ...?
HISUI

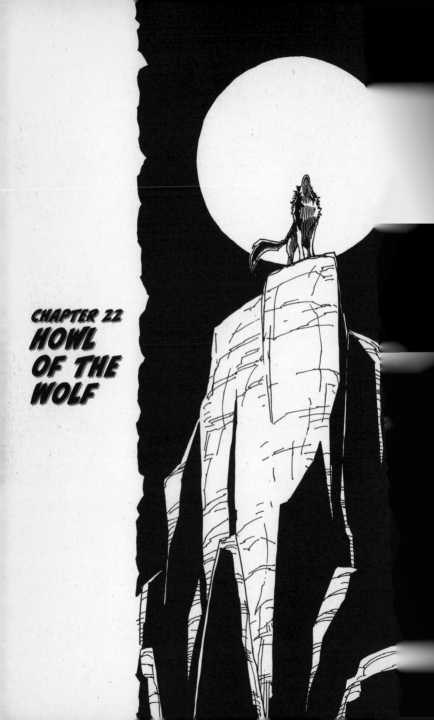

CHAPTER 22
HOWL OF THE WOLF

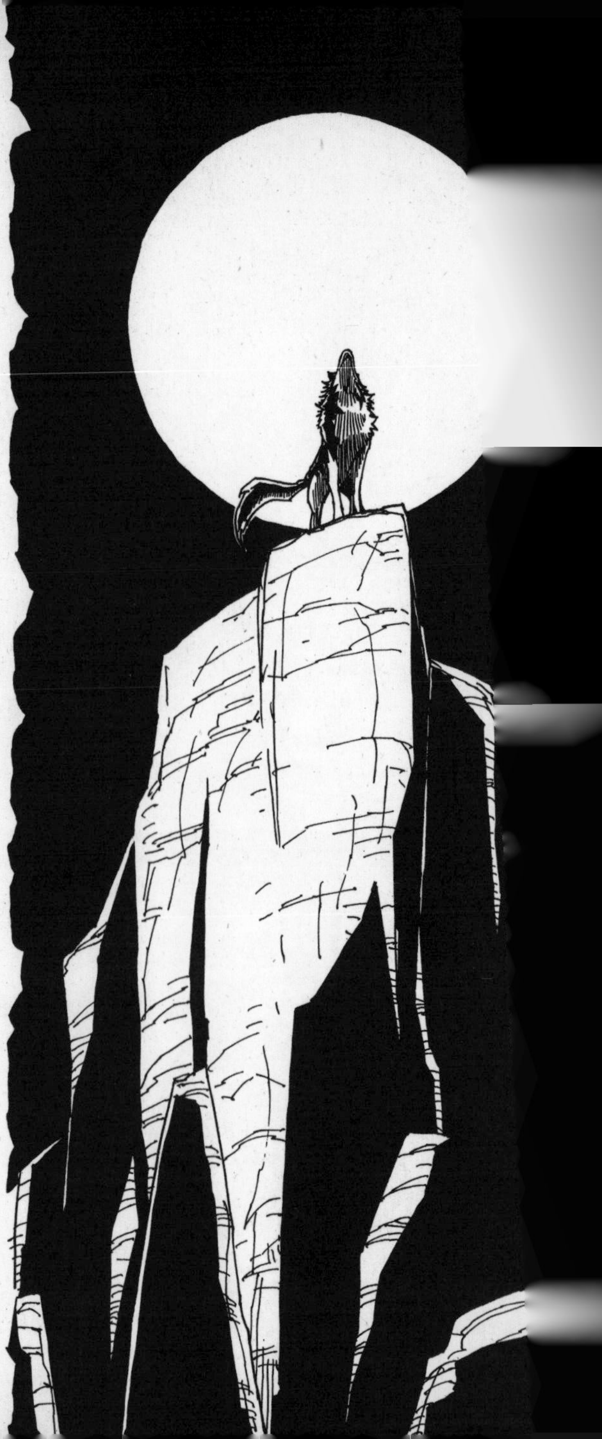

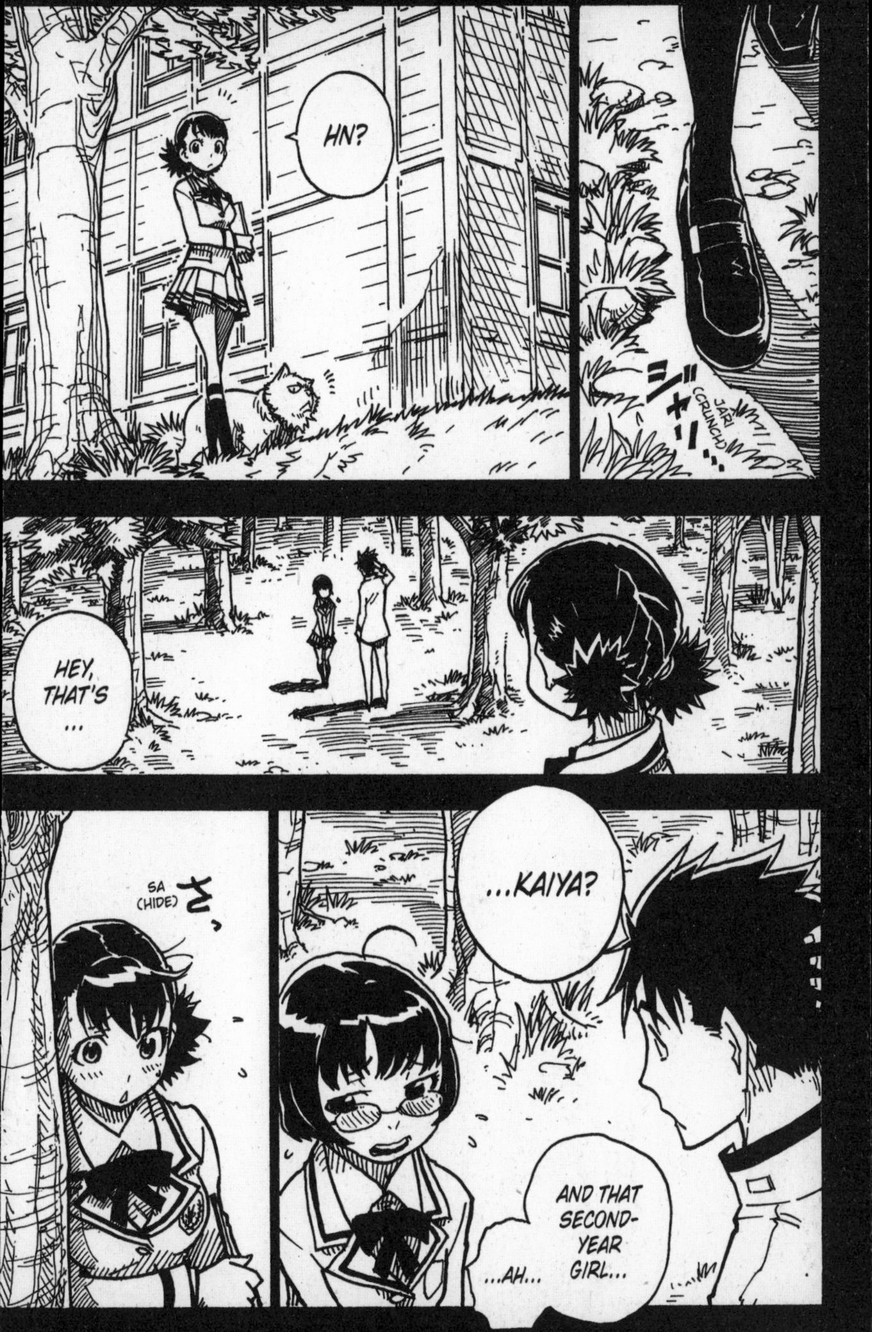
ジャリ…
JARI (CRUNCH)
HN?
HEY, THAT'S ...
...KAIYA?
AND THAT SECOND-YEAR GIRL...
...AH...
さ
SA (HIDE)

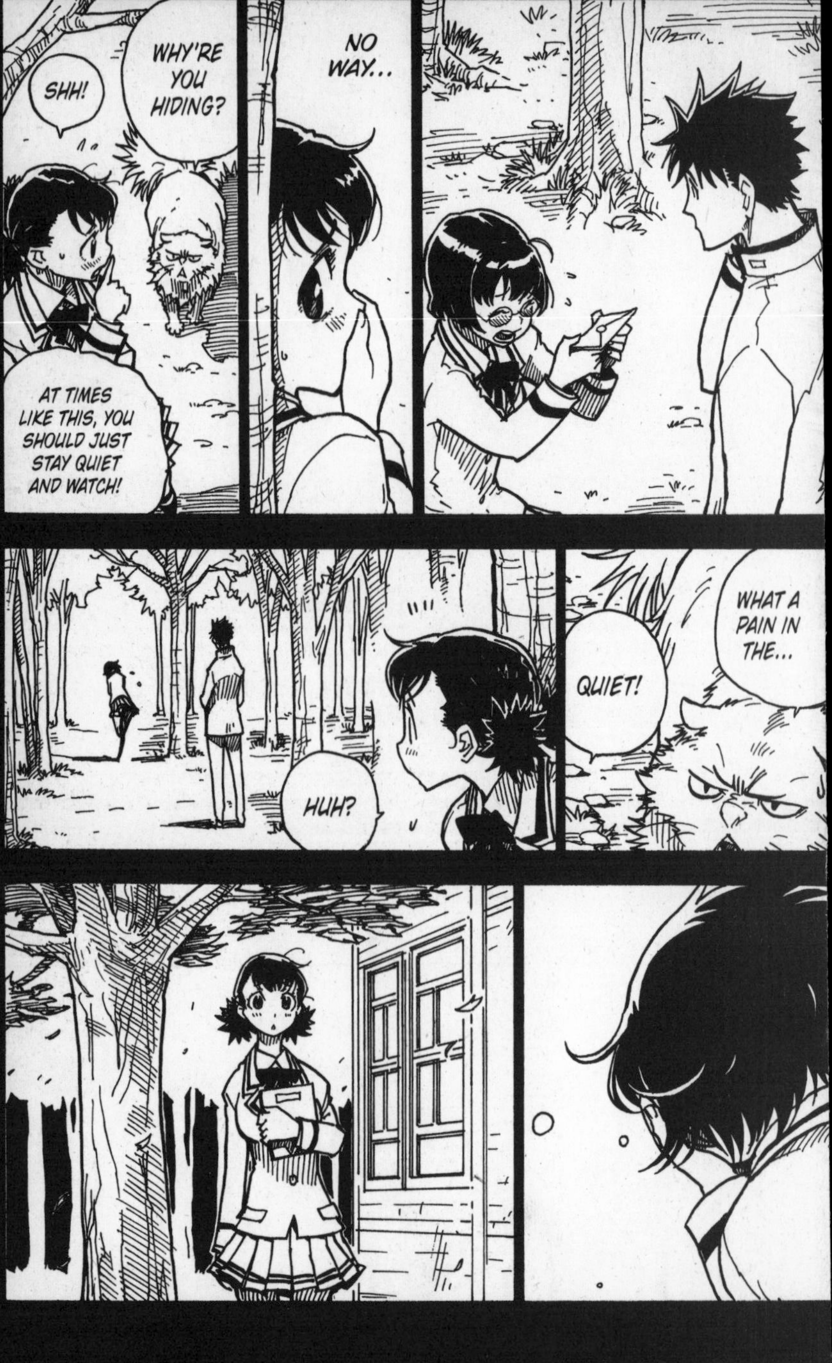
NO WAY...
WHY'RE YOU HIDING?
SHH!
AT TIMES LIKE THIS, YOU SHOULD JUST STAY QUIET AND WATCH!
WHAT A PAIN IN THE...
QUIET!
HUH?

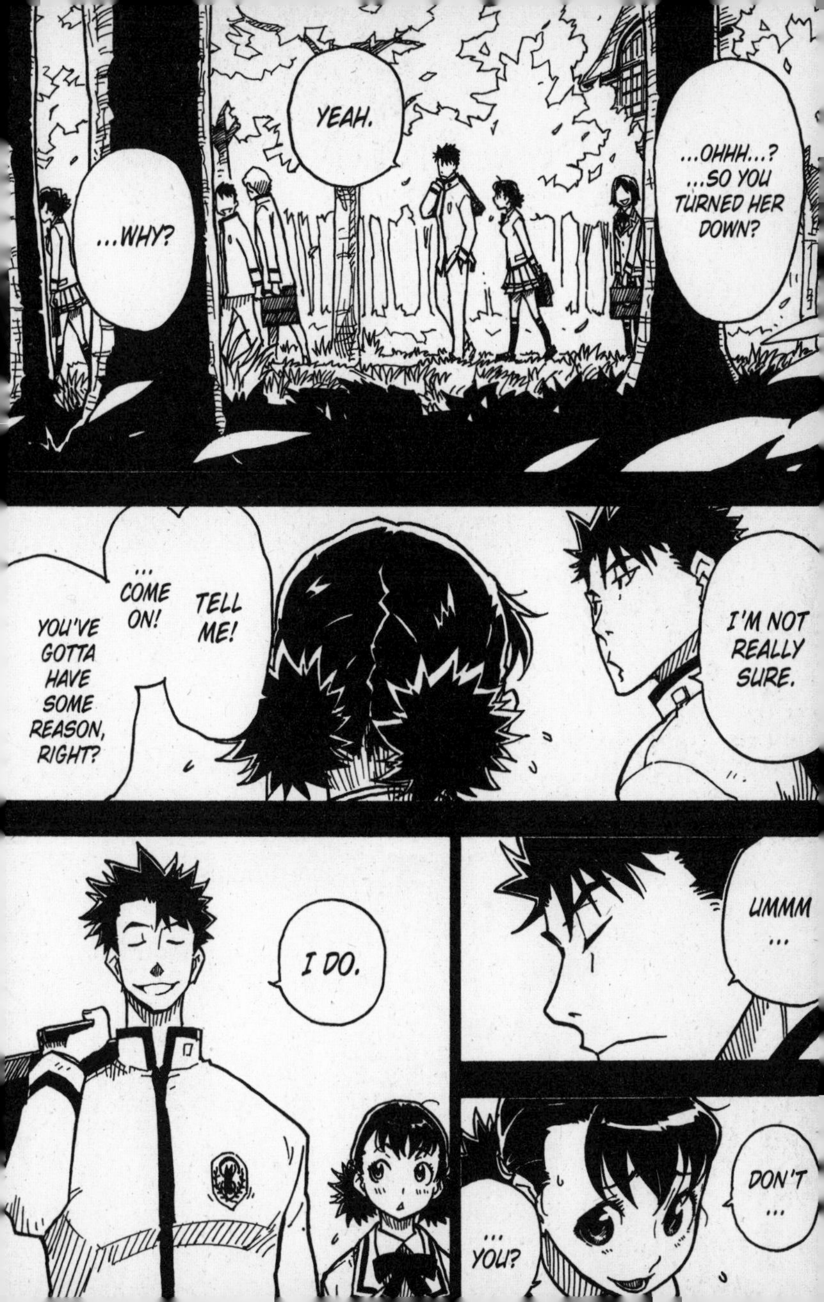
...OHHH...? ...SO YOU TURNED HER DOWN?
YEAH.
...WHY?
I'M NOT REALLY SURE.
TELL ME!
... COME ON!
YOU'VE GOTTA HAVE SOME REASON, RIGHT?
UMMM ...
DON'T ...
... YOU?
I DO.

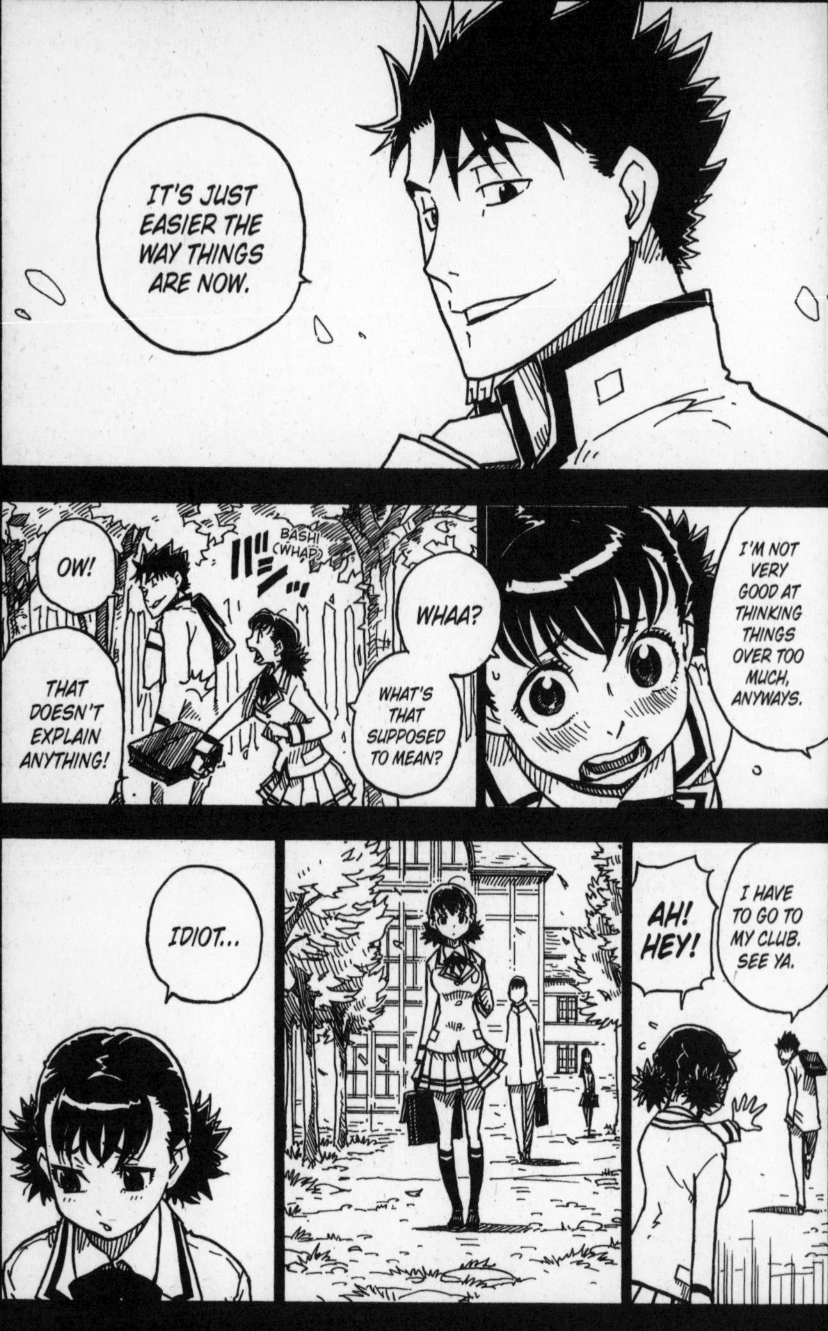
IT'S JUST EASIER THE WAY THINGS ARE NOW.
I'M NOT VERY GOOD AT THINKING THINGS OVER TOO MUCH, ANYWAYS.
WHAA?
WHAT'S THAT SUPPOSED TO MEAN?
BASHI (WHAP)
OW!
THAT DOESN'T EXPLAIN ANYTHING!
I HAVE TO GO TO MY CLUB. SEE YA.
AH! HEY!
IDIOT...

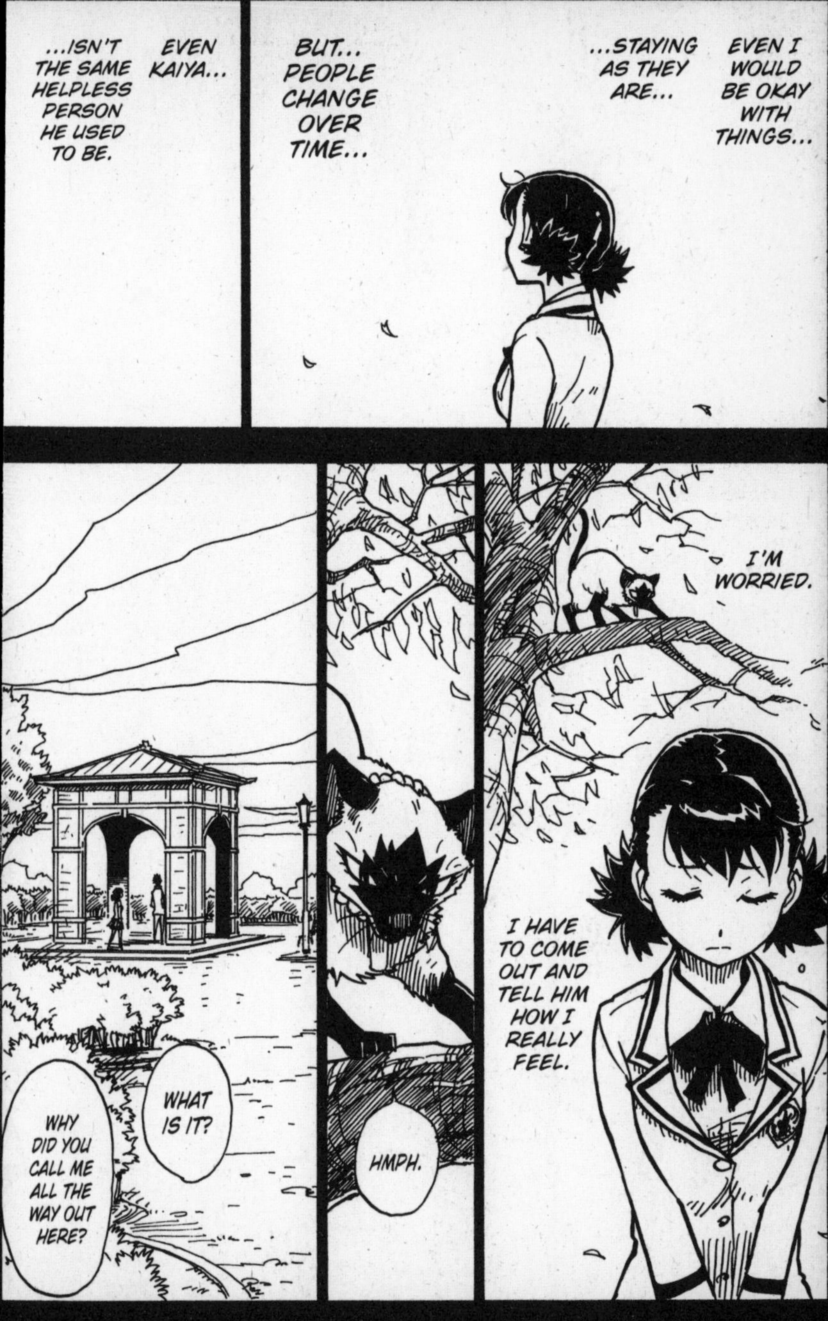
EVEN I WOULD BE OKAY WITH THINGS...
...STAYING AS THEY ARE...
BUT... PEOPLE CHANGE OVER TIME...
EVEN KAIYA...
...ISN'T THE SAME HELPLESS PERSON HE USED TO BE.
I'M WORRIED.
I HAVE TO COME OUT AND TELL HIM HOW I REALLY FEEL.
HMPH.
WHAT IS IT?
WHY DID YOU CALL ME ALL THE WAY OUT HERE?

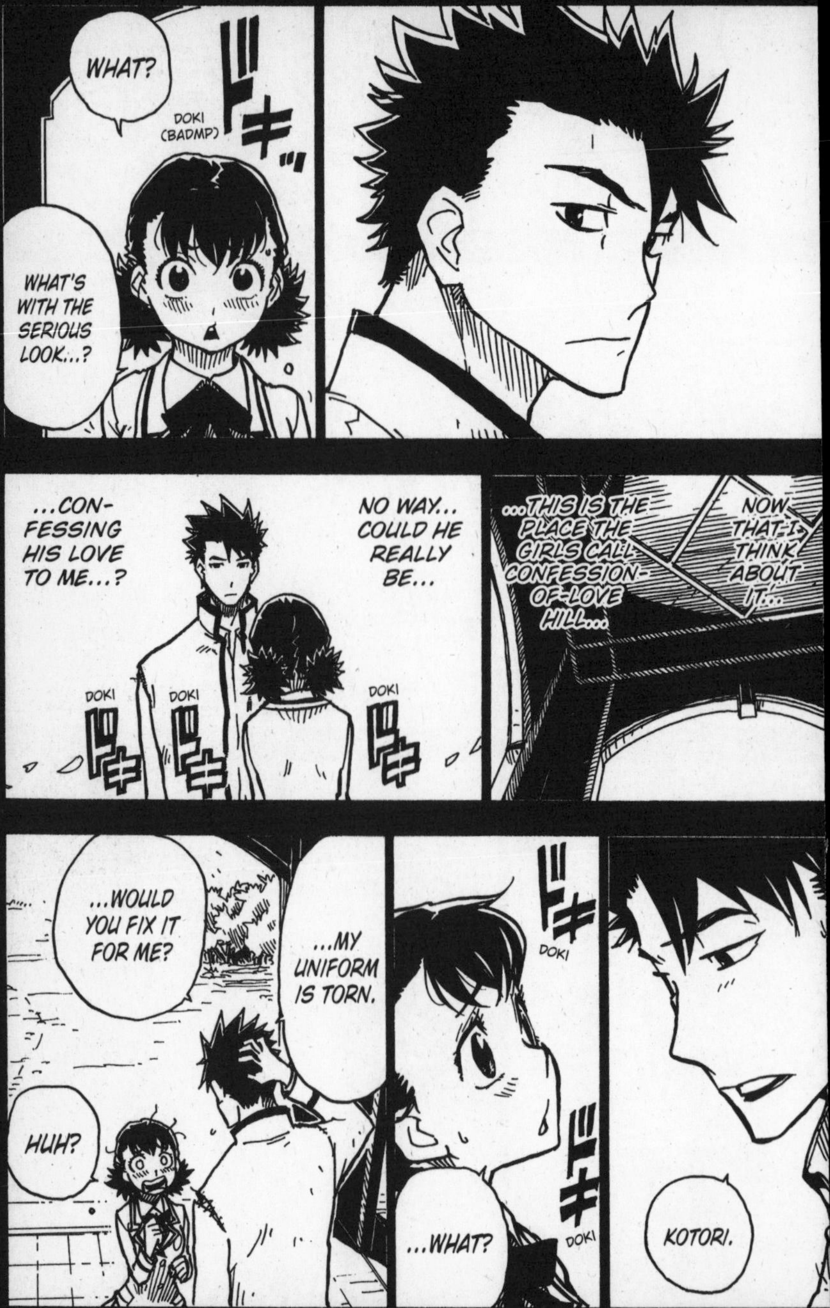
WHAT?
DOKI (BADMP)
WHAT'S WITH THE SERIOUS LOOK...?
NOW THAT I THINK ABOUT IT...
...THIS IS THE PLACE THE GIRLS CALL CONFESSION-OF-LOVE HILL...
NO WAY... COULD HE REALLY BE...
...CON-FESSING HIS LOVE TO ME...?
DOKI
DOKI
DOKI
KOTORI.
DOKI
...WHAT?
DOKI
...MY UNIFORM IS TORN.
...WOULD YOU FIX IT FOR ME?
HUH?

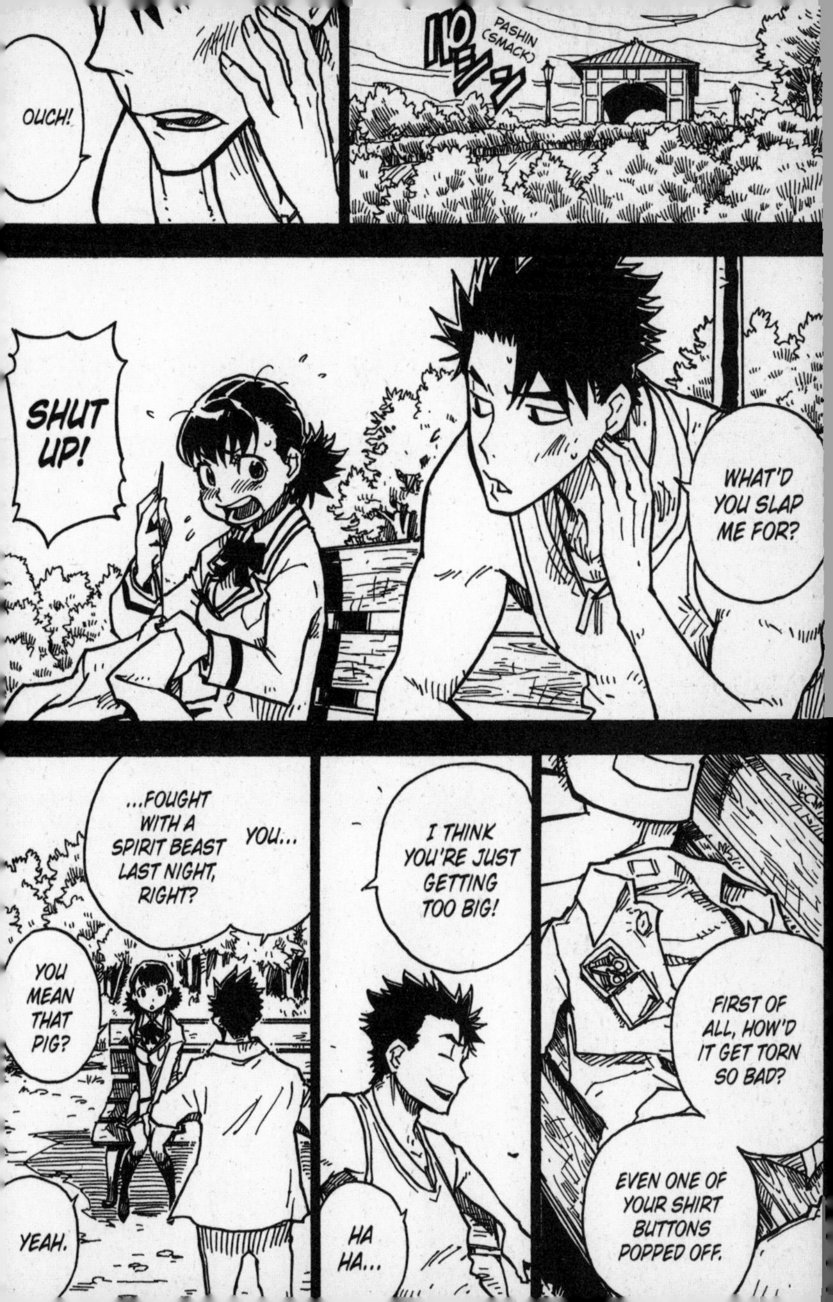
PASHIN (SMACK)
OUCH!
WHAT'D YOU SLAP ME FOR?
SHUT UP!
FIRST OF ALL, HOW'D IT GET TORN SO BAD?
EVEN ONE OF YOUR SHIRT BUTTONS POPPED OFF.
I THINK YOU'RE JUST GETTING TOO BIG!
HA HA...
YOU...
...FOUGHT WITH A SPIRIT BEAST LAST NIGHT, RIGHT?
YOU MEAN THAT PIG?
YEAH.

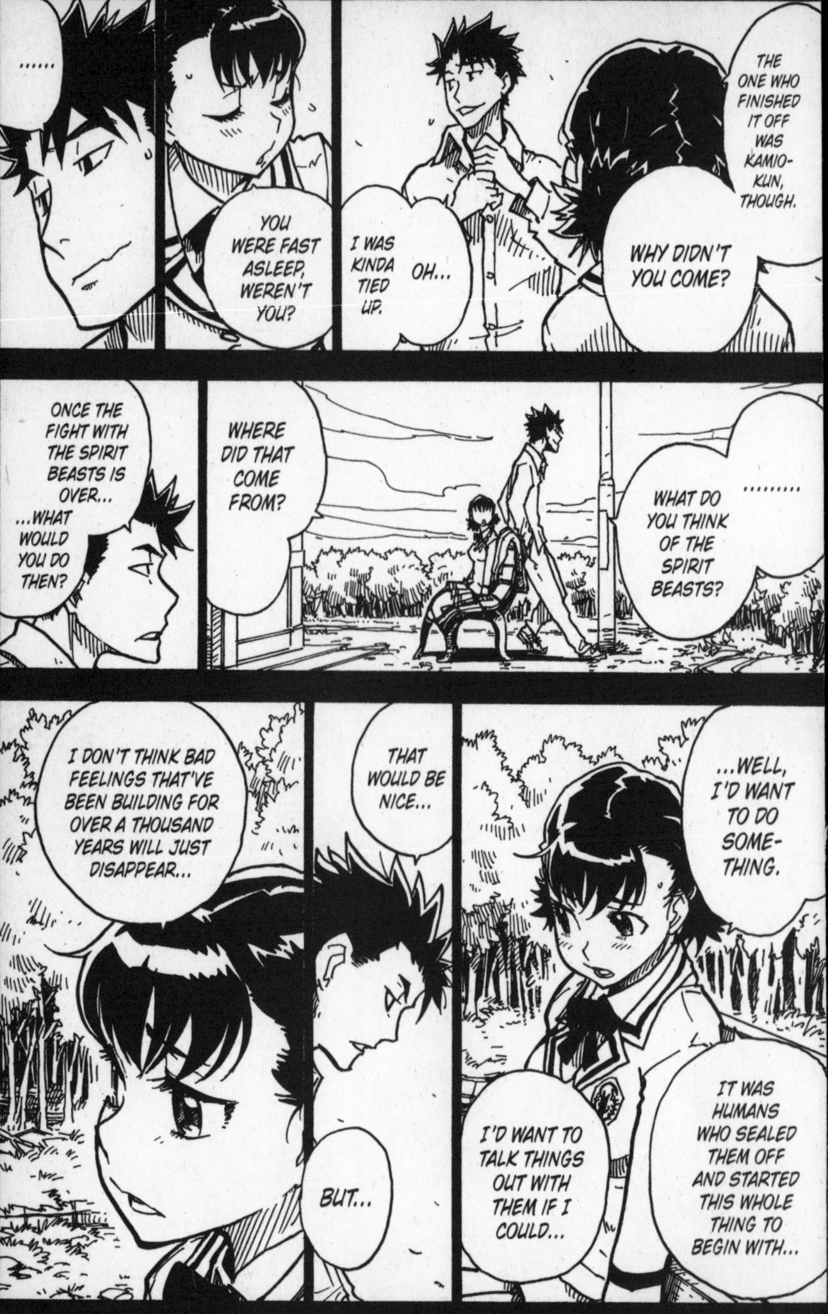
THE ONE WHO FINISHED IT OFF WAS KAMIO-KUN, THOUGH.
WHY DIDN'T YOU COME?
OH...
I WAS KINDA TIED UP.
YOU WERE FAST ASLEEP, WEREN'T YOU?
......
....
WHAT DO YOU THINK OF THE SPIRIT BEASTS?
WHERE DID THAT COME FROM?
ONCE THE FIGHT WITH THE SPIRIT BEASTS IS OVER...
...WHAT WOULD YOU DO THEN?
...WELL, I'D WANT TO DO SOME-THING.
IT WAS HUMANS WHO SEALED THEM OFF AND STARTED THIS WHOLE THING TO BEGIN WITH...
I'D WANT TO TALK THINGS OUT WITH THEM IF I COULD...
THAT WOULD BE NICE...
BUT...
I DON'T THINK BAD FEELINGS THAT'VE BEEN BUILDING FOR OVER A THOUSAND YEARS WILL JUST DISAPPEAR...

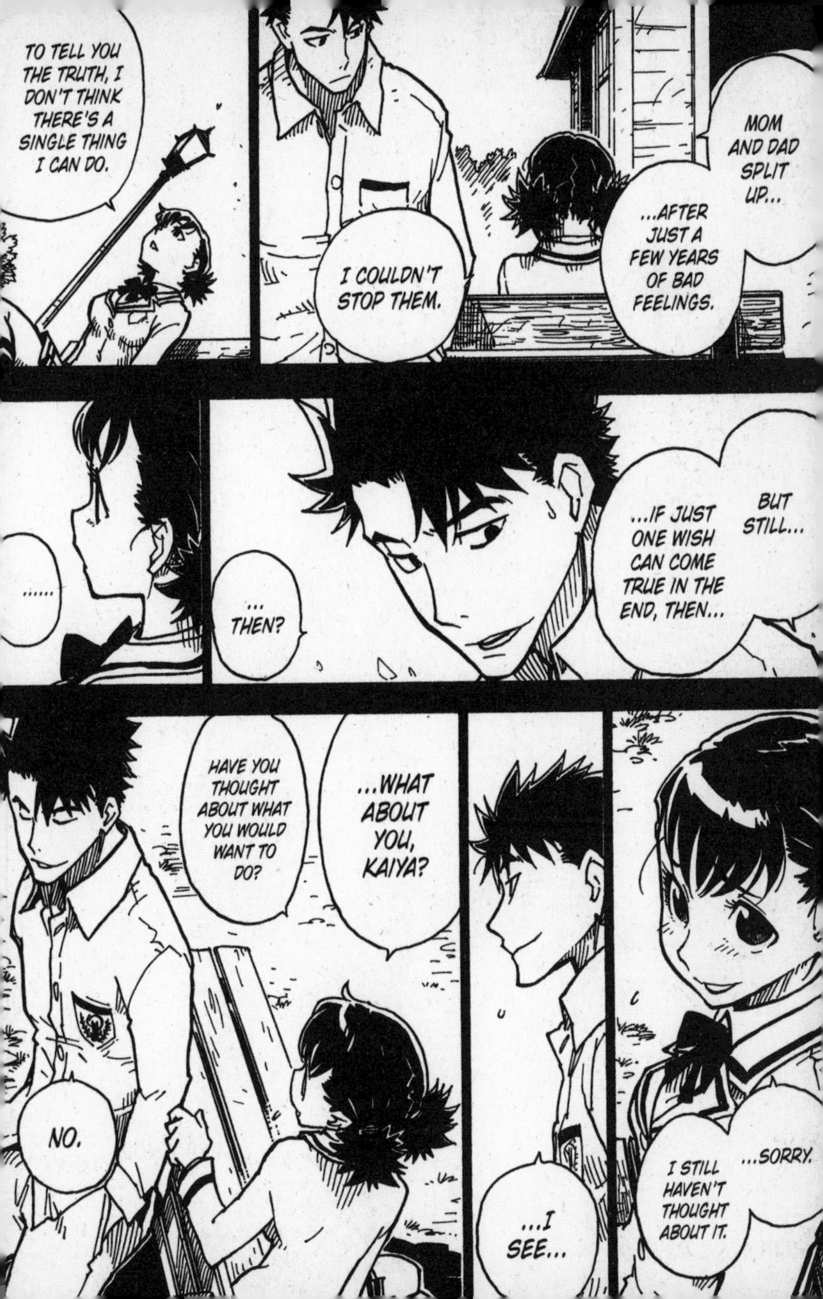
MOM AND DAD SPLIT UP...
...AFTER JUST A FEW YEARS OF BAD FEELINGS.
I COULDN'T STOP THEM.
TO TELL YOU THE TRUTH, I DON'T THINK THERE'S A SINGLE THING I CAN DO.
BUT STILL...
...IF JUST ONE WISH CAN COME TRUE IN THE END, THEN...
...THEN?
......
...SORRY.
I STILL HAVEN'T THOUGHT ABOUT IT.
...I SEE...
...WHAT ABOUT YOU, KAIYA?
HAVE YOU THOUGHT ABOUT WHAT YOU WOULD WANT TO DO?
NO.

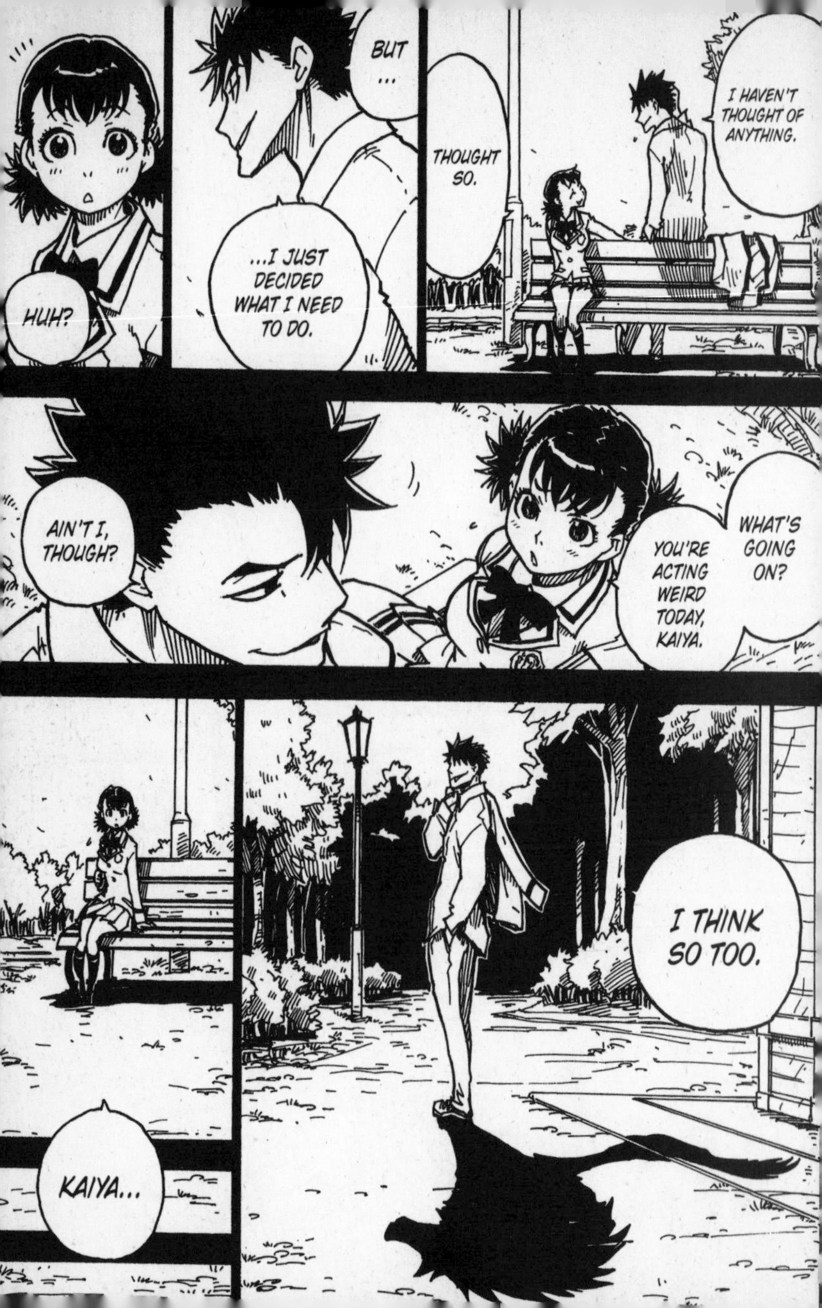
I HAVEN'T THOUGHT OF ANYTHING.
THOUGHT SO.
BUT ...
...I JUST DECIDED WHAT I NEED TO DO.
HUH?
WHAT'S GOING ON?
YOU'RE ACTING WEIRD TODAY, KAIYA.
AIN'T I, THOUGH?
I THINK SO TOO.
KAIYA...

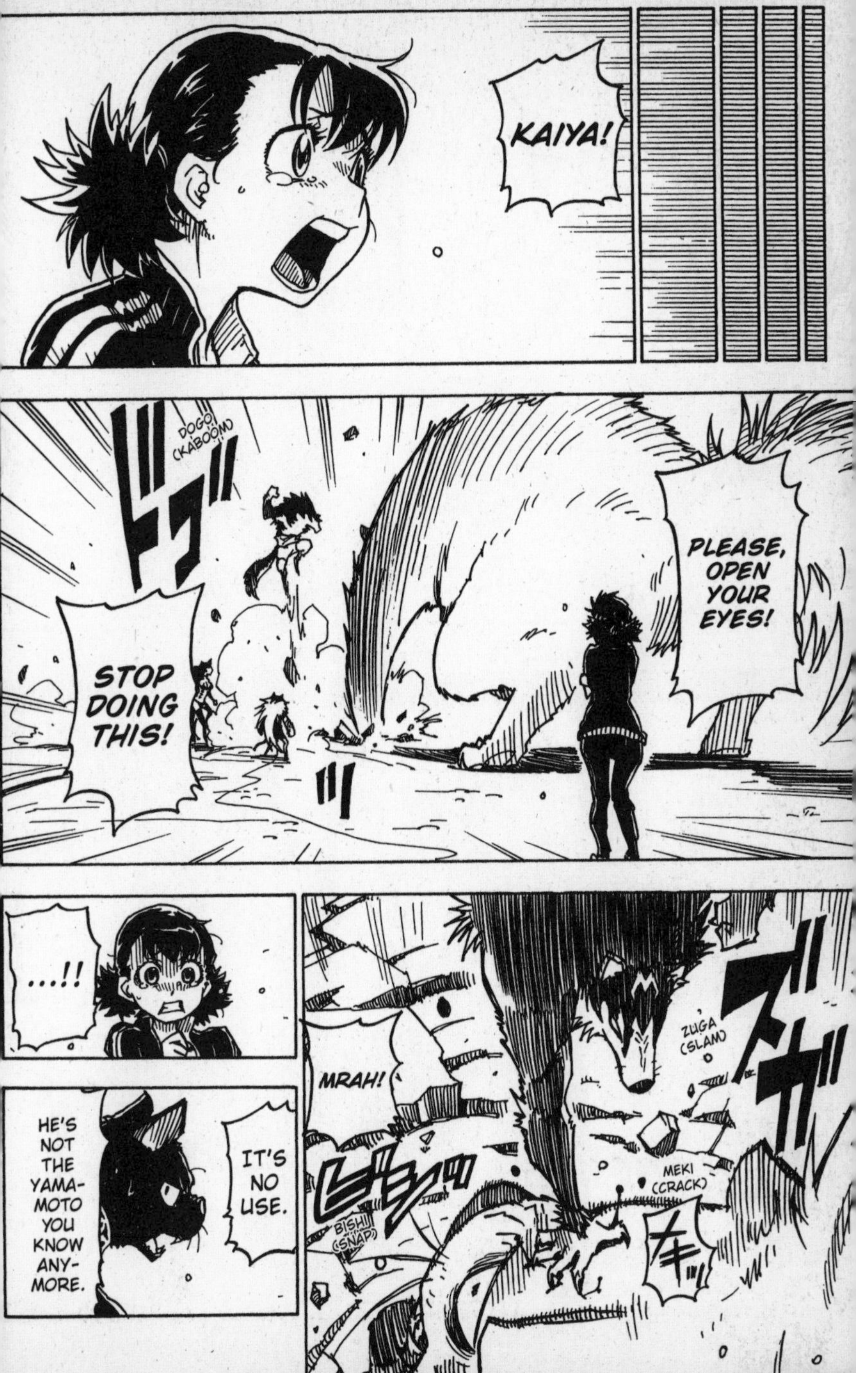
KAIYA!
PLEASE, OPEN YOUR EYES!
DOGO (KABOOM)
STOP DOING THIS!
ZUGA (SLAM)
MRAH!
MEKI (CRACK)
BISHI (SNAP)
...!!
IT'S NO USE.
HE'S NOT THE YAMA-MOTO YOU KNOW ANY-MORE.

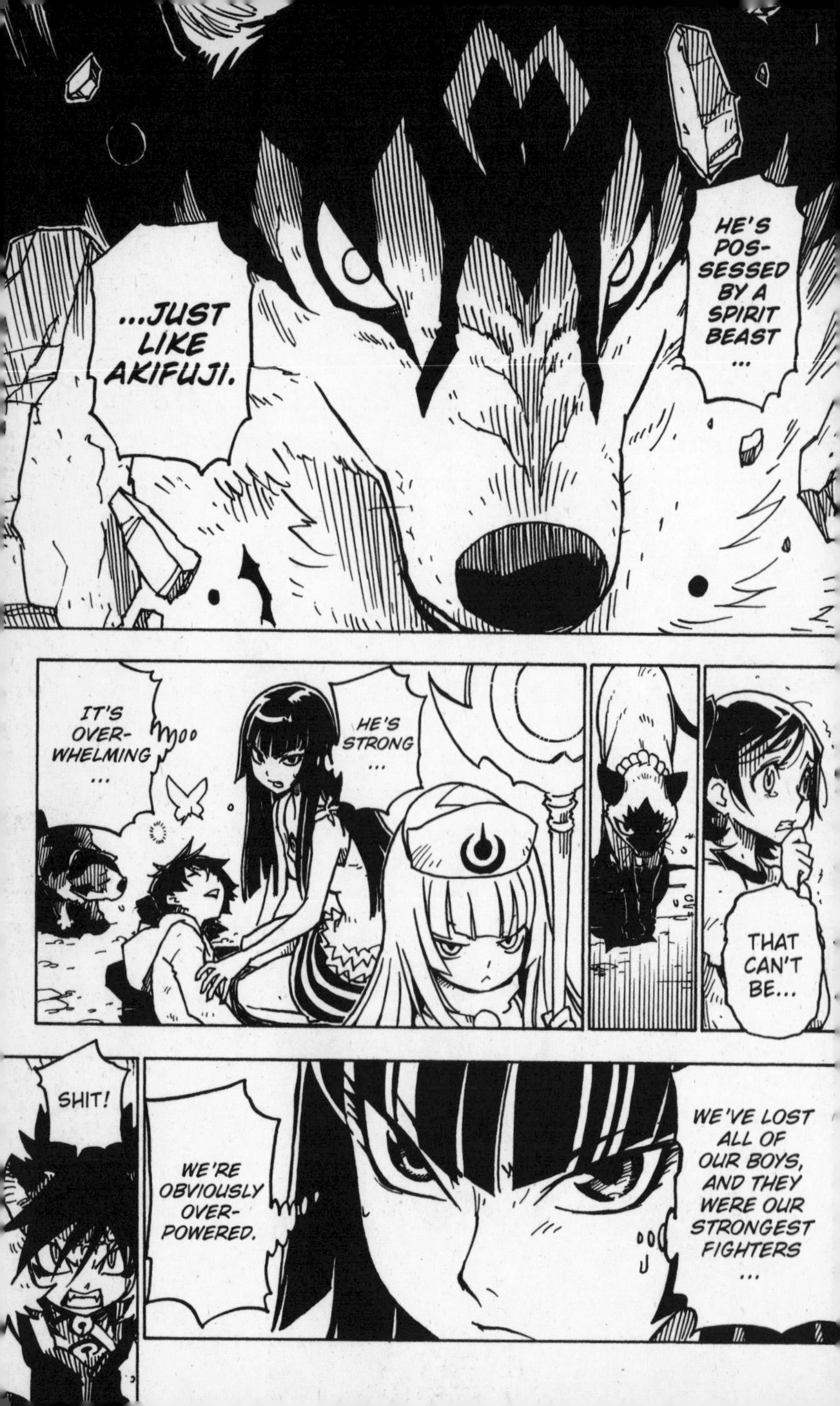
HE'S POS-SESSED BY A SPIRIT BEAST...
...JUST LIKE AKIFUJI.
THAT CAN'T BE...
HE'S STRONG...
IT'S OVER-WHELMING...
WE'VE LOST ALL OF OUR BOYS, AND THEY WERE OUR STRONGEST FIGHTERS...
WE'RE OBVIOUSLY OVER-POWERED.
SHIT!

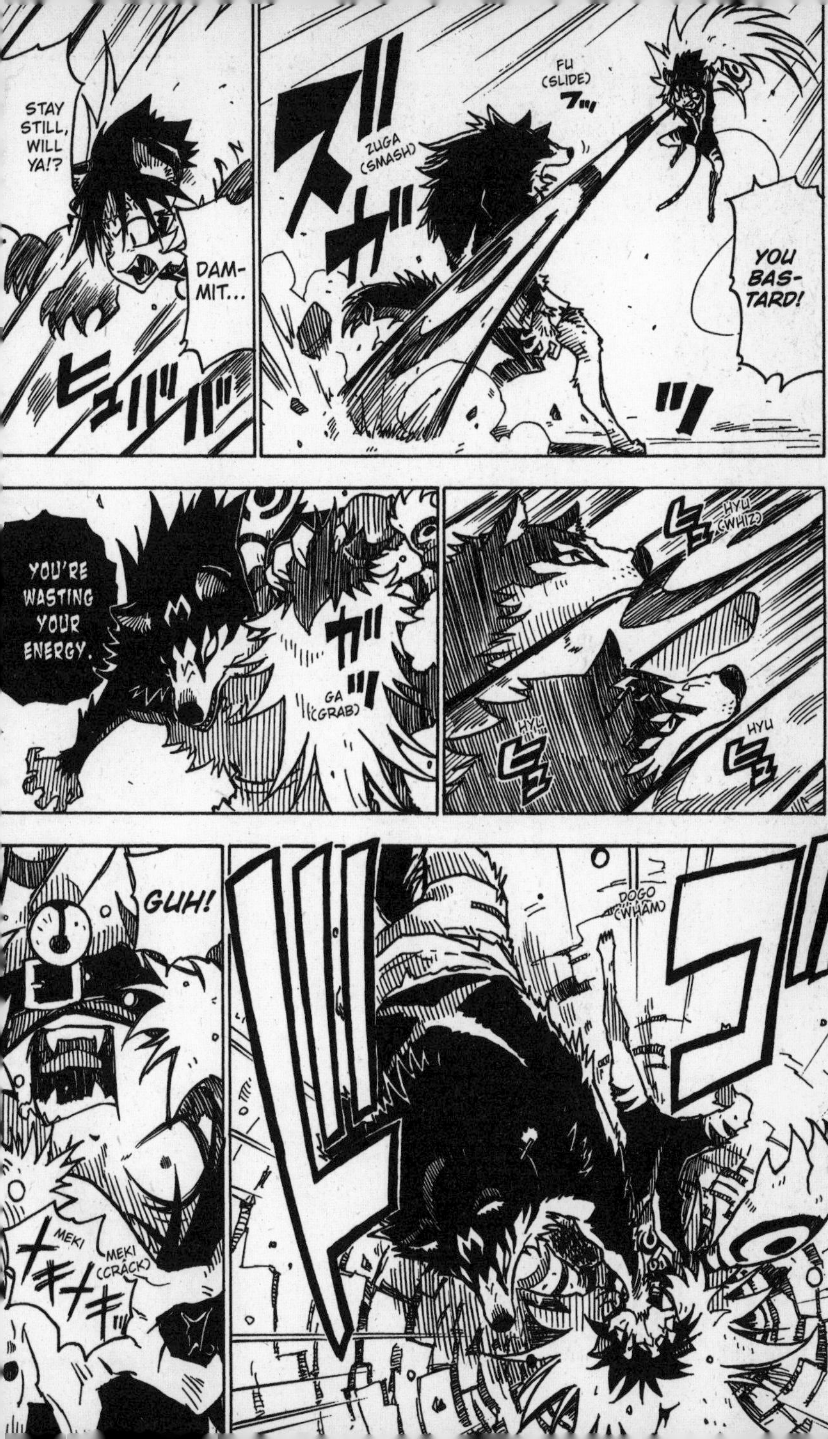
FU (SLIDE)
YOU BAS-TARD!
ZUGA (SMASH)
STAY STILL, WILL YA!?
DAM-MIT...
HYU (WHIZ)
HYU
HYU
GA (GRAB)
YOU'RE WASTING YOUR ENERGY.
DOGO (WHAM)
GUH!
MEKI
MEKI (CRACK)

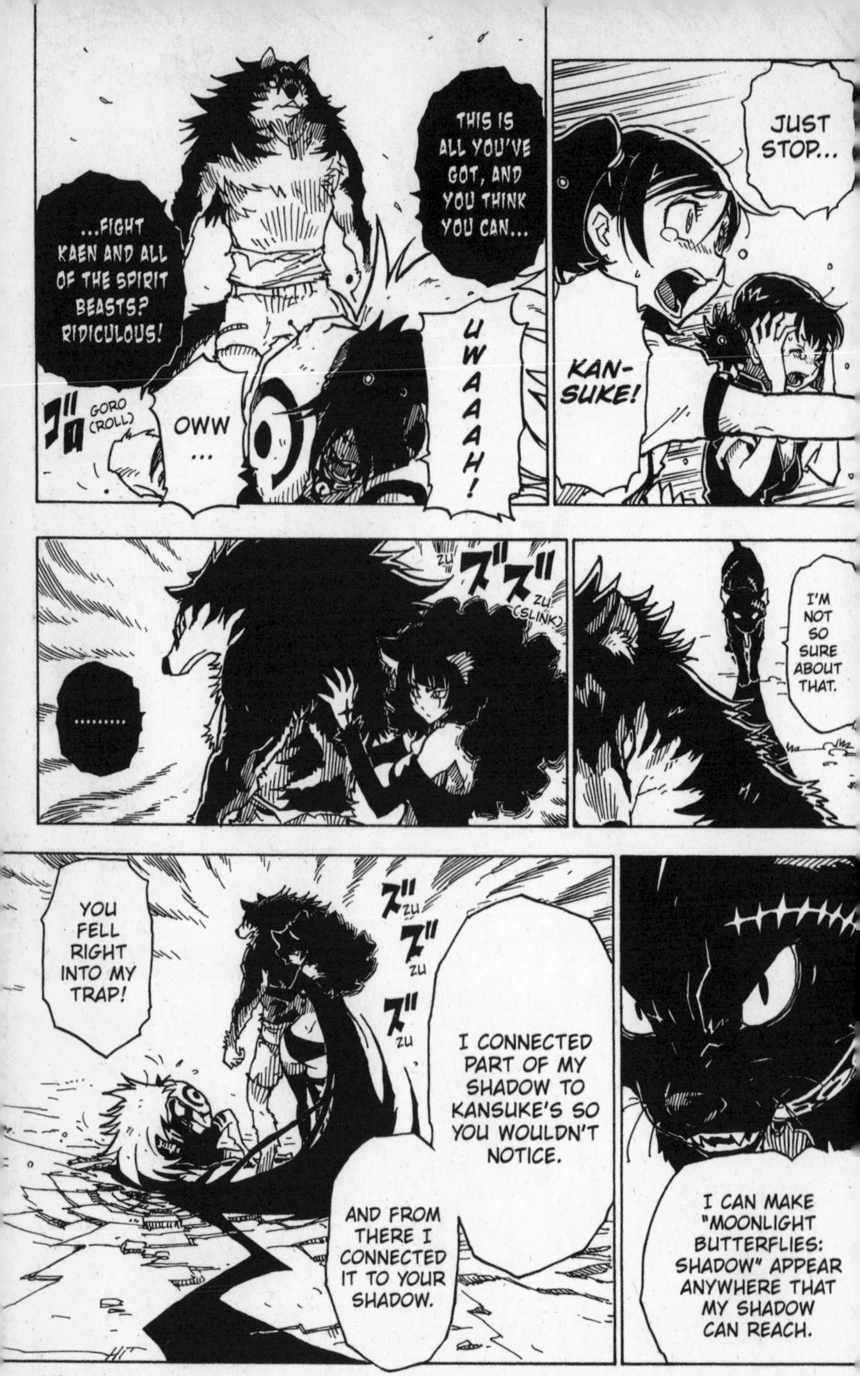
JUST STOP...
KAN-SUKE!
THIS IS ALL YOU'VE GOT, AND YOU THINK YOU CAN...
...FIGHT KAEN AND ALL OF THE SPIRIT BEASTS? RIDICULOUS!
UWAAAAH!
OWW ...
GORO (ROLL)
I'M NOT SO SURE ABOUT THAT.
ZU ZU (SLINK)
....
I CAN MAKE "MOONLIGHT BUTTERFLIES: SHADOW" APPEAR ANYWHERE THAT MY SHADOW CAN REACH.
YOU FELL RIGHT INTO MY TRAP!
ZU
ZU
ZU
I CONNECTED PART OF MY SHADOW TO KANSUKE'S SO YOU WOULDN'T NOTICE.
AND FROM THERE I CONNECTED IT TO YOUR SHADOW.

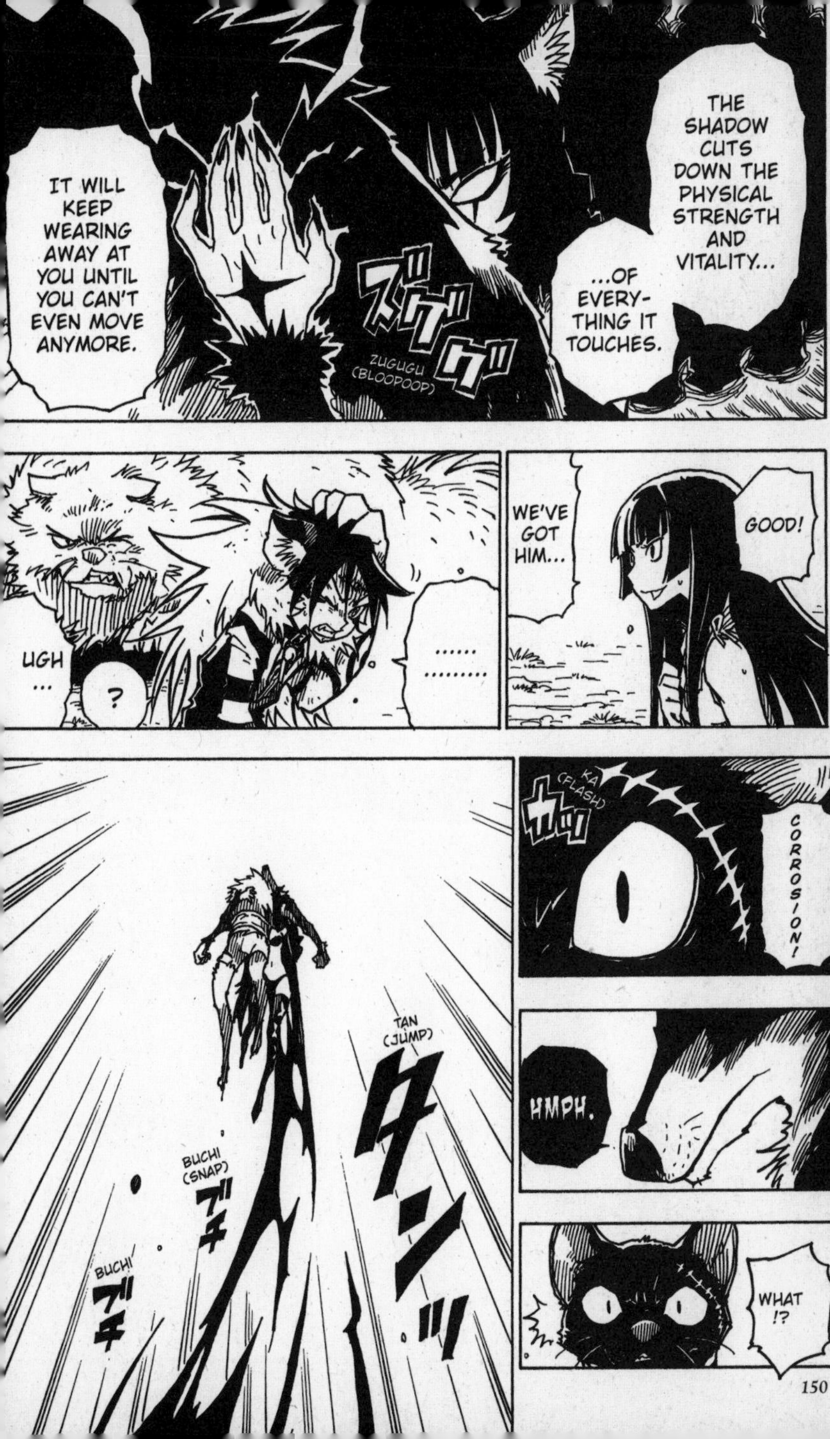
THE SHADOW CUTS DOWN THE PHYSICAL STRENGTH AND VITALITY...
...OF EVERYTHING IT TOUCHES.
ZUGUGU (BLOOPOOP)
IT WILL KEEP WEARING AWAY AT YOU UNTIL YOU CAN'T EVEN MOVE ANYMORE.
GOOD!
WE'VE GOT HIM...
......
....
UGH ...
?
KA (FLASH)
CORROSION!
HMPH.
WHAT !?
TAN (JUMP)
BUCHI (SNAP)
BUCHI

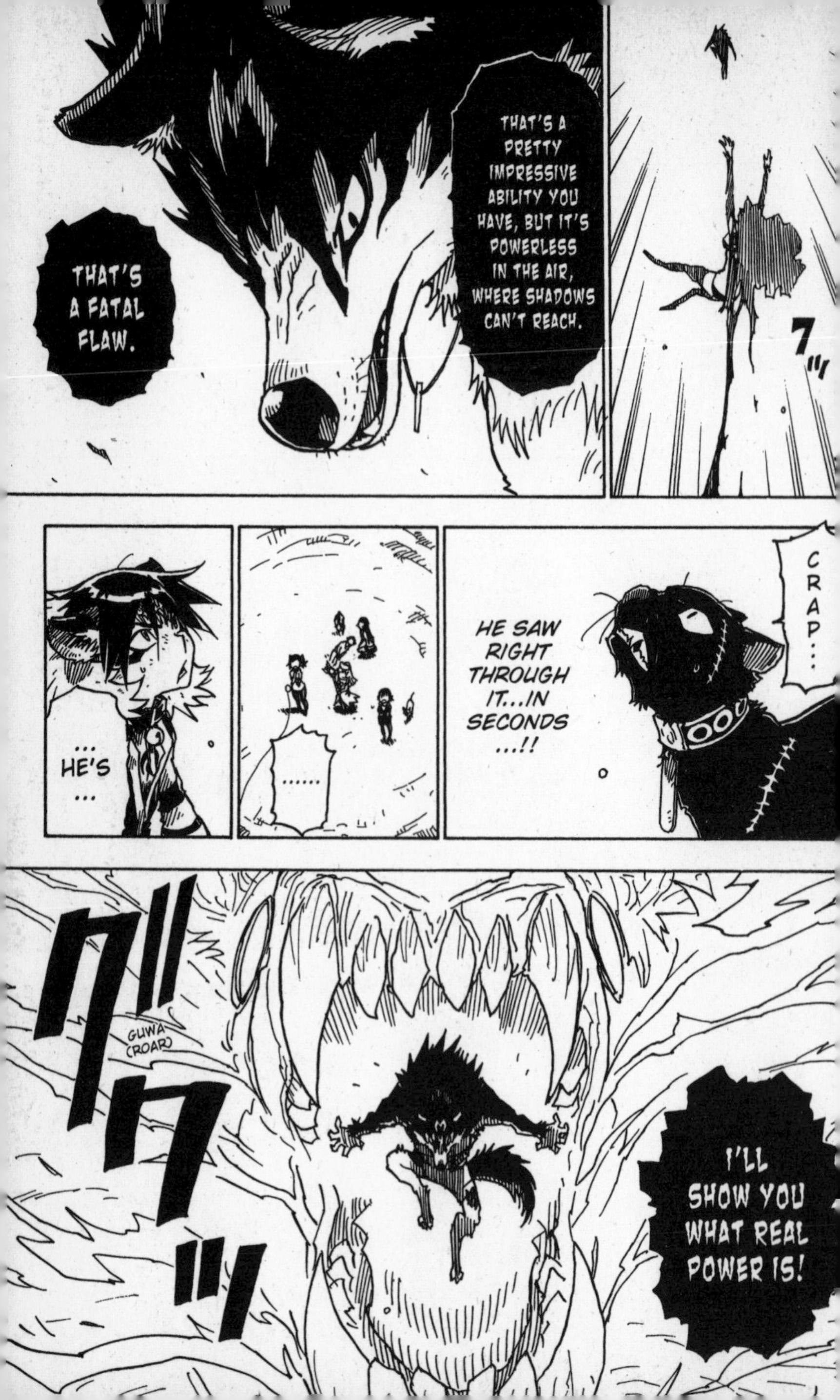
THAT'S A PRETTY IMPRESSIVE ABILITY YOU HAVE, BUT IT'S POWERLESS IN THE AIR, WHERE SHADOWS CAN'T REACH.
THAT'S A FATAL FLAW.
CRAP...
HE SAW RIGHT THROUGH IT...IN SECONDS...!!
......
...HE'S...
I'LL SHOW YOU WHAT REAL POWER IS!
GUWA (ROAR)

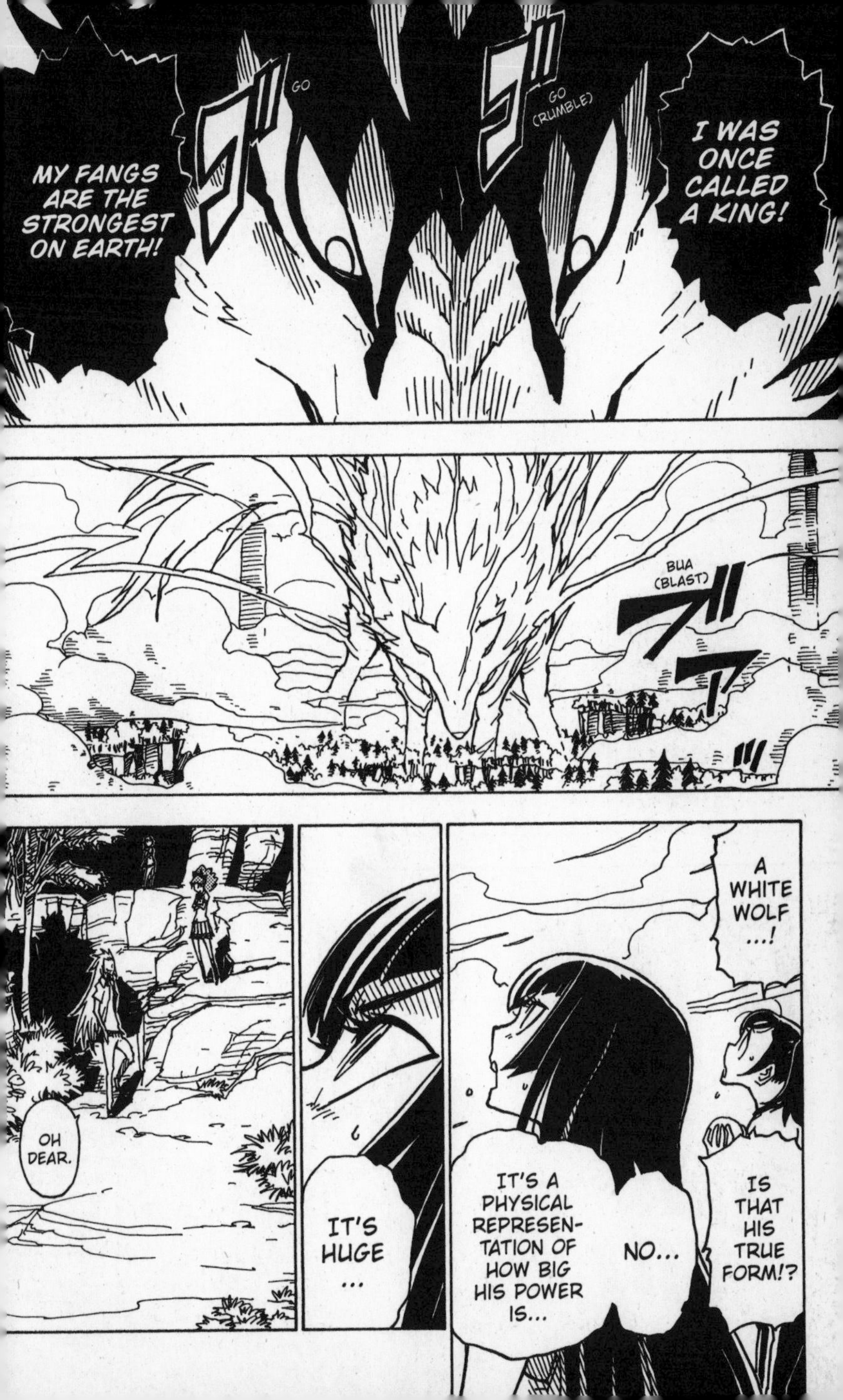
I WAS ONCE CALLED A KING!
ゴ
GO (RUMBLE)
ゴ
GO
MY FANGS ARE THE STRONGEST ON EARTH!
ブァ
BUA (BLAST)
A WHITE WOLF ...!
IS THAT HIS TRUE FORM!?
NO...
IT'S A PHYSICAL REPRESEN-TATION OF HOW BIG HIS POWER IS...
IT'S HUGE ...
OH DEAR.

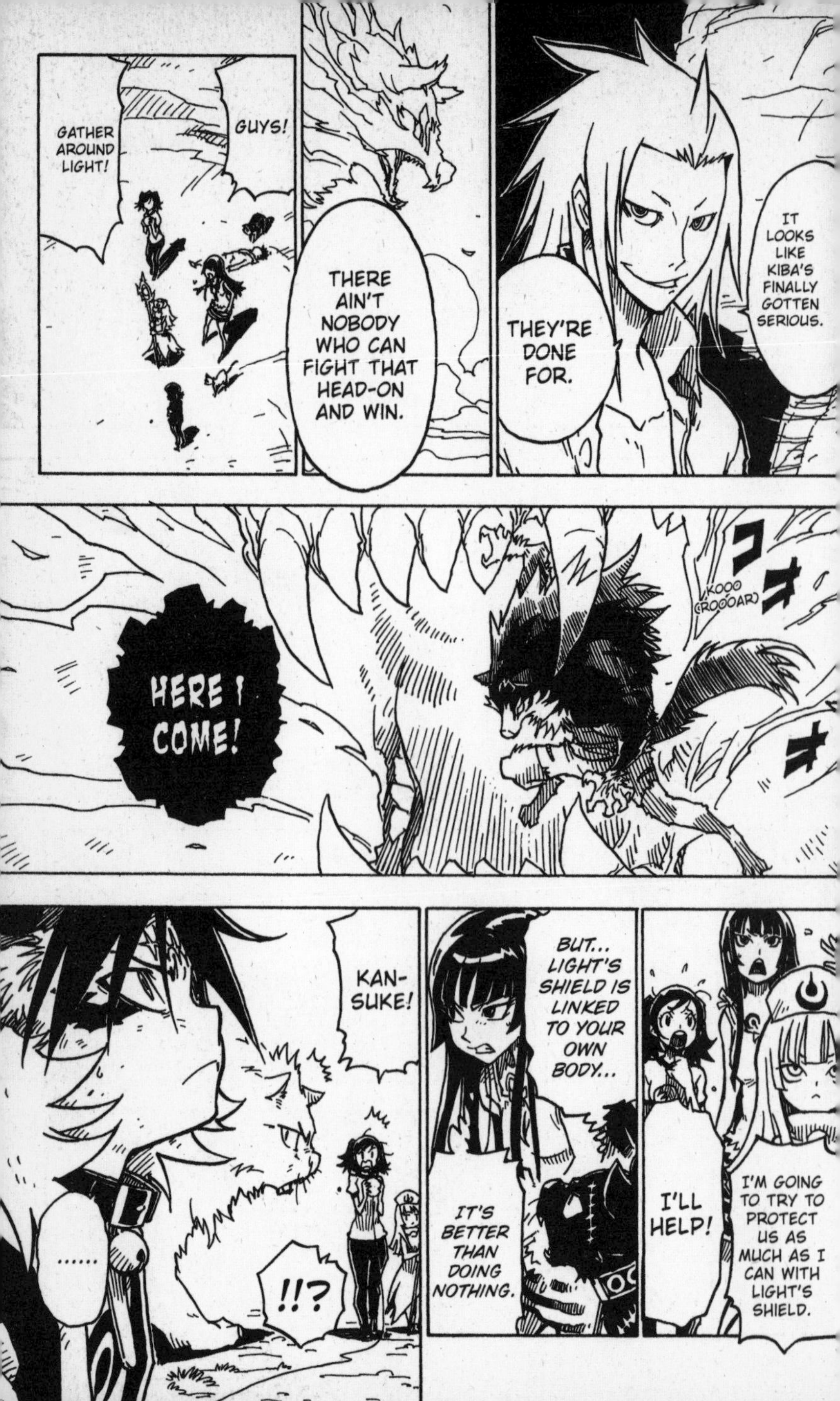
IT LOOKS LIKE KIBA'S FINALLY GOTTEN SERIOUS.
THEY'RE DONE FOR.
THERE AIN'T NOBODY WHO CAN FIGHT THAT HEAD-ON AND WIN.
GUYS!
GATHER AROUND LIGHT!
コオオ
KOOO (ROOOAR)
HERE I COME!
I'M GOING TO TRY TO PROTECT US AS MUCH AS I CAN WITH LIGHT'S SHIELD.
I'LL HELP!
BUT... LIGHT'S SHIELD IS LINKED TO YOUR OWN BODY...
IT'S BETTER THAN DOING NOTHING.
KAN-SUKE!
!!?
......

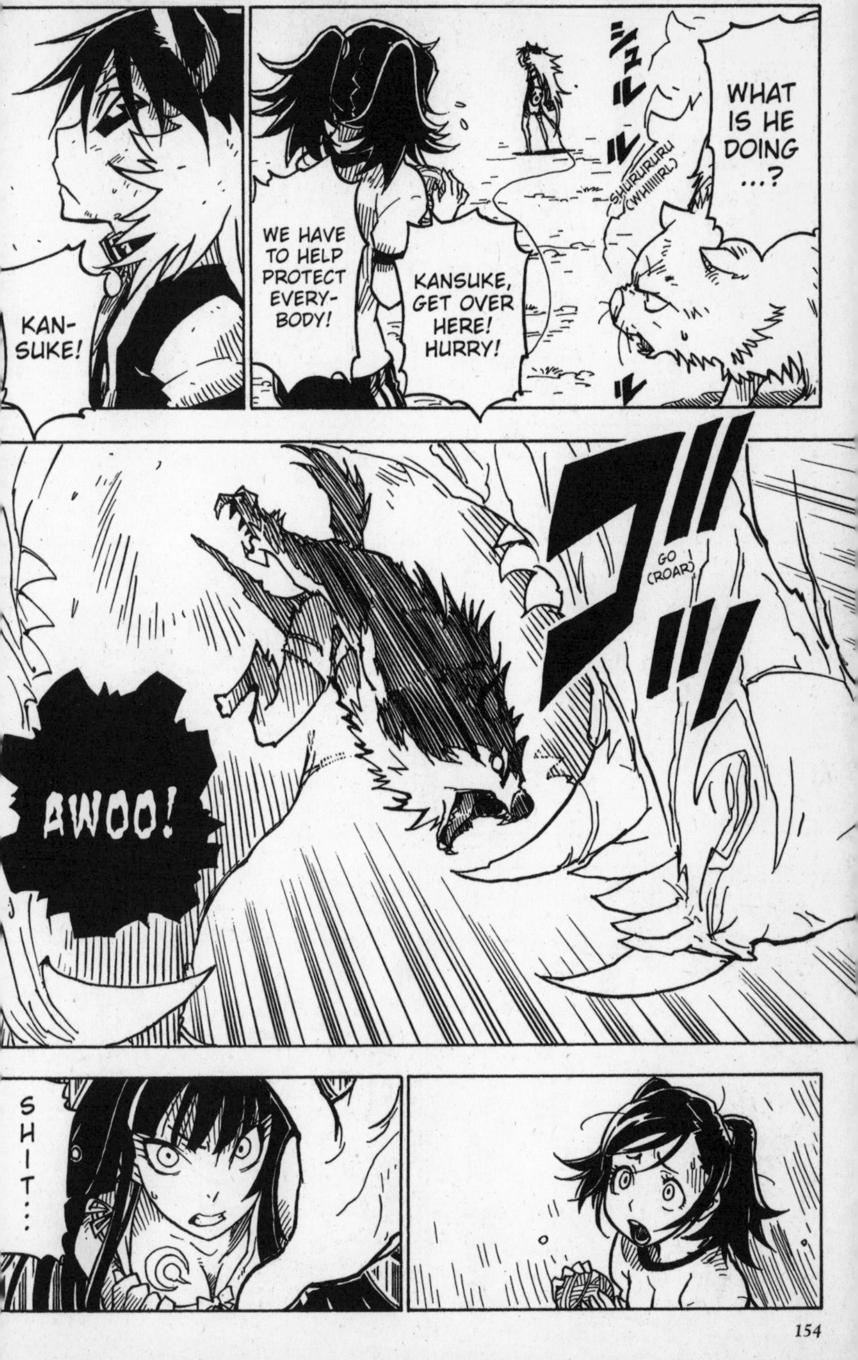
WHAT IS HE DOING ...?
SHURURURU (WHIIIIIRL)
KANSUKE, GET OVER HERE! HURRY!
WE HAVE TO HELP PROTECT EVERY-BODY!
KAN-SUKE!
GO (ROAR)
AWOO!
SHIT...

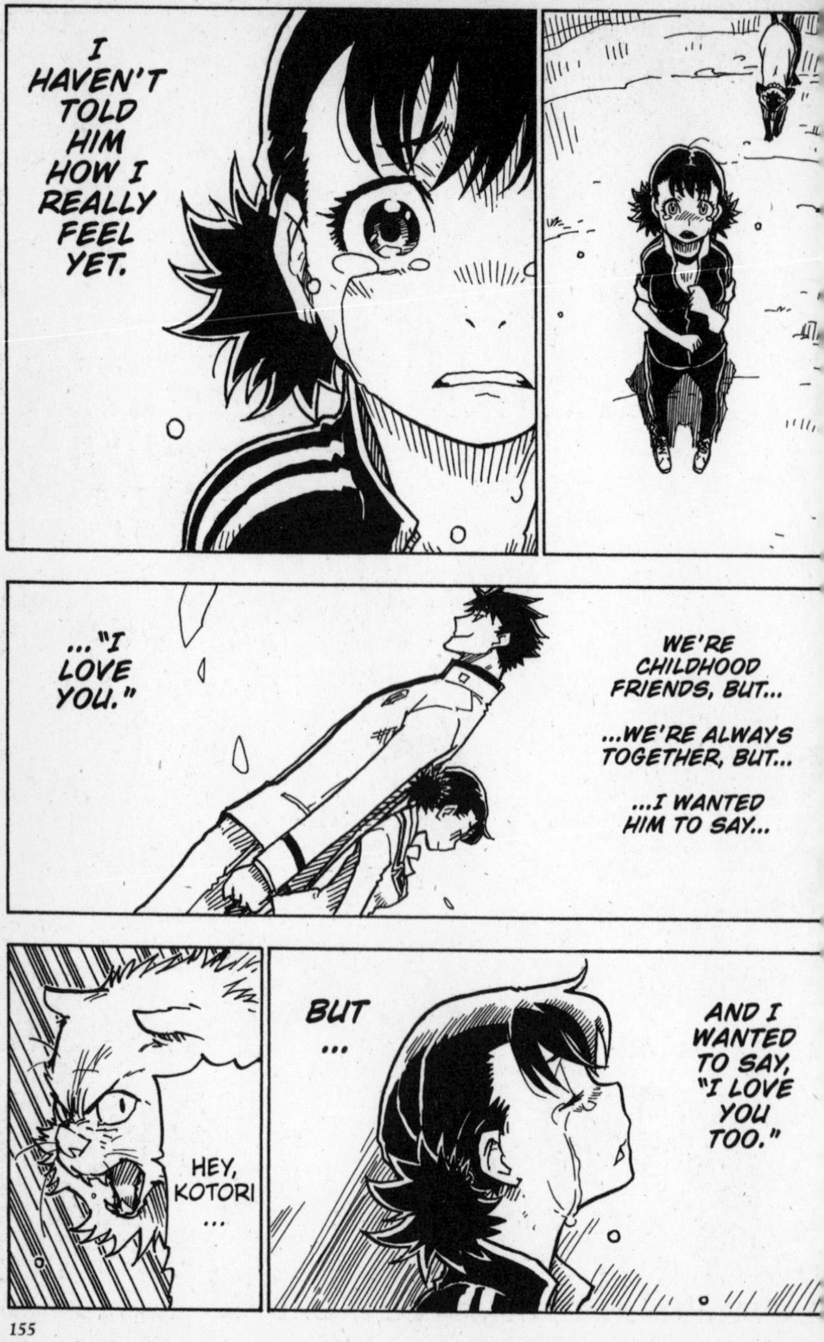
I HAVEN'T TOLD HIM HOW I REALLY FEEL YET.
WE'RE CHILDHOOD FRIENDS, BUT...
...WE'RE ALWAYS TOGETHER, BUT...
...I WANTED HIM TO SAY...
..."I LOVE YOU."
AND I WANTED TO SAY, "I LOVE YOU TOO."
BUT ...
HEY, KOTORI ...

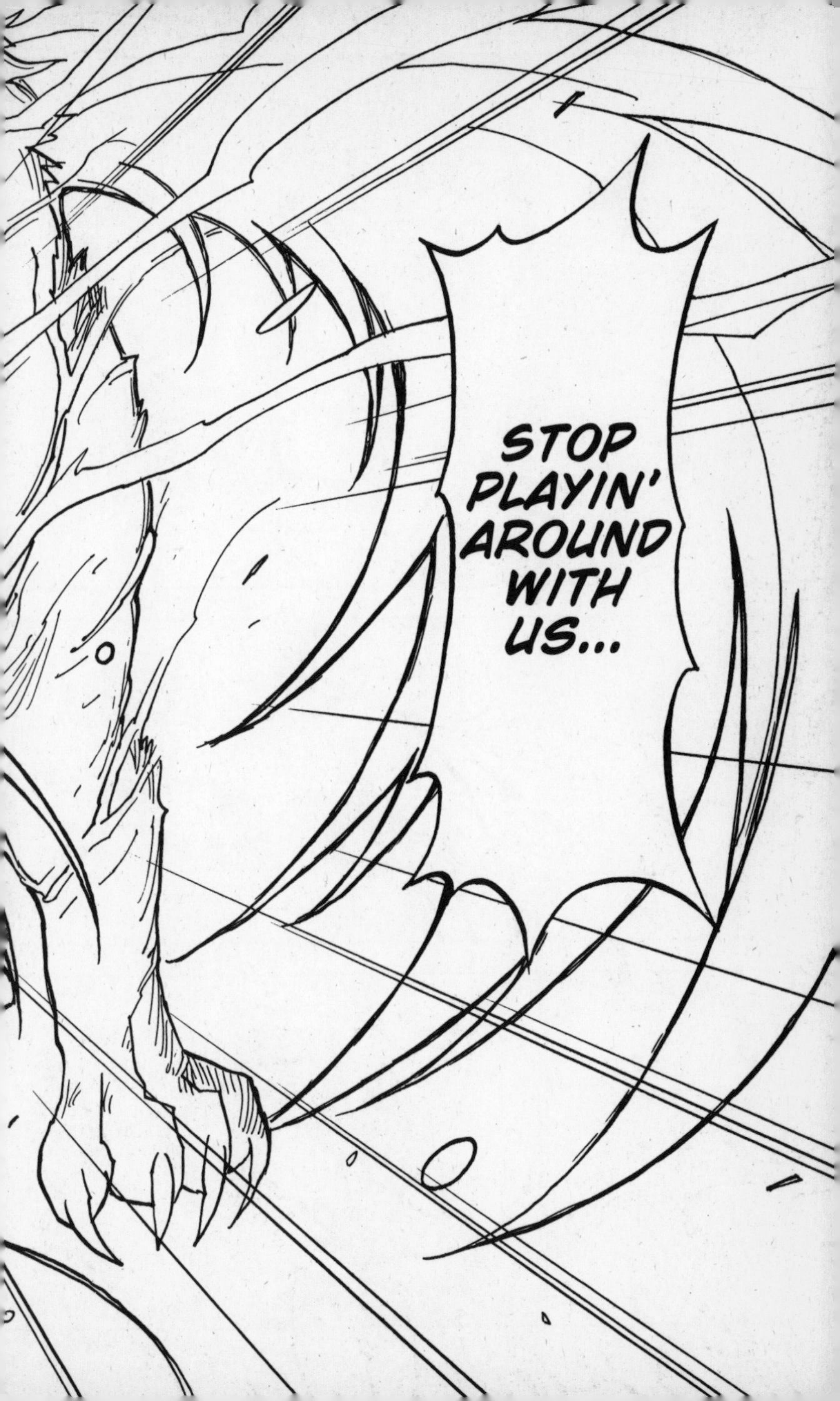
STOP PLAYIN' AROUND WITH US...

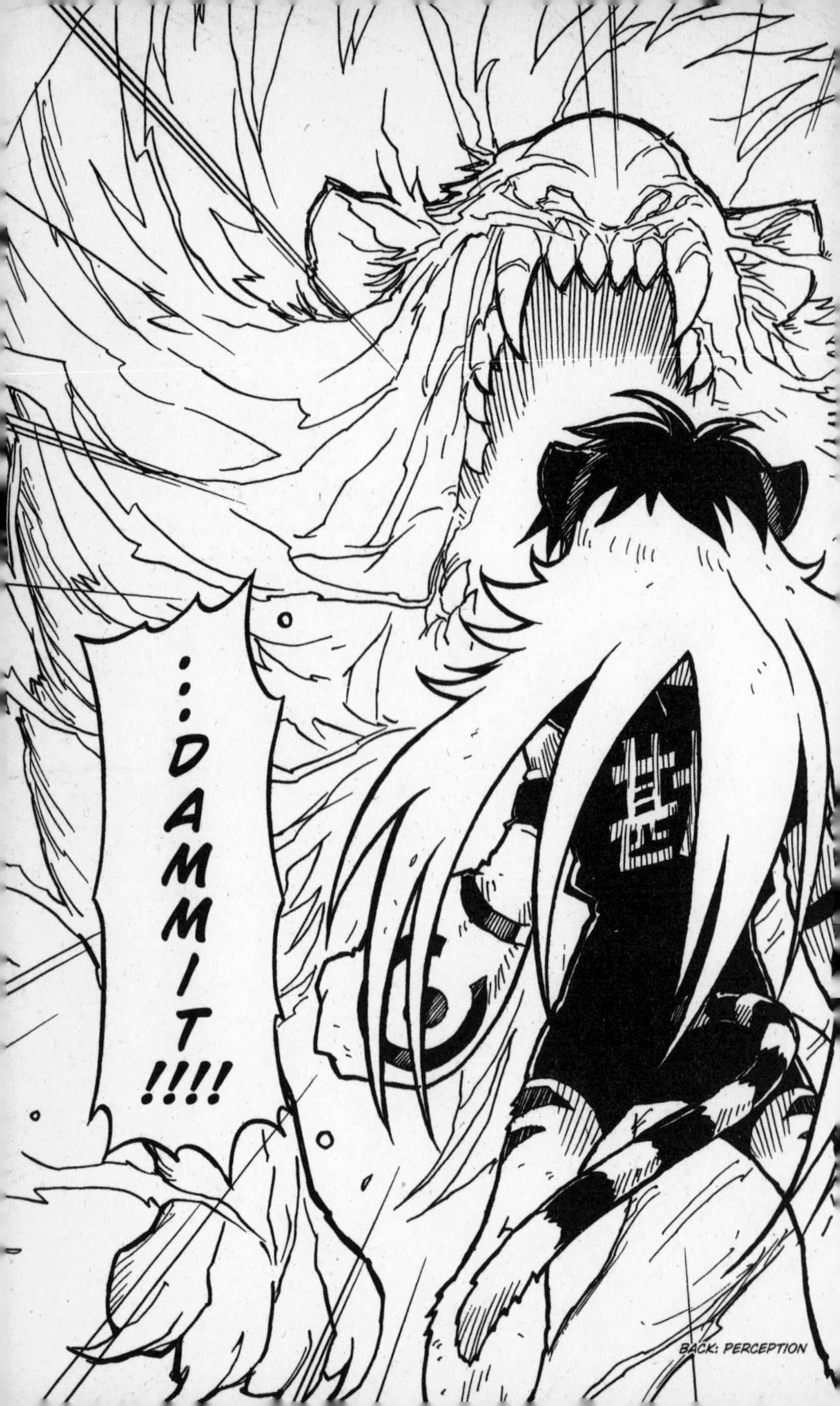
...DAMMIT!!!!
BACK: PERCEPTION

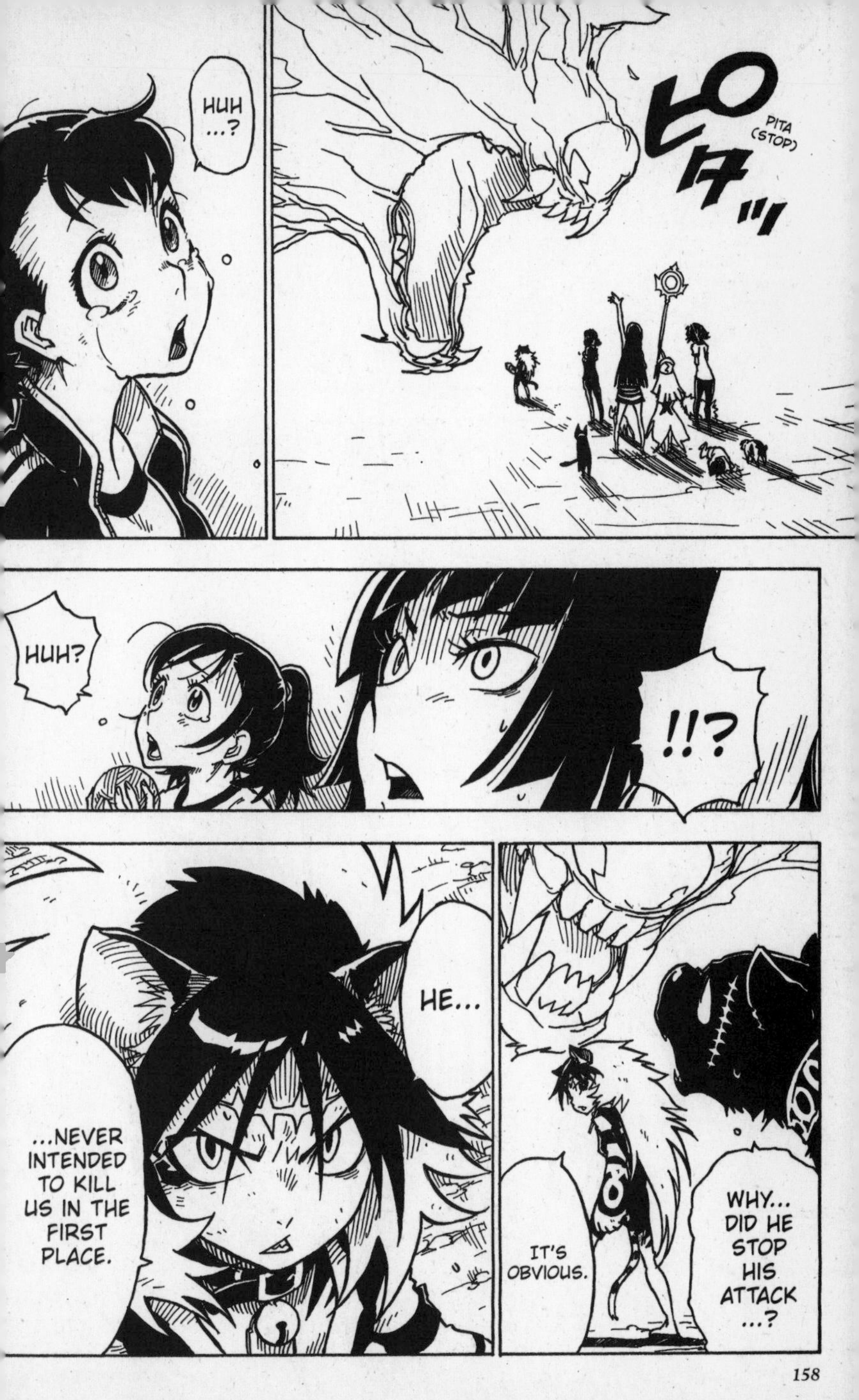
ピタッ
PITA (STOP)
HUH ...?
!!?
HUH?
WHY... DID HE STOP HIS ATTACK ...?
IT'S OBVIOUS.
HE...
...NEVER INTENDED TO KILL US IN THE FIRST PLACE.

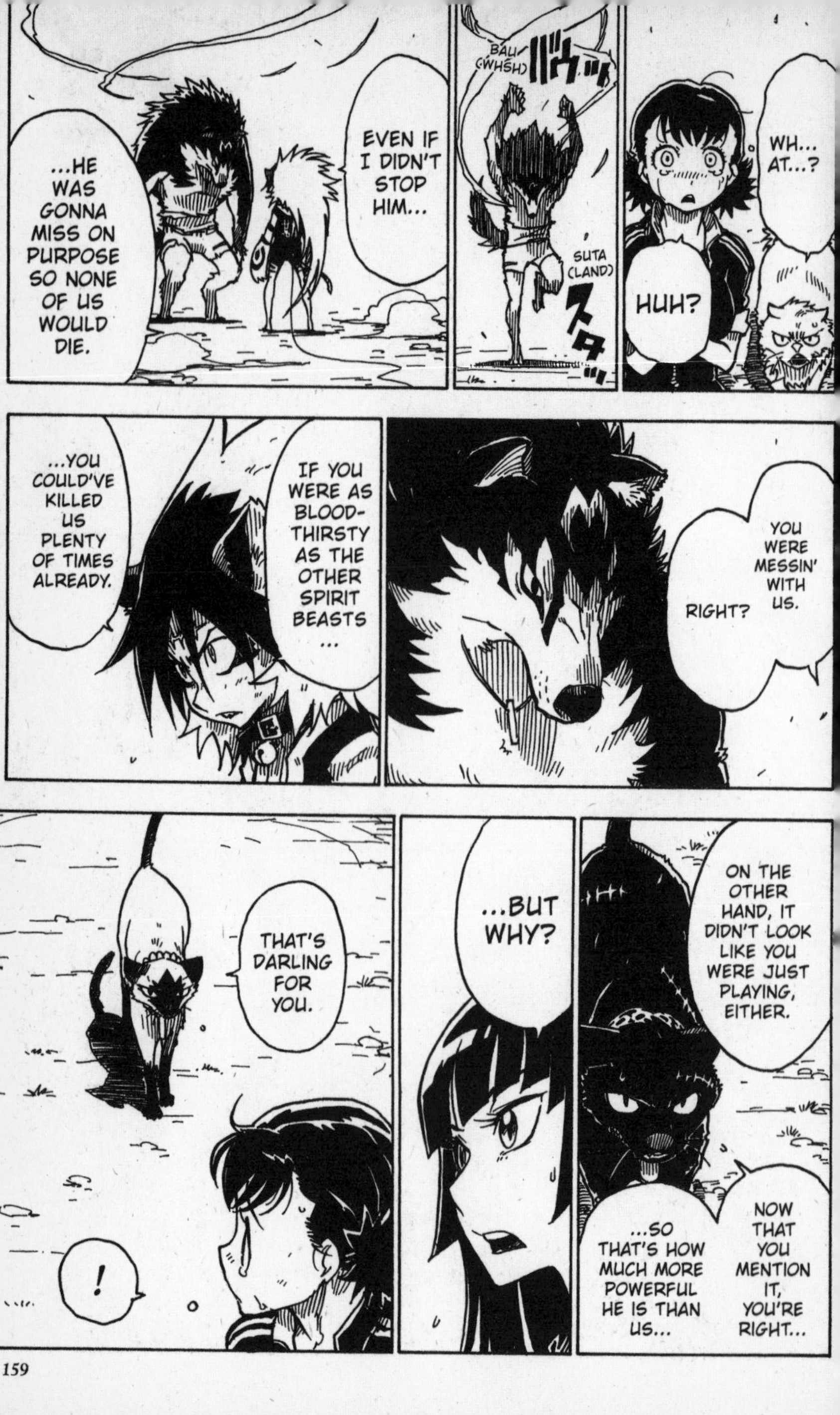
WH... AT...?
HUH?
BAU (WHSH)
SUTA (LAND)
EVEN IF I DIDN'T STOP HIM...
...HE WAS GONNA MISS ON PURPOSE SO NONE OF US WOULD DIE.
YOU WERE MESSIN' WITH US.
RIGHT?
IF YOU WERE AS BLOOD-THIRSTY AS THE OTHER SPIRIT BEASTS...
...YOU COULD'VE KILLED US PLENTY OF TIMES ALREADY.
ON THE OTHER HAND, IT DIDN'T LOOK LIKE YOU WERE JUST PLAYING, EITHER.
NOW THAT YOU MENTION IT, YOU'RE RIGHT...
...SO THAT'S HOW MUCH MORE POWERFUL HE IS THAN US...
...BUT WHY?
THAT'S DARLING FOR YOU.
!

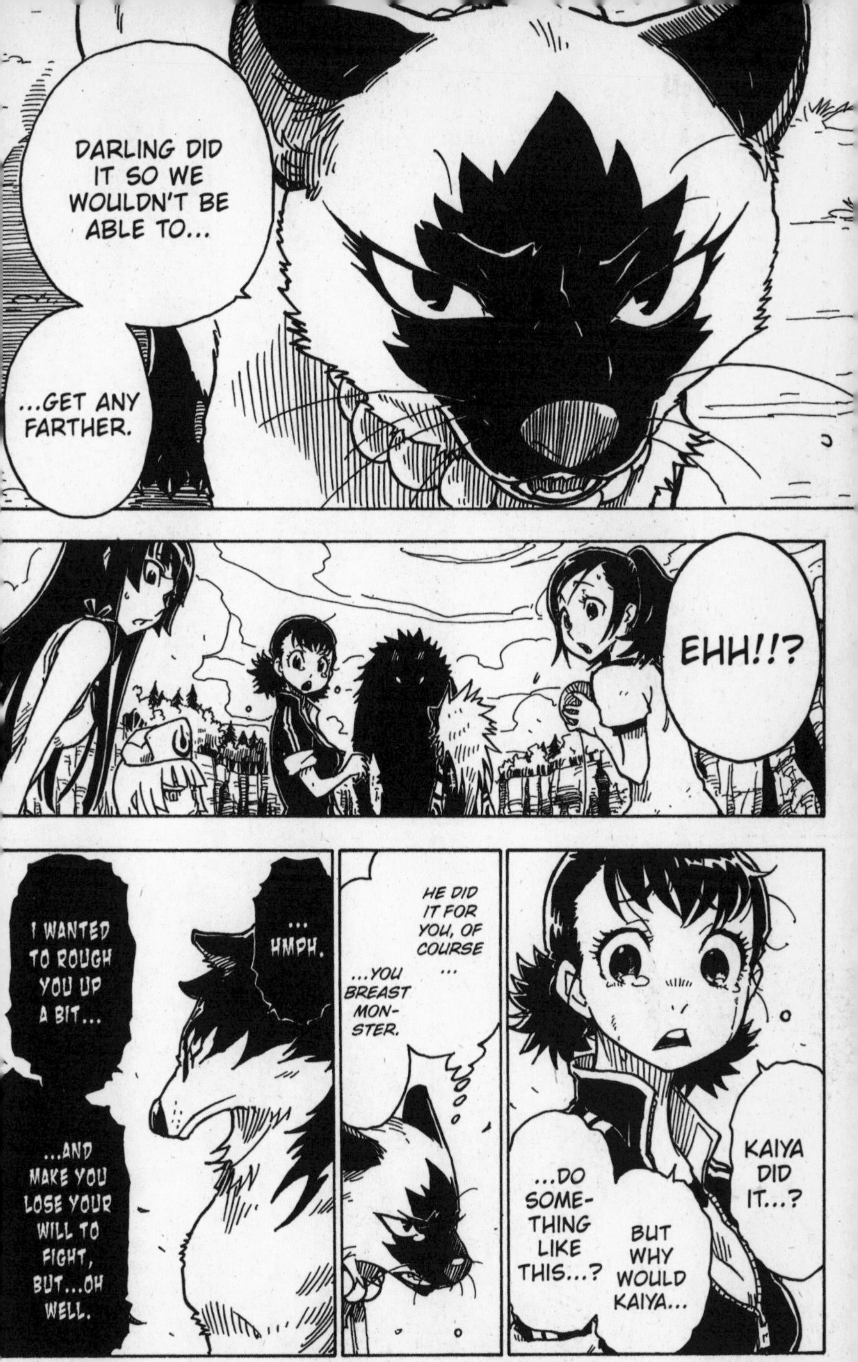
DARLING DID IT SO WE WOULDN'T BE ABLE TO...
...GET ANY FARTHER.
EHH!!?
KAIYA DID IT...?
BUT WHY WOULD KAIYA...
...DO SOMETHING LIKE THIS...?
HE DID IT FOR YOU, OF COURSE...
...YOU BREAST MONSTER.
...HMPH.
I WANTED TO ROUGH YOU UP A BIT...
...AND MAKE YOU LOSE YOUR WILL TO FIGHT, BUT...OH WELL.

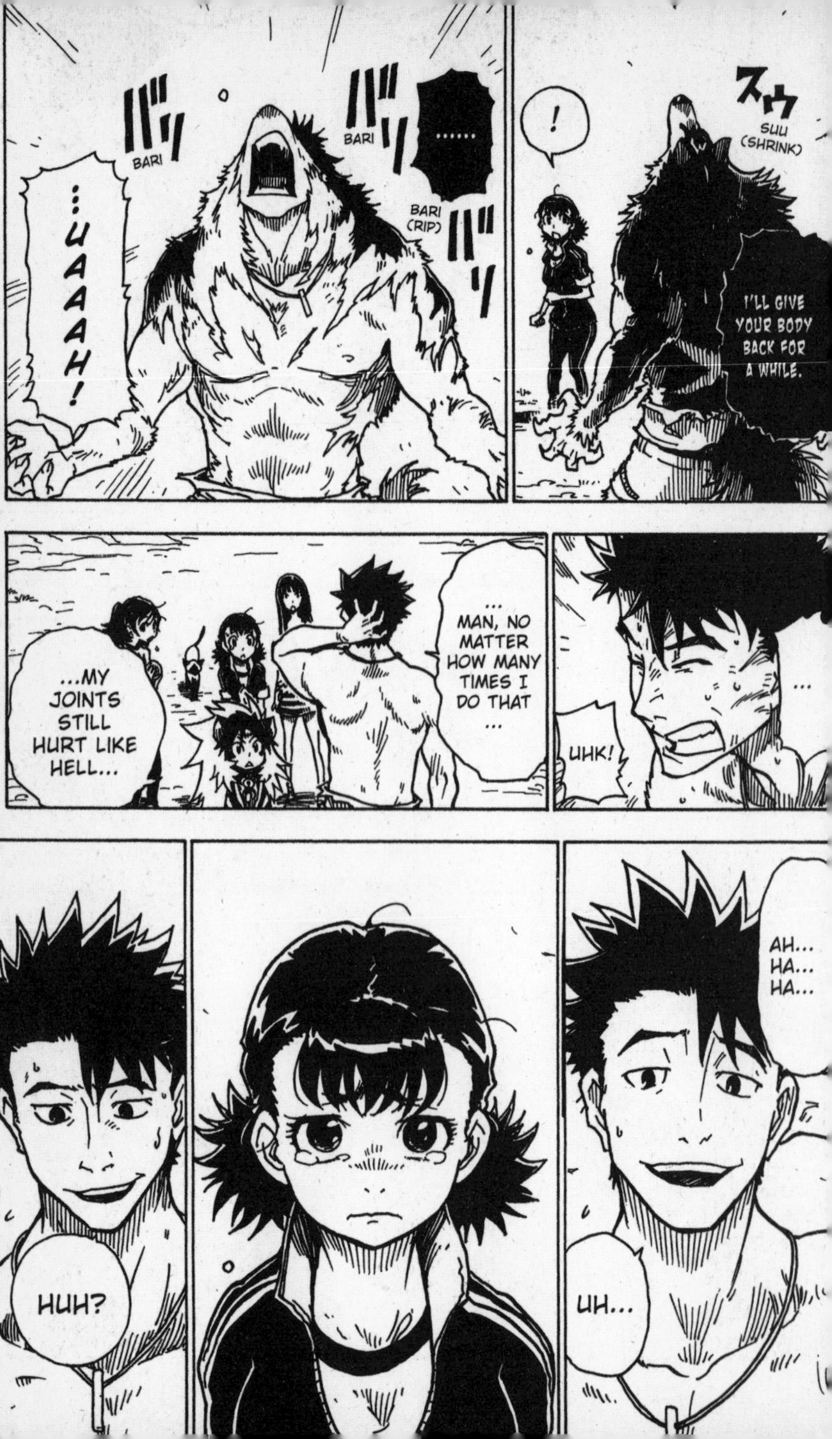
スウ
SUU (SHRINK)
!
I'LL GIVE YOUR BODY BACK FOR A WHILE.
......
バリ
BARI
バリ
BARI (RIP)
バリ
BARI
...UAAAAH!
...
UHK!
... MAN, NO MATTER HOW MANY TIMES I DO THAT ...
...MY JOINTS STILL HURT LIKE HELL...
AH... HA... HA...
UH...
HUH?

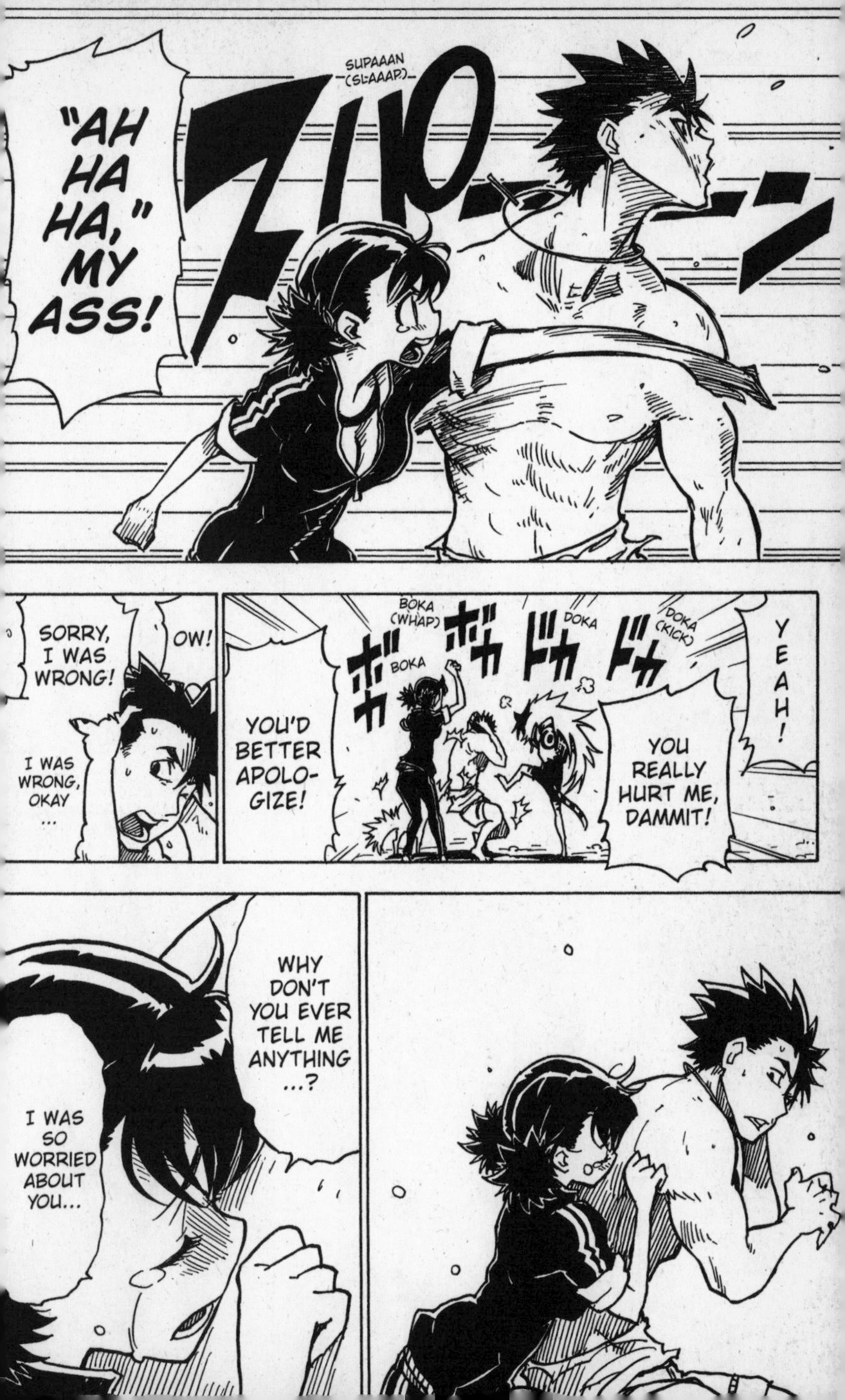
SUPAAAN (SLAAAP)
"AH HA HA," MY ASS!
YEAH!
DOKA (KICK)
DOKA
YOU REALLY HURT ME, DAMMIT!
BOKA (WHAP)
BOKA
YOU'D BETTER APOLOGIZE!
OW!
SORRY, I WAS WRONG!
I WAS WRONG, OKAY...
WHY DON'T YOU EVER TELL ME ANYTHING...?
I WAS SO WORRIED ABOUT YOU...

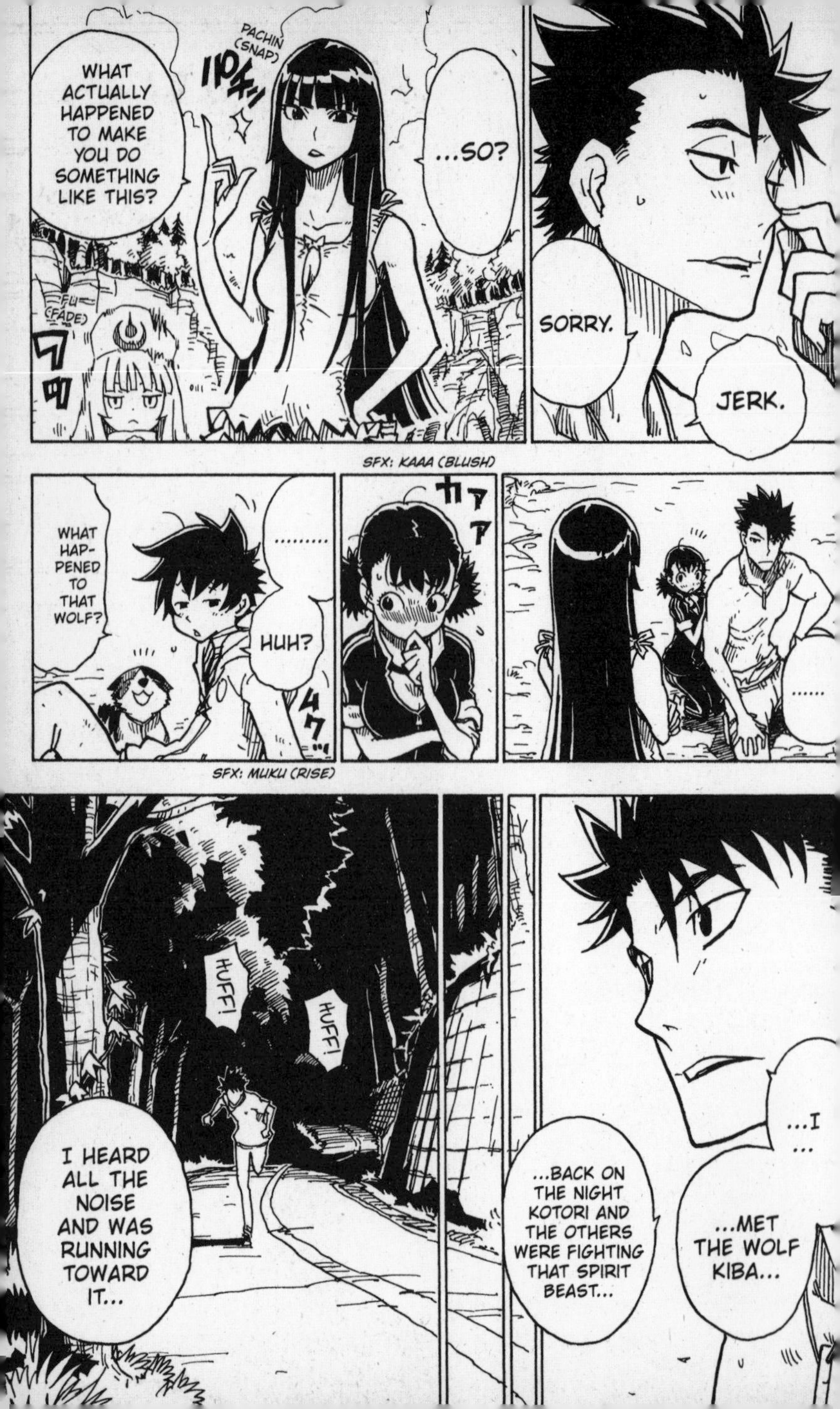
SORRY.
JERK.
...SO?
PACHIN (SNAP)
WHAT ACTUALLY HAPPENED TO MAKE YOU DO SOMETHING LIKE THIS?
FU (FADE)
SFX: KAAA (BLUSH)
......
....
HUH?
WHAT HAP-PENED TO THAT WOLF?
SFX: MUKU (RISE)
...I ...
...MET THE WOLF KIBA...
...BACK ON THE NIGHT KOTORI AND THE OTHERS WERE FIGHTING THAT SPIRIT BEAST...
HUFF!
HUFF!
I HEARD ALL THE NOISE AND WAS RUNNING TOWARD IT...

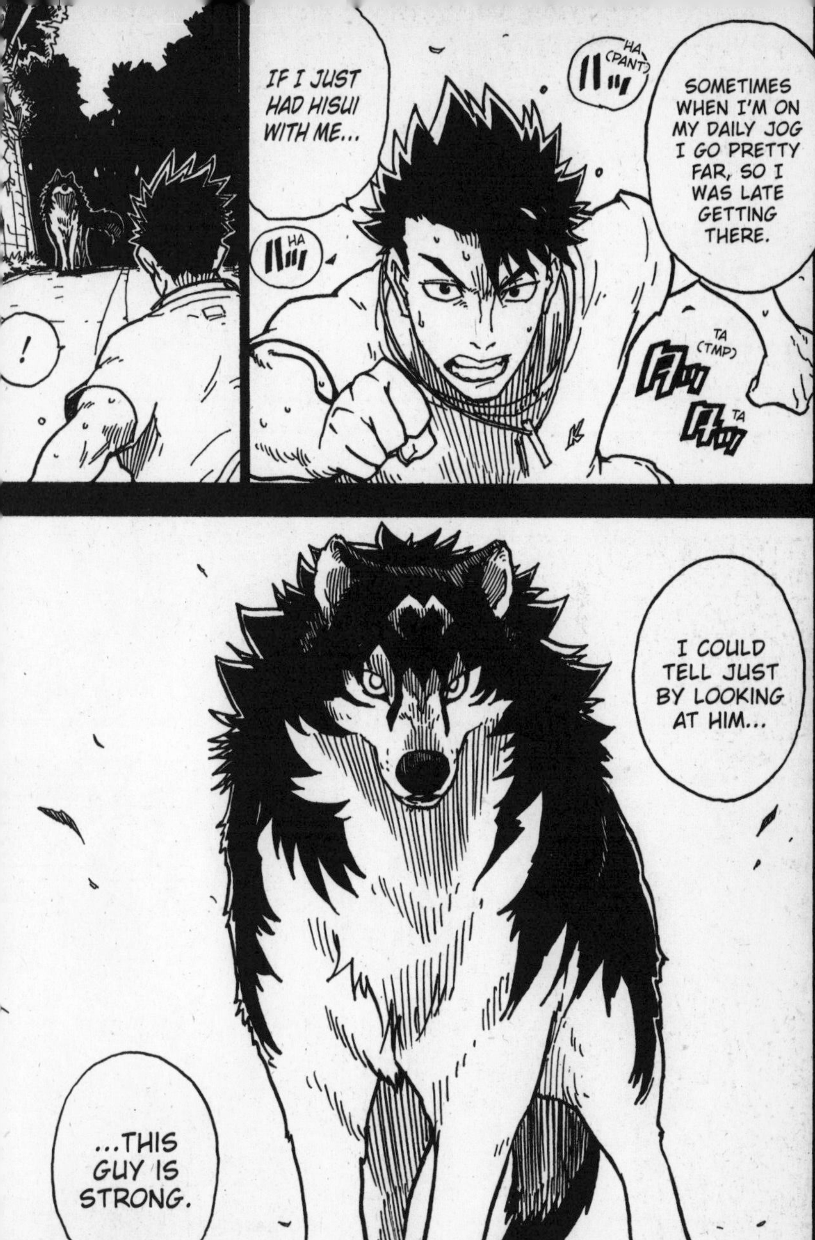
SOMETIMES WHEN I'M ON MY DAILY JOG I GO PRETTY FAR, SO I WAS LATE GETTING THERE.
HA (PANT)
IF I JUST HAD HISUI WITH ME...
HA
TA (TMP)
TA
!
I COULD TELL JUST BY LOOKING AT HIM...
...THIS GUY IS STRONG.

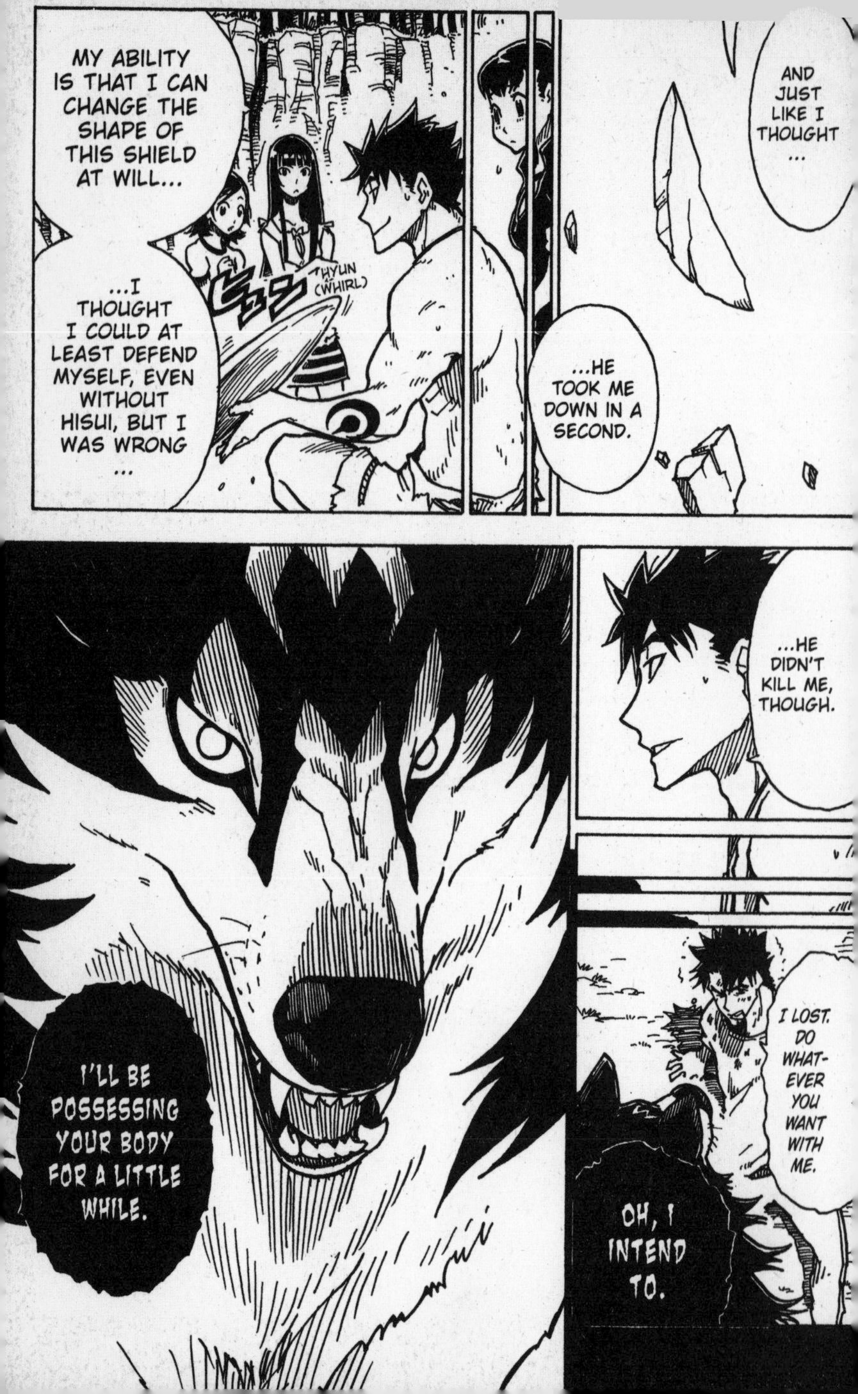
AND JUST LIKE I THOUGHT ...
...HE TOOK ME DOWN IN A SECOND.
MY ABILITY IS THAT I CAN CHANGE THE SHAPE OF THIS SHIELD AT WILL...
HYUN (WHIRL)
...I THOUGHT I COULD AT LEAST DEFEND MYSELF, EVEN WITHOUT HISUI, BUT I WAS WRONG ...
...HE DIDN'T KILL ME, THOUGH.
I LOST. DO WHAT-EVER YOU WANT WITH ME.
OH, I INTEND TO.
I'LL BE POSSESSING YOUR BODY FOR A LITTLE WHILE.

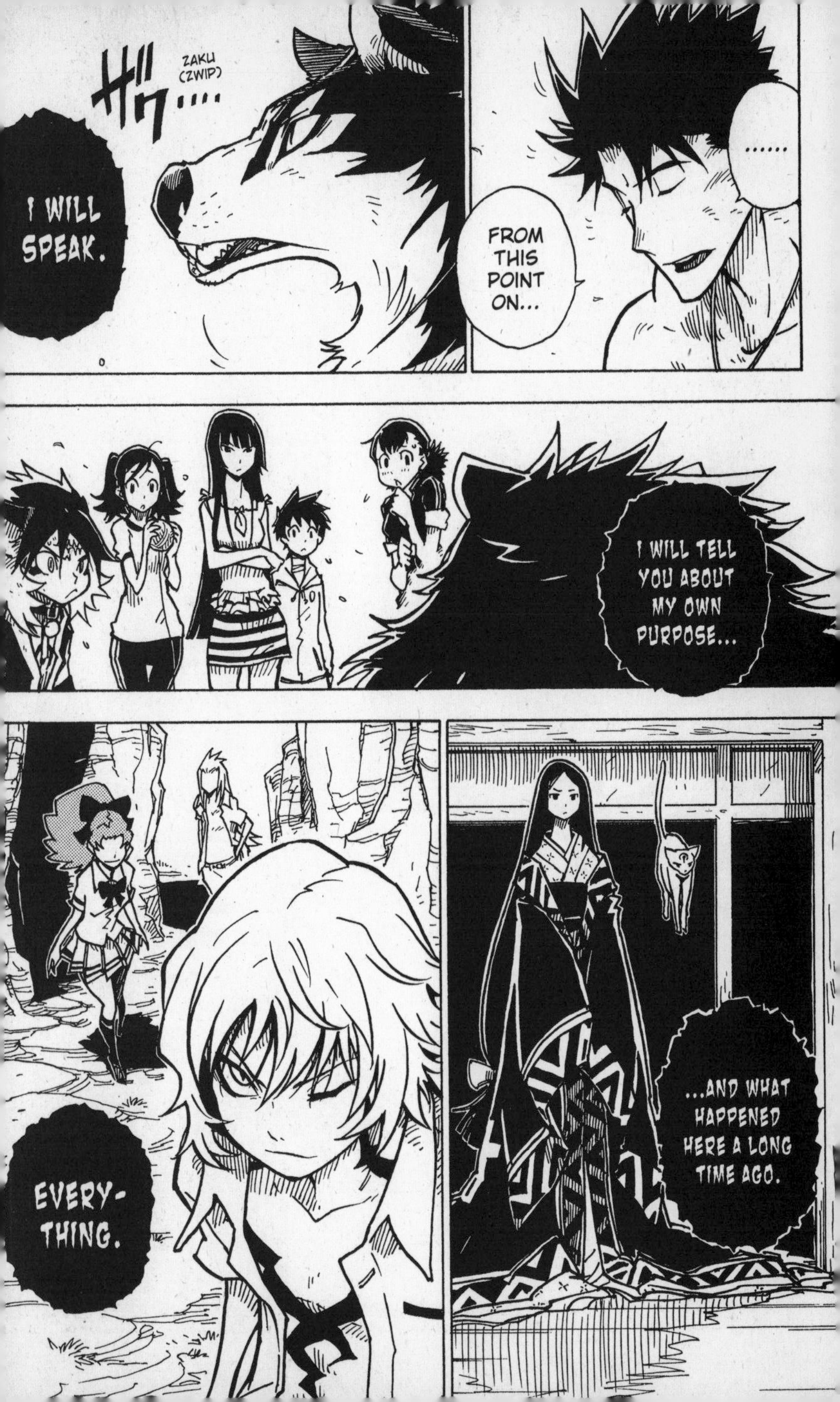
......
FROM THIS POINT ON...
ザク....
ZAKU (ZWIP)
I WILL SPEAK.
I WILL TELL YOU ABOUT MY OWN PURPOSE...
...AND WHAT HAPPENED HERE A LONG TIME AGO.
EVERY-THING.

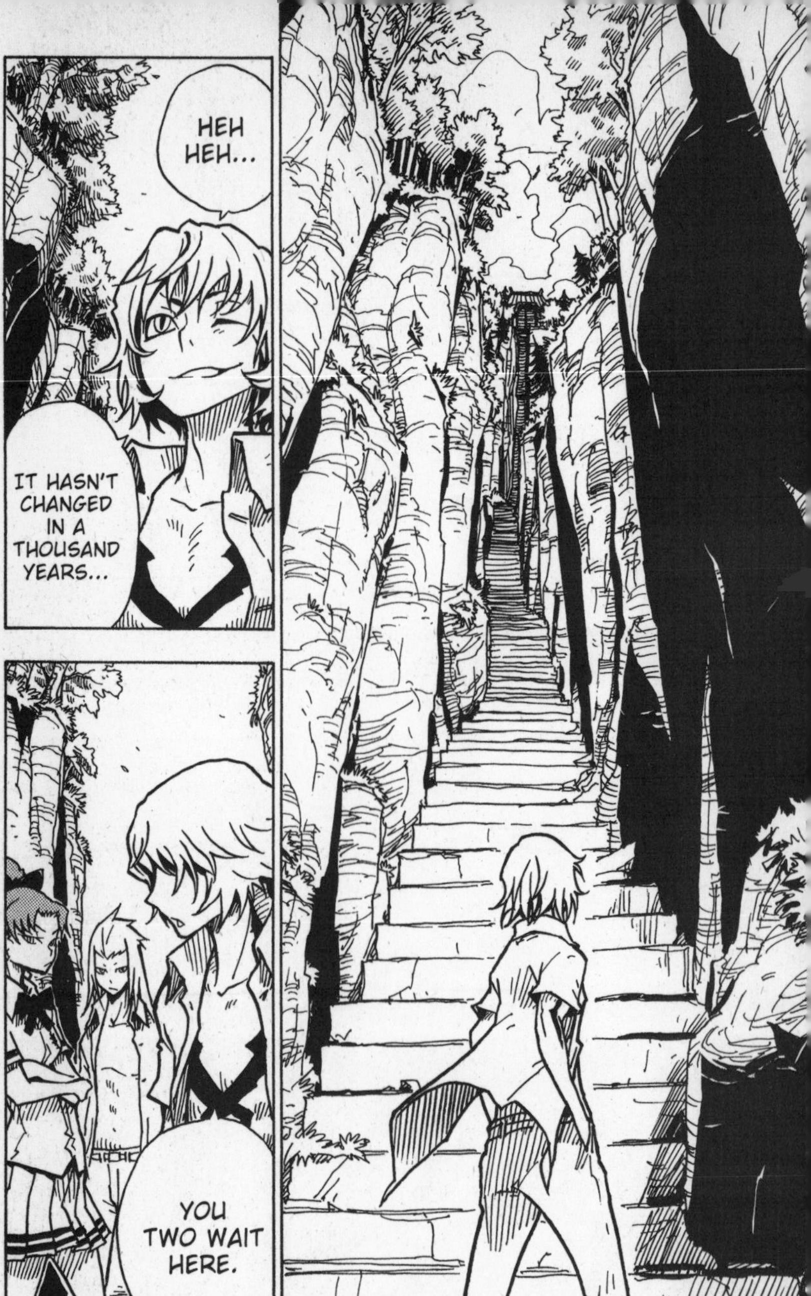
HEH HEH...
IT HASN'T CHANGED IN A THOUSAND YEARS...
YOU TWO WAIT HERE.

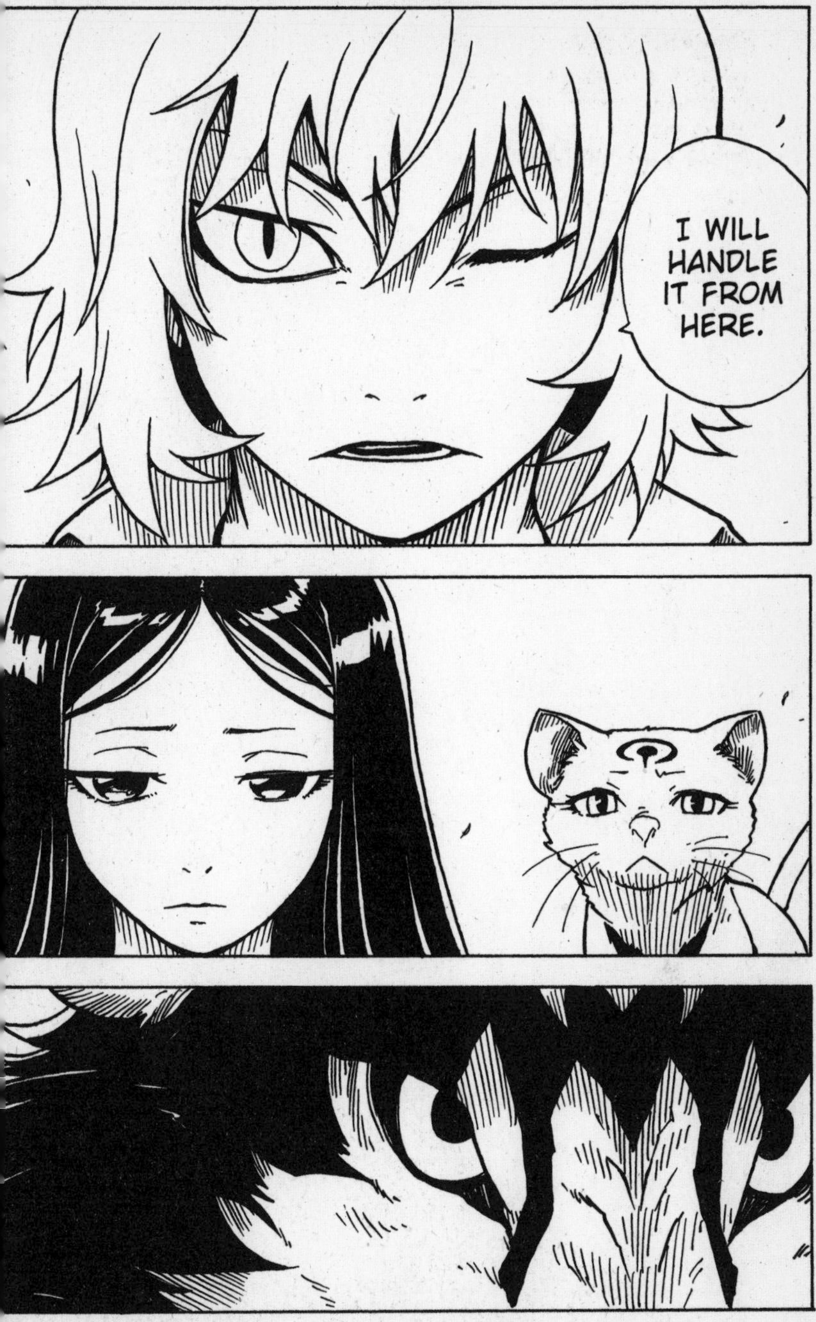
I WILL HANDLE IT FROM HERE.

CHAPTER 23
TALE OF LONG AGO

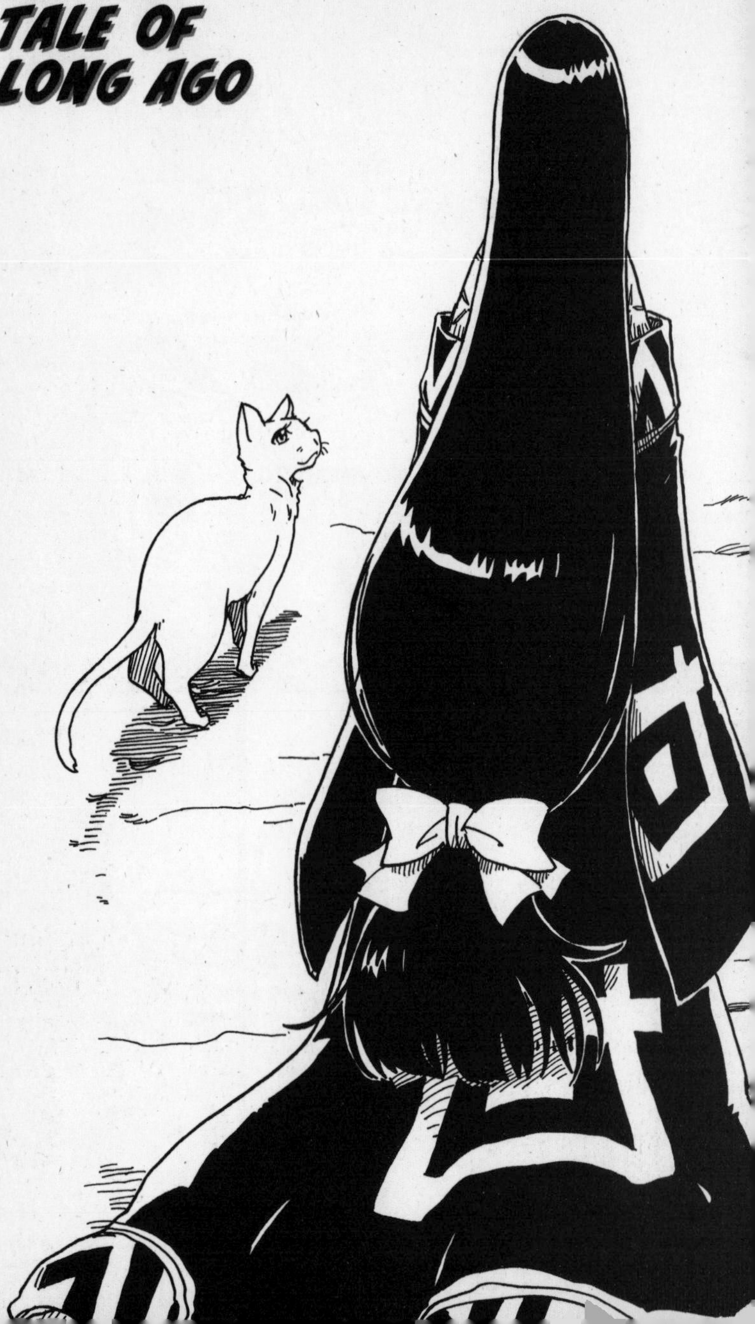

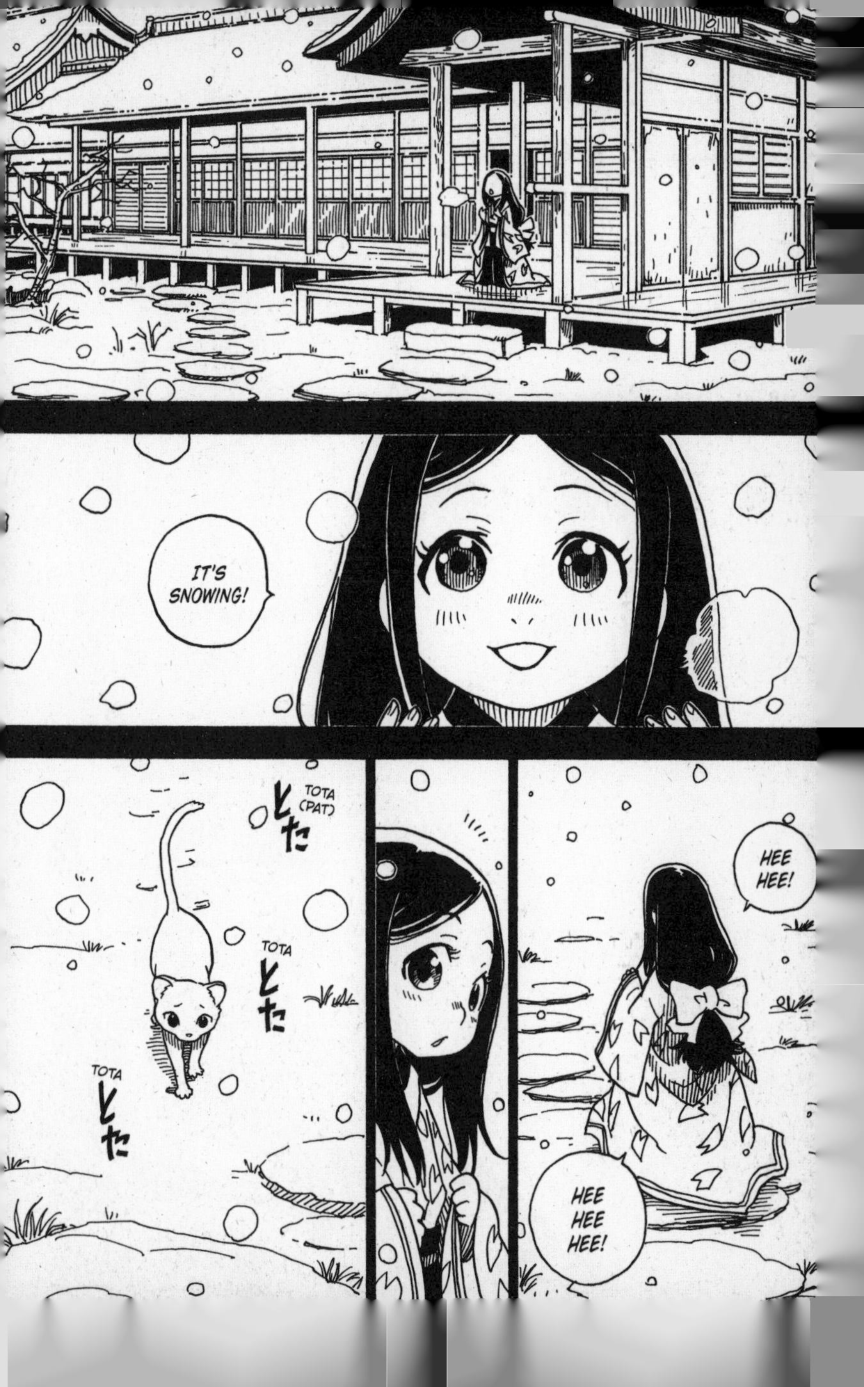
IT'S SNOWING!
HEE HEE!
HEE HEE HEE!
とた
TOTA (PAT)
とた
TOTA
とた
TOTA

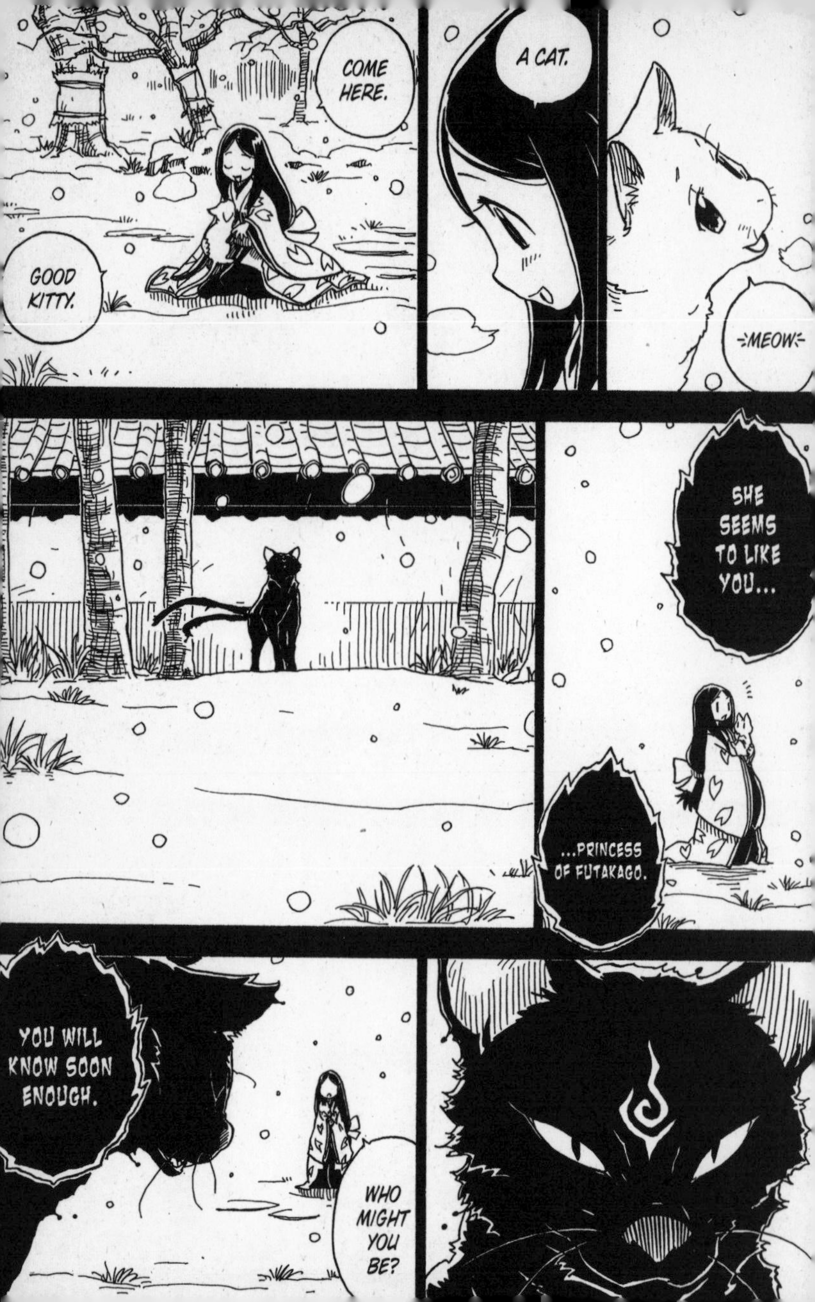
-MEOW-
A CAT.
COME HERE.
GOOD KITTY.
SHE SEEMS TO LIKE YOU...
...PRINCESS OF FUTAKAGO.
WHO MIGHT YOU BE?
YOU WILL KNOW SOON ENOUGH.

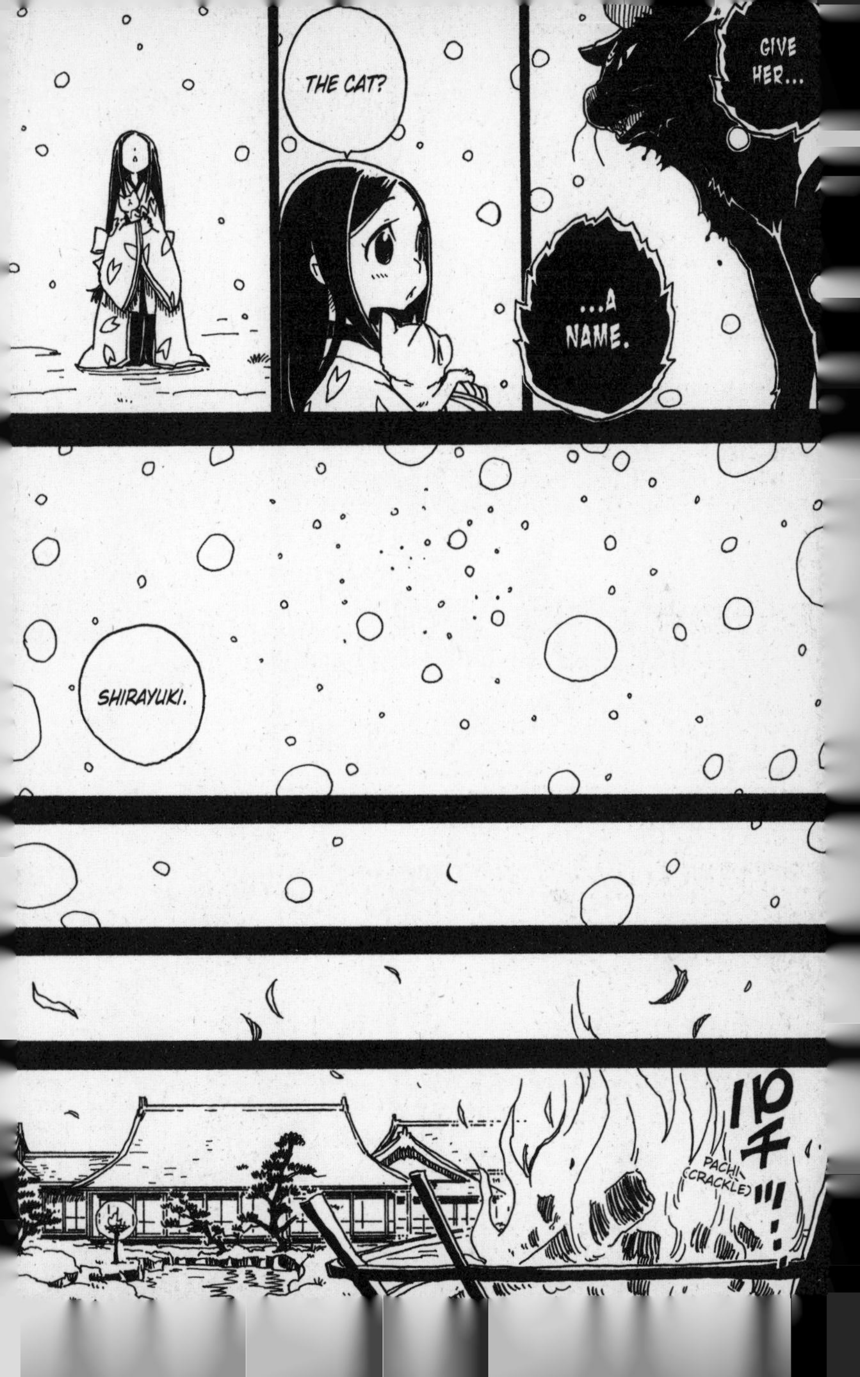
GIVE HER...
...A NAME.
THE CAT?
SHIRAYUKI.
パチ
PACH! (CRACKLE)

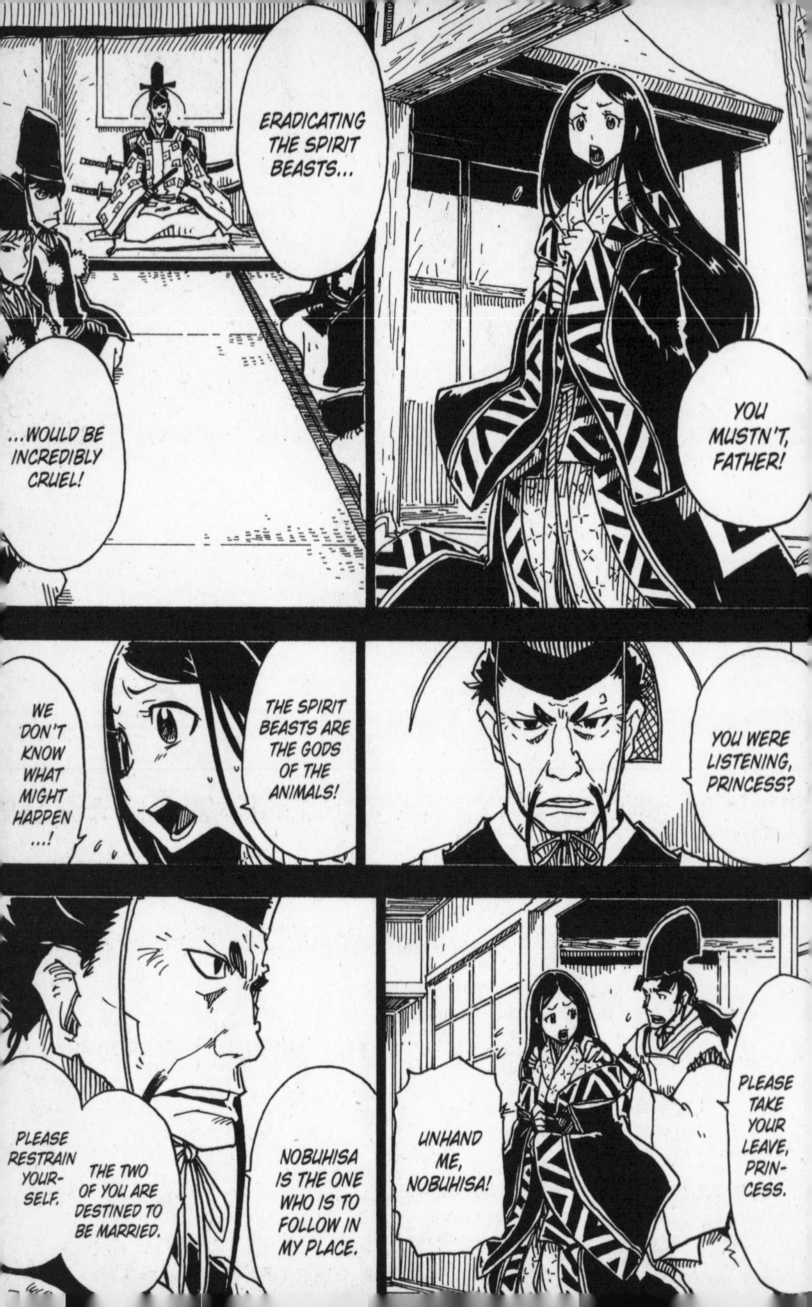
YOU MUSTN'T, FATHER!
ERADICATING THE SPIRIT BEASTS...
...WOULD BE INCREDIBLY CRUEL!
YOU WERE LISTENING, PRINCESS?
THE SPIRIT BEASTS ARE THE GODS OF THE ANIMALS!
WE DON'T KNOW WHAT MIGHT HAPPEN ...!
PLEASE TAKE YOUR LEAVE, PRIN-CESS.
UNHAND ME, NOBUHISA!
NOBUHISA IS THE ONE WHO IS TO FOLLOW IN MY PLACE.
THE TWO OF YOU ARE DESTINED TO BE MARRIED.
PLEASE RESTRAIN YOUR-SELF.

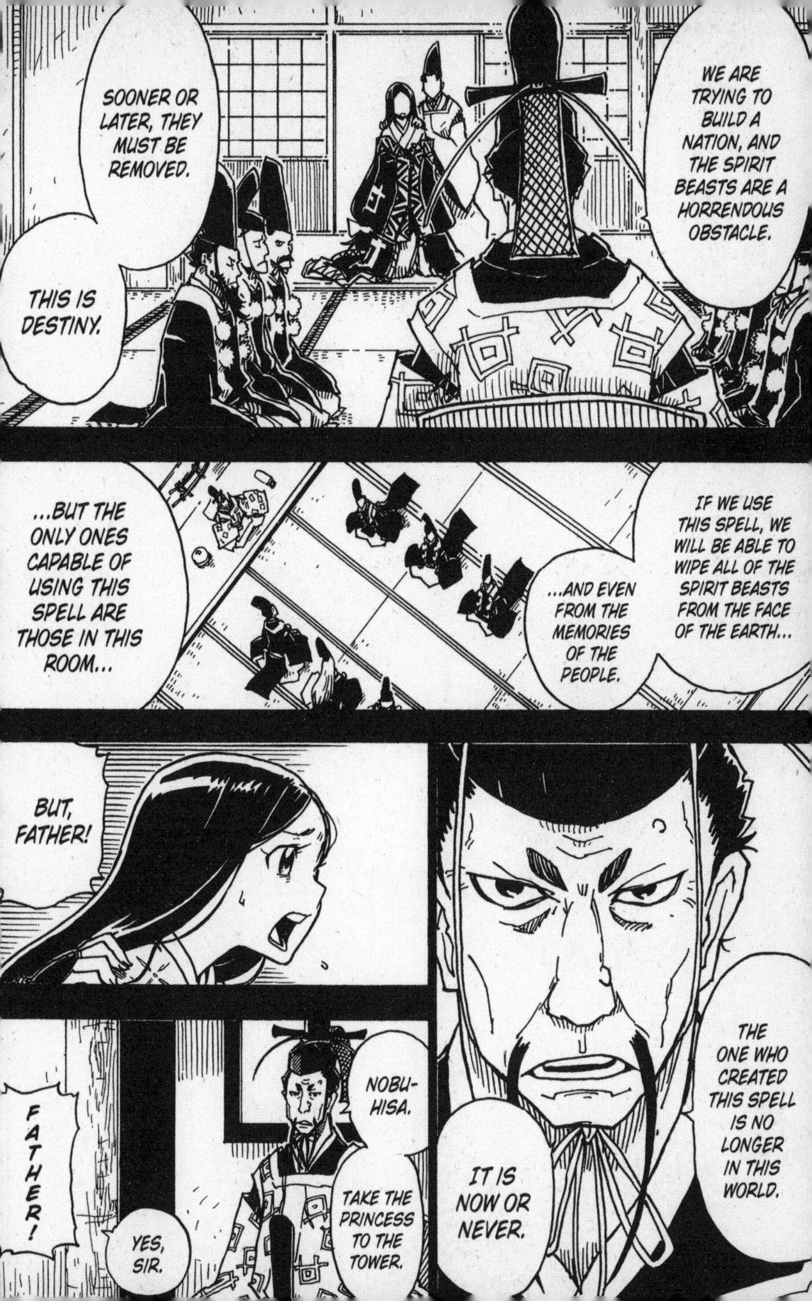
WE ARE TRYING TO BUILD A NATION, AND THE SPIRIT BEASTS ARE A HORRENDOUS OBSTACLE.
SOONER OR LATER, THEY MUST BE REMOVED.
THIS IS DESTINY.
IF WE USE THIS SPELL, WE WILL BE ABLE TO WIPE ALL OF THE SPIRIT BEASTS FROM THE FACE OF THE EARTH...
...AND EVEN FROM THE MEMORIES OF THE PEOPLE.
...BUT THE ONLY ONES CAPABLE OF USING THIS SPELL ARE THOSE IN THIS ROOM...
THE ONE WHO CREATED THIS SPELL IS NO LONGER IN THIS WORLD.
IT IS NOW OR NEVER.
BUT, FATHER!
NOBU-HISA.
TAKE THE PRINCESS TO THE TOWER.
YES, SIR.
FATHER!

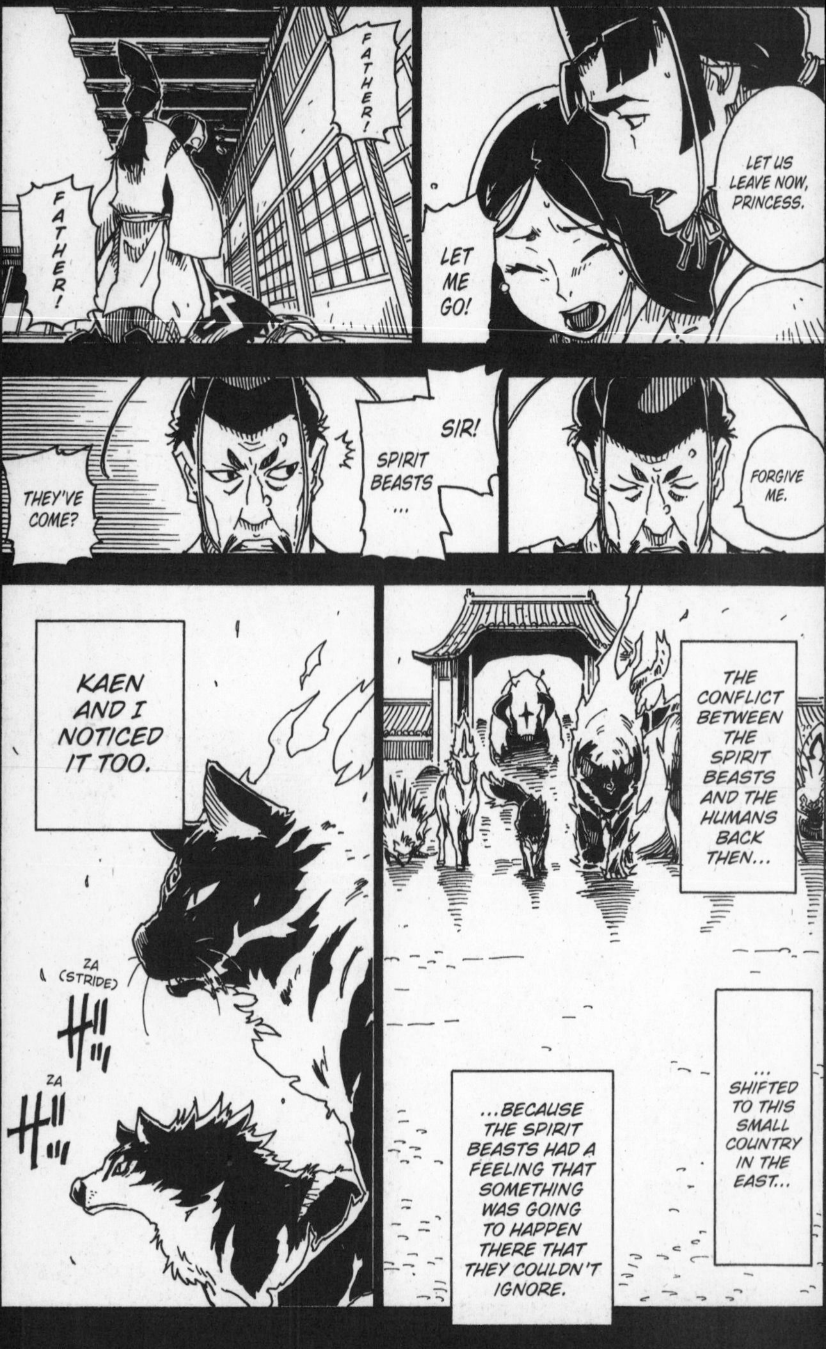
LET US LEAVE NOW, PRINCESS.
LET ME GO!
FATHER!
FATHER!
FORGIVE ME.
SIR!
SPIRIT BEASTS...
THEY'VE COME?
THE CONFLICT BETWEEN THE SPIRIT BEASTS AND THE HUMANS BACK THEN...
...SHIFTED TO THIS SMALL COUNTRY IN THE EAST...
...BECAUSE THE SPIRIT BEASTS HAD A FEELING THAT SOMETHING WAS GOING TO HAPPEN THERE THAT THEY COULDN'T IGNORE.
KAEN AND I NOTICED IT TOO.
ZA (STRIDE)
ZA

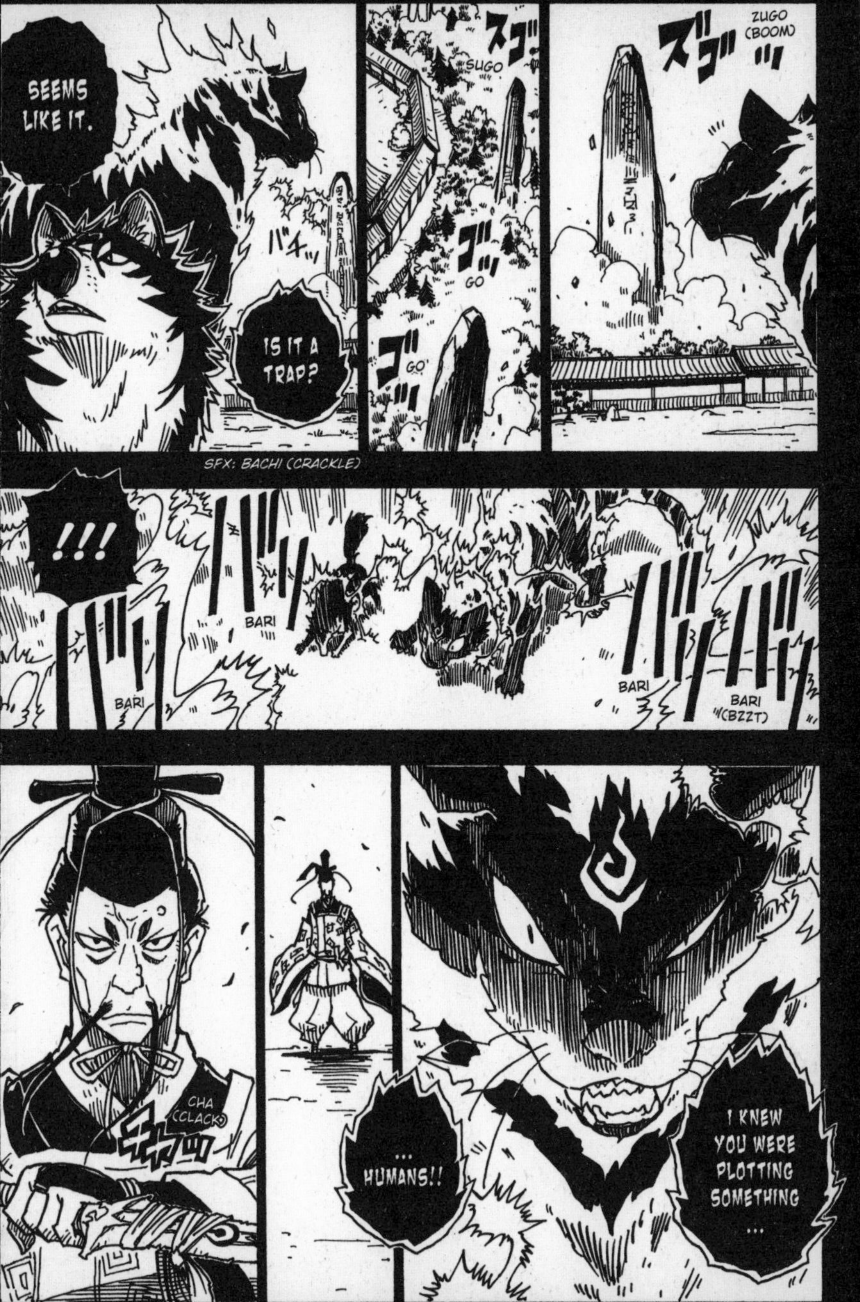
ZUGO (BOOM)
SUGO
GO
GO
IS IT A TRAP?
SEEMS LIKE IT.
SFX: BACHI (CRACKLE)
BARI (BZZT)
BARI
BARI
!!!
BARI
I KNEW YOU WERE PLOTTING SOMETHING ...
... HUMANS!!
CHA (CLACK)

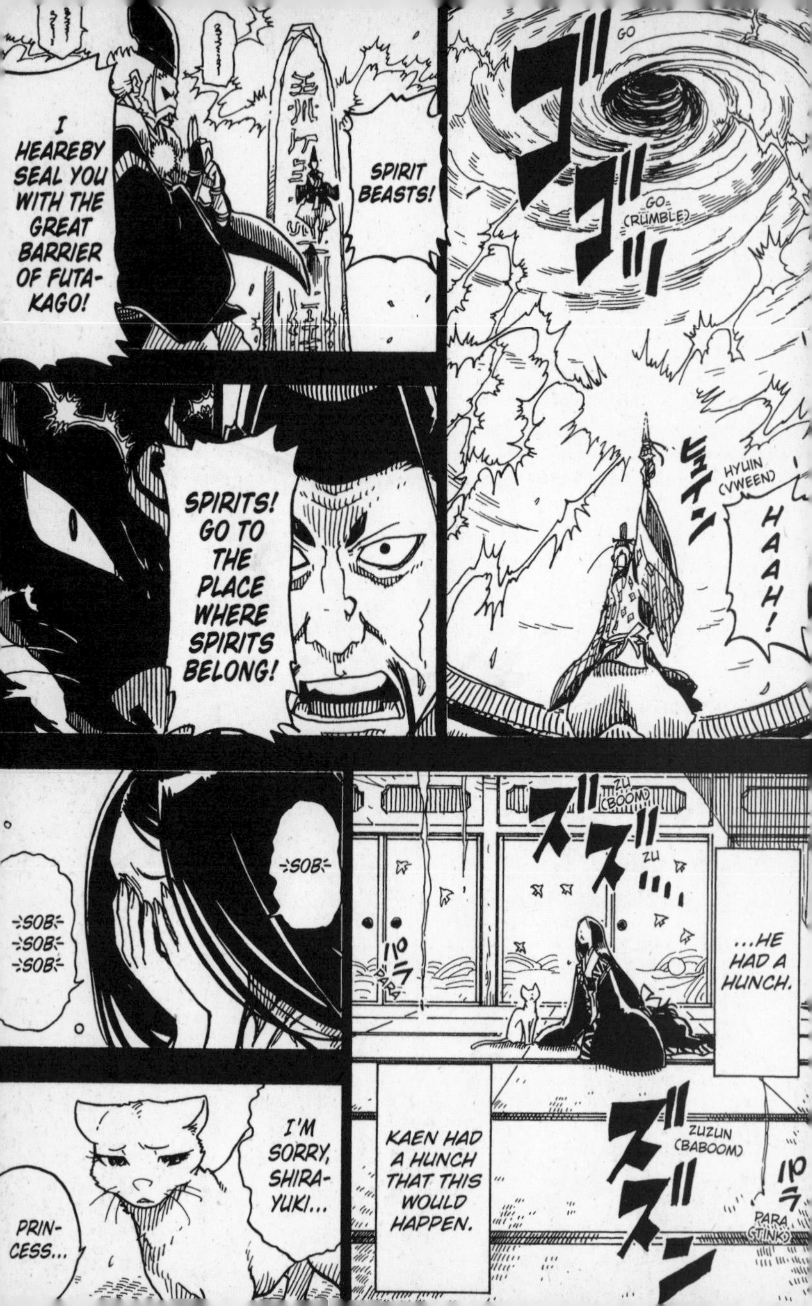
GO
GO (RUMBLE)
HYUIN (VWEEN)
HAAAH!
SPIRIT BEASTS!
I HEAREBY SEAL YOU WITH THE GREAT BARRIER OF FUTA-KAGO!
SPIRITS! GO TO THE PLACE WHERE SPIRITS BELONG!
ZU (BOOM)
ZU
PARA
...HE HAD A HUNCH.
SOB
SOB SOB SOB
ZUZUN (BABOOM)
PARA (STINK)
KAEN HAD A HUNCH THAT THIS WOULD HAPPEN.
I'M SORRY, SHIRA-YUKI...
PRIN-CESS...

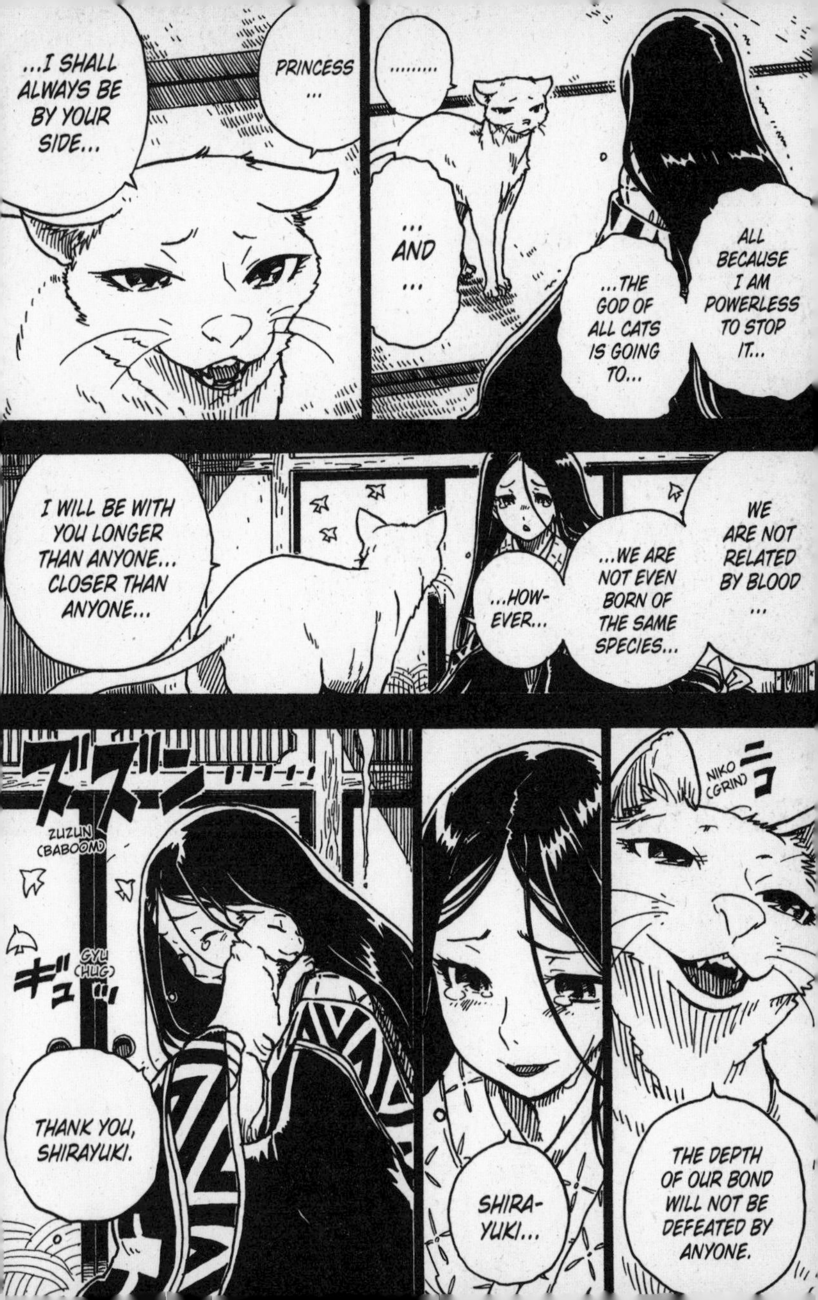

....
...AND...
...THE GOD OF ALL CATS IS GOING TO...
ALL BECAUSE I AM POWERLESS TO STOP IT...
PRINCESS...
...I SHALL ALWAYS BE BY YOUR SIDE...
WE ARE NOT RELATED BY BLOOD...
...WE ARE NOT EVEN BORN OF THE SAME SPECIES...
...HOW-EVER...
I WILL BE WITH YOU LONGER THAN ANYONE... CLOSER THAN ANYONE...
NIKO (GRIN)
THE DEPTH OF OUR BOND WILL NOT BE DEFEATED BY ANYONE.
SHIRA-YUKI...
ZUZUN (BABOOM)
GYU (HUG)
THANK YOU, SHIRAYUKI.

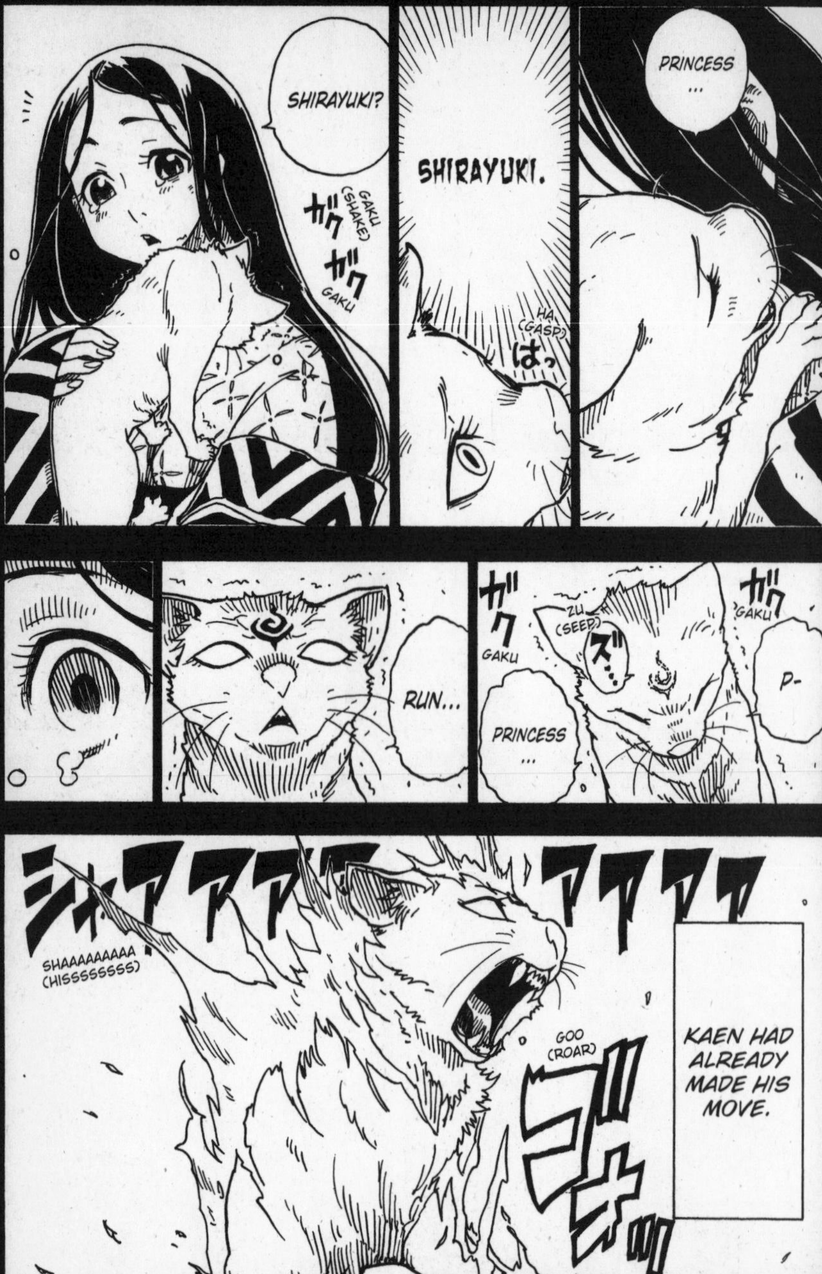
PRINCESS ...
SHIRAYUKI.
HA (GASP) はっ
SHIRAYUKI?
GAKU (SHAKE) ガク
ガク GAKU
ガク GAKU
P-
ZU (SEEP) ズ...
ガク GAKU
PRINCESS ...
RUN...
KAEN HAD ALREADY MADE HIS MOVE.
GOO (ROAR) ゴォッ
シャアアア アアアア
SHAAAAAAAAA (HISSSSSSSS)

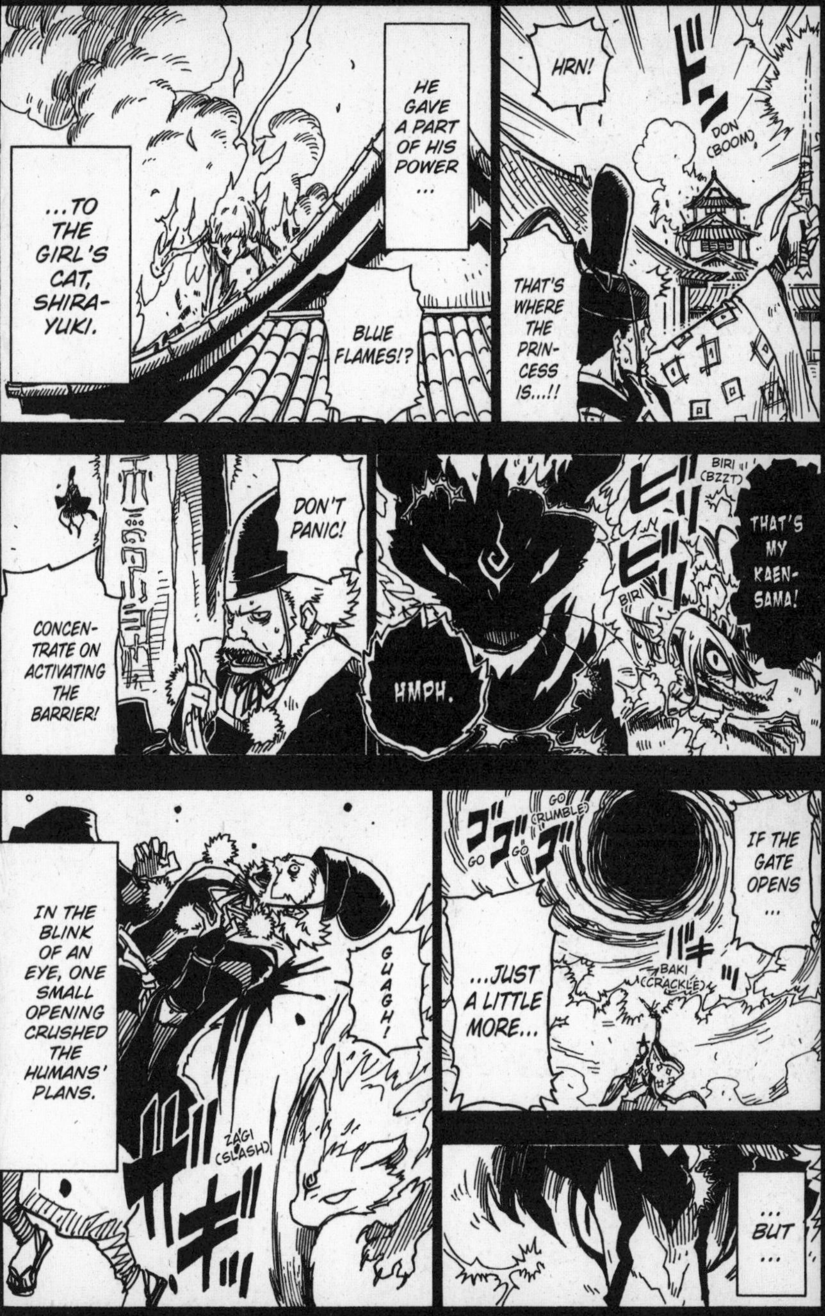
HRN!
DON (BOOM)
THAT'S WHERE THE PRINCESS IS...!!
HE GAVE A PART OF HIS POWER...
...TO THE GIRL'S CAT, SHIRAYUKI.
BLUE FLAMES!?
BIRI (BZZT)
BIRI
THAT'S MY KAEN-SAMA!
HMPH.
DON'T PANIC!
CONCENTRATE ON ACTIVATING THE BARRIER!
GO (RUMBLE)
GO GO
IF THE GATE OPENS...
BAKI (CRACKLE)
...JUST A LITTLE MORE...
...BUT...
IN THE BLINK OF AN EYE, ONE SMALL OPENING CRUSHED THE HUMANS' PLANS.
GUAGH!
ZAGI (SLASH)

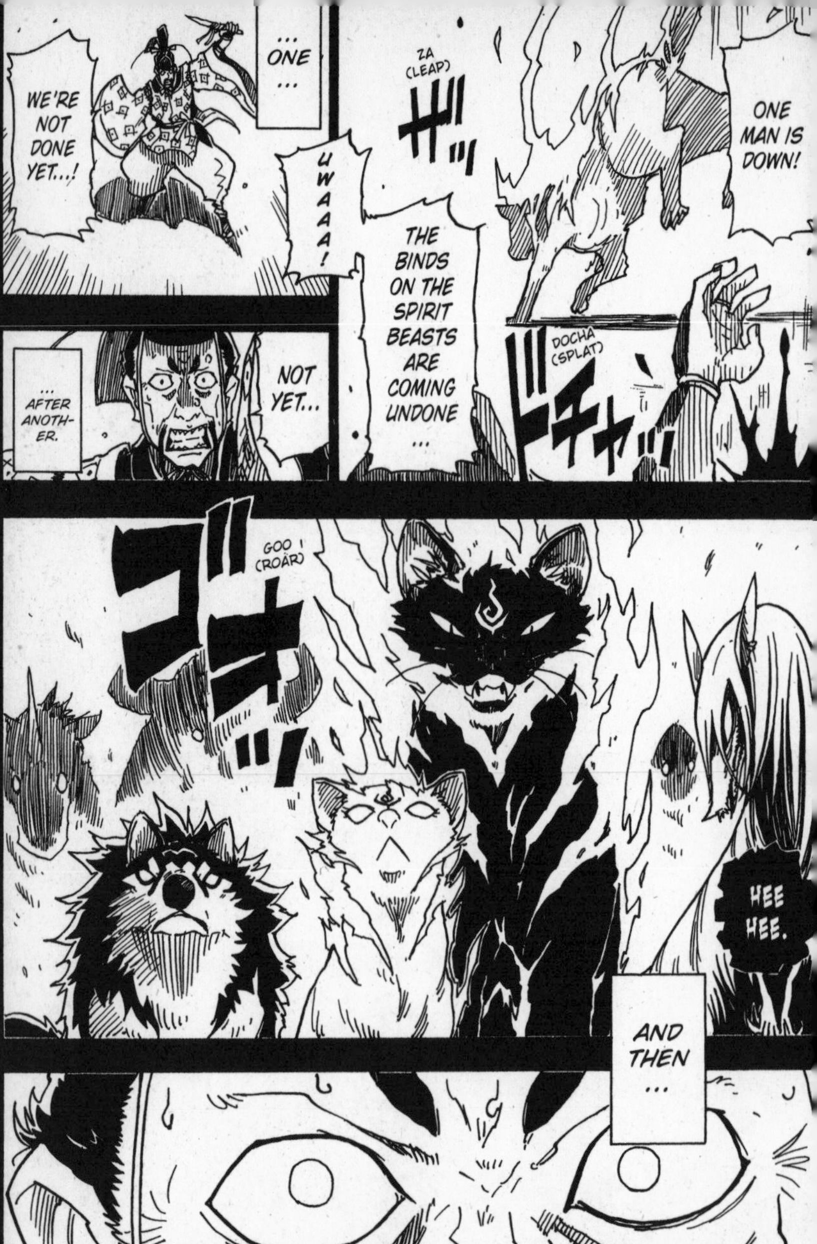

ONE MAN IS DOWN!
ZA (LEAP)
ザッ
THE BINDS ON THE SPIRIT BEASTS ARE COMING UNDONE ...
DOCHA (SPLAT)
ドチャッ
... ONE ...
WE'RE NOT DONE YET...!
UWAAAA!
NOT YET...
... AFTER ANOTHER.
GOO ! (ROAR)
ゴオッ
HEE HEE.
AND THEN ...

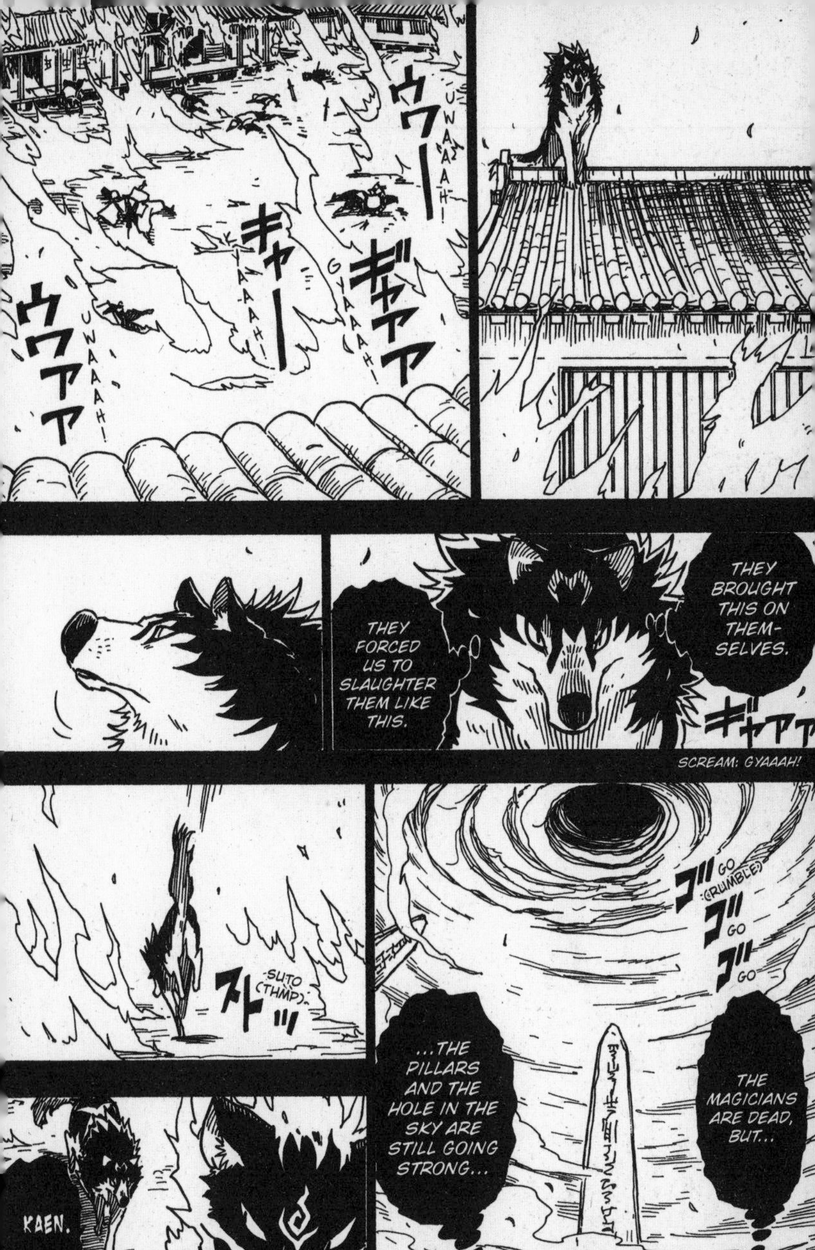
ウワー
UWAAAH!
ギャアア
GYAAAAH!
キャー
KYAAAH!
ウワアア
UWAAAH!
THEY BROUGHT THIS ON THEM-SELVES.
THEY FORCED US TO SLAUGHTER THEM LIKE THIS.
ギャアア
SCREAM: GYAAAH!
ゴゴゴ
GO (RUMBLE) GO GO
THE MAGICIANS ARE DEAD, BUT...
...THE PILLARS AND THE HOLE IN THE SKY ARE STILL GOING STRONG...
ストッ
SUTO (THMP)
KAEN.

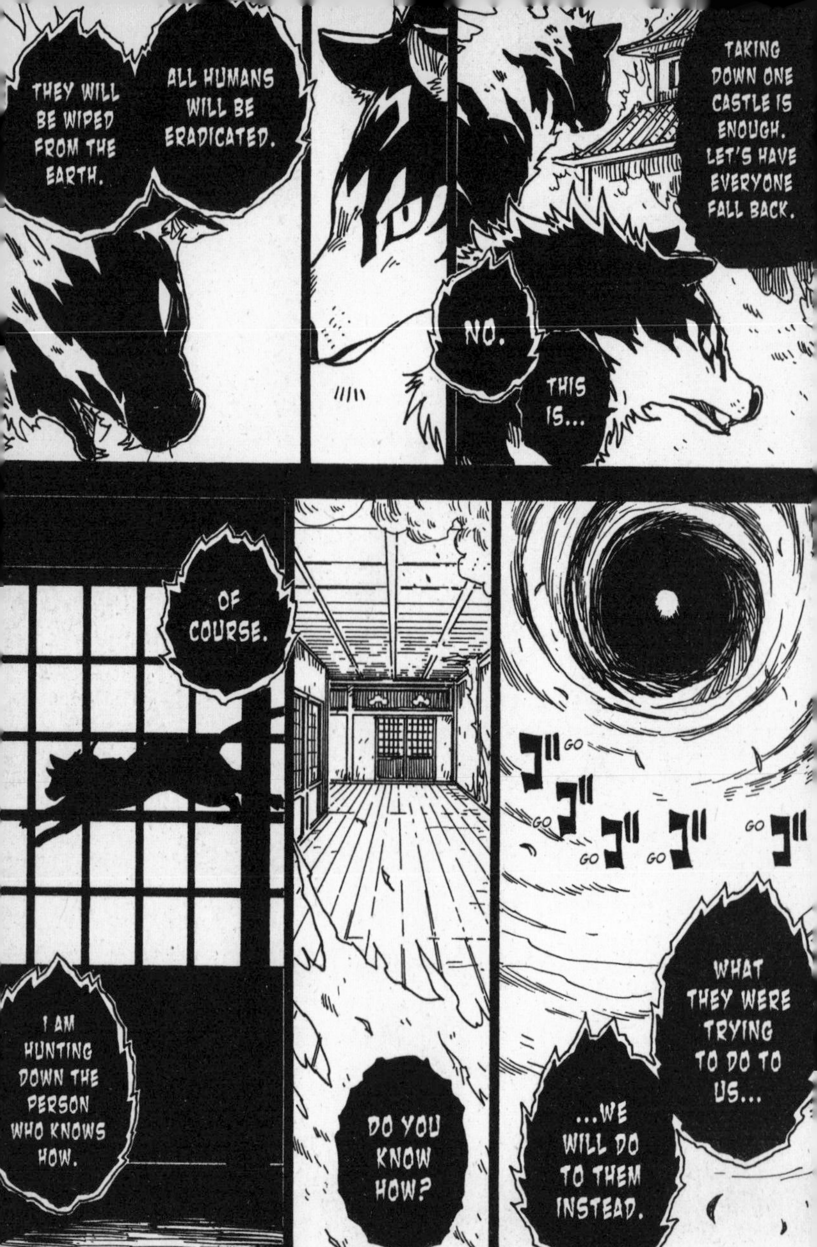
TAKING DOWN ONE CASTLE IS ENOUGH. LET'S HAVE EVERYONE FALL BACK.
NO.
THIS IS...
ALL HUMANS WILL BE ERADICATED.
THEY WILL BE WIPED FROM THE EARTH.
ゴ GO ゴ GO ゴ GO ゴ GO ゴ GO
WHAT THEY WERE TRYING TO DO TO US...
...WE WILL DO TO THEM INSTEAD.
DO YOU KNOW HOW?
OF COURSE.
I AM HUNTING DOWN THE PERSON WHO KNOWS HOW.

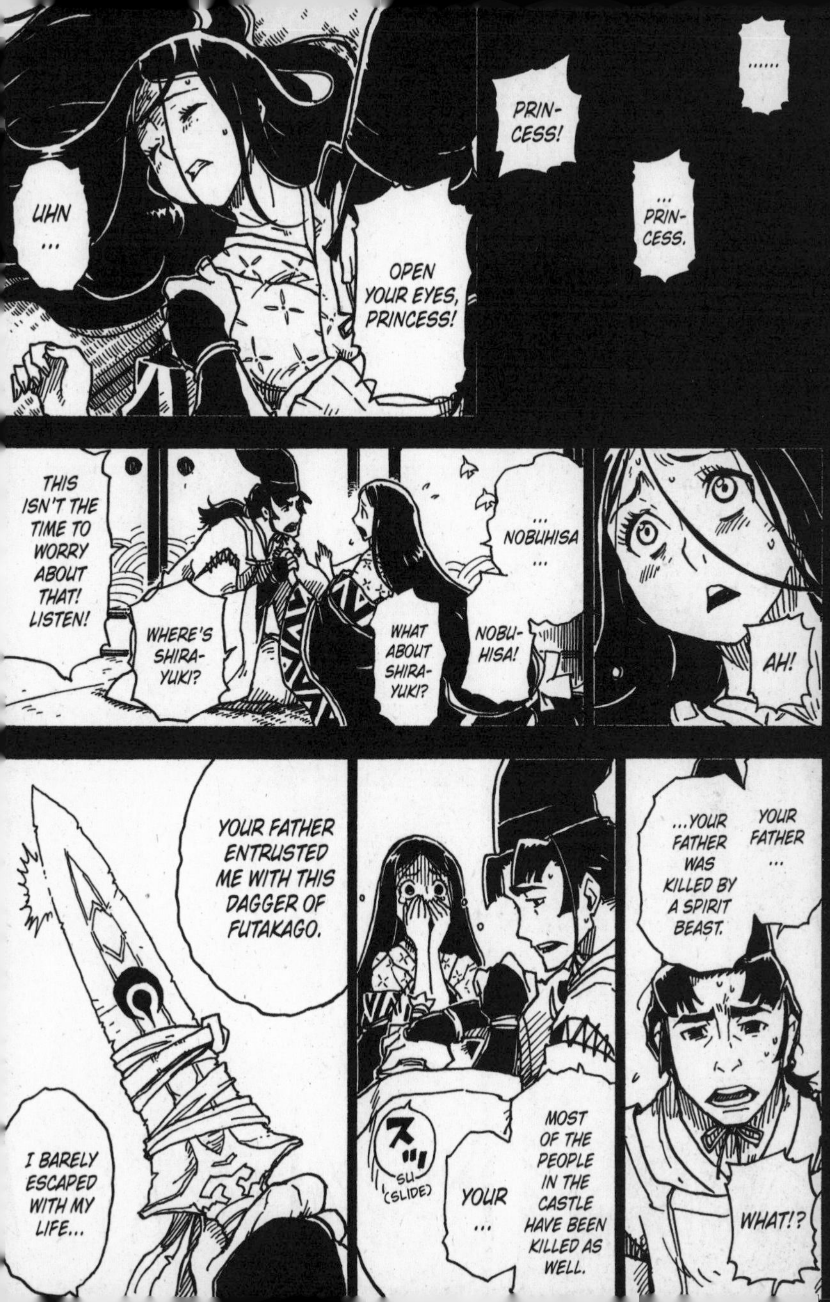
......
PRIN-CESS!
... PRIN-CESS.
OPEN YOUR EYES, PRINCESS!
UHN ...
AH!
... NOBUHISA ...
NOBU-HISA!
WHAT ABOUT SHIRA-YUKI?
WHERE'S SHIRA-YUKI?
THIS ISN'T THE TIME TO WORRY ABOUT THAT! LISTEN!
YOUR FATHER ...
...YOUR FATHER WAS KILLED BY A SPIRIT BEAST.
WHAT!?
MOST OF THE PEOPLE IN THE CASTLE HAVE BEEN KILLED AS WELL.
YOUR ...
スッ
SU (SLIDE)
YOUR FATHER ENTRUSTED ME WITH THIS DAGGER OF FUTAKAGO.
I BARELY ESCAPED WITH MY LIFE...

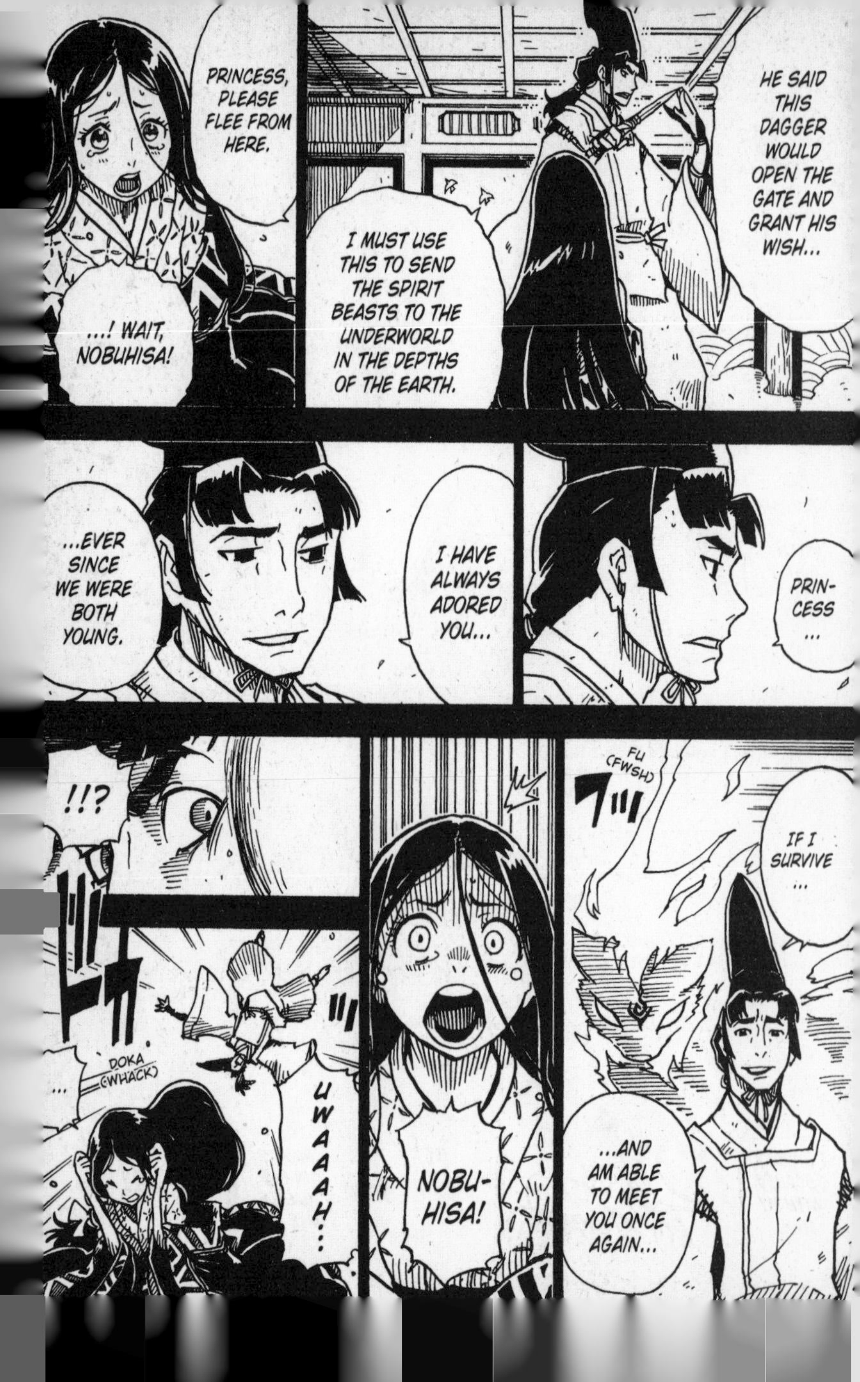
HE SAID THIS DAGGER WOULD OPEN THE GATE AND GRANT HIS WISH...
I MUST USE THIS TO SEND THE SPIRIT BEASTS TO THE UNDERWORLD IN THE DEPTHS OF THE EARTH.
PRINCESS, PLEASE FLEE FROM HERE.
...! WAIT, NOBUHISA!
PRIN-CESS ...
I HAVE ALWAYS ADORED YOU...
...EVER SINCE WE WERE BOTH YOUNG.
FU (FWSH)
IF I SURVIVE ...
...AND AM ABLE TO MEET YOU ONCE AGAIN...
NOBU-HISA!
!!?
DOKA (WHACK)
...
UWAAAAH...

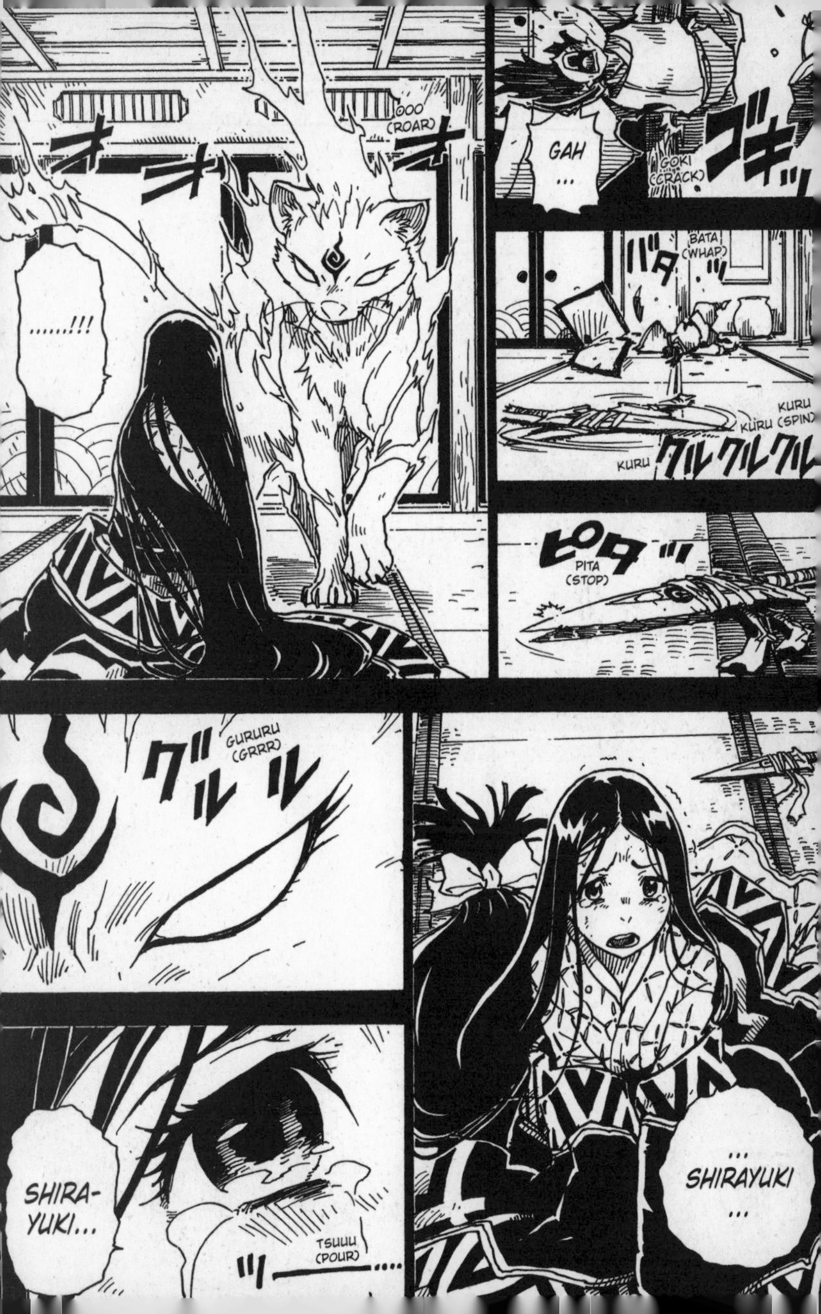
GAH ...
GOKI (CRACK)
BATA (WHAP)
KURU KURU KURU (SPIN)
PITA (STOP)
OOO (ROAR)
......!!!
... SHIRAYUKI ...
GURURU (GRRR)
SHIRA-YUKI...
TSUUU (POUR)

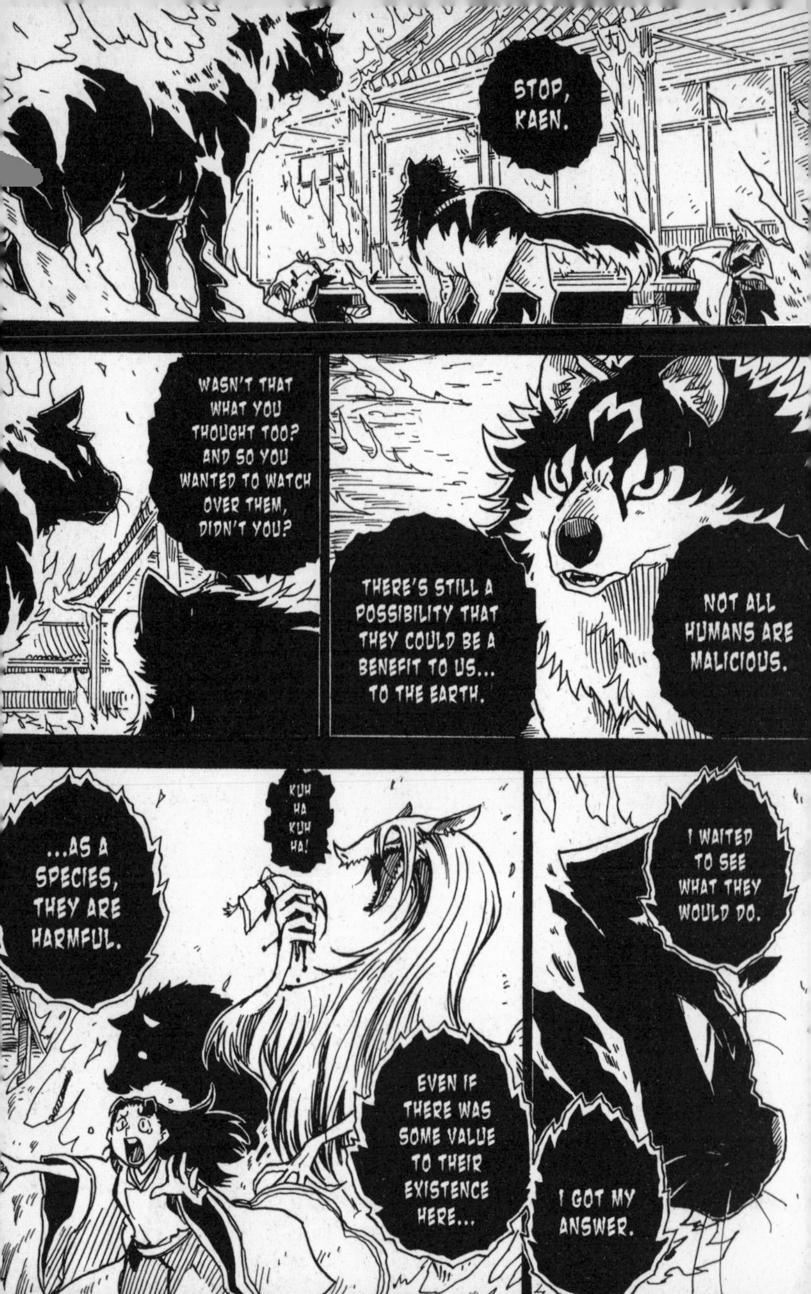
STOP, KAEN.
NOT ALL HUMANS ARE MALICIOUS.
THERE'S STILL A POSSIBILITY THAT THEY COULD BE A BENEFIT TO US... TO THE EARTH.
WASN'T THAT WHAT YOU THOUGHT TOO? AND SO YOU WANTED TO WATCH OVER THEM, DIDN'T YOU?
I WAITED TO SEE WHAT THEY WOULD DO.
I GOT MY ANSWER.
KUH HA KUH HA!
EVEN IF THERE WAS SOME VALUE TO THEIR EXISTENCE HERE...
...AS A SPECIES, THEY ARE HARMFUL.

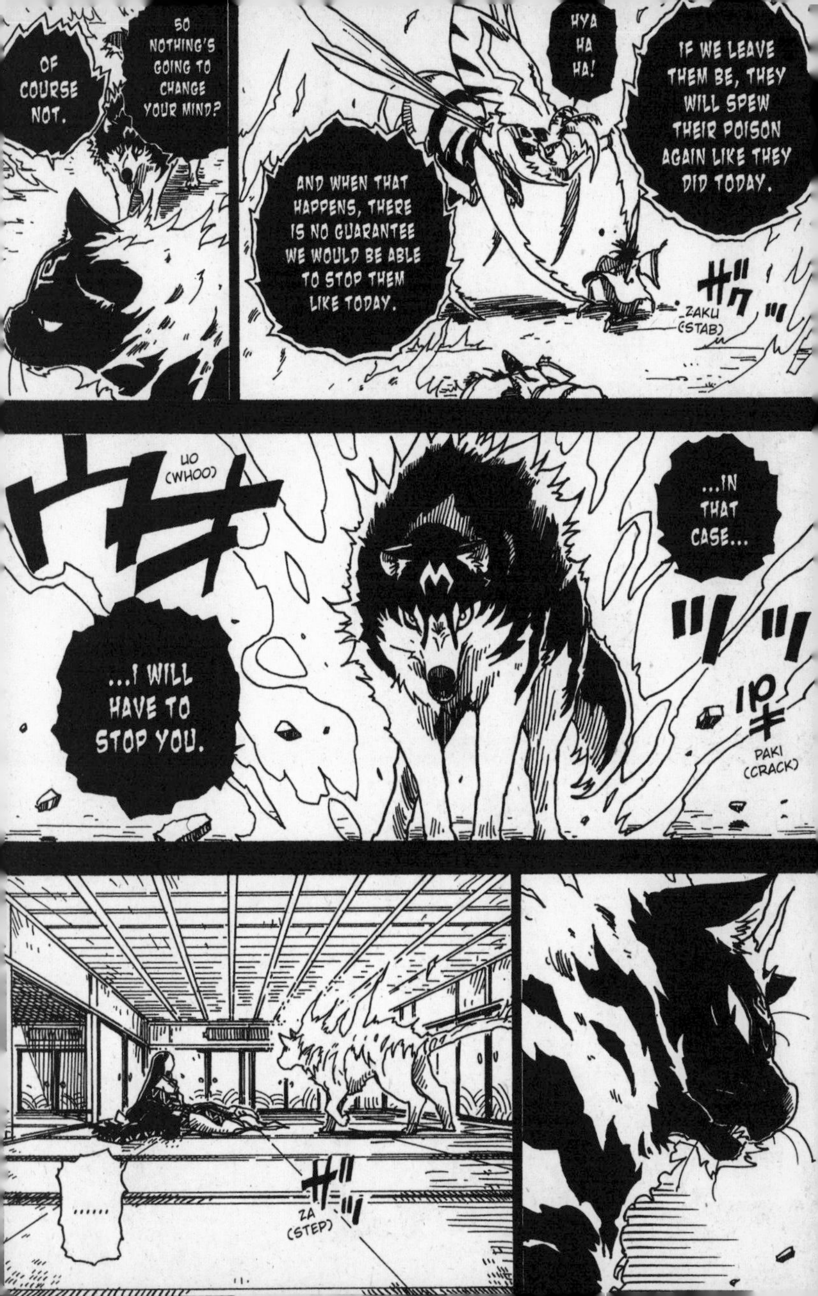
IF WE LEAVE THEM BE, THEY WILL SPEW THEIR POISON AGAIN LIKE THEY DID TODAY.
HYA HA HA!
AND WHEN THAT HAPPENS, THERE IS NO GUARANTEE WE WOULD BE ABLE TO STOP THEM LIKE TODAY.
ZAKU (STAB)
SO NOTHING'S GOING TO CHANGE YOUR MIND?
OF COURSE NOT.
...IN THAT CASE...
PAKI (CRACK)
UO (WHOO)
...I WILL HAVE TO STOP YOU.
ZA (STEP)
......

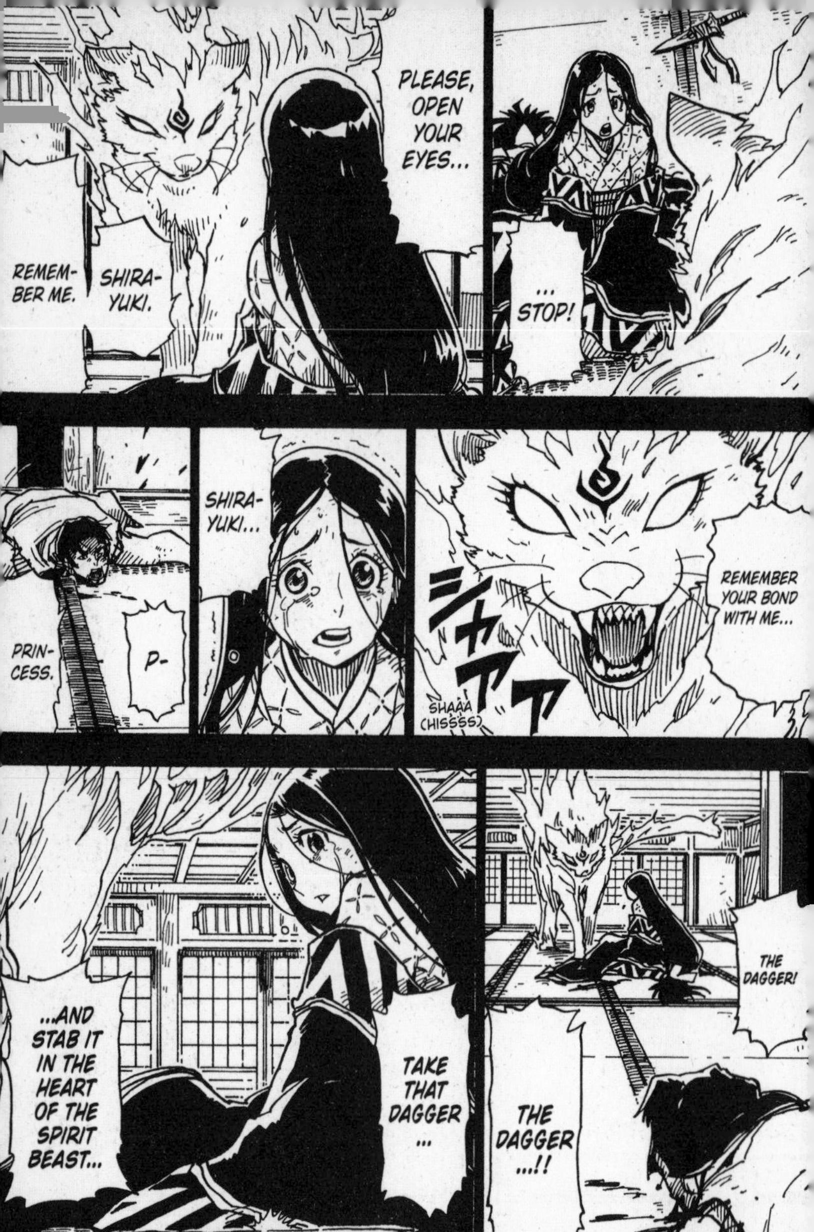
...STOP!
PLEASE, OPEN YOUR EYES...
SHIRA-YUKI.
REMEM-BER ME.
REMEMBER YOUR BOND WITH ME...
シャアア
SHAAA (HISSSS)
SHIRA-YUKI...
P-
PRIN-CESS.
THE DAGGER!
THE DAGGER ...!!
TAKE THAT DAGGER ...
...AND STAB IT IN THE HEART OF THE SPIRIT BEAST...

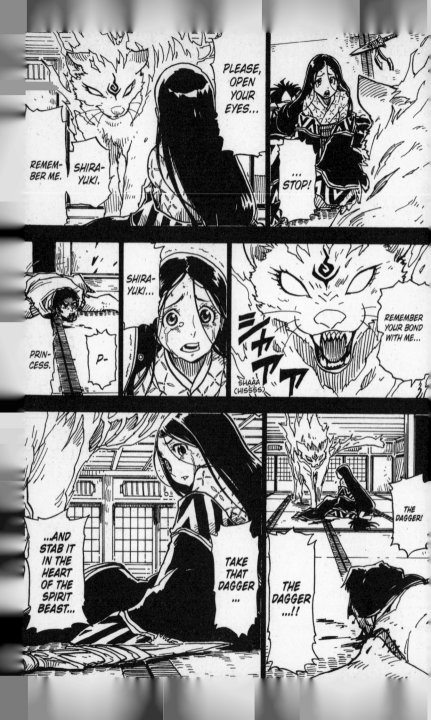

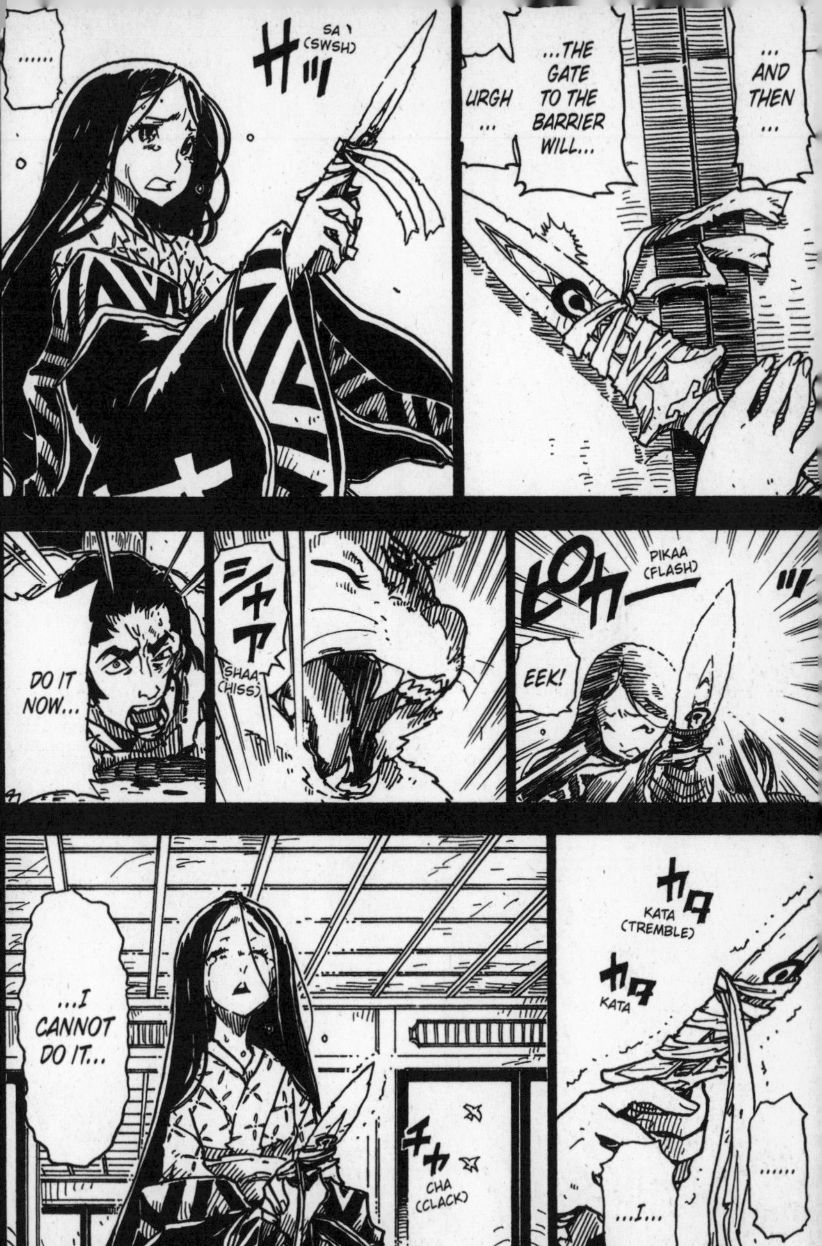
...AND THEN...
...THE GATE TO THE BARRIER WILL...
URGH...
サッ
SA (SWSH)
......
ピカーッ
PIKAA (FLASH)
EEK!
シャア
SHAA (HISS)
DO IT NOW...
カタ
KATA (TREMBLE)
カタ
KATA
......
...I...
...I CANNOT DO IT...
チャ
CHA (CLACK)

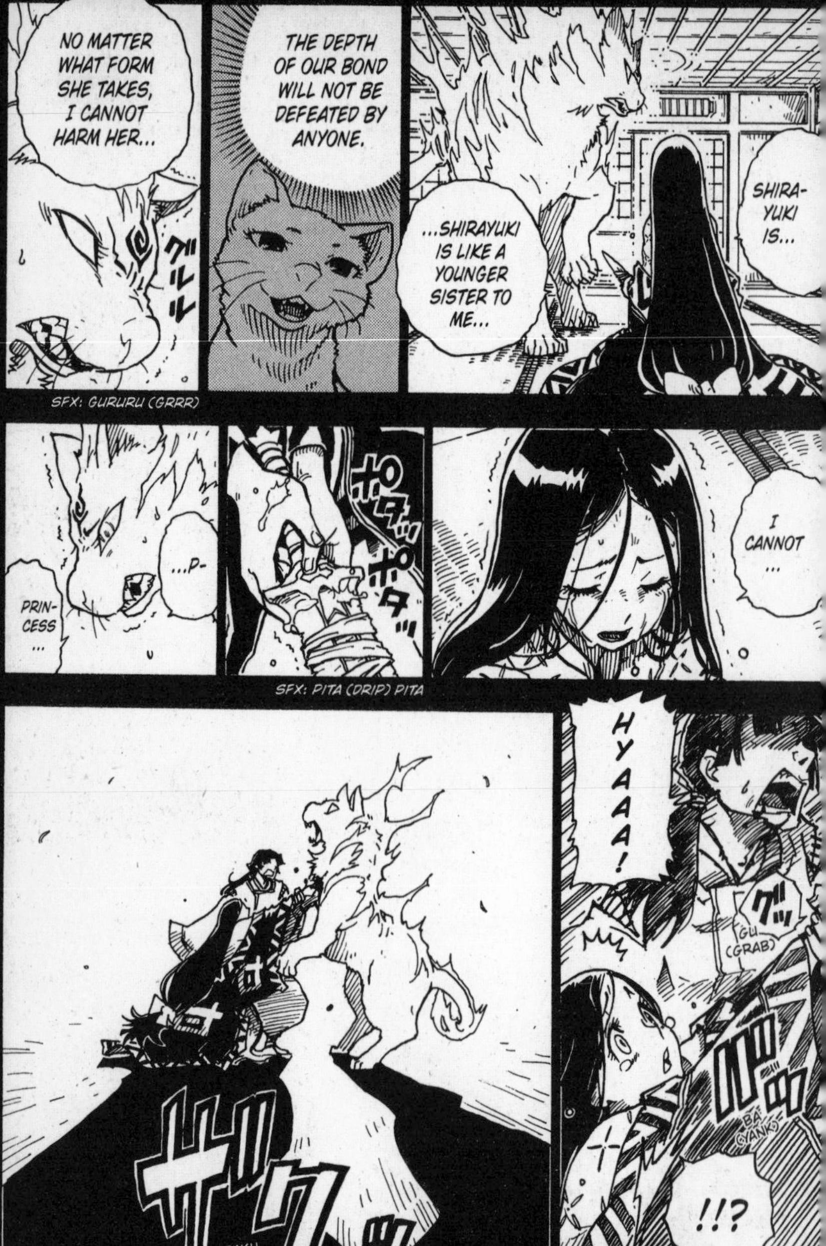
SHIRA-YUKI IS...
...SHIRAYUKI IS LIKE A YOUNGER SISTER TO ME...
THE DEPTH OF OUR BOND WILL NOT BE DEFEATED BY ANYONE.
NO MATTER WHAT FORM SHE TAKES, I CANNOT HARM HER...
SFX: GURURU (GRRR)
I CANNOT ...
SFX: PITA (DRIP) PITA
...P- PRINCESS ...
HYAAAA!
GU (GRAB)
BA (YANK)
!!?
ZAKU (STAB)

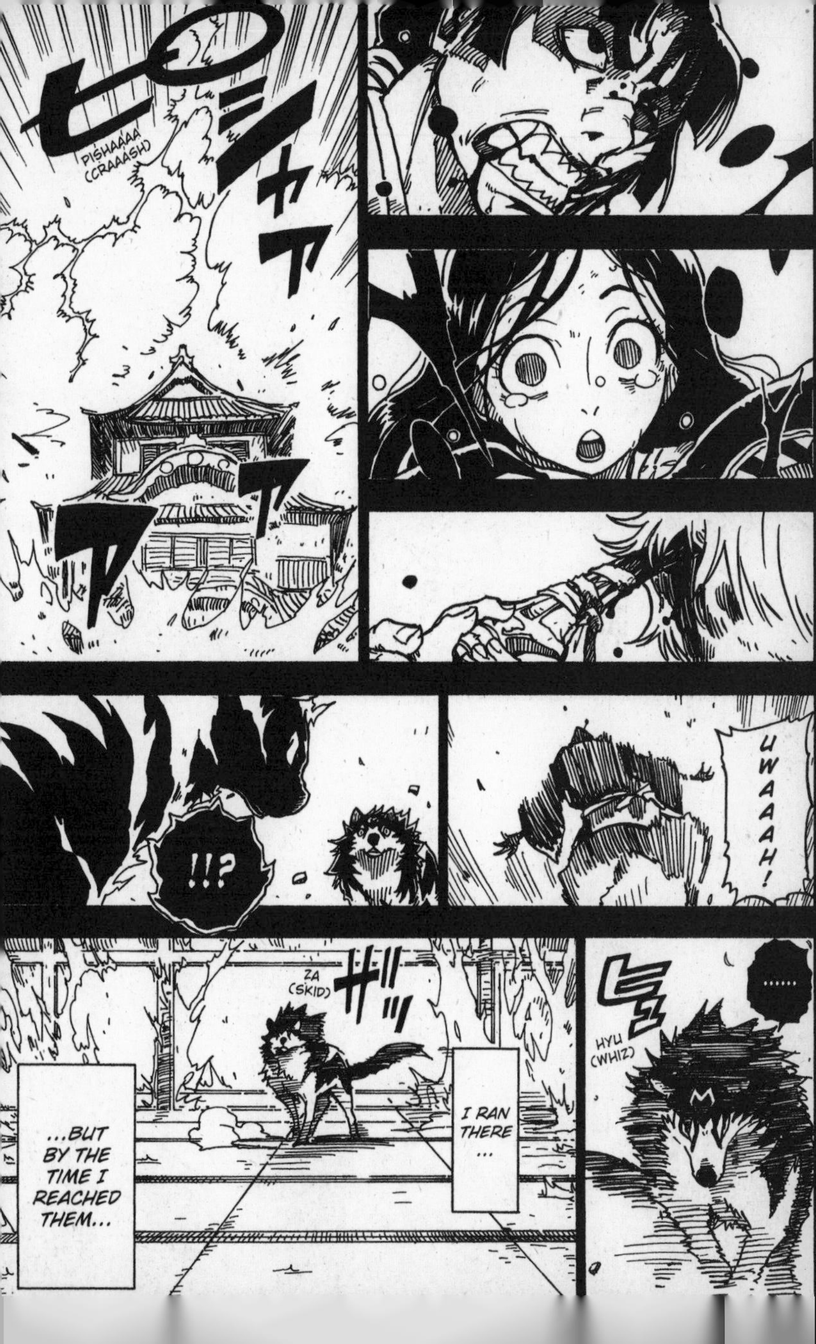

ピシャァァァ
PISHAAAA (CRAAASH)
UWAAAAH!
!!?
ヒュ
HYU (WHIZ)
......
I RAN THERE ...
ザッ
ZA (SKID)
...BUT BY THE TIME I REACHED THEM...

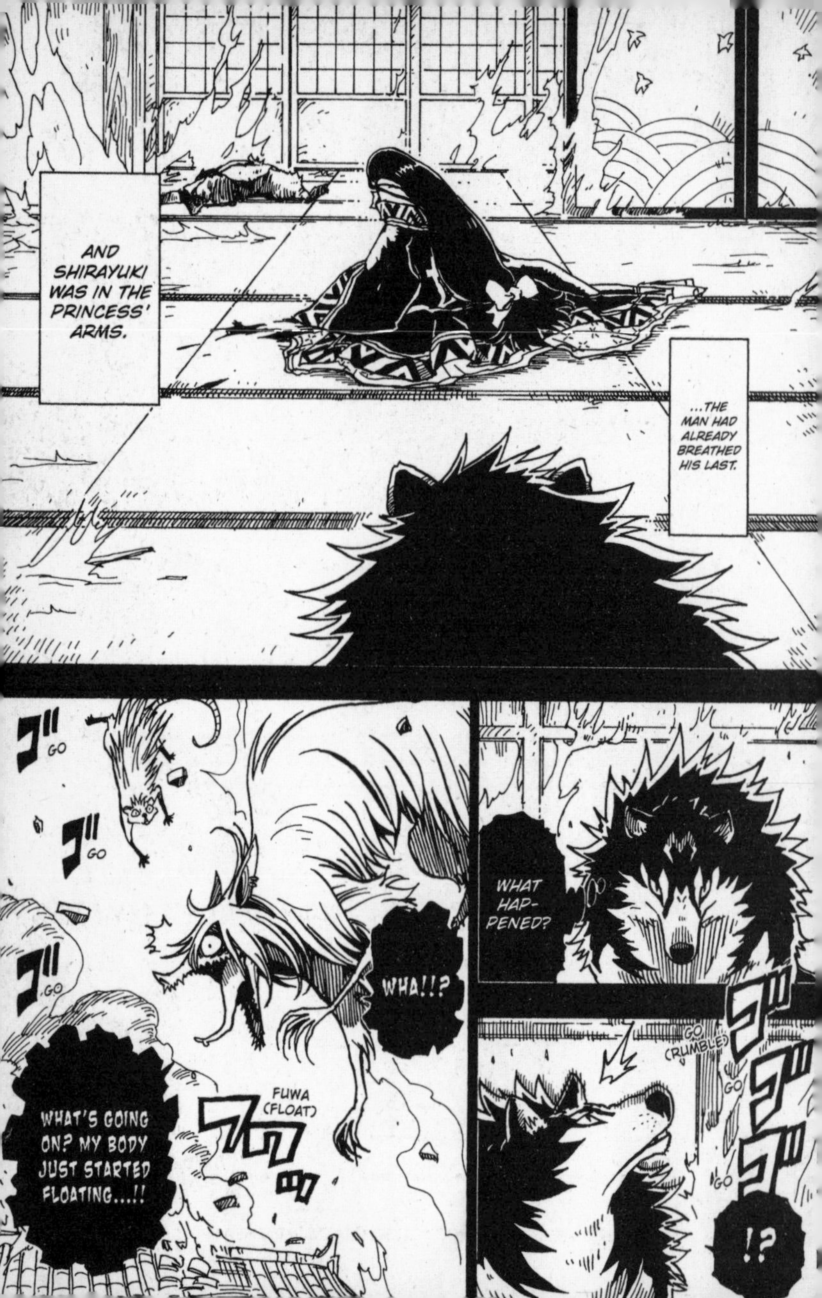
...THE MAN HAD ALREADY BREATHED HIS LAST.
AND SHIRAYUKI WAS IN THE PRINCESS' ARMS.
WHAT HAP-PENED?
GO (RUMBLE)
GO
GO
!?
GO
GO
GO
WHA!!?
FUWA (FLOAT)
WHAT'S GOING ON? MY BODY JUST STARTED FLOATING...!!

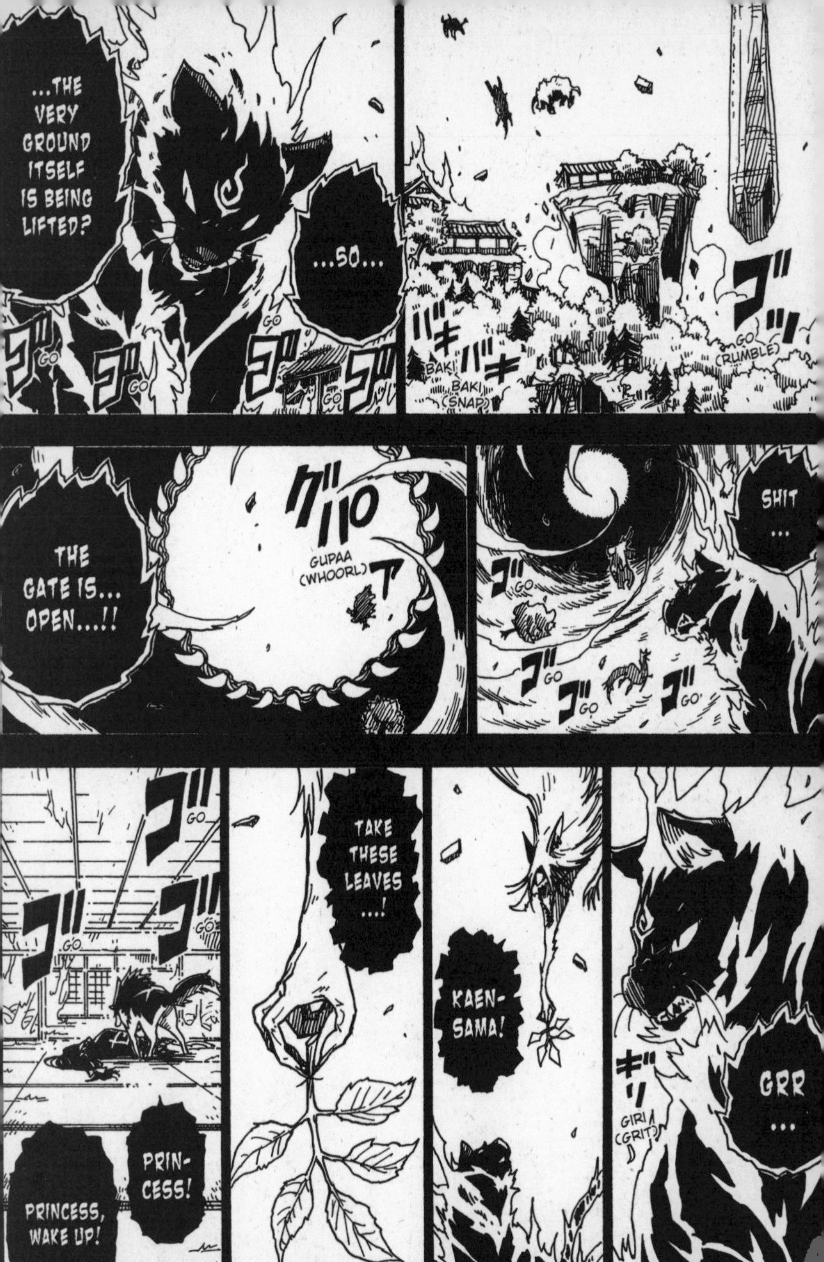
GO (RUMBLE)
BAKI
BAKI (SNAP)
...SO...
...THE VERY GROUND ITSELF IS BEING LIFTED?
GO GO GO GO
SHIT...
GO GO GO GO
GUPAA (WHOORL)
THE GATE IS... OPEN...!!
GRR...
GIRI (GRIT)
KAEN-SAMA!
TAKE THESE LEAVES...!
GO GO GO
PRIN-CESS!
PRINCESS, WAKE UP!

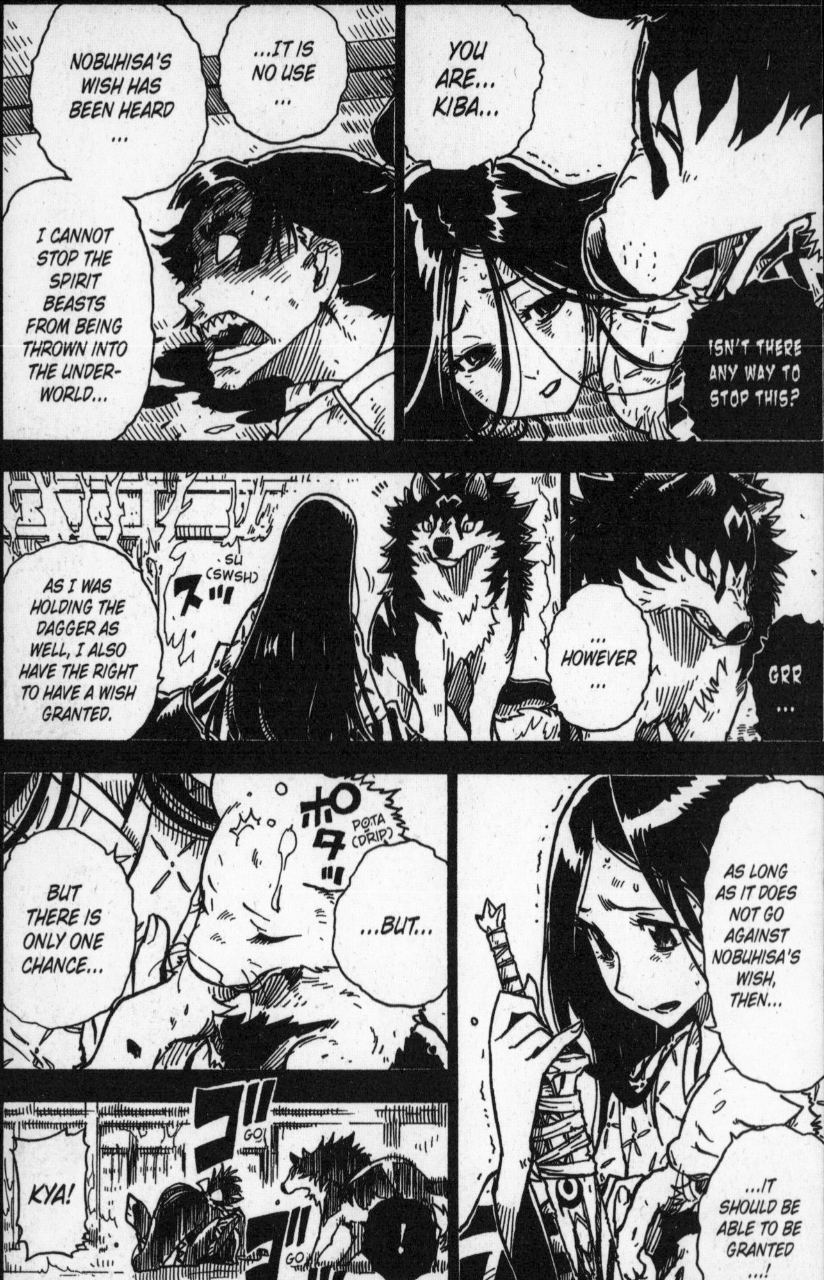
YOU ARE... KIBA...
ISN'T THERE ANY WAY TO STOP THIS?
...IT IS NO USE ...
NOBUHISA'S WISH HAS BEEN HEARD ...
I CANNOT STOP THE SPIRIT BEASTS FROM BEING THROWN INTO THE UNDER-WORLD...
GRR ...
... HOWEVER ...
SU (SWSH)
AS I WAS HOLDING THE DAGGER AS WELL, I ALSO HAVE THE RIGHT TO HAVE A WISH GRANTED.
AS LONG AS IT DOES NOT GO AGAINST NOBUHISA'S WISH, THEN...
...IT SHOULD BE ABLE TO BE GRANTED ...!
...BUT...
POTA (DRIP)
BUT THERE IS ONLY ONE CHANCE...
GO
GO
!
KYA!

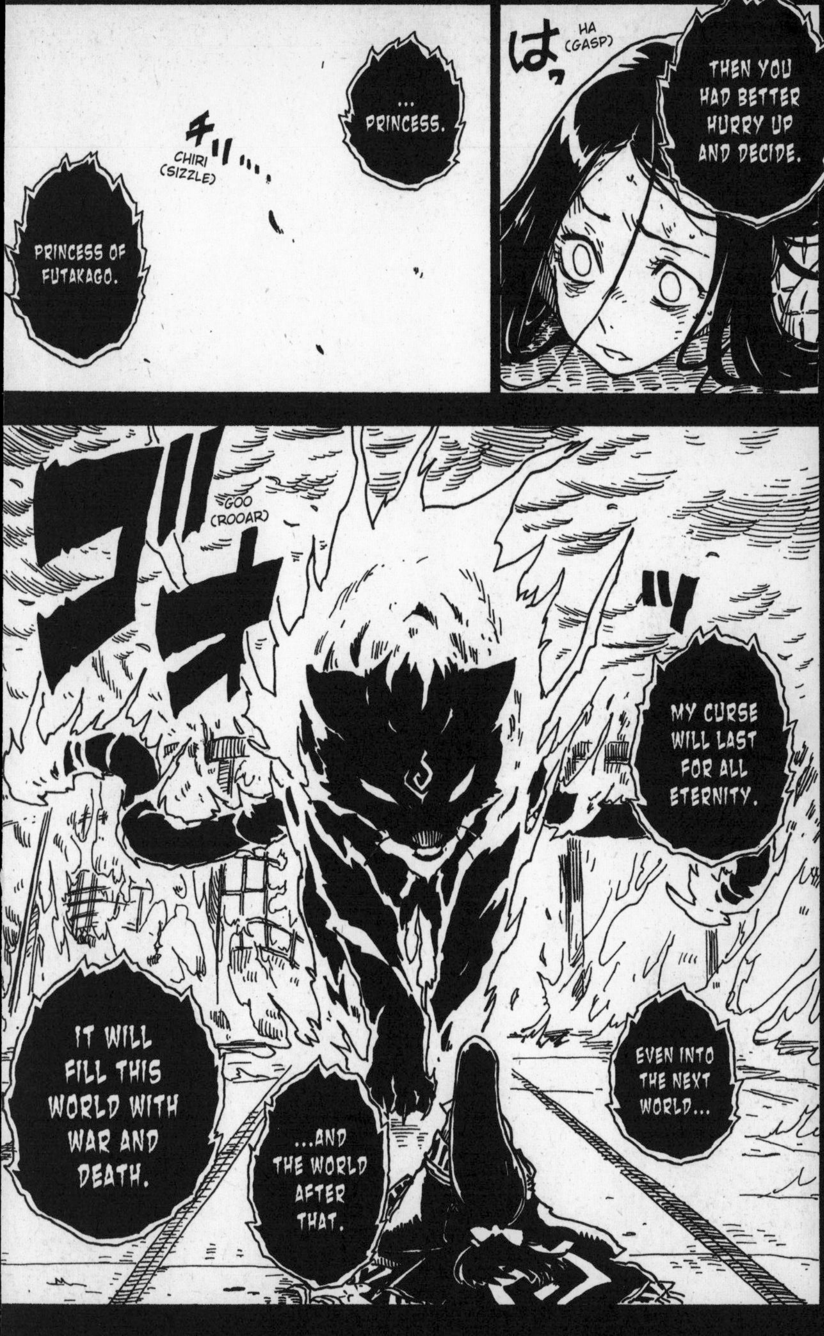
は っ
HA (GASP)
THEN YOU HAD BETTER HURRY UP AND DECIDE.
... PRINCESS.
チリ...
CHIRI (SIZZLE)
PRINCESS OF FUTAKAGO.
ゴオッ
GOO (ROOAR)
MY CURSE WILL LAST FOR ALL ETERNITY.
IT WILL FILL THIS WORLD WITH WAR AND DEATH.
EVEN INTO THE NEXT WORLD...
...AND THE WORLD AFTER THAT.

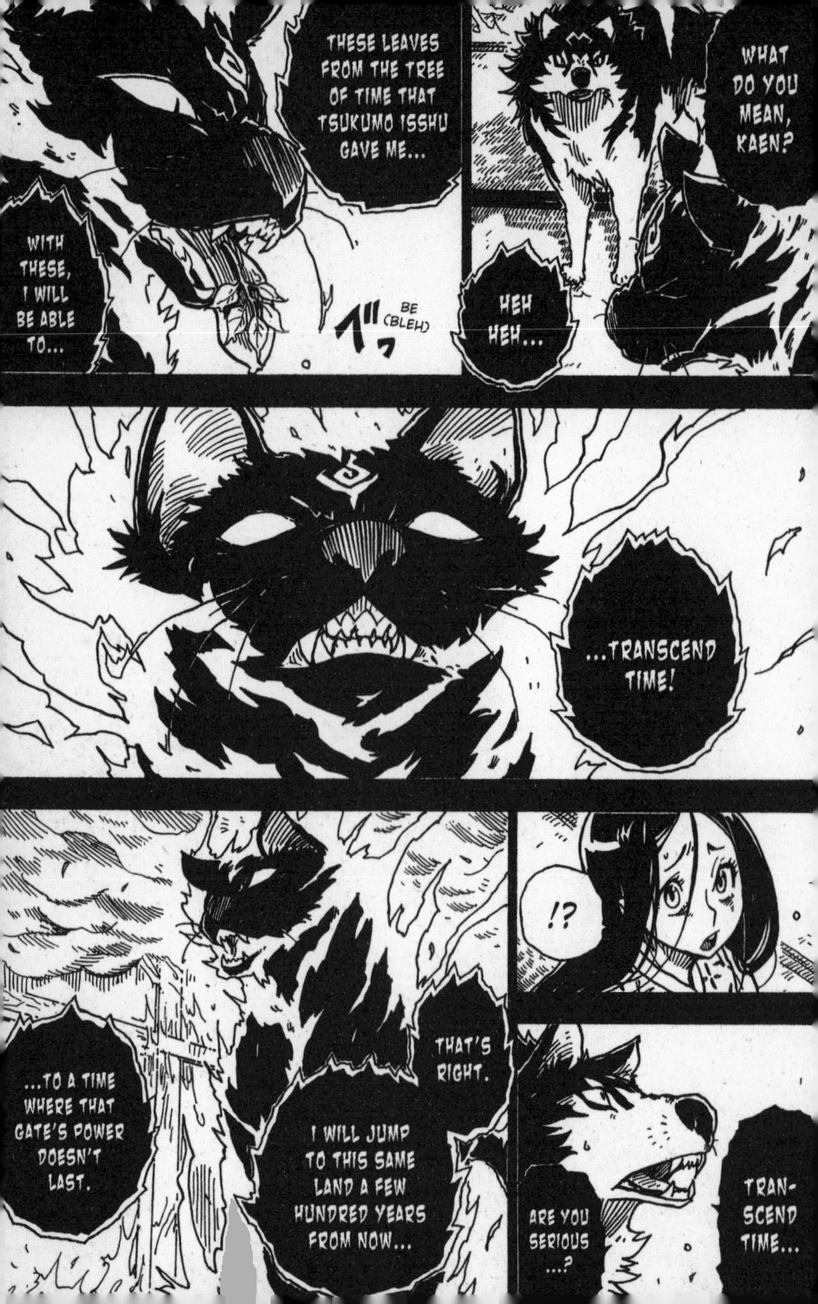
WHAT DO YOU MEAN, KAEN?
HEH HEH...
THESE LEAVES FROM THE TREE OF TIME THAT TSUKUMO ISSHU GAVE ME...
BE (BLEH)
WITH THESE, I WILL BE ABLE TO...
...TRANSCEND TIME!
!?
TRAN-SCEND TIME...
ARE YOU SERIOUS ...?
THAT'S RIGHT.
I WILL JUMP TO THIS SAME LAND A FEW HUNDRED YEARS FROM NOW...
...TO A TIME WHERE THAT GATE'S POWER DOESN'T LAST.

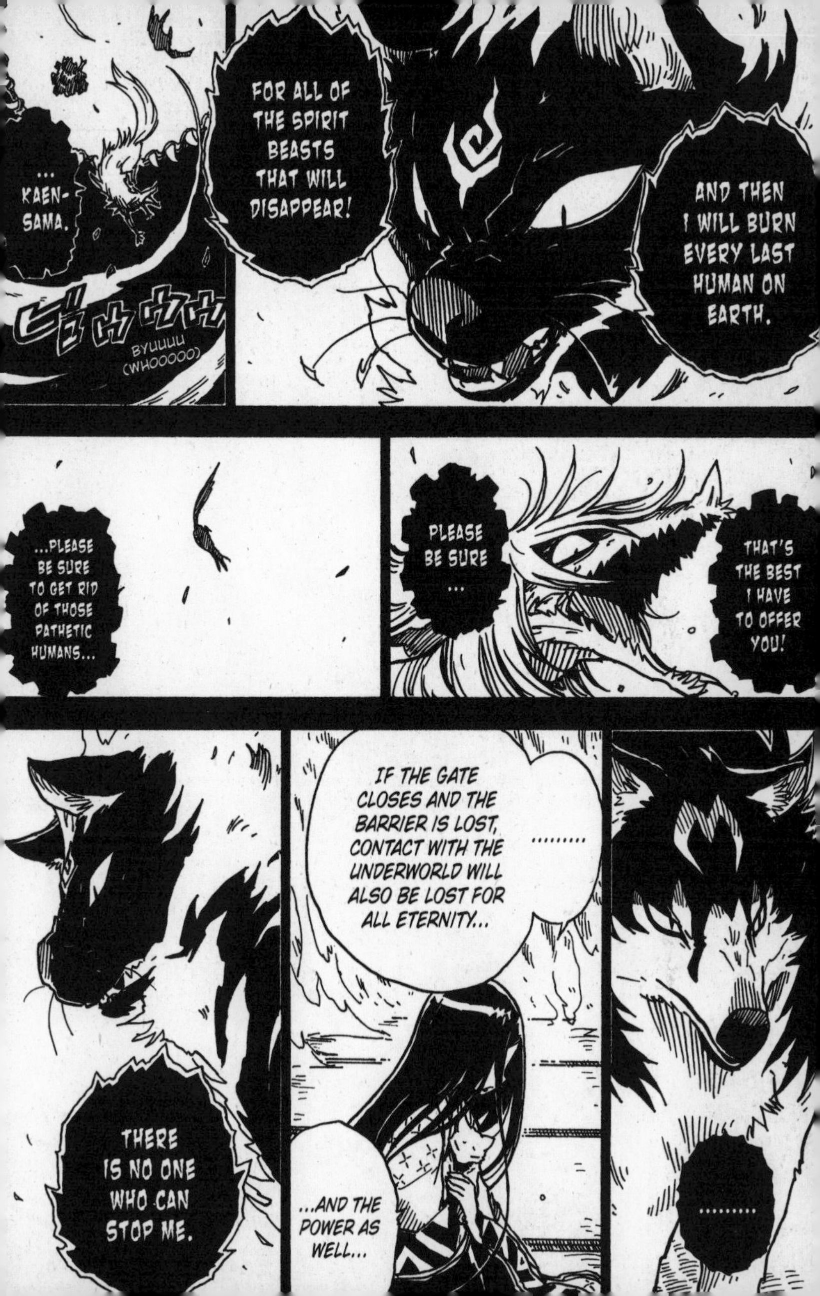
FOR ALL OF THE SPIRIT BEASTS THAT WILL DISAPPEAR!
AND THEN I WILL BURN EVERY LAST HUMAN ON EARTH.
...KAEN-SAMA.
BYUUUU (WHOOOOO)
THAT'S THE BEST I HAVE TO OFFER YOU!
PLEASE BE SURE...
...PLEASE BE SURE TO GET RID OF THOSE PATHETIC HUMANS...
....
....
IF THE GATE CLOSES AND THE BARRIER IS LOST, CONTACT WITH THE UNDERWORLD WILL ALSO BE LOST FOR ALL ETERNITY...
...AND THE POWER AS WELL...
THERE IS NO ONE WHO CAN STOP ME.

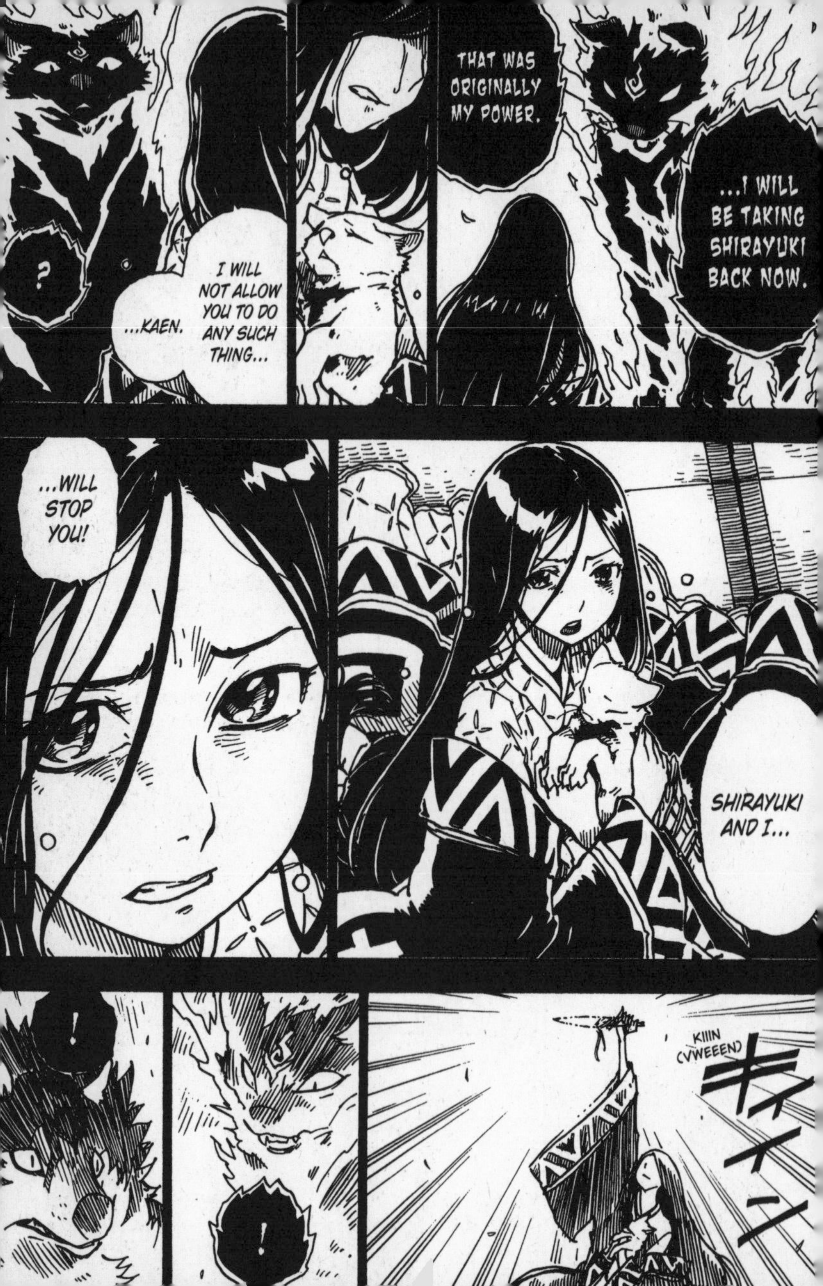
...I WILL BE TAKING SHIRAYUKI BACK NOW.
THAT WAS ORIGINALLY MY POWER.
I WILL NOT ALLOW YOU TO DO ANY SUCH THING...
...KAEN.
?
SHIRAYUKI AND I...
...WILL STOP YOU!
KIIIN (VWEEEN)
!
!

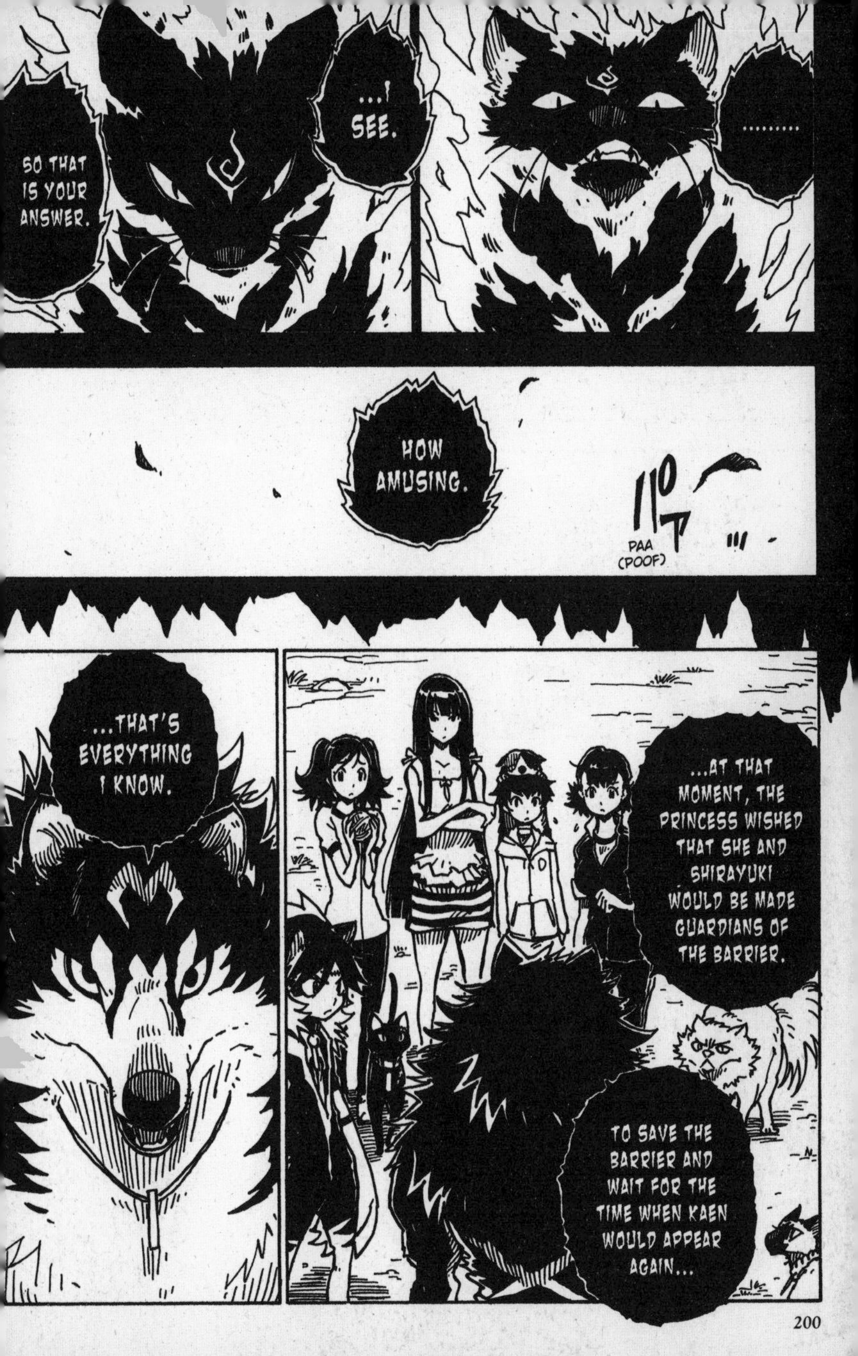
....
...I SEE.
SO THAT IS YOUR ANSWER.
HOW AMUSING.
PAA (POOF)
...AT THAT MOMENT, THE PRINCESS WISHED THAT SHE AND SHIRAYUKI WOULD BE MADE GUARDIANS OF THE BARRIER.
TO SAVE THE BARRIER AND WAIT FOR THE TIME WHEN KAEN WOULD APPEAR AGAIN...
...THAT'S EVERYTHING I KNOW.

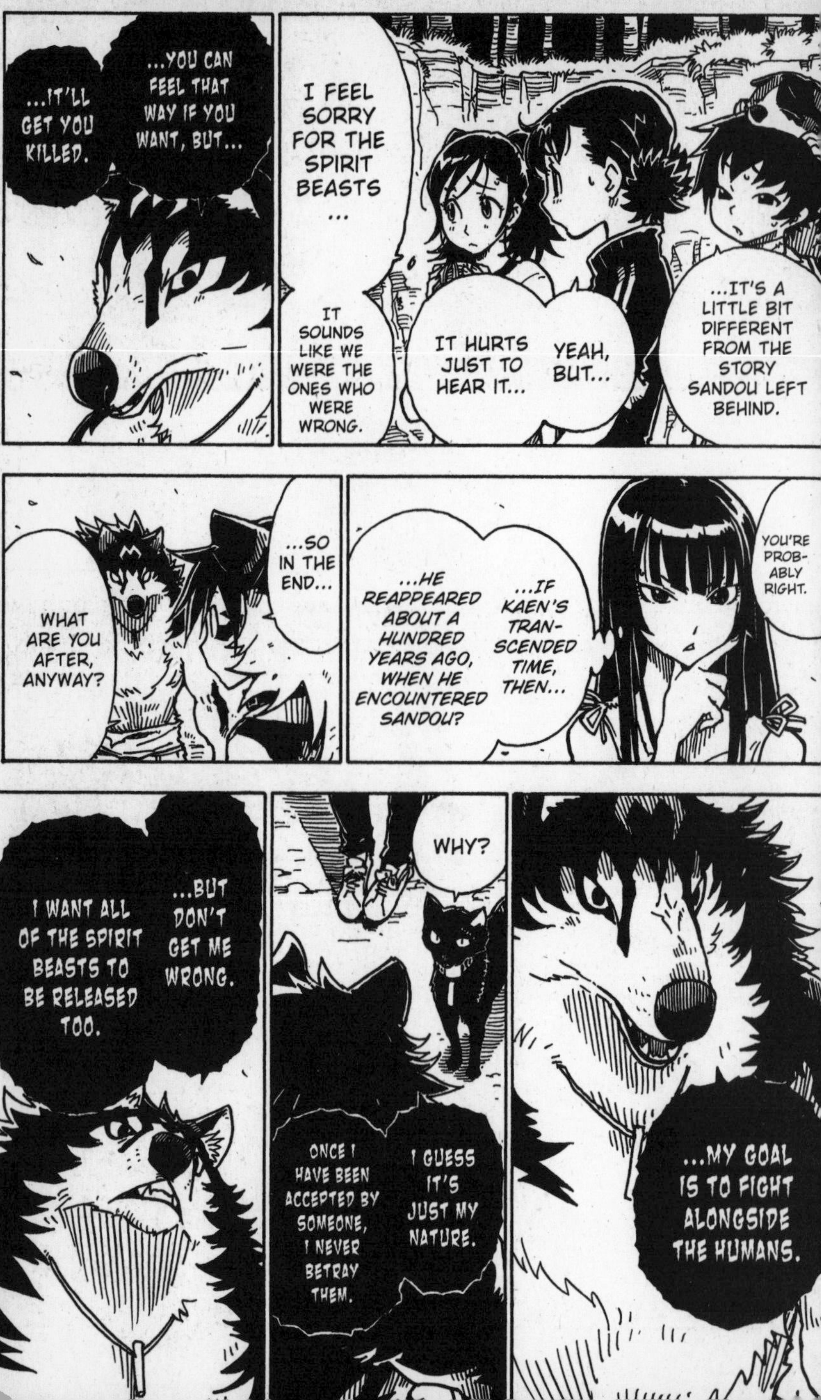

...IT'S A LITTLE BIT DIFFERENT FROM THE STORY SANDOU LEFT BEHIND.
I FEEL SORRY FOR THE SPIRIT BEASTS...
YEAH, BUT...
IT HURTS JUST TO HEAR IT...
IT SOUNDS LIKE WE WERE THE ONES WHO WERE WRONG.
...YOU CAN FEEL THAT WAY IF YOU WANT, BUT...
...IT'LL GET YOU KILLED.
YOU'RE PROBABLY RIGHT.
...IF KAEN'S TRANSCENDED TIME, THEN...
...HE REAPPEARED ABOUT A HUNDRED YEARS AGO, WHEN HE ENCOUNTERED SANDOU?
...SO IN THE END...
WHAT ARE YOU AFTER, ANYWAY?
...MY GOAL IS TO FIGHT ALONGSIDE THE HUMANS.
WHY?
I GUESS IT'S JUST MY NATURE.
ONCE I HAVE BEEN ACCEPTED BY SOMEONE, I NEVER BETRAY THEM.
...BUT DON'T GET ME WRONG.
I WANT ALL OF THE SPIRIT BEASTS TO BE RELEASED TOO.

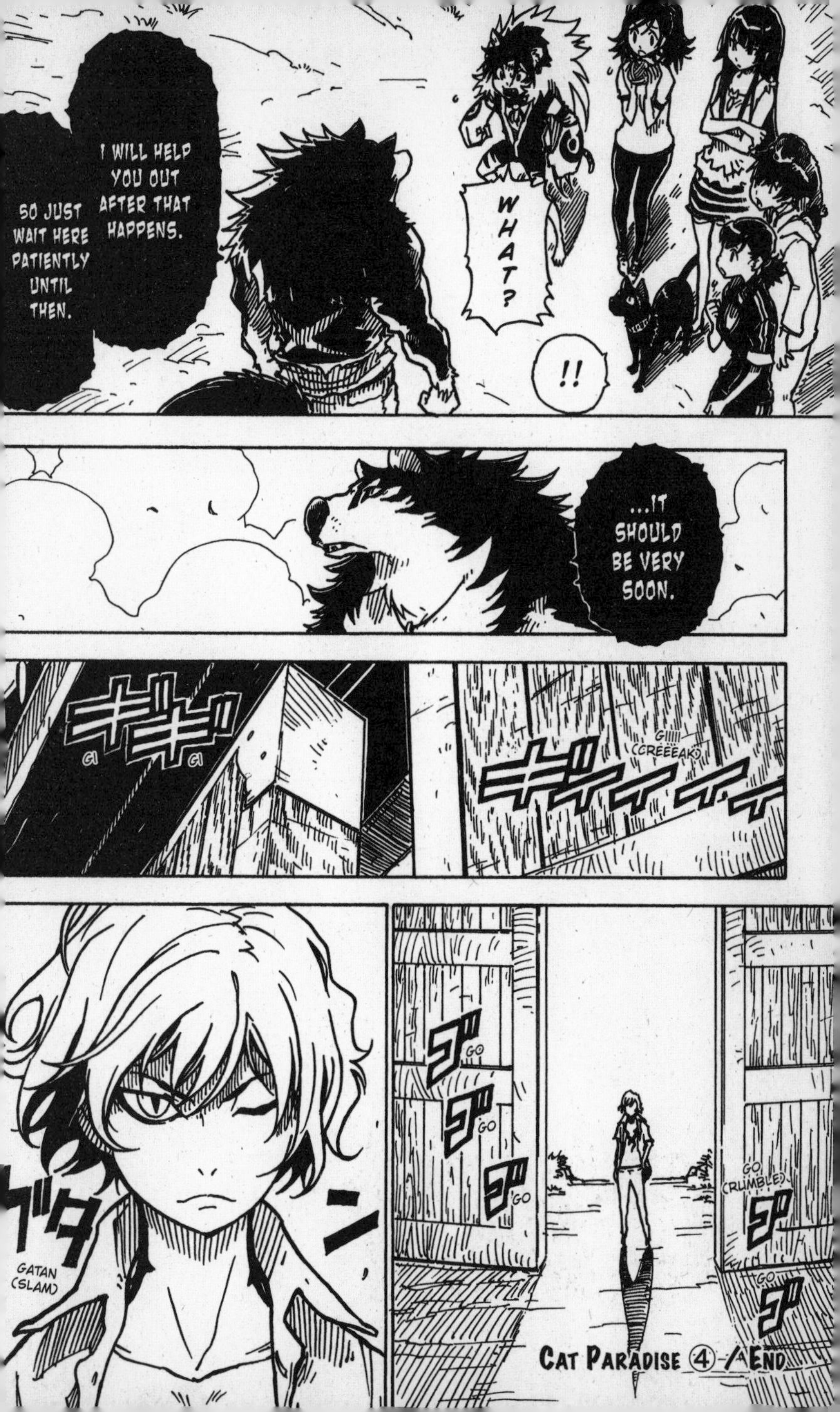
I WILL HELP YOU OUT AFTER THAT HAPPENS.
SO JUST WAIT HERE PATIENTLY UNTIL THEN.
WHAT?
!!
...IT SHOULD BE VERY SOON.
GI!!!! (CREEEEAK)
GI
GI
GO (RUMBLE)
GO
GO
GO
GO
GATAN (SLAM)
CAT PARADISE ④ / END

CAT PARADISE

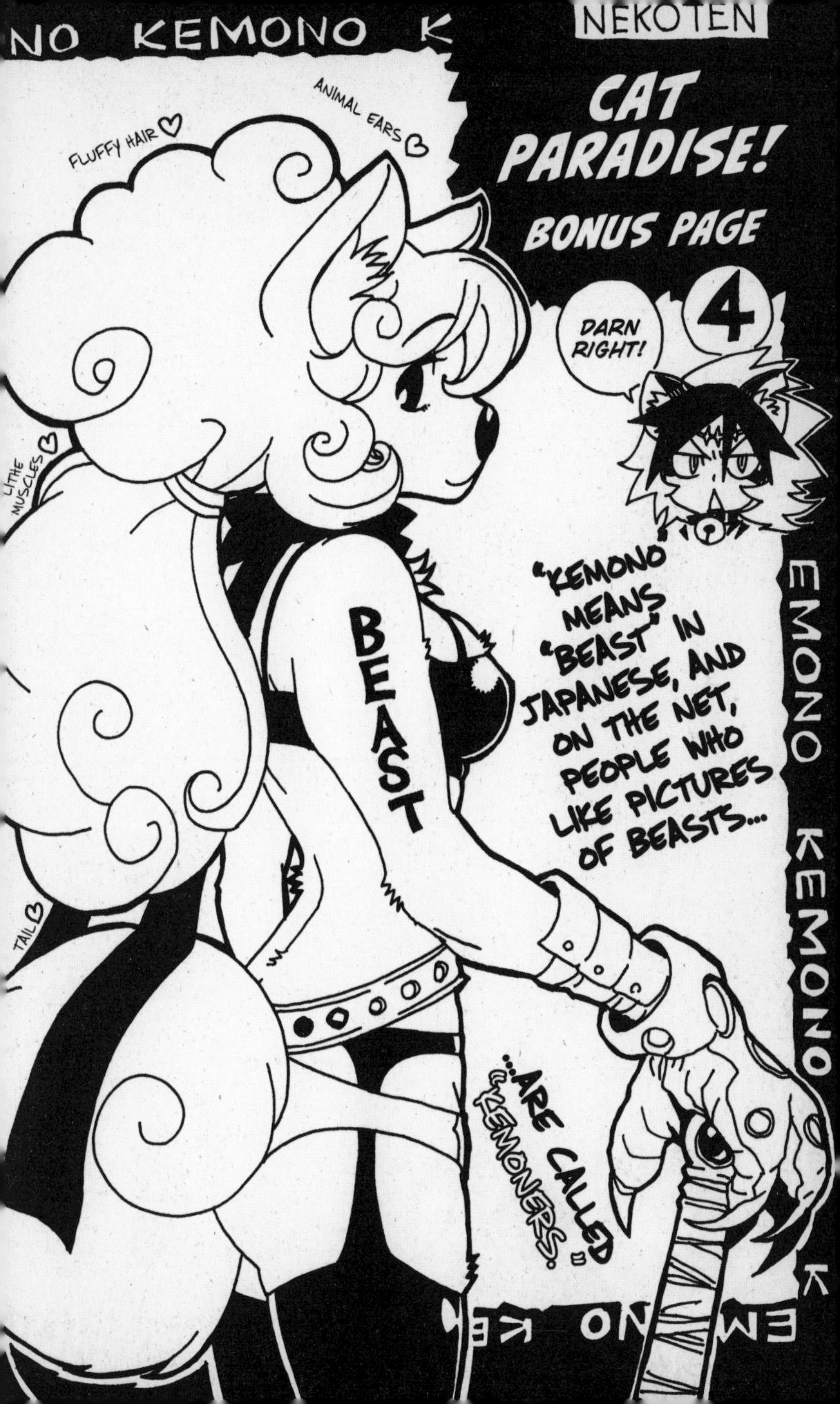

NEKOTEN
CAT PARADISE! BONUS PAGE
4
NO KEMONO K
ANIMAL EARS♡
FLUFFY HAIR♡
LITHE MUSCLES♡
TAIL♡
BEAST
DARN RIGHT!
"KEMONO MEANS "BEAST" IN JAPANESE, AND ON THE NET, PEOPLE WHO LIKE PICTURES OF BEASTS...
...ARE CALLED "KEMONERS."
EMONO KEMONO K

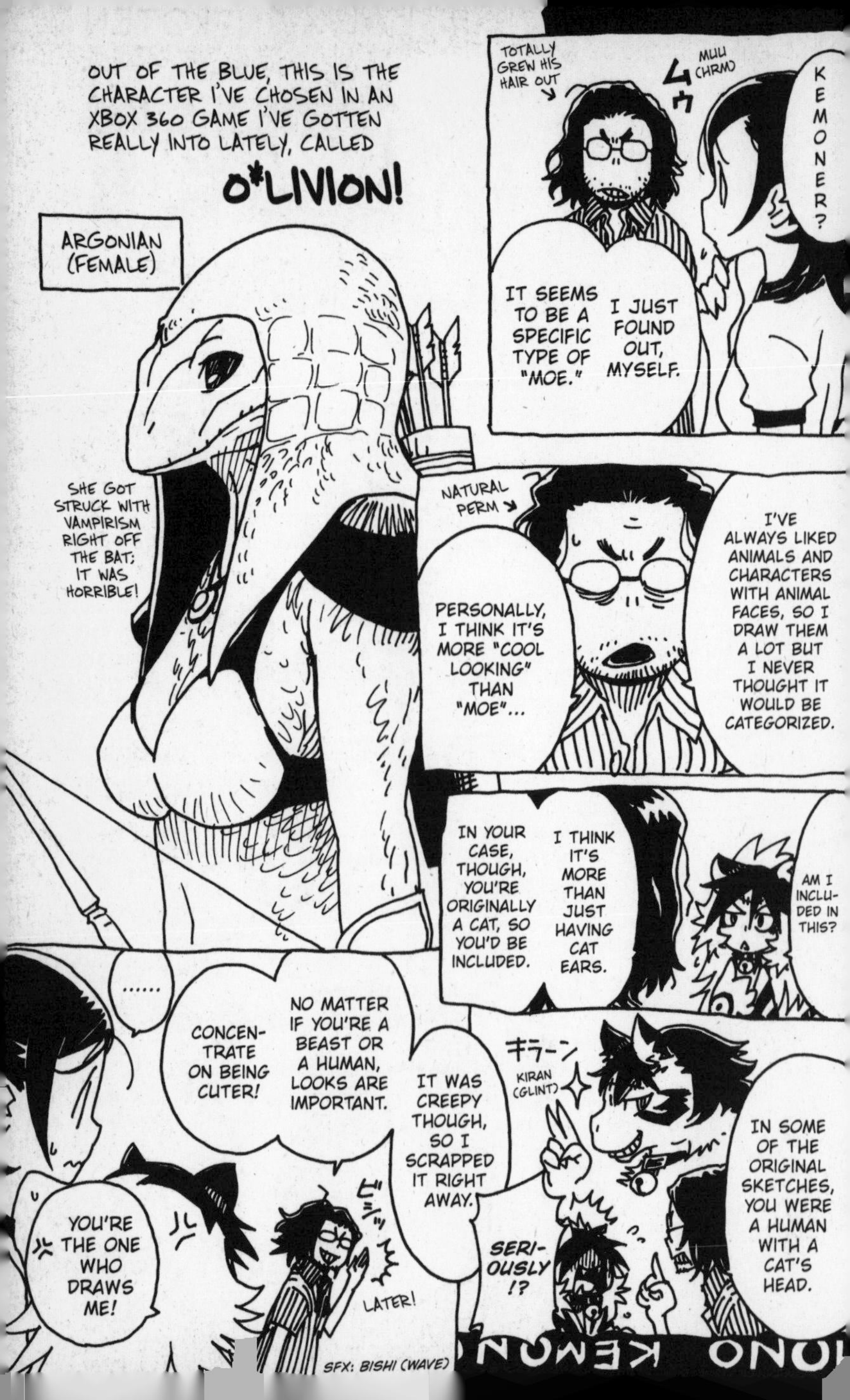
KEMONER?
ムウ
MUU (CHRM)
TOTALLY GREW HIS HAIR OUT
I JUST FOUND OUT, MYSELF.
IT SEEMS TO BE A SPECIFIC TYPE OF "MOE."
I'VE ALWAYS LIKED ANIMALS AND CHARACTERS WITH ANIMAL FACES, SO I DRAW THEM A LOT BUT I NEVER THOUGHT IT WOULD BE CATEGORIZED.
NATURAL PERM
PERSONALLY, I THINK IT'S MORE "COOL LOOKING" THAN "MOE"...
AM I INCLUDED IN THIS?
I THINK IT'S MORE THAN JUST HAVING CAT EARS.
IN YOUR CASE, THOUGH, YOU'RE ORIGINALLY A CAT, SO YOU'D BE INCLUDED.
OUT OF THE BLUE, THIS IS THE CHARACTER I'VE CHOSEN IN AN XBOX 360 GAME I'VE GOTTEN REALLY INTO LATELY, CALLED
O*LIVION!
ARGONIAN (FEMALE)
SHE GOT STRUCK WITH VAMPIRISM RIGHT OFF THE BAT; IT WAS HORRIBLE!
IN SOME OF THE ORIGINAL SKETCHES, YOU WERE A HUMAN WITH A CAT'S HEAD.
キラーン
KIRAN (GLINT)
SERIOUSLY!?
IT WAS CREEPY THOUGH, SO I SCRAPPED IT RIGHT AWAY.
NO MATTER IF YOU'RE A BEAST OR A HUMAN, LOOKS ARE IMPORTANT.
......
CONCENTRATE ON BEING CUTER!
LATER!
YOU'RE THE ONE WHO DRAWS ME!
SFX: BISHI (WAVE)

Translation Notes

Pg. 49
Ame-no-Murakumo no Tsurugi can be translated as "Sword of Gathering Clouds in the Heavens." It is a reference to the original name of the Kusanagi no Tsurugi ("Grass-Cutting Sword"), the sword of the Japanese imperial regalia. According to legend, this sword was discovered inside Yamato-no-Orochi (an eight-headed serpent) when the beast was slain by the god Susa-no-o.

Pg. 75
Perception The symbol on Kansuke's back means "perception." It is also pronounced "kan," so it could also be taken as the first symbol in Kansuke's name.

Pg. 104
Dream Box In the Japanese, another possible reading for "Dream Box" is "Dream Barrier."

Pg. 152
"My fangs are the strongest on Earth!" Kiba's name means "fang" in Japanese, so this line is a reference to his name.

Pg. 172
Shirayuki means "white snow."

Pg. 205
O*livion The mangaka is talking about the game *Elder Scrolls IV: Oblivion*, which was released for PC and Xbox 360 in 2006. It is a first-person action/role-playing game.